Lecture Notes
in Business Information Processing 133

Series Editors

Wil van der Aalst
Eindhoven Technical University, The Netherlands
John Mylopoulos
University of Trento, Italy
Michael Rosemann
Queensland University of Technology, Brisbane, Qld, Australia
Michael J. Shaw
University of Illinois, Urbana-Champaign, IL, USA
Clemens Szyperski
Microsoft Research, Redmond, WA, USA

T0280285

Dietmar Winkler
Stefan Biffl
Johannes Bergsmann (Eds.)

Software Quality

Increasing Value in Software and Systems Development

5th International Conference, SWQD 2013
Vienna, Austria, January 15-17, 2013
Proceedings

 Springer

Volume Editors

Dietmar Winkler
Vienna University of Technology
Institute of Software Technology
and Interactive Systems
Vienna, Austria
E-mail: dietmar.winkler@tuwien.ac.at

Stefan Biffl
Vienna University of Technology
Institute of Software Technology
and Interactive Systems
Vienna, Austria
E-mail: stefan.biffl@tuwien.ac.at

Johannes Bergsmann
Software Quality Lab GmbH
Linz, Austria
E-mail: johannes.bergsmann@software-quality-lab.at

ISSN 1865-1348   e-ISSN 1865-1356
ISBN 978-3-642-35701-5   e-ISBN 978-3-642-35702-2
DOI 10.1007/978-3-642-35702-2
Springer Heidelberg Dordrecht London New York

Library of Congress Control Number: 2012954060

ACM Computing Classification (1998): D.2, K.6

Typesetting: Camera-ready by author, data conversion by Scientific Publishing Services, Chennai, India

Printed on acid-free paper

Springer is part of Springer Science+Business Media (www.springer.com)

Message from the General Chair

The Software Quality Days (SWQD) conference and tools fair started in 2009 and has grown to one of the biggest conferences on software quality in Europe within a strong community. The program of the SWQD conference is designed to encompass a stimulating mixture of practical presentations and new research topics in scientific presentations as well as tutorials and an exhibition area for tool vendors and other organizations in the area of software quality.

This professional symposium and conference offers a range of comprehensive and valuable opportunities for advanced professional training, new ideas, and networking with a series of keynote speeches, professional lectures, exhibits, and tutorials.

The SWQD conference is suitable for anyone with an interest in software quality, such as test managers, software testers, software process and quality managers, product managers, project managers, software architects, software designers, user interface designers, software developers, IT managers, development managers, application managers, and others with similar roles.

January 2013   Johannes Bergsmann

Message from the Scientific Program Chair

The 5th Software Quality Days (SWQD) Conference and Tools Fair brought together researchers and practitioners from business, industry, and academia working on quality assurance and quality management for software engineering and information technology. The SWQD conference is one of the largest software quality conferences in Europe.

Over the past years a growing number of scientific contributions were submitted to the SWQD symposium. Starting in 2012 the SWQD symposium included a dedicated scientific track published in scientific proceedings. For the second year we received an overall number of 18 high-quality submissions from researchers across Europe which were each peer-reviewed by three or more reviewers. Out of these submissions, the editors selected seven contributions as full papers, yielding an acceptance rate of 39%. Authors of the best papers will be invited to submit extended versions of their papers to a special section in the *Software Quality* journal. Further, six short papers, which represent promising research directions, were accepted to spark discussions between researchers and practitioners at the conference.

Main topics from academia and industry focused on systems and software quality management methods, improvements of software development methods and processes, latest trends in software quality, and testing and software quality assurance.

This book is structured according to the sessions of the scientific track following the guiding conference topic "Increasing Value in Software and Systems Development":

- Risk Management
- Software and Systems Testing
- Test Processes
- Model-Based Development
- Process Improvement and Measurement

January 2013   Stefan Biffl

Organization

SWQD 2013 was organized by the Software Quality Lab GmbH and the Vienna University of Technology, Institute of Software Technology and Interactive Systems, and the Christian Doppler Laboratory "Software Engineering Integration for Flexible Automation Systems."

Organizing Committee

General Chair

Johannes Bergsmann   Software Quality Labs GmbH

Scientific Chair

Stefan Biffl   Vienna University of Technology

Proceedings Chair

Dietmar Winkler   Vienna University of Technology

Organizing and Publicity Chair

Petra Bergsmann   Software Quality Labs GmbH

Program Committee

SWQD 2013 established an international committee of well-known experts in software quality and process improvement to peer-review the scientific submissions.

Maria Teresa Baldassarre	University of Bari, Italy
Armin Beer	University of Applied Sciences, Vienna, Austria
Ruth Breu	University of Innsbruck, Austria
Deepak Dhungana	Siemens Corporate Technology Research, Austria
Schahram Dustdar	Vienna University of Technology, Austria
Frank Elberzhager	Fraunhofer IESE, Germany
Michael Felderer	University of Innsbruck, Austria
Gordon Fraser	Saarland University, Germany
Christian Frühwirth	Aalto University, Finland

Marcela Genero	University of Castilla-La Mancha, Spain
Harald Gruber	Johannes Kepler Universität Linz, Austria
Paul Grünbacher	Johannes Kepler University Linz, Austria
Volker Gruhn	Universität Duisburg-Essen, Germany
Jens Heidrich	Fraunhofer IESE, Germany
Slinger Jansen	Utrecht University, The Netherlands
Petri Kettunen	University of Helsinki, Finland
Mahvish Khurum	Blekinge Institute of Technology, Sweden
Eda Marchetti	ISTI-CNR Pisa, Italy
Juergen Münch	University of Helsinki, Finland
Simona Nica	Graz University of Technology, Austria
Markku Oivo	University of Oulu, Finland
Mauro Pezzè	University of Milan Bicocca/Lugano, Italy/Switzerland
Dietmar Pfahl	Pika Research Inc., Canada
Rick Rabiser	Johannes Kepler University, Austria
Rudolf Ramler	Software Competence Center Hagenberg GmbH, Austria
Andreas Rausch	Technische Universität Clausthal, Germany
Barbara Russo	Free University of Bolzano/Bozen, Italy
Klaus Schmid	University of Hildesheim, Germany
Wikan Sunindyo	Vienna University of Technology, Austria
Rini van Solingen	Delft University of Technology, The Netherlands
Stefan Wagner	University of Stuttgart, Germany
Dietmar Winkler	Vienna University of Technology, Austria

Additional Reviewers

Asim Abdulkhaleq
Michael Deynet
Jaap Kabbedijk
Ravi Khadka

Table of Contents

Keynotes

Software Quality: From Requirements to Architecture 1
  Manfred Broy

The Consortium for IT Software Quality (CISQ) 3
  Richard Mark Soley and Bill Curtis

Risk Management

Experiences and Challenges of Introducing Risk-Based Testing in an
Industrial Project 10
  Michael Felderer and Rudolf Ramler

Project Progress and Risk Monitoring in Automation Systems
Engineering 30
  Wikan Sunindyo, Thomas Moser, Dietmar Winkler, and
  Richard Mordinyi

Software and Systems Testing

WebMate: Generating Test Cases for Web 2.0 55
  Valentin Dallmeier, Martin Burger, Tobias Orth, and Andreas Zeller

Testing Web Services in the Cloud 70
  Harry M. Sneed

Model-Based Strategies for Reducing the Complexity of Statistically
Generated Test Suites 89
  Winfried Dulz

Hazard Analysis for Technical Systems............................ 104
  Mario Gleirscher

Test Processes

Using Defect Taxonomies to Improve the Maturity of the System Test
Process: Results from an Industrial Case Study 125
  Michael Felderer and Armin Beer

Model-Based Development

A Transformation of Business Process Models into Software-Executable
Models Using MDA   147
   Nuno Santos, Francisco J. Duarte, Ricardo J. Machado, and
   João M. Fernandes

Aligning Domain-Related Models for Creating Context for Software
Product Design   168
   Nuno Ferreira, Nuno Santos, Ricardo J. Machado, and
   Dragan Gašević

Process Improvement and Measurement

Mapping CMMI and RUP Process Frameworks for the Context of
Elaborating Software Project Proposals   191
   Paula Monteiro, Ricardo J. Machado, Rick Kazman, Ana Lima,
   Cláudia Simões, and Pedro Ribeiro

Development and Evaluation of Systems Engineering Strategies:
An Assessment-Based Approach   215
   Fritz Stallinger, Reinhold Plösch, Robert Neumann,
   Stefan Horn, and Jan Vollmar

Improving Completeness of Measurement Systems for Monitoring
Software Development Workflows   230
   Miroslaw Staron, Wilhelm Meding, and Micael Caiman

Exploiting Natural Language Definitions and (Legacy) Data
for Facilitating Agreement Processes   244
   Christophe Debruyne and Cristian Vasquez

Author Index   259

Software Quality: From Requirements to Architecture

Manfred Broy

Institut für Informatik, Technische Universität München, Germany
broy@in.tum.de

Extended Abstract

Software systems today are an existential part of technical systems, processes, and infrastructure. They are the backbone of assistance, communication, and information systems. Their reliable operation and long-term evolution of their technology is of outstanding importance for industry and society.

Against this background attention should be paid to the question of the quality of software systems. However, the concept of quality of software is very versatile. This has its foundation in the particularities of software. Software is a less tangible than other products of the engineering disciplines. It is highly abstract in its development, usually describes complex behavior and in its long-term operation and development it is subject to its own laws. In many applications software is tightly integrated into products and processes and determines their quality to a large extent.

However, software quality is a multi-faceted notion.

Against this background, it is far from obvious what quality of a software system is accurate for its specific purpose. In consequence, it is necessary to develop a differentiated concept of software quality. Such a sophisticated concept of software quality can be captured, for example, in so-called quality models that allow structured and detailed views onto the quality of software systems. In such models, quality criteria for software systems are defined and the comprehensive concept of software quality is broken down into a number of specific aspects and features. Outstanding examples of such aspects of software quality are functional adequacy, usability, reliability, functional safety, information security, performance, maintainability and many more.

Just as the concept of quality as such, each of these terms addresses complex concepts by itself. To get a more objective understanding of these concepts, there are several approaches. One possibility is a further breakdown each of the quality aspects into even finer sub-features. A second approach is to define a couple of metrics that make the quality and quality characteristics measureable. Measures and metrics follow the idea of making quality comparable. A third approach is the concretization of quality concepts by operational measures, where we relate the quality aspects to consequences in handling the software. For instance, we might measure maintainability by the overhead in maintaining software in a particular usage and evolution scenario.

D. Winkler, S. Biffl, and J. Bergsmann (Eds.): SWQD 2013, LNBIP 133, pp. 1–2, 2013.
© Springer-Verlag Berlin Heidelberg 2013

All these approaches lead to specific forms and instances of quality models. The reactions of operational aspects based on the idea that quality is less a matter of judgment, but rather a question of the expense necessary in the usage, operation, evolution, and marketing of a software system.

However, there is another problem. There is not an independent isolated concept of evaluating software quality. Software quality is always related to the usage context of a software system. Hence for a software system there are always two aspects of quality, the quality of the software system as it is and the required quality. Strictly speaking, it does not make sense to consider these two different aspects separately and independently. In short, a reasonable quality assessment must always be in relation to specific software quality requirements.

This shows that comprehensive, highly differentiated models of software quality requirements have to be considered. In other words, good quality models support structuring of the specific quality requirements in terms of guidelines and serve as guidelines for capturing quality-related requirements.

A second milestone for software systems is their architecture. Architecture refers to the structure of a system from different perspectives. Classically, architecture addresses the decomposition of systems into subsystems often referred to as modules or components. These subsystems cooperate to provide the desired functionality of a software system.

Quality requirements have to address two levels. First, there is a quality concept of the software system as it is defined in the interfaces of a behaving system as a whole. This concerns in particular the suitability of the functionality and usability of the interface. We speak of "quality in use". Much of the other quality items manifest itself closely in the architecture. As an example, software reliability is of course a notion of the overall system concerns, and coupled to the availability of the required functionality, but to ensure that quality is a result of an adequate design of the architecture. That is, the reliability of the components and the question of how the components are matched to potential problems of either the context of the software system, such as special features of the execution platform or operating environment or of issues and problem inside the architecture of the software system.

Against this background, the Technical University of Munich worked out an approach to a comprehensive quality model as a guideline for structuring the requirements and how to use the quality model for creating the design of the architecture and to support the evaluation of its quality. The consistency and appropriateness of the quality model manifests itself in the question to what extent it provides the option to relate requirements, functional specification, and architecture to support traceability, validation, and verification of quality properties.

The Consortium for IT Software Quality (CISQ)

Richard Mark Soley[1] and Bill Curtis[2]

[1] Object Management Group
soley@omg.org
[2] Consortium for IT Software Quality
curtis@acm.org

Abstract. Standards and guidelines are the backbone to support efficient and effective projects in software engineering with respect to quality aspects. The Consortium for IT Software Quality (CISQ) represents a consortium of end-user and vendor organizations working together under the Object Management Group (OMG) process to produce standards for measuring and reporting software quality independently of the process used to produce that software. This paper introduces to CISQ and presents the main contributions to software quality for end-users and vendors.

Keywords: Standardization, software quality metrics, CISQ.

1 Introduction

CISQ exists to address a significant challenge: the lack of visibility IT executives have into the structural quality and risk of their critical business applications. A fundamental assumption underlying CISQ is that global standards for measuring the attributes of software, especially at the source code level, are fundamental to meeting this challenge. The IT industry needs standard measures to support the use of quality attributes in benchmarking and controlling software acquisition. Currently software measures are too often manual, expensive, and based on inconsistent or even subjective definitions. In order to improve the discipline of application development CISQ has set four initial objectives presented in Table 1.

Table 1. CISQ Rationales

1	Raise international awareness of the critical challenge of structural quality in business-critical IT software
2	Define standard, automatable measures for evaluating the non-functional, structural quality of IT software
3	Promote global acceptance of the standard in acquiring IT software
4	Develop an infrastructure of authorized assessors and products using the standard

D. Winkler, S. Biffl, and J. Bergsmann (Eds.): SWQD 2013, LNBIP 133, pp. 3–9, 2013.
© Springer-Verlag Berlin Heidelberg 2013

2   CISQ Mission

CISQ bases its mission, strategies, and tactics on the following premises:

- IT application quality is a critical business issue as more business processes are committed to software
- The current quality of IT application software exposes the business to unacceptable levels of risk and loss
- Businesses do not have governance structures sufficient to manage the risks to which poor quality application software exposes them
- Customers and providers of IT application software do not have a common basis for describing and managing the quality of delivered application software
- Business and government and their providers need a common voice to drive attention to and improvements in IT application software

CISQ will pursue the following measureable goals:

- 75% of the Global 1000 have an IT application software quality governance structure that involves the business
- 75% of Global 1000 use a common IT application software structural quality standard in contractual agreements with their suppliers/outsourcers
- 50% of the Global 1000 have established baselines and business value propositions for IT application software structural quality

3   Work Products

To pursue its second objective, i.e., developing standard, automatable measures and anti-patterns for evaluating IT software quality, CISQ has formed technical working groups for each of the high priority software attributes decided by the membership. CISQ technical working groups have defined standard quality measures and software anti-patterns characterizing the software attributes of highest priority to CISQ members. Software anti-patterns represent vulnerabilities, weaknesses, and violations of good coding and architectural practice related to these high priority attributes. These working groups will produce four products described in **Table 2** that will be submitted to the Object Management Group (OMG) standards process.

Based on the content of CISQ products, we anticipate that their final form will be of repositories of measures and anti-patterns that are maintained under configuration management. These measures and anti-patterns will be associated with rules and guidelines for adapting them to different languages, platforms, technologies, and uses. CISQ will also develop rules and guidelines for aggregated measures from the component to the application level.

Table 2. CISQ Work Products

Product	Description	Availability
Software measures	Standard definitions at the source code level with tailoring guidelines for application to different languages and technologies	Repository
Software anti-patterns	Anti-patterns defined to a level that can be recognized in source code	Repository
Scoring rules	Rules for aggregating software measures from the component to the application level and other guidelines as necessary for manipulating measures of software attributes	Document
Usage guidelines	Methods for adopting and using software attribute measures and anti-patterns in developing, acquiring, or benchmarking applications	Document

4   CISQ-Related Standards

The most relevant existing standard is ISO/IEC 9126, now being replaced by the ISO/IEC 25000 series, which describes a model of software quality attributes (ISO/IEC 25010). OMG supports several standards that CISQ will use to accelerate the development of standard measures of software attributes. These include the Knowledge Discovery Meta-Model which describes the elements resulting from a parse that provide the countable elements for quality metrics and the Structured Metrics Meta-model that provides a standard format for representing metrics. OMG is currently working on a standard for representing anti-patterns, vulnerabilities, weaknesses, and violations of good coding practice. CISQ will support the development and evolution of these standards.

5   Developing Standard Quality Characteristic Measures

CISQ conducted three Executive Forums – in Frankfurt, Germany in Fall 2009, in Arlington, VA Fall 2009, and in Bangalore, India June, 2010. The quality issues raised by the executives in attendance grouped into four categories; 1) specific quality attributes to be defined as quality measures in the CISQ standard, 2) primary uses for these quality measures, 3) support required for using quality measures effectively, and 4) methods for integrating quality measures into life cycle and acquisition processes.

Participants wanted to prioritize the focus on application software, but did not want to artificially exclude system or embedded software. They prioritized five initial target measures for CISQ which are summarized in Table 3. Primary uses for the measures emerging from these groups included controlling internal development, managing the quality of externally supplied software, estimating maintenance effort/costs, managing application portfolios, and assessing business disruption risk.

Table 3. CISQ Automatable Measures

Measure	Description
Functional Size	Develop a definition for automating Function Points
Maintainability	Measure factors affecting maintenance cost, effort, and duration
Reliability	Measure factors affecting availability and recoverability of operations
Performance	Measure factors affecting responsiveness to users
Security	Measure factors affecting vulnerability and leverage existing work in the assurance community

Several Technical Workgroups were formed to address these five areas of measurement. Work groups launched their activities in onsite meetings held during the first quarter of 2010. Meetings were held by bi-yearly through Fall 2011 and the completed measurement standards for the four quality characteristics (excluding Functional Size) were published on the CISQ website in September 2012.

The objective of the Functional Sizing workgroup was to create a definition of Function Points that is as close to IFPUG counting rules as possible, while resolving the issues necessary to enable fully automated counting at the source code level. This group has completed it work and the standard for automated Function Points is currently undergoing OMG's process for becoming a supported specification. Possible future objectives will be to define functional measures for areas where current definitions may be weak such as Web interfaces or heavily algorithmic software.

The workgroups creating automatable definitions for the Quality Characteristics of Reliability, Performance Efficiency, Security, and Maintainability have recently completed their work. In September 2012 CISQ published the standards for these measures in the Member's Area of the CISQ Website (www.it-cisq.org). Membership in CISQ is free since it is now sponsored by vendors who intend to implement the CISQ standards. The following paragraphs describe each of the four Quality Characteristics measures and some examples of the measurable elements included in each.

Reliability: According to ISO/IEC 25010, Reliability concerns "the degree to which a system or component performs its required functions under stated conditions for a specified period of time." This definition is consistent with ISO/IEC/IEEE 24765-2010 which provides a common vocabulary for software and systems engineering. Assessing reliability requires checks of at least the following software engineering best practices and technical attributes whose violations will be measured:

Architecture Practices
– Multi-layer design compliance
– Software manages data integrity and consistency

Coding Practices
– Error & exception handling
– Protecting state in multi-threaded environments

– Safe use of inheritance and polymorphism
– Patterns that lead to unexpected behaviors
– Resource bounds management
– Managing allocated resources
– Timeouts
– Built-in remote addresses
– Complex code

Performance Efficiency: According to ISO/IEC 25010, Performance Efficiency concerns "the performance relative to the amount of resources used under stated conditions for a specified period of time." Assessing Performance Efficiency requires checking at least the following software engineering best practices and technical attributes whose violations will be measured:

Architecture Practices
– Appropriate interactions with expensive and/or remote resources
– Data access performance and data management
– Memory, network and disk space management
– Centralized handling of client requests
– Use of middle tier components versus stored procedures or database functions

Coding Practices
– Compliance with Object-Oriented best practices
– Compliance with SQL best practices
– Expensive computations in loops
– Static connections versus connection pools
– Compliance with garbage collection best practices

Security: According to ISO/IEC 25010, Security concerns "the degree of protection of information and data so that unauthorized persons or systems cannot read or modify them and authorized persons or systems are not denied access to them." This definition is consistent with ISO/IEC 12207-2008 Systems and Software Engineering—Software Lifecycle Processes. Assessing Security requires at least checking the following software engineering best practices and technical attributes whose violations will be measured:

Architecture Practices
– Multi-layer design compliance
– Input Validation
– SQL Injection
– Cross-Site Scripting
– Failure to use vetted libraries or frameworks

Coding Practices
– Error & Exception handling
– Use of hard-coded credentials

- Buffer overflows
- Broken or risky cryptographic algorithms
- Improper validation of array index
- Missing initialization
- References to released resources
- Improper locking
- Uncontrolled format string

Maintainability: According to ISO/IEC 25010, Maintainability concerns "the degree to which the product can be modified." This definition is consistent with ISO/IEC/IEEE 24765-2010 which provides a common vocabulary for software and systems engineering. Assessing maintainability requires checking the following software engineering best practices and technical attributes whose violations will be measured:

Architecture Practices
- Strict hierarchy of calling between architectural layers
- Excessive horizontal layers

Coding Practices
- Compliance with Object-Oriented best practices
- Unstructured code
- Duplicated code
- Tightly coupled modules
- Controlled level of dynamic coding
- Cyclomatic complexity
- Over-parameterization of methods
- Encapsulated data access
- Commented out instructions
- Hard coding of literals
- Excessive component size

6   Summary

Standards for software quality will benefit end-users (by providing a consistent, reliable measure of quality for software both packaged and bespoke, and allowing purchasers to make better-informed decisions) as well as software vendors (by providing a way to improve software and prove to purchasers the quality of that product in a consistent fashion). Software integrators and other development organizations get a way to differentiate by proving product quality in a visible fashion. CISQ addresses these needs with well-defined, clearly focused, neutrally-developed international standards for software quality focused on the *software artifacts* rather than the process used to produce them. This important distinction allows differentiation of product without regard to implementation process.

It might be thought that this approach would obviate the need to measure and re-port software production process quality (à la the Software Engineering Institute's CMMI). Nothing could be further from the truth—software quality and software process quality go hand-in-hand, which is why the CISQ effort was launched by the Object Management Group and Software Engineering Institute together. The best products will exhibit both high software process maturity and high artifact quality.

Most importantly, the CISQ process is open, neutral and international. Systems integrators, offshore development organizations, software vendors and myriad software users participate in the production and test of these standards, and there is always room for participation by other interested parties.

References

1. OMG: Object Management Group, Inc. - Website, http://www.omg.org
2. CISQ: Consortium for IT Software Quality – Website, http://it-cisq.org

Experiences and Challenges of Introducing Risk-Based Testing in an Industrial Project

Michael Felderer[1] and Rudolf Ramler[2]

[1] Institute of Computer Science University of Innsbruck, Austria
michael.felderer@uibk.ac.at
[2] Software Competence Center Hagenberg, Austria
rudolf.ramler@scch.at

Abstract. Risk-based testing has a high potential to improve the software test process as it helps to optimize the allocation of resources and provides decision support for the management. But for many organizations the integration of risk-based testing into an existing test process is a challenging task. In this paper we present a generic risk-based testing methodology and a procedure how it can be introduced in a test process. Based on this procedure we derive four stages of risk-based test integration, i.e., initial risk-based testing, risk-based test reporting, risk-based test planning, and optimization of risk-based testing. We then discuss how this procedure could be applied based on an industrial project and identify several challenges and lessons learned in introducing risk-based testing.

Keywords: software testing, risk-based testing, test management, system testing.

1   Introduction

In many application domains, system testing has to be done under severe pressure due to limited resources and time constraints with the consequence that only a subset of all relevant test cases can be executed. In this context, risk-based testing approaches that include risks to manage all phases of the test process are more and more considered to improve testing. The appropriate application of risk-based testing may have several benefits. Risk-based testing optimizes the allocation of resources (budget, time, persons), is a means for mitigating risks, helps to early identify critical areas, and provides decision support for the management. For many organizations the most challenging task to realize the benefits of risk-based testing is the initial integration of risk-based testing into an existing test process as there is so far no clear methodological support for it.

In this paper we therefore present an approach for the stepwise integration of risk-based testing into an existing system test process and apply it to an industrial project. The procedure for introducing risk-based testing is based on a generic risk-based testing methodology that is aligned with the standard test process as defined by the *International Standard Testing Qualifications Board* (ISTQB) [1]. The procedure

D. Winkler, S. Biffl, and J. Bergsmann (Eds.): SWQD 2013, LNBIP 133, pp. 10–29, 2013.

itself consists of seven steps, i.e., (1) analysis and planning of the integration, (2) identification of risk items, (3) assessment procedure for risks, (4) design and execution of test cases based on risks, (5) consideration of risks in test reports, (6) consideration of risks for test planning, and (7) continuous evaluation and improvement of risk-based testing. To adapt this procedure to the needs of organizations, we distinguish four stages of risk-based test integration depending on the number of implemented steps. The first stage 'initial risk-based testing' implements steps (1) to (4), the second stage 'risk-based test reporting' additionally implements step (5), the third stage 'risk-based test planning' additionally implements step (6), and finally the fourth stage 'optimization of risk-based testing' additionally implements step (7). Based on an industrial project, we then discuss how the initial stage of risk-based testing could be introduced and identify several challenges and lessons learned from this integration.

In sum, this paper contributes to the integration of risk-based testing into implemented standard test processes in several ways. First, we provide a procedure for introducing risk-based testing which defines clear steps and is aligned with standard test processes. From this procedure we then derive four stages of risk-based test integration, tailoring the integration to the needs of specific development organizations. Finally, we show how the risk-based test integration could be performed in an industrial project and draw conclusions.

The remainder of this document is structured as follows. In the next section we present a standard-aligned risk-based testing methodology. In Section 3 we explain a procedure how the risk-based testing methodology can be introduced into an existing standard test process and derive stages of risk-based test integration. In Section 4 we apply this procedure to an industrial project, and in Section 5 we present related work. Finally, in Section 6 we summarize the challenges of introducing risk-based testing, draw conclusions and present future work.

2   Risk-Based Testing Methodology

Risk-based testing is a type of software testing that considers risks of the software product as the guiding factor to solve decision problems in the design, selection and prioritization of test cases [2]. A risk is the chance of injury, damage or loss and typically determined by the probability of its occurrence and its impact. The standard risk model also applied in our methodology is based on the two factors *probability* (P), determining the likelihood that a failure assigned to a risk occurs, and *impact* (I), determining the cost of a failure if it occurs in operation.

Mathematically, the risk (coefficient) R of an arbitrary risk item a can be determined based on the probability P and the impact I in the following way:

$$R(a) = P(a) \circ I(a)$$

The binary operator $\circ$ that connects P and I is typically the multiplication of two numbers or the cross product of two numbers or arbitrary characters (but not restricted to these operations).

Risk-based testing can be considered in all steps of a system test process. Our risk-based testing methodology extends the risk-based test process defined by Felderer et al. [3] and is based on the standard test process as defined by the ISTQB. It contains the phases *test planning and control, test analysis and design, test implementation and execution, test evaluation and reporting*, and *test closure activities*. Test planning is the activity of establishing or updating a test plan. A test plan is a document describing the scope, approach, resources, and schedule of intended test activities. In test control, the actual progress is compared against the plan which often results in concrete measures. During the test analysis and design phase the general testing objectives defined in the test plan are transformed into tangible test conditions and test cases. Test implementation contains remaining tasks like preparing test harnesses and test data, or writing automated test scripts which are necessary to enable the execution of the implementation-level test cases. The tests are then executed and all relevant details of the execution are recorded in a test log. During the test evaluation and reporting phase, the exit criteria are evaluated and the logged test results are summarized in a test report. During the test closure phase, data is collected from completed activities to consolidate experience, test ware, facts, and numbers.

Our generic risk-based test process additionally considers the phases risk identification and risk assessment. The generic risk-based test process is shown in Fig. 1 and consists of the phases *Risk Identification, Test Planning and Control, Risk Assessment, Test Analysis and Design, Evaluation and Reporting*, and *Test Closure Activities*.

In the *Risk Identification* phase *risk items* are identified and a list of risk items covering the whole system under test is compiled. Risk items are elements to which tests are assigned and for which the risk is calculated. Therefore risk items need to be concrete to enable risk calculation and the assignment of tests. The risk identification is typically performed by the project manager and the test manager.

In the *Test Planning and Control* phase the *test plan* is defined and controlling, which is an ongoing activity in parallel to the other activities in the of software testing process, is initiated. The test plan contains test prioritization criteria, test methods, exit criteria and the test effort under consideration of risk aspects. Although our approach is independent of a concrete test plan, we assume that a given test plan contains a basic risk classification scheme [3]. The test planning is typically performed by a test manager.

In the *Risk Assessment* phase the risk coefficient is calculated and classified for each risk item based on probability and impact factors. To distribute and improve the estimation of the factors P and I, they can be refined by sub-characteristics which are then determined by predefined metrics as proposed in software quality models like Factor-Criteria-Metrics [4] or ISO 25000 [5]. The probability typically considers *technical criteria* of a product such as complexity or the maturity of used technologies, and the impact considers *business criteria* such as monetary loss, reputation or importance of a feature in general. For instance, in a concrete industrial project the probability criteria complexity, visibility and third-party software, and the impact criteria importance, availability, and usage were considered. Based on the risk coefficient, a risk level is assigned to each risk item defining a *risk classification* for all risk items. A concrete risk assessment procedure based on this model is explained in [3]. The risk assessment can be performed by various stakeholders possessing the know-how needed to estimate business or technical factors, e.g., the importance of feature can be estimated by a product manager and the maturity of a technology by a software architect.

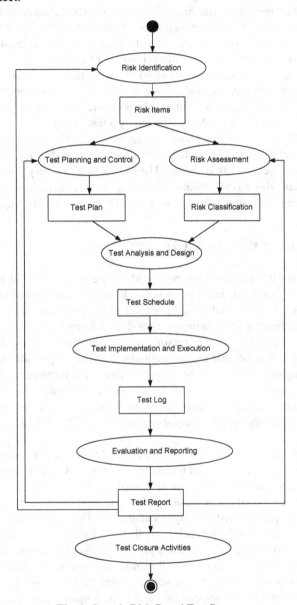

Fig. 1. Generic Risk-Based Test Process

In the *Test Analysis and Design* phase a concrete test schedule is defined based on the test plan and the risk classification. The *test schedule* contains a list of test cases that has been designed under consideration of risk aspects defined in the test plan, the risk classification and the given resources. The test analysis and design is typically performed by testers and test managers.

In the *Test Implementation and Execution* phase the test schedule is executed. The execution of the test cases is determined by their risk-based priority and the resource limitations. As a result of the test execution, a *test log* is created. The test implementation and execution is typically performed by testers.

In the *Test Evaluation and Reporting* phase the test log data is evaluated and a *test report* is created to support decisions of the test or project management. The report emphasizes an estimation of the mitigated risks and the residual risks. The test evaluation and reporting is typically performed by a test manager.

In the *Test Closure Activities* phase experiences from the actual test project are evaluated, e.g., the severity of the observed failures is related to the risk assessment procedure, to improve risk-based testing. The test closure is a very important activity to steadily adapt risk-based testing according to the experiences of the test organization. The test closure activities are typically led by a test manager.

3   Introducing Risk-Based Testing

The risk-based testing methodology presented before shows the full integration of risk-based testing into the standard test process. In industry, risk-based testing is often limited to test prioritization and its full potential to improve software quality and the test process by mitigating risks, estimating residual risks and optimizing test resource allocation is not exploited. A main reason for the limitation of risk-based testing to test prioritization is the fact that testing methodologies do not provide instructions for the stepwise implementation of risk-based testing. If an organization intends to evaluate and improve its test process based on Test Maturity Model integration (TMMi) [6] identifying and controlling product risks - which can be ensured by integrating risk-based testing into the test process - is necessary to reach TMMi level 2: managed.

In this section we define the steps how risk-based testing can be introduced into a test process following our risk-based testing methodology. Based on these instructions we indicate stages fostering the introduction of risk-based testing. As we define several stages of risk-based test integration, our approach is more concrete concerning the integration of product risk management than TMMi where this integration is considered on several maturity levels in so called specific goals and specific practices (SP), e.g., on TMMi level 2 (SP perform a generic product risk assessment, SP define product risk categories and parameters, SP identify product risks, SP analyzes product risks, SP monitor product risks, SP identify and prioritize test cases), TMMi level 3 (SP perform product risk assessment [in context of a master test plan], SP identify non-functional product risks, SP analyze non-functional product risks, SP identify and prioritize non-functional test cases), and TMMi level 4 (SP revise the product risks as appropriate). But TMMi does not provide concrete steps for risk-based test integration. In this respect, our approach substantiates the practices specified in TMMi and defines a concrete workflow for risk-based test integration.

The seven steps for introducing risk-based testing based on the test process presented in the previous section are shown in Fig. 2. These steps are (1) *Analysis and Planning of the Integration*, (2) *Identification of Risk Items*, (3) *Assessment Procedure for Risks*, (4) *Design and Execution of Test Cases based on Risks*, (5) *Consideration of Risks in Test Reports*, (6) *Consideration of Risks for Test Planning*, and (7) *Continuous Evaluation and Improvement of Risk-Based Testing*. Step 3 contains the three sub-steps (3.1) *Definition of Business Criteria*, (3.2) *Definition of Technical Criteria*, and (3.3) *Definition of a Risk Assessment Procedure*. In the following paragraphs we explain these steps in more detail.

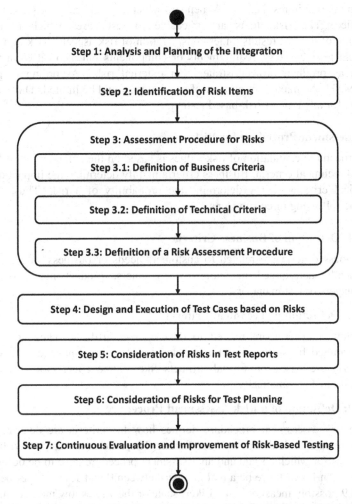

Fig. 2. Steps for Introducing Risk-Based Testing into Risk-Based Testing Methodology

Step 1: Analysis and Planning of the Integration

Before implementing risk-based testing in a test process, it has to be evaluated whether the integration of risk-based testing in a test process is feasible and beneficial. For instance, if one detects an inhomogeneous distribution of faults in projects, risk-based testing may be a measure to detect faults more effectively and more efficiently. But if the estimated resources for conventional risk-neutral testing are smaller than for performing a risk assessment, the integration of risk-based testing does not make sense. Additionally, in this step the overall integration of risk-based testing has to be planned, e.g., by creating a time plan and providing the resources needed for the integration.

Step 2: Identification of Risk Items

In this step the risk items, i.e., the elements to which risk values are assigned, have to be identified. The risk items are traceable to test cases which enables the interpretation of the test results under consideration of risk aspects. Risk items can be development artifacts, e.g., requirements or components but also different types of risks such as product, project, strategic or external risks. According to practical experiences [7], the maximum number of risk items should be limited. This step is the prerequisite for any type of risk-based testing.

Step 3: Assessment Procedure for Risks

In our approach the calculation of risk values is based on the combination of business criteria and technical criteria. Business criteria mainly determine the impact of a risk, and technical criteria mainly determine the probability of a risk. Thus, this step contains the following three sub-steps.

Step 3.1: Definition of Business Criteria

Business criteria are related to customers-needs or business value. They are typically determined manually by customers, product managers, project managers or test managers.

Step 3.2: Definition of Technical Criteria

Technical criteria are related to development artifacts. They are typically determined by software architects, developers or test managers. If technical criteria are based on formal artifacts like source code, they can even be determined automatically.

Step 3.3: Definition of a Risk Assessment Procedure

The risk assessment procedure defines how the criteria are determined and combined to calculate a risk coefficient. The criteria are calculated based on metrics for which a scale and an assessment procedure have to be defined. The value can for instance be a real number between 0 and 1, an integer between 0 and 9 possibly measured on a Likert scale or the values low/medium/high. The assessment can for instance be performed automatically, e.g., based on a static analysis tool but also manually based on forms, individual interviews or workshops. For the manual assessment, guidelines how to determine values may be useful to guarantee that the risk coefficients are estimated in a realistic way. For instance, there may be a guideline on how the importance of a feature is scored to guarantee that the customer does not assign the value "high" to the importance of each feature. Additionally, it has to be defined how to combine the criteria values to an overall risk value. For instance, weights for the different criteria may be considered to calculate the risk values as the weighted mean value of the criteria values.

Step 4: Design and Execution of Test Cases based on Risks

In this step, test cases are designed and executed under consideration of risks. The test design and execution is not based on an elaborated risk-based test plan but only considers risk for roughly deciding whether and how many test cases are designed and executed for a risk item.

Step 5: Consideration of Risks in Test Reports

In this step, risks are considered in test reports. Such risk-based test reports provide additional information for decision makers like project or test managers [8]. Risk-based test reports such as risk burn-down charts or traffic light reports visualize test results and risks in a combined way. An additional estimation of residual risks based on the available project data like risk and defect data is valuable to control the release quality [9].

Step 6: Consideration of Risks for Test Planning

In this step, risks are considered to define an elaborated risk-based test plan. The risk-based test plan is based on a risk classification. For each risk category in the risk classification specific test design techniques, exit criteria or test automation degrees that take the risk level into account are defined. Differing from step 3, the test cases are systematically not informally designed and executed based on the risk-based test plan defined as part of the overall test plan.

Step 7: Continuous Evaluation and Improvement of Risk-Based Testing

As risk-based testing is very specific for a domain and a test organization, the implemented risk-based test methodology has to be evaluated and improved after a test cycle or a test project has to be finished. For instance, if one observes that several failures of severity critical occur in tests of risk items with a low risk value, the risk assessment procedure or the test plan may not be optimal.

According to inhomogeneous distribution of faults in software [7] and the fact that failures have different consequences if occurring in different parts of a software product, already the application of the steps 1 to 4 may significantly improve the test process. Based on this initial level of risk-based test integration, three other stages with growing maturity of risk-based test integration can be defined by incrementally adding Steps 5, 6 and 7. The resulting four stages of risk-based test integration, i.e.,

(1) *Initial Risk-Based Testing*, (2) *Risk-Based Test Reporting*, (3) *Risk-Based Test Planning*, and (4) *Optimization of Risk-Based Testing* are shown in Fig. 3 and explained in the following paragraphs.

(1) **Initial Risk-Based Testing.** This stage comprises the basic integration of risk-based testing into a standard test process. It contains the analysis and planning of the integration, the identification of risk items, a risk assessment procedure, and the design and execution of test cases based on risks (Steps 1, 2, 3 and 4 of procedure for introducing risk-based testing). On this level, the risk values assigned to risk items are used informally, i.e., not based on a formal risk-based test plan, to control the design and execution of test cases. The assigned risk values can for instance be used to distribute resources for test design or to prioritize test cases for test execution.

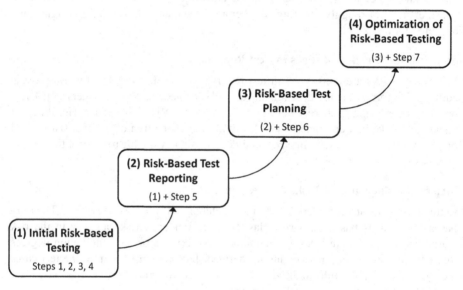

Fig. 3. Stages of Risk-Based Test Integration

(2) **Risk-Based Test Reporting.** This stage is based on stage (1) and additionally considers risks for test reporting (Step 5 of procedure for introducing risk-based testing). Risk-based test reporting is valuable to control the test and release quality.

(3) **Risk-Based Test Planning.** This stage is based on stage (2) and additionally considers risks for test planning (Step 6 of procedure for introducing risk-based testing). On this level, the test plan formally takes risks into account, e.g., for selecting appropriate test design techniques or exit criteria. Thus, at this stage risk-based test activities of the lower stages are formalized.

(4) **Optimization of Risk-Based Testing.** This stage is based on stage (3) and optimizes risk-based testing by continuous evaluation and improvement (Step 7 of procedure for risk-based testing).

4   Discussion in Context of an Industrial Application

In order to realize the benefits of risk-based testing in a real-world setting, the applied testing approach has to be brought into alignment with the risk-based test process. For every step outlined in the previous section, testing has to be adopted to provide the necessary prerequisites. In this section we illustrate the practical challenges involved in introducing the initial stage of risk-based testing by describing the context of an industrial project for which a risk-based testing approach has been considered.

The project has been concerned with the development of a Web-based application part of a large information system, which was developed by the same team of about ten people over the last years. The project had a duration of about one year and was structured in two iterations, each divided in a development and a stabilization phase. An iteration is characterized by a defined set of features, which is implemented throughout the development phase in a number consecutive sprints. Once the implementation has been completed, the feature-freeze milestone marks the transition to the stabilization phase. Although testing has been an important activity throughout all phases of the project, system testing and fixing of the detected issues is central in the stabilization phase. At the end of the iteration, the application containing the new features is released and handed over to a separate service and maintenance organization.

System testing in the stabilization phase is an important and valuable yet also a resource-intensive and time-consuming activity. Therefore, a risk-based testing approach has been considered to improve testing efficiency and effectiveness. To determine the suitability of the project for risk-based testing, a retrospective analysis of the first project iteration has been conducted. In the following the key issues in introducing risk-based testing are explored.

4.1   Distribution of Faults

An essential prerequisite for risk-based testing is the inhomogeneous distribution of faults over the different severity classes and the various parts of the system. In the stabilization phase of the first iteration, a total of 53 faults have been detected by testing, which were rated as high severity (9 faults), medium severity (27 faults) and low severity faults (17).

Fig. 4 shows the distribution of these faults to the application's implementation in terms of about 200 source code files. Faults involve one or several files (the maximum $max = 29$ files, the average $avg = 5$ files with a standard deviation $s = 6.5$).

The faults showed a typical Pareto distribution with the majority of the faults concentrating in a small fraction of the files [10]. Considering all files of the application, 80 % of the associations between faults and files were found in 19 % of the files (marked by a dashed vertical line in Fig. 4). The most critical file was associated to 24 different faults. However, while in total 41 % of the files were found to be faulty, more than half of them (59 %) did not contain any fault. Furthermore, only 11.6 % of all files were associated to high severity faults.

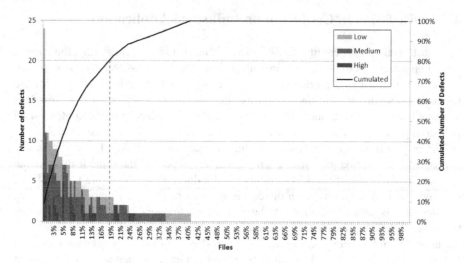

Fig. 4. Distribution of Faults to Implementation Files

This distribution clearly indicates that testing may benefit from a risk-based approach if the testing effort can be directed to those files that have associated faults, especially when these faults also have a high severity rating.

4.2   Identification of Risk Items

One of the first steps in risk-based testing involves the identification of risk items such as functional components or features that can be associated to business and technical criteria values as well as test cases. In the described project, different risk considerations were related to different viewpoints on how to structure the application.

— *Functional viewpoint:* The user requirements as well as the derived acceptance criteria relevant for setting priorities in testing were based on the application's observable functionalities. They were structured according to the main use cases and the associated Web pages that provide the corresponding functionality. In total about 40 Web pages were distinguished. The detailed specification of the graphical layout and the navigation structure included in the requirements emphasizes the importance of the usage related aspects of this viewpoint. The specified use cases and Web pages correspond to the implementation of the client side of the application, which encompasses about two third of the source code files. However, a considerable part of the files concerns the implementation of the backend (server side of the application), which cannot be directly associated to the application's functional structure expressed by the use cases or Web pages.

— *Architectural viewpoint:* The application's architecture distinguishes between client side and server side components and reflects the implementation details more accurately. An approximate relationship between observable functionality and components may be established at least for the client side components. Still, however, the architecture recognizes several shared components and libraries – also for the client side – that cannot be directly linked to the functionality due to the numerous potential dependencies between these components. Furthermore, this viewpoint introduces external dependencies to related parts of the overall system.

— *Development viewpoint:* Several different technologies have been applied for the implementation of the Web-based application, which were assumed to be associated with different risk levels due to various reasons such as degree of technological expertise, available tool support or quality assurance measures applied throughout development. The applied technologies evident in the source code files include JavaScript (45 % of all files), Java (29 %), Java Server Pages (19 %), Cascading Style Sheets (2 %) as well as various others (5 %). Closely linked to the different technologies are non-functional aspects such as compatibility or security as related issues are often dependent on the applied technology. Many of these non-functional aspects are particular critical for Web-based applications and bear a considerable additional risk.

The relevant artifacts in focus of the different viewpoints are illustrated in Fig. 5. While the *Functional View* is concerned with the user requirements, the *Architectural View* provides information about the hierarchical decomposition of the application into components. The link between the functional and the architectural view is maintained by the implements relation between use cases in the specified requirements and client side UI components constituting Web pages tangible for the user. From the architectural viewpoint, the information provided by the *Development View* can be considered a subset that, nevertheless, includes additional aspects, i.e., information about the components' properties.

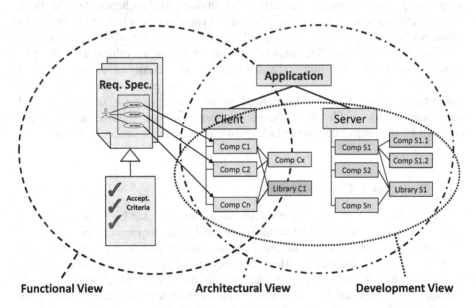

Fig. 5. Different Viewpoints on the Application Under Test

A reconciliation of the different viewpoints showed that there is no single structure of the application that can completely capture all risk aspects. For the studied project, the most comprehensive structure is provided by the architectural viewpoint and is derived from the application's component model. The risk aspects indicated by the other viewpoints should be related to the components and may be maintained as additional properties used in calibrating the risk model. However, it still remains an open question how the mostly vague relationships can be formalized into a complete and consistent model.

4.3   Exploration of Business Criteria

Once the architectural components have been defined as risk items, the associated risks can be assessed. Assessing business criteria is strongly associated to an estimation of the business value of the application's functionality.

As previously indicated, however, in the studied project a direct link between the functionality and the application's components can only be established for the client side. The server side components constitute the backend of the application and, thus, build the basis for any observable functionality provided by the application. Neither their business value nor the associated business criteria can be reliably estimated. An initial approximation of the impact based on business criteria may be derived from the weighted average of the acceptance criteria associated to the client side components.

In the studied project, the specified acceptance criteria contained a non-conformance classification based on the business value of the application's functionality. This classification was therefore proposed as relevant source for determining related business criteria. The classification schema defined three principal classes denoted as high (critical), mid (major) and low (minor) to which the application's functionality was mapped. However, the actual mapping simply classified the main usage scenarios of the base functions as critical and all other scenarios as major. Anything related to layout was classified as minor. As a consequence, the homogeneous classification of major parts for the application's functionality (more than 75 %) showed to be inadequate for deriving a well discriminated risk profile. Nevertheless, a more elaborate classification was not provided by the project due to the lack of an established assessment approach in the organization.

4.4   Exploration of Technical Criteria

Usually a wide range of potential influence factors are available for the assessment of technical criteria, which may be identified by analyzing the project's history. Since our study was based on the first development iteration, no data from previous versions of the application was available. Hence, in order to acquire an approximation of the involved technical criteria, we decided to tab into the experience of involved architects and developers by conducting structured interviews once the feature-freeze milestone had been achieved. The main focus of the interviews was to gain insights about which components part of application's architecture were considered fault-prone. The participants were asked (1) to rate the risk that the different components may contain faults as either high, medium, or low and (2) to explain how they came to their ratings in order to understand possible risk factors specific for the studied project. Six people involved in the development of the application as architects or developers participated in the interviews.

Although the interviews were conducted in an informal way and mainly subjective opinions of the interview participants were collected, the accumulated results provided insights about 36 different architectural components: 8 received ratings that indicated an above medium risk of being fault-prone. Furthermore, 14 components were considered of low risk. The ratings for these high and low risk components were consistent across the interview participants. The main reasons mentioned for high risk ratings were high complexity of the control structure, lack of test tool support for some of the applied technologies, as well as frequently changing and poorly documented external interfaces.

Deriving a risk estimation from interviews were involved several challenges.

— First, since factors determining technical criteria still had to be explored, the rating conducted in the interviews was mainly driven by the discussion of possible influence factors and their potential impact. Thus, the risk ratings were most often subjective estimates and the interview participants felt not confident to express these estimates on a more fine-grained scale other than high, medium or low.

— Second, the application's architecture is composed by a hierarchical component structure. Thus, since the identified components were associated to different levels in this component structure, the resulting hierarchical dependencies had to be considered in the component rating. The rating of a higher order component depended on its specific properties as well as on the rating of its subcomponents. In many cases the interview participants explained the risks by "zooming into" the components, sometimes even until the file level. However, the low degree of formality of the architectural specification did not allow a more formal rating approach.

— Third, the interviews were conducted with key members of the project who were closely involved in development and who had detailed knowledge as well as a good overview of the whole application. As a consequence, the availability of these key people was limited and scheduling interviews was a challenge in itself. More time consuming estimation techniques that would include several interview cycles or group discussions to consolidate disagreements in ratings had to be omitted due to time constraints.

4.5   Risk Assessment

The overall risk is determined by the combination of business criteria and technical criteria. In our case, however, the initial exploration of potential criteria did not provide a consistent basis for a structured risk assessment. In particular, the first estimates of the business criteria were not considered an adequate input for such an assessment due to the lack of data concerning server side components and the mostly homogeneous rating of the client side components.

To investigate the applicability of the results achieved from exploring the technical criteria, the provided estimates were compared to the actual defects identified with the applied conventional testing approach. The actual defect counts per component were retrieved from the retrospective analysis of the first iteration. Fig. 6 shows the resultant confusion matrix for the estimated risk classes.

The estimations achieved an overall accuracy of 52.8 %. Nevertheless, the classes *high* and *low* are of particular importance, as for components in these classes a corresponding high or low testing effort may be recommended. The estimations concerning the class *high* showed a precision of 87.5 % and a recall of 46.7 %. The precision was achieved as almost all components estimated to have a high risk of being fault-prone actually contained faults; several even contained high severity faults. However, the low recall indicates that the estimation missed several of the critical components. While in the estimation only 8 components were considered of high risk, actually 15 components fall into this class. The number of misclassification has to be considered as critical for the class *low*, which showed a precision of 57.1 % and a recall of 66.7 %. Two components estimated to have a low risk of being faulty were actually found to have a high number of faults. Both even contained a high severity fault.

		estimated			
		high	medium	low	
actual	high	**7**	**6**	**2**	15
	medium	**1**	**4**	**4**	9
	low	**0**	**4**	**8**	12
		8	14	14	36

Fig. 6. Confusion Matrix for the Estimated Risk Classes

In general, these results confirmed that a risk-based testing approach can be applied in the studied project. However, the outcome of the initial risk assessment based on informal estimates is not sufficient to proceed with the next steps in introducing risk-based testing. Therefore, further effort has to be invested in identify a consistent set of relevant risk criteria that can be assembled to a reliable risk model for calculating the associated risk values.

5 Related Work

The importance of risk management for software engineering [11] has been addressed in several risk management approaches tailored to software engineering processes. For instance, Karolak [12] proposes a risk management process for software engineering that contains the activities risk identification, risk strategy, risk assessment, risk mitigation, and risk prediction. Risk-based testing is a test-based approach to risk management. In the literature, several risk-based testing approaches have been proposed.

Amland [13] defines a risk-based testing approach that is based on Karolak's risk management process comprising the following steps and the corresponding risk management activities: planning (risk identification and risk strategy), identification of risk indicators (part of risk assessment), identification of the cost of a failure (part of risk assessment), identification of critical elements (part of risk assessment), test execution (risk mitigation), and estimation of completion (risk reporting and risk prediction). Differing from our methodology the approach is not aligned with the standard test process.

Bach [14] presents a pragmatic approach to risk-based testing grounded on a heuristic software risk analysis. Bach distinguishes inside-out risk analysis starting with details about a situation and identifying associated risk, and outside-in risk analysis starting with a set of potential risks and matching them to the details of the situation. In our approach we generalize and integrate the concepts of Bach by introducing generic risk items and risk assessment.

Redmill provides a thorough discussion of risk-based testing [15] as well as a proposal for practical application suggesting a single factor risk assessment, either for probability of for impact, or a two-factor risk assessment, in which probability and impact are combined [16]. The application of the resulting risk classification in the test process, e.g., for test planning, design, execution or reporting, is beyond the scope of the approach.

Stallbaum and Metzger [17] introduce a model-driven risk-based system testing approach that is based on the Factor-Criteria-Metrics model [4]. The focus of their approach is the annotation of risk assessment data in UML-based models, however, without a standard-aligned risk-based testing methodology and without an approach for its introduction in existing test processes.

Risk-based testing is an essential component in a value-based testing strategy [18]. In their work on value-based software testing, Li et al. [19, 20] introduce a method that integrates business importance, quality risk and testing cost to determine testing priorities at the level of features for test panning and controlling. In contrast to our approach, an alternative way for risk assessment is used: The relative business importance is determined via a requirements prioritization approach based on expert judgment of positive/negative impact of the presence/absence of features [21]. The quality risk is based on quantitative and qualitative risk factors derived from past projects and experience. Weights for quality risks are defined using the Analytical Hierarchy Process (AHP) method [22] from multi-criteria decision-making. Together with the developers, the test manager estimates the relative risk for each feature and, finally, calculates the risk probability values that are set in relation to testing costs. Thus, on the one hand, this method goes beyond our approach as the underlying value-based perspective integrates the potential benefits of testing with the costs of testing. On the other hand, the proposed integration into the software testing process considers mainly test planning and controlling as target activities.

A further risk-based testing approach that is similar to ours is the Practical Risk-Based Testing Approach (PRIMSA) [7]. It distinguishes business and technical risks determined by weighted criteria to calculate the overall risk of risk items. Additionally, PRISMA defines a process consisting of concrete activities, i.e., initiating, planning, kick-off meeting, extended risk identification, individual preparation, processing individual scores, consensus meeting, and define differentiated risk-based testing approach. The activities are defined in a very concrete way with detailed instructions. Thus, the PRISMA approach is highly specific and not as adaptable as our approach. Furthermore, PRISMA does also not define stages of risk-based test integration. Differing from our approach, all other mentioned risk-based testing approaches including PRISMA do not provide a systematic in-depth discussion of the challenges of introducing the approach.

We base our work on the standard testing process according to the definition of the ISTQB [1]. In Spillner et al. [23] as well as Black [24] risk-based testing is integrated into the standard test process. The focus of this integration is, however, on risk assessment and no process or guidelines for improving the test process by a stepwise integration of risk-based testing is offered such as in our approach.

Maturity models like CMMI [25] or SPICE [26] have successfully been applied to assess and improve software development processes in general. In the meanwhile, also special maturity models for test processes are available like Test SPICE [27], Test Process Improvement (TPI Next) [28, 29] or Test Maturitiy Model integration (TMMi) [6]. Test approaches for process improvement propose different structural concepts such as areas, processes, process groups and stages. Risk-based testing or at least specific steps of the risk-based testing approach proposed in this paper can be mapped to areas or processes. However, Test SPICE, TPI/TPI Next and TMMi do not consider stages of risk-based testing itself such as our approach.

6   Conclusion and Future Work

In this paper we presented experiences and challenges of introducing risk-based testing in an industrial project. We first explained a generic risk-based testing methodology and a procedure how it can be introduced incrementally in a test process. We then showed how this procedure could be applied in an industrial project. Numerous challenges and lessons learned in introducing risk-based testing on the initial stage have been identified:

- A consolidation of perspectives on the system under test (e.g., functional viewpoints, architectural viewpoints, development viewpoints etc.) is required in order to identify an appropriate set of risk items. However, none of the different viewpoints may be sufficient to completely cover all relevant risk items, calling for a combination or integration that relates the various properties of the different viewpoints into a complete model.

— If not explicitly developed in the requirements engineering phase, many projects will not have a clear understanding about the business value of the system's functionality. Thus, these projects can neither provide accurate values for individual functions nor are they able to thoroughly estimate the associated business criteria.

— When a more technical structure of the system (e.g., components of the system architecture) is maintained as basis for the risk items, it is often hard to consistently map the value of system functions and the associated business criteria to the risk items. The mapping is made difficult in particular due to items with many dependencies leading to high risk exposure (e.g., shared components).

— Technical structures (e.g., component structures) are often hierarchically organized and the involved people understand and discuss the overall system in terms of these hierarchies. However, hierarchical dependencies introduce a further level of complexity in calculating and associating risk values to risk items. When derived from informal models described with UML, the resultant structures may often be incomplete and inconsistent.

— From a technical perspective, a wide range of potential influence factors can be easily identified, for example, size and complexity of components, dependencies between components and to external entities, coverage by static and dynamic quality assurance measures, and applied development technologies. Many of them can even be supported by automated collection of related metric values. In previous studies on defect prediction [30] it has been found that selecting adequate sources for extracting metric values is essential to produce useful results. Furthermore, usually only a subset of the large number of available metric values is sufficient to develop an operable risk model. However, selecting a suitable subset of the potentially large amount of available metrics that best represents the criteria is an open question.

— Ideally, metric values can be collected from a project's development history spanning several iterations. New projects lacking such a historic track record may derive a representative data basis from related parallel or previous projects. Otherwise, estimation approaches leveraging the experience of the involved project members have to be applied.

— Risk estimations involving several project members require a structured and well-defined approach to provide objective and reliable results. Without prior experience of the involved participants, it may still require several iterations to converge to a common perception of the procedures and a calibrated risk model. However, it has to be noted that the overall effort can be quite high, especially when several key members of a project should be involved in the risk assessment. Their limited availability may impose serious restrictions concerning the possible risk estimation and consolidation approaches. Matters get even worse when such estimates need to be conducted frequently throughout the lifecycle of a project.

In this paper we have introduced four stages of risk-based test integration, i.e., initial risk-based testing, risk-based test reporting, risk-based test planning, and optimization of risk-based testing. But in the industrial application we have only discussed challenges for risk-based test integration at the initial stage. In future, we will also introduce the other stages in industrial projects and present appropriate challenges and lessons learned. To provide better support for initial integration of risk-based testing we plan several measures. First, we will perform a detailed cost-benefit analysis to improve the step analysis and planning of the risk-based test integration. Then, we plan to conduct and compile a survey on risk-based testing in industry to provide a comprehensive collection of best practices and techniques supporting practitioners in identifying risk items and assessing risks. Finally, we will consider data mining techniques to construct prediction models used for risk estimation from a large set of metric values that considers non-obvious interdependencies between a large set of metric values. Thereby, the necessary training data values are derived from the project's development history.

Acknowledgments. This work has been supported by the project QE LaB – Living Models for Open Systems (www.qe-lab.at) funded by the Austrian Federal Ministry of Economics (Bundesministerium für Wirtschaft und Arbeit) as well as the competence network Softnet Austria (www.soft-net.at) funded by the Austrian Federal Ministry of Economics (Bundesministerium für Wirtschaft und Arbeit), the province of Styria, the Steirische Wirtschaftsförderungsgesellschaft mbH (SFG), and the city of Vienna's Center for Innovation and Technology (ZIT).

References

1. ISTQB: Standard glossary of terms used in software testing. Version 2.1 (2010)
2. Gerrard, P., Thompson, N.: Risk Based E-Business Testing. Artech House. Inc., Norwood (2002)
3. Felderer, M., Haisjackl, C., Breu, R., Motz, J.: Integrating Manual and Automatic Risk Assessment for Risk-Based Testing. Software Quality Days, 159–180 (2012)
4. Cavano, J.P., McCall, J.A.: A framework for the measurement of software quality. ACM SIGMETRICS Performance Evaluation Review 7(3-4), 133–139 (1978)
5. ISO: ISO/IEC 25000 Software and system engineering-Software product Quality Requirements and Evaluation (SQuaRE)-Guide to SQuaRE. International Organization for Standarization (2005)
6. van Veenendaal, E., Goslin, A., Olsen, K., O'Hara, F., Miller, M., Thompson, G., Wells, B.: Test Maturity Model integration (TMMi) Version 1.0, TMMi Foundation (2008)
7. van Veenendaal, E.: The PRISMA Approach, Uitgeverij Tutein Nolthenius (2012)
8. Ramler, R., Kopetzky, T., Platz, W.: Value-Based Coverage Measurement in Requirements-Based Testing: Lessons Learned from an Approach Implemented in the TOSCA Testsuite. In: 38th Euromicro Conference on Software Engineering and Advanced Applications, SEAA 2012 (2012)
9. Cangussu, J.W., Karcich, R.M., Mathur, A.P., DeCarlo, R.A.: Software release control using defect based quality estimation. In: 15th International Symposium on Software Reliability Engineering (2004)

10. Fenton, N.E., Ohlsson, N.: Quantitative analysis of faults and failures in a complex software system. IEEE Transactions on Software Engineering 26(8), 797–814 (2000)
11. Pfleeger, S.L.: Risky business: what we have yet to learn about risk management. Journal of Systems and Software 53(3), 265–273 (2000)
12. Karolak, D.W., Karolak, N.: Software Engineering Risk Management: A Just-in-Time Approach. Wiley-IEEE Computer Society Press (1995)
13. Amland, S.: Risk-based testing: Risk analysis fundamentals and metrics for software testing including a financial application case study. Journal of Systems and Software 53(3), 287–295 (2000)
14. Bach, J.: Heuristic risk-based testing. Software Testing and Quality Engineering Magazine 11, 99 (1999)
15. Redmill, F.: Exploring risk-based testing and its implications. Softw. Test. Verif. Reliab. 14(1), 3–15 (2004)
16. Redmill, F.: Theory and practice of risk-based testing: Research Articles. Softw. Test. Verif. Reliab. 15(1), 3–20 (2005)
17. Stallbaum, H., Metzger, A.: Employing Requirements Metrics for Automating Early Risk Assessment. In: Workshop on Measuring ss, pp. 1–12 (2007)
18. Ramler, R., Biffl, S., Grünbacher, P.: Value-based Management of Software Testing. In: Biffl, S., Aurum, A., Boehm, B., Erdogmus, H., Grünbacher, P. (eds.) Value-Based Software Engineering, pp. 225–244. Springer (2006)
19. Li, Q., Li, M., Yang, Y., Wang, Q., Tan, T., Boehm, B., Hu, C.: Bridge the Gap between Software Test Process and Business Value: A Case Study. In: Wang, Q., Garousi, V., Madachy, R., Pfahl, D. (eds.) ICSP 2009. LNCS, vol. 5543, pp. 212–223. Springer, Heidelberg (2009)
20. Li, Q., Yang, Y., Li, M., Wang, Q., Boehm, B., Hu, C.: Improving Software Testing Process: Feature Prioritization to Make Winners of Success-critical Stakeholders. J. Softw. Maint. Evol. Res. Pract. (2010)
21. Wiegers, K.E.: First things first: Prioritizing requirements. Software Development 7(10), 24–30 (1999)
22. Saaty, T.L.: The Analytic Hierarchy Process. McGraw-Hill (1980)
23. Spillner, A., Rossner, T., Winter, M., Linz, T.: Software Testing Practice: Test Management: A Study Guide for the Certified Tester Exam ISTQB Advanced Level, Rocky Nook (2007)
24. Black, R.: Advanced Software Testing. Guide to the ISTQB Advanced Certification as an Advanced Test Manager, vol. 2. Rocky Nook (2009)
25. Ahern, D., Clouse, A., Turner, R.: CMMI distilled: a practical introduction to integrated process improvement. Addison-Wesley Professional (2008)
26. Dorling, A.: SPICE: Software process improvement and capability determination. Software Quality Journal 2(4), 209–224 (1993)
27. Steiner, M., Blaschke, M., Philipp, M., Schweigert, T.: Make Test Process Assessment Similar to Software Process Assessment–the Test SPICE Approach. Journal of Software: Evolution and Process 24(5), 471–480 (2012)
28. Koomen, T., Pol, M.: Test process improvement: a practical step-by-step guide to structured testing. Addison-Wesley Professional (1999)
29. Koomen, T., van der Aalst, L., Broekman, B., Vroon, M.: TMap Next, For Result-driven Testing. UTN Publishers (2006)
30. Ramler, R., Larndorfer, S., Natschläger, T.: What Software Repositories Should Be Mined for Defect Predictors? In: 35th Euromicro Conference on Software Engineering and Advanced Applications, SEAA 2009 (2009)

Project Progress and Risk Monitoring
in Automation Systems Engineering

Wikan Sunindyo, Thomas Moser, Dietmar Winkler, and Richard Mordinyi

Christian Doppler Laboratory "Software Integration for Flexible Automation Systems"
Vienna University of Technology
Vienna, Austria
{Wikan.Sunindyo,Thomas.Moser,Dietmar.Winkler,
Richard.Mordinyi}@tuwien.ac.at

Abstract. Current Automation Systems Engineering (ASE) projects consist of heterogeneous engineering workflows for managing processes that are executed in different engineering fields, e.g., mechanical, electrical, or software engineering. Project managers and engineers typically create and use their own specific engineering workflows for managing objects across the borders of heterogeneous engineering fields, such as development artifacts, change requests or signals. Major challenges in the context of addressing risk awareness for engineering workflow validation are the unawareness regarding risks of other project stakeholders and limited scalability of risk estimation approaches. In this paper, we propose the Engineering Service Bus (EngSB) framework for flexible and efficient object change management processes and risk-aware engineering workflow validation. The object change management here means the management of signal changes in an industry showcase. The workflow validation involves the activity to validate the real-world engineering project data with the designed workflow. Based on real-world engineering project data from a hydro power plant systems integrator we propose the definition of risk factors on project management and engineering levels to increase risk awareness. First results of the industry case study show that the inclusion of risk factors can enhance the overall engineering project quality, thus enabling risk mitigation in ASE projects.

Keywords: Automation Systems Engineering, Project Progress Monitoring, Risk Monitoring.

1   Introduction

Automation Systems Engineering (ASE) project management typically involves heterogeneous engineering fields, e.g., mechanical, electrical, or software engineering, which should work together to reach common goals such as delivering high quality automation systems using an efficient and effective automation systems development process [30]. However, engineers from different engineering fields typically use their own tools and data models for performing specific tasks within their specific engineering fields. The heterogeneity of data models hinders efficient project progress

D. Winkler, S. Biffl, and J. Bergsmann (Eds.): SWQD 2013, LNBIP 133, pp. 30–54, 2013.

monitoring and risk management. Hence project managers need an integrated view coping with the semantic heterogeneities of the different involved heterogeneous engineering fields.

For communicating, disseminating, and managing objects, e.g., development artifacts, change requests or objects used for common engineering activities such as signals, across the borders of different engineering fields, engineers typically create and use their own specific engineering workflows [2][3] with limited interaction capabilities between the different fields. An engineering workflow (usually the part of more generic company-wide engineering processes) has its main focus on observation and monitoring of a set of individual engineering steps (within one discipline), while business processes usually provide a comprehensive view on the entire project. The goal of using engineering workflows is to support engineers and project managers with suitable information on the implementation and enactment of processes running in the system. Unlike typical business workflows, engineering workflows not necessarily are connected directly to customers [31]. Examples for typical engineering workflows are Integrated Product Development (IPD).

In addition, current approaches for managing engineering workflows still do not satisfactorily address risk awareness during process analysis. This leads to analysis results which are hard to justify from a business management perspective, e.g., risks arising from the fact that the costs of changes are typically higher if performed at a later stage of an engineering process [29]. Current solutions only provide limited capabilities to analyze and present change management process data across disciplines.

With focus on raising the risk awareness of object change management workflows, the key questions for project management and engineers are (a) how changes can be handled more efficiently and (b) how relevant change requests can be passed to the involved engineers. Thus, there exists the need for flexible and comprehensive engineering process support across disciplines to enable collaboration and interaction between disciplines, tools, and data models. In the context of addressing risk awareness for engineering workflow validation, i.e. getting an comprehensive project overview at anytime of the project and independent of the involved engineering tools, the major challenges are (a) different stakeholders of ASE projects, who need to be able to identify and mitigate risks efficiently, and (b) different stakeholders of ASE projects, who need to classify their specific risk factors based on their requirements.

This paper presents the Engineering Service Bus (EngSB) framework – a middleware platform for supporting collaboration across disciplines and domain borders – which bridges the gap between heterogeneous disciplines by providing semantic integration of data models [3, 5, 22] based on the technical integration of domain-specific tools [4]. The integrated view on heterogeneous engineering environments enables the implementation of a flexible and efficient object change management process and demonstrates the ability for risk-aware engineering workflow validation based on real-world engineering project data from a hydro power plant systems integrator. In addition, we propose the definition of risk factors on project management and engineering levels to increase risk awareness on both levels. First empirical [28] results show that the ability of capturing and analyzing data from different data sources across various engineering fields enables comprehensive observation and monitoring of the engineering process and risk factors, which can enhance the overall engineering project quality and enables risk mitigation in ASE. The findings on the results have been discussed with the industry experts to enhance the validity of the results and the analysis approach.

In this work, the EngSB framework can be seen as a kind of Integrated Product Development (IPD) approach, as it also tries to provide a systematic approach to product development which increases customer satisfaction through a timely collaboration of necessary disciplines throughout the development life-cycle [23].

The remainder of this paper is structured as follows: Section 2 presents related works on Automation Systems Engineering (ASE), the Engineering Service Bus (EngSB) Approach, the Engineering Cockpit prototype, and on risk management. Section 3 identifies the research issues, while section 4 presents the use case. Section 5 describes the solution approach. Section 6 presents the evaluation results, which are discussed in section 7 with regard to the research issues. Finally, section 8 concludes and identifies future work.

2   Related Work

This section summarizes background information on Automation Systems Engineering, the Engineering Service Bus (EngSB), the Engineering Cockpit (EngCo) prototype, and on risk management.

2.1   Automation Systems Engineering

Automation systems, e.g., complex industrial automation plants for manufacturing, steel mills, or power plants include a set of heterogeneous engineering environments, e.g., mechanical, electrical, and software engineering disciplines who should collaborate and interact for successfully completing ASE projects [3]. The project in our case is an automation systems engineering project which involves heterogeneous stakeholders from different engineering domains to collaborate and achieve a particular goal. Expert knowledge is embodied in domain-specific standards, terminologies, people, processes, methods, models, and tools [21][20]. Nevertheless, individual disciplines including discipline specific tools and data models are isolated and/or with limited support for interaction and collaboration [4]. Thus, a major challenge is to synchronize specification data and plans from a wide range of engineering aspects in the overall engineering process, e.g., physical plant design, mechanical and electrical engineering artifacts, and process and project planning [34].

Fig. 1 illustrates a basic engineering process, observed at in a hydro power plant as our industry partner, including five phases in sequential order: initial, drawing started, customer approval, factory tests, and customer commissioning. Note that these phases (i.e., project states) correspond to the individual states of engineering objects. A more detailed view on the sequential steps, e.g., during the phase "drawing started", showed that engineers follow their own (isolated) engineering processes within their assigned discipline or domain. In addition, engineers from individual disciplines work in parallel on similar engineering objects from different perspectives [34]. Thus, they have to synchronize and exchange data to keep the engineering project consistent. Note that similar processes apply for all engineering phases. The risk elements in these processes are hidden in each step and can be categorized into domain specific risks, collaboration risks, and project management risks.

Changes from disciplines have to be passed to related engineers who might be affected by those changes. For instance changing a sensor from hardware perspective might have an impact on electrical engineers (how to connect the sensor) and to the software engineer (how to control and analyze sensor data). Observations in industry projects showed a less frequent and informal synchronization process, executed by experts manually. Because of a high effort of human experts, who are familiar with at least two engineering disciplines, this synchronization process is executed less frequently and, thus, include a high risk regarding the consistency of engineering objects and the impact of changes. The high effort of the human experts are often needed in resolving changes in the engineering project, however their availabilities are somehow limited.

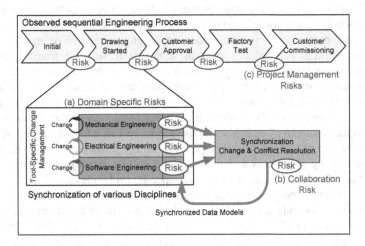

Fig. 1. Management and Engineering Risks from Process Perspective [34]

Based on our observation we found a set of risks in the ASE which can have a major impact on the individual engineers and on the project: (a) *Domain specific risks* focus on individual and isolated disciplines, where engineers apply well-established risk management approaches, e.g., RiskIt [17] for the software engineering domain. As individual disciplines can apply appropriate countermeasures which have effects on these disciplines, related disciplines might be affected by these measures; (b) *Collaboration risks* focus on the need for frequent synchronization of individual artifacts and engineering objects coming from different disciplines. Because of a high manual effort for synchronization (if not automated) the frequency of data exchange is quite low; e.g., once per month. If done less frequently the number of changes might be very high leading to additional risks with respect to related disciplines in case of changes; (c) *project management risks* focus on project monitoring and control challenges, which usually depend on the capability to capture and analyze project data and draw appropriate solutions. Because of a lack of synchronization and limited access to comprehensive data additional risks arise, even if the data are available very late in the project. Thus, late changes, e.g., during the factory test or during the commissioning phase at the customers' site, result in inefficient, error-prone and risky engineering processes [29].

To overcome risks on (1) management level, i.e., enabling project observation and control across disciplines and domain borders and (2) on engineering level, i.e., supporting efficient change management and frequent synchronization across disciplines, the Engineering Service Bus [4] supports interaction of related stakeholder within a heterogeneous engineering environments with respect to improving (i) engineering processes and change management, (ii) quality assurance activities, and (iii) risk management in the ASE domain.

2.2   Engineering Service Bus

Current developers of software systems use a wide range of tools from software vendors, open source communities, and in-house developers. Getting these tools to work together to support a development process in an engineering environment remains challenging as there is a wide variety of standards these tools follow [15]. Any integration approach has to address the levels of technical heterogeneity, i.e., how to connect systems that use different platforms, protocols, etc., so they can exchange messages [7][12][25]; and semantic heterogeneity, i.e., how to translate the content of the messages between systems that use different local terminologies for common concepts in their domain of discourse, so these systems can understand each other and conduct a meaningful conversation [1][9][24][11][21]. Particularly in ASE, integration of engineering systems is a challenge as typically a broad range of engineering tools from different vendors are used to solve specific problems [26].

Biffl and Schatten proposed a platform called Engineering Service Bus (EngSB), which integrates not only different tools and systems but also different steps in the software development lifecycle [5][4]. The platform aims at integrating software engineering disciplines e.g., mechanical, electrical or software engineering, rather than individual services [7]. The EngSB consists of the following main components: (1) engineering discipline specific tools to be integrated, and (2) so called connectors which enable communication between the bus and the specific engineering tool which consist of a technical specific and a technical neutral interface. The technical specific interface is implemented within the engineering tool while the technical neutral interface (i.e. tool domain) represents a standardization of connectors of a specific engineering tool type. This seems possible since different tools, developed to solve the same problem have, more or less, similar interfaces. For example, the source code management (SCM) tools Subversion and CVS both provide similar functionality, which allows describing these tools as instances of the SCM tool domain. This concept allows the EngSB to interact with a tool domain without knowing which specific tool instances are actually present. Note that tool domains do not implement tool instances but provide the abstract description of events and services, which have to be provided by concrete connectors of tool instances to the EngSB. This implies that the EngSB not only facilitates data integration but more importantly functional integration as well (3) the Engineering Database [22] and the Engineering Knowledge Base [20] which enable versioning of common data used and an automated transformation of common concepts represented differently in the various engineering tools. (4) project relevant added-value applications like the Engineering Cockpit [19] for efficient project monitoring or the Engineering Object Editor [18] for quality assured integration of data sources. (5) a workflow engine executing engineering processes which describe a configurable sequence of process steps satisfying project integration requirements. The workflow engine is an engine which generates event logs based on designed workflow and its relevant rules for further analysis. The engine is responsible for the correct management of the workflow relevant rules and events while the configuration of it makes use of the modeled concepts of tool instances and tool domains in the Engineering Knowledge Base.

2.3   Engineering Cockpit

The Engineering Cockpit (EngCo) is a social-network-style collaboration platform for automation system engineering project managers and engineers, applying technical [4] and semantic integration [6, 16, 29] approaches for bridging gaps between heterogeneous ASE project data sources as foundation for comprehensive project monitoring and management, which was first introduced in [19]. It builds on semantic web technology, the Engineering Knowledge Base (EKB) and semantic integration framework [20], to explicitly link the data model elements of several heterogeneous ASE project data sources based on their data semantic definitions.

The EngCo is generic framework for project reporting across tool and domain boundaries, and shows the prototypic implementation to demonstrate how to calculate a set of metrics for project managers and engineers, e.g., number of signals and their project phase. In [19] a general EngCo concept has been described and discussed by taking into account concrete evaluation data from industry. The feasibility of the EngCo prototype was evaluated by performing a set of project-specific queries across engineering discipline boundaries for information on current and historic project activities based on real-world ASE project data from our industry partner in the hydro power plant engineering domain.

Major results were that EngCo (a) enables the definition of project-specific queries across engineering discipline boundaries and therefore minimizes the effort for near-time analysis of the project progress, (b) automatically shows the current view on project progress as soon as the engineering groups send their local changes to planning data to the common data basis, and (c) enables early risk detection and analysis, e.g., an unexpectedly large number of changes to engineering objects late in the project.

2.4   Risk Management

A risk is a random event that may possibly occur and, if it would occur, it would have a negative impact on the goals of the organization. A risk is composed of three elements, namely the scenario, its probability of occurrence, and the size of its impact if it would occur (either a fixed value or a distribution) [32]. Webster's dictionary[1] defines "risk" as "the possibility of loss or injury". In risk management's fundamental concept, this definition can be translated into risk exposure or "risk impact" or "risk factor".

Risk exposure is defined by the relationship of RE = P(UO) * L(UO) where RE is the risk exposure, P(UO) is the probability of an unsatisfactory outcome and L(UO) is the loss of the parties affected if the outcome is unsatisfactory.

Risk management is defined as the identification, assessment, and prioritization of risks followed by coordinated and economical application of resources to minimize, monitor, and control the probability and/or impact of unfortunate events or to maximize the realization of opportunities [13]. Boehm [6] classified risk management into two primary steps, namely risk assessment and risk control. The first step, risk assessment, involves risk identification, risk analysis, and risk prioritization. The second step, risk control, involves risk-management planning, risk resolution, and risk monitoring. Recent works on general risk management, for example by Ropponen and Lyytinen [27].

This risk management classification helps to specify a deeper step in risk mitigation for automated software engineering. Risk mitigation/risk reduction itself is defined as a systematic reduction in the extent of exposure to a risk and/or the likelihood of its occurrence. Vose [32] classified risk management options into several groups, namely (a) acceptance, i.e. nothing is done to control the risk, (b) increase, i.e. reduce the level of protection and allocate the resources to manage other risks in order to achieve a superior overall risk efficiency, (c) get more information, i.e. acquiring more information to decrease the level of uncertainty, (d) avoidance, i.e. changing a method of operation, a project plan, an investment strategy, etc., so that the identified risk is no longer relevant, (e) reduction (mitigation), involves a range of techniques, which may be used together, to reduce the probability of the risk, its impact or both, (f) contingency planning, devised to optimize the response to risks if they occur, (g) risk reserve, to add some reserve (buffer) to cover the risk should it occur, (h) insurance, insure for risks that have an impact outside our comfort zone to an insurance company, and (i) risk transfer, which involves manipulating the problem so that the risk is transferred from one party to another.

Risk management and business process management play an important role in the current economy. The continuous improvement of economic aspects of a company's business processes is the foundation to stay competitive. It is not surprising that Gartner [10] puts business process improvement as the top priority in its CIO report. Jakoubi and Tjoa [16] define risk aware business process management as the integration of a risk perspective into business process management. They propose a set of extension required for the business process and risk management domain in order to consider risks in business processes in an integrated way.

Becker et al [2] proposed a strategy called SIQinU (Strategy for understanding and Improving Quality in Use) to improve the quality of the products in an organization. This strategy allows the recognition of quality problems in use through evaluation and proposes product improvements by understanding and applying changes on product

[1] http://www.merriam-webster.com

attributes. There are two steps to improve the quality of products, namely (a) under-standing the quality of current product version, and (b) making appropriate changes to increase the quality of new version of improvement actions were needed. This work supports our effort to design and implement a framework for involving risk factors in the automation systems. This involvement of risk factors increases the automation systems quality by (a) increasing the risk-awareness of project managers and engi-neering team, (b) avoiding possible risk in the systems, e.g., potential losses of the systems, and (c) designing the mitigation plan for the systems, if risks happen.

3   Research Issues

Current engineering process analysis in ASE typically does not take into considera-tion risk factors. This makes the systems less robust against certain classes of risks and/or systems changes. By including risk factors, such as incomplete or incorrect engineering object changes on an engineering level or over-budgeting or delays in the schedule on a project management level, into the engineering process analysis, it is expected that the main systems stakeholders (i.e., project managers and engineers in the context of this paper) will be more aware of urgent risks in the system.

The involvement of risk factors in ASE itself can be classified into stakeholders coming from different levels and which interact directly with the system. In this work, we identified and classified two types of users, namely project managers and engi-neers. Each type of user may have different kinds of risk factors according to their requirements and goals. Furthermore, typically both project managers and engineers are only focusing on the risks from their specific environment without being aware about the risks of the overall business system.

From this situation, we derive two major research issues regarding the involvement of risk factors in the ASE process to improve the efficiency and effectiveness of engi-neering process analysis.

RI-1: How to identify and mitigate risks by using engineering workflows in ASE projects. Current approaches for identifying risks and increasing risk-awareness have been successfully researched and applied for business entities in the business process management, e.g., the RiskIt approach [17]. In this research issue, we want to elabo-rate whether these concepts, e.g., risk identification and mitigation in risk manage-ment workshops, can also be applied to an engineering context such as ASE, and furthermore want to identify any differences or limitations of this application domain.

Based on the observed engineering processes and the need for interaction, collabora-tion, and synchronization of engineering artifacts across disciplines, we identified the EngSB framework as major platform for supporting efficient and effective risk mitiga-tion. In this context, the main question is how to measure and analyze engineering processes with respect to change management processes and project monitoring and control (project observation). In this paper we focus on the analysis of process events and data with respect to identifying the number of changes based on individual change types.

RI-2: How to classify the risk factors based on different types of stakeholders. The sources of changes in the automation systems can be from internal or external stakeholders. Both types of stakeholders have different kinds of risk factors which depend on the focus of typical tasks and requirements originating from both types of stakeholders. In this paper, we want to elaborate on the focus of risk factors from these stakeholder types in order to increase the risk awareness and provide suggestions on the mitigation actions necessary to take when the risks occur. We collect the data of changes in the automation systems and analyze the amount of changes caused by internal/external stakeholders in different project phases.

4   Use Case

This section presents a multi-disciplinary engineering use case– based on an industry case study – from an industrial partner developing, creating, and maintaining hydro power plants, and demonstrates a typical process related to the management of signal changes during the life cycle of the power plant. Depending on the size of the commissioned power plant there are about 40 to 80 thousand signals to be managed and administrated in different tools of different engineering disciplines. Signals consist of structured key value pairs created by different hardware components and represent one of the base artifacts in the course of developing power plants. Signals include process interfaces (e.g., wiring and piping), electrical signals (e.g., voltage levels), and software I/O variables. Today's integrated tool suites often consist of a predefined set of tools and a homogeneous common data model, which work well in their narrow scope but do not easily extend to other tools in the project outside the tool's scope. Therefore, system integrators in multi-disciplinary engineering projects want to be able to conduct automated change management across all tools that contribute project-level data elements regardless of the origin of the tool and data model.

The current life cycle of a power plant is divided into several phases, each of them reflecting the progress in building the system and the states of the signals. Highly simplified, the following steps are retrieved from the experiences of the industrial partner: (1) First of all engineers start with the requirement & specification phase. In this phase the required data is gathered, such as signals for turbines and generators. It results in the number of sensors, signals and types of sensors. (2) From this data the typology of the system can be created. The output of this step is a number of I/O cards and a network typology. (3) In the next step the circuit diagram is designed. It produces the allocation plan for mechanical resources. (4) Finally the hardware design is finished to be assembled. (5) After this step the Programmable Logic Controller (PLC) software is created to map hardware pin to software pin addresses. (6) Finally the system can be rolled out. In overall these phases are mapped on one of the following signal status: Initial (1), Drawing Started (2, 3), Approved (4) Factory Test Completed (5) and Commissioned (6). These 6 states are generally applicable in the automation systems engineering.

At least there are two different types of stakeholders of the system who are responsible for changes in the power plant system, namely external and internal stakeholders. The external stakeholders, e.g., the customers or the business managers may introduce new requirements or new rules/regulations that affect to the signal changes. The internal stakeholders, e.g., the internal engineers or the project managers also have their own requirements to change the signals in the systems. The previously described process refers to a perfect scenario, whereas in general 25% of all signals change due to changing customer requirements at any point in the life cycle of the development of the power plant. However, the later signals are changed, the more effort has to be invested in coordination with other disciplines and thus the more costs are created. Project managers would welcome monitoring tools allowing them to identify risks in the different phases of development. The combination of data sources from different disciplines may provide information about e.g., customer behavior due to the number of change request per project phase, difficult and complex areas in construction due to high number of explicit and implicit changes. A specific type of risk may be related to the source of changes. For example if there are more than 5% of changes from external stakeholders, it triggers an alarm to revise the budget. Hence the project manager should measure the sources of the signals change and calculate the percentage of overall change for risk mitigation.

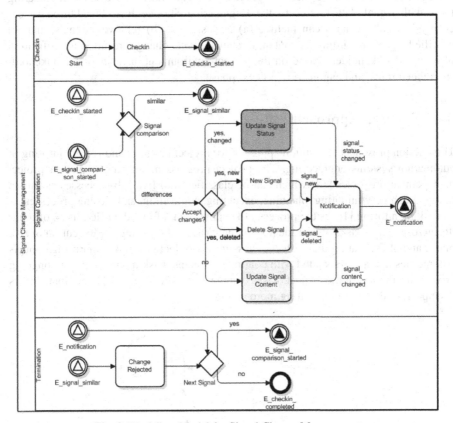

Fig. 2. Workflow Model for Signal Change Management

Fig. 2 presents a basic change management process, a signal check-in workflow. It shows a BPMN notation of signal change management workflow which consists of checkin, signal comparison and termination activities. After checking in, a signal will be compared to decide the next action, whether the signal is updated (signal status or signal content), accepted, or deleted. The notification of action will be reported to the project manager.

The process refers to the fact that collaboration between heterogeneous disciplines and tools requires common concepts for mapping individual models and activities and that system integrators have to synchronize engineering data from those tools.

Signal as a common concept link information across different engineering disciplines. Consequently, management of signals face important challenges like: (a) make signal handling consistent, (b) integrate signals from heterogeneous data models/tools, and (c) manage versions of signal changes across engineering disciplines. The check in workflow supports handling of such challenges by tracking changes on signals and notifying particular engineers.

Note that changes are defined within modified signal lists derived from individual engineering tools to be synchronized with the current overall signal list. Thus, change management refers to the merging process of signal lists provided by engineering tools with signal data known to the Engineering Service Bus. In addition to unchanged signal, changes can include (a) new signals, (b) removed signals, and (c) modified signals regarding its content or status. Signal changes result in a notification of involved stakeholders based on the project environment, e.g., involved stakeholders, related roles, and engineering process phase.

5   Solution Approach

This section presents the solution approach for project progress and risk monitoring in automation systems engineering. The project progress monitoring is part of project management processes [14] which can be classified into five sub-processes as shown in Fig. 3., namely initiating, planning, executing, controlling, and closing processes.

Risk monitoring [14] is the process of keeping track of the identified risks, of monitoring of residual risks and of identifying new risks, of ensuring the execution of risk plans, and of evaluating their effectiveness in risk-reduction. Risk monitoring collects risk metrics that are associated with contingency plans. Risk monitoring is an ongoing process for the life of the project. Risks change as new risks develop, anticipated risks disappear, or the project is getting more mature.

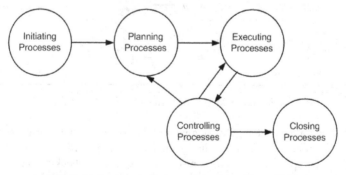

Fig. 3. Links Among Process Groups in a Phase [14]

5.1 Risk Factors Analysis

The scope of the risk factor analysis framework is to support multidisciplinary engineering teams that add, update and delete signals as well as project managers to support monitoring and decision making process. Each discipline has specific engineering models and tools. These engineering models work well for the specific discipline or expert, but are not well designed for interdisciplinary cooperation. The goal of this framework is to support risk factor analysis across different types of stakeholders, e.g., engineers and project managers, and to fulfill different requirements of different types of stakeholders.

The target audiences of this risk factor analysis framework are two types of stakeholders, namely engineers and project managers. Engineers, e.g., mechanical engineers, electrical engineers, or software engineers, want to effectively and efficiently analyze risk factors of their engineering process in signal change management, e.g., incorrectness or incompleteness of signals in the change process. However, often problems of integrity appear due to heterogeneous data models and formats used in those different engineering fields. Incorrect signals refer to e.g., mutually contradicting values or values outside specific thresholds. Incomplete signals refer to missing values or values with partly missing information (e.g., 3 digits representation of a complete information, whereas the third digit is not set).

Knowledge beneficiaries, such as project managers, want to monitor, control and improve engineering processes such that the processes do not violate risk factors like over budgeting or late project deliveries. This intention is often complicated by the required high effort for performing cross-domain risk factors analyses, e.g., to know which parties should be responsible for over budgeting or project delays.

The major precondition for using the risk factor analysis framework is a working communication link between the engineering tools to be integrated, such as Engineering Service Bus [4], Enterprise Service Bus [7], or point-to-point integration.

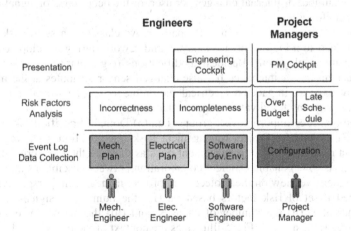

Fig. 4. Risk Factor Analysis Framework

Fig. 4 shows the framework for risk factor analysis which consists of two types of stakeholders, namely engineers and project managers. Engineers give inputs in the form of event log data which are based on their own development environments. The configuration of the event log is set up by project managers.

This event log is useful for further risk factors analysis in the next layer, which is distributed into two parts, namely the engineers' part and the project managers' part. Engineers are more concerned about the correctness and completeness of the signal changes between different engineering fields, and consider the incorrectness and incompleteness of the changed signals as risk factors between the engineers. In contrast, project managers are more concerned about budget and project schedule, such that the risk factors for the project managers are related to over budgeting and project delays. The results of this risk factor analysis are presented in the engineering cockpit to show the risks that should be mitigated by each type of stakeholder.

5.2   Risk Factors Classification

This section further classifies risk factors based on different stakeholder types. The types of risks classified here are related to the data of specific projects and specific level which may be defined beforehand. The risk analysis can be based on the phases (e.g., timeline of the project) or on the related tools (e.g., EPlan[2], logi.DOC[3]). Source of changes in the project could be an option for risk analysis, e.g., 5% of changes may originate from external partners, if the number of changes exceeds 5 %, then a new contract needs to be negotiated and thus the budget is affected. Any change by a project-related tool is considered as an internal change, while any change using the Engineering Object Editor (EOE[4]) [18] is considered as external change. The EOE is an Excel Add-on to support efficient quality assurance activities for contributions from external project partners.

Risk analysis could also be done to analyze project values based on the experience of different stakeholders, e.g., to analyze the data of multiple comparable projects or to analyze the number of changes per component. Other types of risk analyses can be based on the number of internal changes per user, or the occurrence of signal changes in late project phases.

From the discussion with our industry partner, we classified a set of risk factors, which often lead to a high effort for analysis and rework during development, commissioning, and deployment. Besides, modifications (e.g., change of a sensor) are critical issues during maintenance because changed sensor attributes at the mechanical site may have an impact on electrical requirements (e.g., wiring) and software requirements (e.g., modified value ranges as data input).

Based on the three important risk groups, i.e., (a) Domain Specific Risks, (b) Collaboration Risks, and (c) Project Management Risks (see Section 2.1), we focus on collaboration risks and project management risks as they are the most critical aspects in ASE projects to (1) enable efficient collaboration between disciplines and (2) enable a comprehensive view on the project from project management perspective. Thus, we identified a set of risk factors based on (i) the number of signals as project progress indicator, (ii) the number of changes, and (iii) the periods of engineering object changes (i.e., signals). Fig. 5 illustrates the context of the investigated risks.

---

[2] EPlan Electric: http://www.eplan.de
[3] Logi.DOC: http://www.logicals.com
[4] http://cdl.ifs.tuwien.ac.at/files/CDL-Flex_ASB_UC31_EOE_en.pdf

Project Progress Overview. The project progress overview presents the overall number of the signals grouped by engineering phase over time. It illustrates the fluctuation of the number of signals available in a certain phase based on operations applied to (a subset of) signals. If signals are added, it means that the number of signals in a certain phase is increasing. If some signals are deleted, it means that the number of signals in certain phase is decreasing. Updates include two different types of changes: (a) modifications of signal content (non-status updates) and (b) status updates (i.e., upgrading individual signals or groups of signals to the next sequential engineering phase). Signal status updates do not have any impact on the numbers of signals; if a signal has been modified (content change) its status is reset to initial. Based on this setting, we can observe how the signal change operations affect the number of signals available in certain phases, and how the signal updates change signals from an initial phase to a commissioned/final phase. In a healthy project, we could expect a continuous increase of the number of signals (i.e., added signals) and increasing signal status information (i.e., the signals are passing individual phases) over time. On the opposite a decreasing number of signals and the reset of signals from advanced states to initial might indicate risks.

Impact of Stakeholders. Changes might be initiated from different sources, e.g., by the internal engineers and the project managers or externally by the customer. A high number of external changes (even late in the project) might lead to high risks; a high number of internal changes (especially removed and updated signals) might indicate issues in the engineering process of a related discipline. Thus the source of change is an important measure for risk identification. We identify the sources of signal changes to analyze the potential risks, e.g., *what's the most frequent signal changes source? What's the trend of signal changes across different types of stakeholders?* Or *how signal changes can be displayed over time?*

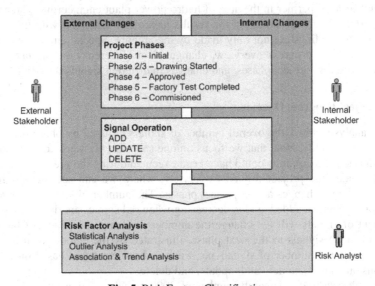

Fig. 5. Risk Factors Classification

Impact on Project Phases. Projects can be divided into several phases, namely initial, drawing started, approved, factory test completed, and commissioned (see Section 2.1 for details). Risks arise if signals are changed very often, especially late in the engineering project, e.g., a sensor has to be changed during the commissioning phase. Thus the related signals have to be changes as well. In addition, related disciplines might be affected by this change as well. Modification of signals results in resetting the signal state to initial (i.e., the starting phase) and all other phases have to be processed again. Thus, signals assigned to a project phase might be an indicator for risk assessment. As risk, we identify the number of signal changes for each phase across the period of time. From this analysis, we can observe the fluctuation of signal changes across time, depending on the project phase. Some signals can be changed from a phase to next phase, and it is expected that at the end of a project all signals will be in the final phase (commissioned).

Impact of Signals Operations. Operations on signals increase (add new signals) or decrease (deletion of signals) the number of signals available in the project. Signal updates will not change the number of signals but either the signal content or the assignment to a project phase. The update operation itself can be divided further into updates of a signal status or updates without signal status changes, i.e. signal content updates. In this type of risk factor analysis, we observe the relationship between the types of signal change operations over time. The results of this analysis can be used to measure possible risks that could happen during signal changes, e.g., the number of deletion should always less than or equal to the number of available signals.

6   Results

This section presents the empirical results of the risk factor analysis based on the data from our industrial partner in the area of hydro power plant engineering. The analysis was performed by the authors, but the results have been discussed with the industry experts, so the findings are not only made by the authors. Special emphasis is put on monitoring project progress overview, changes from different type of stakeholders, changes in different project phases, and changes in different signals operation.

6.1   Project Progress Overview

The first analysis shows the overall number of signals grouped by phase per commit which is done weekly. Note that we focus on one snapshot per week for analysis purposes. Thus several commits could have been executed during the previous week. The result illustrates the project progress overview, where we can see the progress of numbers of signal changes across project phases. The number of signals is increasing when new signals are added, and is decreasing when old signals are deleted. Updating the content of signals will not change the number of changes. Updates of the signal status will move signals to the next phase, illustrated by the colors given in Fig. 6. Fig. 6 presents the number of signals per week and project phase based on different operations on signals, namely add, update, and delete.

The results showed an overall number of 3000 signals (after week 44) when the project is completed and strong variations of the number of signals along the project course, e.g., a large number of removed signals in week 19 and a smaller number of removed signals in week 25 and 30 A more detailed investigation showed reconstruction activities during project reviews.

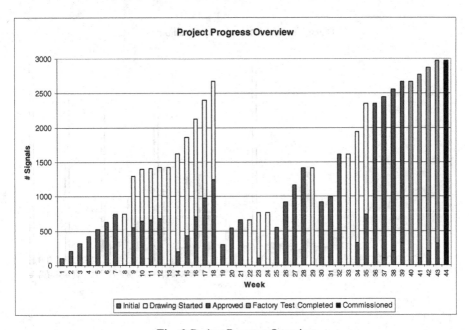

Fig. 6. Project Progress Overview

The number of signals is increasing from week 1 to 7, and then the signals are upgraded to the next phase (*drawing started*). From week 9 to 12, new signals are added and then upgraded to the next phase (*drawing started*) in week 13. From week 14 to 18, new signals are introduced and then deleted in week 19. From week 19 to 21, new signals are added and then upgraded to the next phase in week 22. Some new signals are added in week 23 and upgraded to the *drawing started* phase in week 24, and then deleted in week 25. From week 25 to 28, new signals are introduced, upgraded to the next phase in week 29, and deleted in week 30. From week 30 to 32, new signals are introduced and upgraded to the next phase (*drawing started*) in week 33. Some new signals are still added, until week 35, and then upgraded to the phase *approved* in week 36. The signals are changed to the phase *factory test completed* in week 40, and in week 44 all signals available are upgraded to the phase *commissioned*. Note that – starting from week 36, a high share of signals passed all sequential phases to the final phase *commissioning completed*.

Nevertheless it is notable that in week 19 a very high number of signals (about 80%) have been removed. A more detailed investigation of the results showed that the engineers used templates of components and also reused components from other projects without adjusting them to the current project. Thus, these components have been removed during a project review. A smaller but similar effect happens in week 25 and week 29. Thus this analysis supports project managers and engineers in better assessing the current project state over time. The project state refers to the state of individual signals per project phase, i.e., initial, drawing started, customer approval, factory tests, and customer commissioning (see Section 2.1 for details).

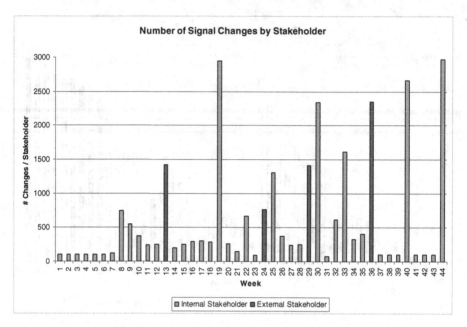

Fig. 7. Number of Signal Changes by Stakeholders

6.2   Number of Signal Changes by Stakeholder Group

The second analysis focuses on the impact of changes by different stakeholders, i.e., internal (engineers and project managers) and external stakeholders (customer). Signal changes originate from external stakeholders, if the customers ask for signal changes based on their requirements. Signal changes are coming from internal stakeholders, if engineers add new signals, update signals, or delete signals used in the project. Signal changes between both stakeholder groups become transparent during synchronization processes and are communicated to related stakeholders by applying an Engineering Ticket, e.g., a notification E-Mail.

Fig. 7 illustrates the bar graph of the number of signal changes by stakeholder. Most of the changes were introduced by the engineering company and their engineers, typically add, update, and signal changes. Infrequent changes were introduced by the customer e.g., caused by reviewing processes or status meetings. The external stakeholder passes signal changes to the project during a certain period, for example in week 13, week 24, week 29, and week 36, while the other regular changes originate from internal stakeholders. A more detailed investigation of the external changes showed that typical changes focuses on signal description changes rather than on critical changes by the customer. Nevertheless, it is notable that in week 36 - very late in the project – a high number of external changes happens. As late changes make

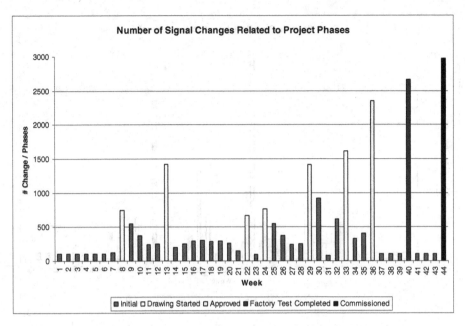

Fig. 8. Number of Signal Changes Related to Project Phases

projects more critical, error-prone and risky, this analysis results supports project managers in better negotiating changes with the customer.

6.3   Number of Signal Changes Related to Project Phases

The impact of signal changes on the project state is another critical issue, as all signal changes (i.e., content changes) require a reset to the initial state and all phases/reviews (i.e. signal status upgrades) have to be repeated. As this process requires some effort and might delay the project, these analysis results help project managers in better understanding possible delays of the project.

Fig. 8 illustrates the bar graph of the number of signal changes related to the project phases. Most of the signal changes are done during the *initial* phases, while some are also done during *drawing started, approved,* and *factory test completed.* At the end of our observation (week 44), all signals are upgraded to the final phase (*commissioned*). It is notable that until week 35 almost all signals and changes are in a very early stage, i.e., in the initial and the drawing started phase. This indicates that the requirements are not well-defined and/or the customer (see Section 6.2) initiated a set of changes. In week 36 we observed a high number of external changes and also the approval by the customer. This indicates that these minor changes were implemented and approved within a very short time interval, i.e., one week. As the project proceeds, short iterations and interaction with the customer could be observed, i.e., adding a small set of new signals by the engineering company and signal status updates in week 40 of about 2600 signals. Finally a similar effect could be observed in weeks 41-44, in which the project has been completed.

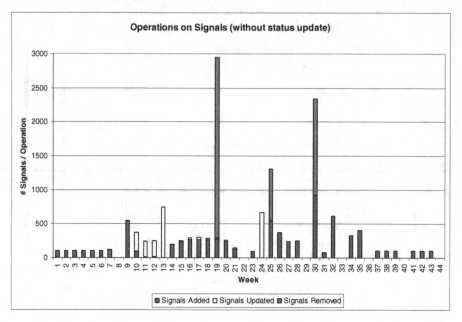

Fig. 9. Operations on Signals (without status update)

6.4   Operations on Signals

Another interesting aspect focuses on the impact of operations, i.e., the amount of operations applied to the signals (i.e., signals added, signals updated, and signals removed). Two different types of operations are introduced, i.e., content updates of signals and signal status updates. Content updates do not change the status/phase of signals and focus on changing the content of signals, e.g., range of devices, device description, tool names, hardware addresses, and path used. Status updates refer to the upgrade of signal stati/phases from one phase to the next phase. All signal content changes result in a reset of the signal status to initial.

Fig. 9 illustrates the stack-bar chart of the number of signals grouped by operations (i.e., add, delete, and update content). Similar to the previous analysis results, we observed added signals along the project duration until the very end of the project, i.e. in week 43. In addition we observed two other issues: (a) a relatively low number of signal content updates, mainly between week 10 to 13 (early in the project) and in week 24. An explanation for this process could be that engineers applied templates and reused components from previous projects; in addition they modified them according to new project requirements. Anyway, as the amount of changes is rather high, a large number of components and signals has been removed in week 19, 25 and 30. After this clarification and cleanup steps the new (and correct) signal have been introduced. There are only few changes on the already available signals.

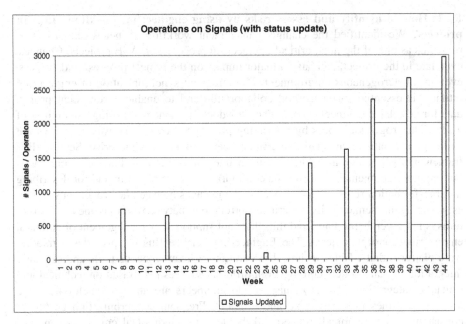

Fig. 10. Operations on Signals (with status update)

Finally the last evaluation focuses on the impact of signal status updates (see Fig. 10 for details). It is notable that signal status updates are typically executed periodically, e.g., once a month during project progress meetings. Fig. 10 shows that the number of signal status updates is increasing in the project, especially during week 24 to week 44. In general, signal status updates are performed monthly.

7   Discussion

This section summarizes the major findings of our risk-based approach for ASE projects based on the initial evaluation of real-world industry data derived from a large-scale engineering company in the hydro power plant domain. We identified three different risk groups: (a) Domain specific risks, (b) Collaboration risks, and (c) Project management risks.

While *domain specific risks* are typically addressed by domain specific tools and methods, e.g., RiskIt method in software engineering [17], we observed strong limitations regarding risk assessment in the ASE domain focusing on heterogeneous engineering environments. *Collaboration risks* typically focus on the synchronization of data models, engineering objects (e.g., signals) and engineering artifacts where engineering propagate changes – the most critical engineering process in ASE projects, especially if various stakeholders from various disciplines are involved – to related engineers in other disciplines. In addition we observed strong limitations on a comprehensive view on the overall engineering project from the project management perspective *(Project Management Risks)*.

RI 1: How to identify and assess risks by using engineering workflows in ASE projects? We identified the change management workflow in heterogeneous environments as one of the most critical engineering processes in ASE projects. Changes, even late in the project, can have a major impact on the project progress and success, even in a heterogeneous environment. Thus frequent synchronization of engineering artifacts is essential for successful collaboration and to enable a consistent project data for all related engineers. Tools like Flowdock[5] provide monitoring capabilities of a set of heterogeneous tools by presenting propagated events. However, it does not facilitate semantical correlation between them. Standard Enterprise Service Bus frameworks [7] enable a technically clean integration between heterogeneous tools, but require high manual effort for the configuration of the platform and for describing the transformation rules needed to exchange messages between heterogeneous services. Once again, semantically described correlations between various message structures is not given beforehand and thus does not support easy management of common engineering concepts/objects. The Engineering Service Bus [4] provides a middleware platform that enables technical integration of heterogeneous tools and semantic integration of data models coming from different sources [3]. Based on technical and semantic integration, project managers and engineers are able to synchronize data across disciplines more effective and efficient. Frequent synchronization enables a consistent data base for all related stakeholders, i.e., individual engineers can start working on an agreed set of engineering data across disciplines. In addition, metrics on the project progress, i.e., the number of signals already implemented engineering objects, become measurable, an important benefit for project managers for project monitoring and control. In addition the amount and impact of changes of engineering objects become observable. The numbers of changes per engineering object and (b) the initiator of the related changes enable project managers (a) to better understand and control the project progress and (b) to address upcoming risks in ASE projects.

The number of engineering objects (signals) is an important indicator regarding the identification of the project progress with respect to individual project risks. Fig. 5 presented the number of signals per week and project phase in our initial evaluation study. One might assume an increasing number of engineering objects over time. Nevertheless the results showed a rapid decrease of the number of signals between week 18 and week 19. The main reason was that previously engineers reused large components from previous projects (some copy / paste approach). In week 18, an in-depth review takes place where it has been decided that the currently used solution approach was not appropriate. Thus, almost all parts of the components have been removed. Similar effects appear between week 21/22 and week 29/30. An analysis at the customer site identified some critical changes in a few components which have been fixed, i.e., exchanged by more appropriate components. Typically the analysis, illustrated in Fig. 5 highlighted the risk of reusing components to a large extent to reduce effort and cost. Using wrong components will result in high rework effort. Thus, it is required to plan component reuse strategies, i.e., how to apply components, subsystems, or systems from successful past projects, appropriately. In common

---

[5] https://flowdock.com/

industry practice individual components are copied to the new project which can raise a set of issues and risks. This data shows the materialization of a risk, i.e., the risk of reusing components that are inappropriate and thus, eventually, have to be replaced. The risk identification means that the diagram indicated the risk that there are components being reused that might or might not be appropriate. The product line approach might be a candidate solution for effective and efficient reuse of components, subsystems, and systems [8].

RI 2: How to classify Risk Factors based on Different Types of Stakeholders?
Based on observations at our industry partner and results from previous analysis results [29] we identified a set of metrics as promising candidate metrics for project risk assessment.

An overview on the *Project Progress* has already been applied to demonstrate the application of risk assessment, based on the number of engineering objects (i.e., signals) in the engineering database. The concept of the Engineering Cockpit [19] provides a comprehensive view on engineering data from heterogeneous sources. More details on individual components and signals can support project, quality, and risk management. Instable and the frequent changing number of available signals is an indicator for reusing components (copy/paste) approach or some unclear requirements which require high rework effort by engineers and experts.

The *Impact of Changes from various Stakeholders* (e.g., internal engineers or external stakeholder, i.e., the customer) is another important aspect in change management processes and can result in high risks (even if external changes happen frequently). The distinction between internal and external stakeholders is easier to discuss because both parties have different intention and perspectives on managing the signal changes, while the types of engineers have similar goals even though they work in different fields. Because each type of stakeholder can introduce modification to the signal status, especially the external stakeholders who could drop a lot of signals in short time that could lead to the change of requirements in the engineer side. Hence the signal changes should be communicated among related stakeholders.

Fig. 7 presented the number of changes per stakeholder group. The results showed that the external stakeholders introduce changes every two months at the beginning and monthly at the end of the project. These analysis results help project-managers in better discussing the changes with the customer. In our initial evaluation the duration between external changes seems to be appropriate. It is notable that the last pile of changes takes effect in week 36, 2 months before project completion.

Impact on Project Phases. Signal changes, especially signal updates result in a reset of the current project phase based on a rather sequential engineering process. Thus an important information and consequence of changes is an analysis on the impact of changes per phase (see Fig. 8). It is notable that until week 35 almost all signals are in the state "initial" or "drawing started", early phases in the ASE project. After applying the last pile of customer changes (i.e., in week 36) the signal status develop to the project finalization time rapidly, e.g., more than one signal status update per week. Note that the evaluation focuses on snapshots (once a week) for analysis purposes.

Impact of Signal Operation. Finally, it is important to have an idea on the share and type of signal changes, i.e., added signals newly introduced to the system, modified (updated) signals, and – the most critical aspect – removed signals. As discussed before, three main risks apply, (a) in week 19 where almost 80% of signals have been removed; (b) in week 25; and (c) in week 30. Main reason for this large amount of deleted signals was the reuse of components and templates which have to be improved for future projects.

8   Conclusion and FutureWork

Engineers from different engineering fields, as occurring typically in large-scale Automation Systems Engineering (ASE) projects, rely on their own tools and data models to perform their specific tasks of their specific engineering fields. Furthermore, these engineers typically create and use their own specific engineering workflows for communicating, disseminating, and managing objects across the borders of different engineering fields. Thus, there is a need for flexible and comprehensive engineering process support across disciplines to allow risk-aware collaboration and interaction between disciplines, tools, and data models. With this focus on raising the risk awareness of object change management workflows, the key questions for project management and engineers are (a) how changes can be handled more efficient and (b) how relevant change requests can be passed to involved engineers.

This paper presented the Engineering Service Bus (EngSB) framework to provide (a) an efficient change management process and (b) integrated views on heterogeneous engineering environments to better analyze and highlight upcoming risks. Based on real-world engineering project data from a hydro power plant systems integrator, the proposed approach is evaluated and discussed.

First results of the industry case study showed that – based on the change management workflow – the consideration of risk factors can enhance the overall engineering project quality and enables risk mitigation in ASE projects. Based on change management data, we identified four main risk factors context of the initial evaluation: (a) Overall number of signal data in the engineering base; (b) the impact of changes from different stakeholder groups, i.e., internal and external stakeholders; (c) Impact of Changes with respect to signal status within a defined engineering process; and (d) impact of different operations on engineering objects (i.e., add, update, delete, and status updates). The analysis results showed that these initially defined metrics are reasonable for assessing the current ASE project from engineers and management perspective.

Nevertheless, the presentation of data and analysis results is essential for individual stakeholders by providing individual views on the project, e.g., focus on a comprehensive view on the project from project management perspective or focus on individual disciplines from the perspective of individual engineers. In [19] we observed the engineering cockpit, a promising solution to present captured data from the change management process to related engineers and the project managers.

Future Work will include three different directions: (a) more detailed investigation of new risk factors and the development / extension of the identified metrics to enable a better understanding of ASE projects, also in other ASE domains than hydro power plant engineering (b) additional evaluations and case studies including new engineering workflows to verify and validate the presented approach with respect to applicability and scalability; and (c) more detailed investigation on the current need of engineers, managers, and related stakeholders to learn more about ASE projects and the need for measurement, data collection, analysis and presentation with respect to develop an engineering cockpit for better supporting ASE projects.

Acknowledgement. This work has been supported by the Christian Doppler Forschungsgesellschaft and the BMWFJ, Austria

References

1. Aldred, L., van der Aalst, W., Dumas, M., Hofstede, A.T.: Understanding the challenges in getting together: The semantics of decoupling in middleware. BPM Center Report BPM-06-19, BPMcenter. org
2. Becker, P., Lew, P., Olsina, L.: Strategy to improve quality for software applications: a process view. In: International Conference on on Software and Systems Process (ICSSP 2011), pp. 129–138. ACM, Waikiki (2011)
3. Biffl, S., Sunindyo, W., Moser, T.: Bridging Semantic Gaps Between Stakeholders in the Production Automation Domain with Ontology Areas. In: Proceedings of 21st SEKE, USA, pp. 233–239 (2009)
4. Biffl, S., Schatten, A., Zoitl, A.: Integration of heterogeneous engineering environments for the automation systems lifecycle. In: 2009 7th IEEE International Conference on Industrial Informatics, pp. 576–581. IEEE (2009)
5. Biffl, S., Schatten, A.: A Platform for Service-Oriented Integration of Software Engineering Environments. In: Proceedings of SoMeT 2009, pp. 75–92. IOS Press (2009)
6. Boehm, B.W.: Software Risk Management: Principles and Practices. IEEE Software 8(1), 32–41 (1991)
7. Chappel, D.A.: Enterprise Service Bus. O'Reilly Media (2004)
8. Clements, P., Northrop, L.M.: Software Product Lines: Practices and Patterns. Addison-Wesley (2007)
9. Doan, A.H., Noy, N.F., Halevy, A.Y.: Introduction to the special issue on semantic integration. ACM Sigmod Record 33, 11–13 (2004)
10. Gartner Inc.: Gartner EXP Worldwide Survey of More than 1.500 CIOs Shows IT Spending to Be Flat (2009), http://www.gartner.com/it/page.jsp?id=855612
11. Hohpe, G.: 06291 Workshop Report: Conversation Patterns. In: Leymann, F., et al. (eds.) The Role of Business Processes in Service Oriented Architectures. Internationales Begegnungs-und Forschungszentrum für Informatik (IBFI), Schloss Dagstuhl, Germany (2006)
12. Hohpe, G., Woolf, B.: Enterprise integration patterns: Designing, building, and deploying messaging solutions. Addison-Wesley Longman Publishing Co. Inc., Boston (2003)
13. Hubbard, D.: The Failure of Risk Management: Why It's Broken and How to Fix It. John Wiley & Sons (2009)
14. IEEE: IEEE Guide–Adoption of the Project Management Institute (PMI(R)) Standard A Guide to the Project Management Body of Knowledge (PMBOK(R) Guide), 4th edn. (2011)
15. IEEE: IEEE Recommended Practice for CASE Tool Interconnection - Characterization of Interconnections. IEEE Std 1175.2-2006, pp. 1–45 (2007)

16. Jakoubi, S., Tjoa, S.: A reference model for risk-aware business process management. In: Fourth International Conference on Risks and Security of Internet and Systems (CRiSIS 2009), pp. 82–89 (2009)
17. Kontio, J.: Risk Management in Software Development: a technology overview and the RiskIt method. In: 21st ICSE Conference, pp. 679–680 (1999)
18. Mordinyi, R., Pacha, A., Biffl, S.: Quality Assurance for Data from Low-Tech Participants in Distributed Automation Engineering Environments. In: Mammeri, Z. (ed.) Proceeding of the 16th IEEE International Conference on Emerging Technologies and Factory Automation, pp. 1–4 (2011)
19. Moser, T., Mordinyi, R., Winkler, D., Biffl, S.: Engineering project management using the Engineering Cockpit: A collaboration platform for project managers and engineers. In: Proceedings of INDIN 2011, pp. 579–584 (2011)
20. Moser, T., Biffl, S., Sunindyo, W., Winkler, D.: Integrating Production Automation Expert Knowledge Across Engineering Domains. International Journal of Distributed Systems and Technologies (IJDST), Special Issue on Emerging Trends and Challenges in Large-Scale Networking and Distributed Systems 2(3), 88–103 (2011)
21. Moser, T., Mordinyi, R., Mikula, A., Biffl, S.: Making Expert Knowledge Explicit to Facilitate Tool Support for Integrating Complex Information Systems in the ATM Domain. In: International Conference on Complex, Intelligent and Software Intensive Systems, CISIS 2009, pp. 90–97. IEEE Computer Society, Fukuoka (2009)
22. Moser, T., Waltersdorfer, F., Winkler, D., Biffl, S.: Version Management and Conflict Detection across Tools in a (Software+) Engineering Environment. In: Proceedings of the Software Quality Days 2011, pp. 1–4 (2011)
23. Nellore, R., Balachandra, R.: Factors influencing success in integrated product development (IPD) projects. IEEE Transactions on Engineering Management 48(2), 164–174 (2001)
24. Noy, N.F., Doan, A., Halevy, A.Y.: Semantic Integration. AI Mag. 26, 7–10 (2005)
25. Rademakers, T., Dirksen, J.: Open-source ESBs in action. Manning Pub. (2008)
26. Rangan, R.M., Rohde, S.M., Peak, R., Chadha, B.: Streamlining Product Lifecycle Processes: A Survey of Product Lifecycle Management Implementations, Directions, and Challenges. Journal of Computing and Information Science in Engineering 5, 227–237 (2005); ST-Streamlining Product Lifecycle Proce
27. Ropponen, J., Lyytinen, K.: Components of Software Development Risk: How to Address Them? A Project Manager Survey. IEEE Trans. Soft. Eng. 26(2), 98–111 (2000)
28. Runeson, P., Höst, M.: Guidelines for conducting and reporting case study research in software engineering. Empir. Software Eng. 14, 131–164 (2009)
29. Sadiq, S., Orlowska, M., Sadiq, W., Foulger, C.: Data flow and validation in workflow modelling. In: 15th Australasian Database Conference (2004)
30. Schafer, W., Wehrheim, H.: The Challenges of Building Advanced Mechatronic Systems. In: Future of Software Engineering (FOSE 2007), pp. 72–84. IEEE Computer Society, Washington, DC (2007)
31. Sunindyo, W.D., Moser, T., Winkler, D., Mordinyi, R., Biffl, S.: Workflow Validation Framework in Distributed Engineering Environments. In: Meersman, R., Dillon, T., Herrero, P. (eds.) OTM 2011 Workshops. LNCS, vol. 7046, pp. 236–245. Springer, Heidelberg (2011)
32. Vose, D.: Risk Analysis - A Quantitative Study. John Wiley & Sons, Ltd. (2008)
33. Winkler, D., Moser, T., Mordinyi, R., Sunindyo, W., Biffl, S.: Engineering Object Change Management Process Observation in Distributed Automation Systems Projects. In: Proceedings of EuroSPI 2011, pp. 1–12 (2011)
34. Winkler, D., Biffl, S.: Improving Quality Assurance in Automation Systems Development Projects. In: Quality Assurance and Management, pp. 20–40. Intec Publishing (2012)

WebMate: Generating Test Cases for Web 2.0

Valentin Dallmeier, Martin Burger, Tobias Orth, and Andreas Zeller

Saarland University, Computer Science Department, Saarbrücken, Germany
{dallmeier,mburger,orth,zeller}@st.cs.uni-saarland.de
http://www.st.cs.uni-saarland.de/

Abstract. Web applications are everywhere—well tested web applications however are in short supply. The mixture of JavaScript, HTML and CSS in a variety of different browsers makes it virtually impossible to apply static analysis techniques. In this setting, *systematic testing* becomes a real challenge. We present a technique to *automatically generate tests* for Web 2.0 applications. Our approach systematically explores and tests all distinct functions of a web application. Our prototype implementation WEBMATE handles interfaces as complex as Facebook and is able to cover up to 7 times as much code as existing tools. The only requirements to use WEBMATE are the address of the application and, if necessary, user name and password.

Keywords: test case generation, automate testing, Web 2.0, web applications.

1 Introduction

In the software industry there is a strong trend towards replacing classic desktop applications with *web applications*—programs that are accessed via a browser and are typically run on a central server. Web applications are popular because they are easy to use and easy to maintain. The user only needs a browser, and the developer only has to maintain a single installation of the application. As a result, the cost of running a web application is relatively low compared to classic applications. On the other hand, quality assurance for web applications is difficult.

The user interface of a web application typically consists of JavaScript, HTML and CSS. This technology mix is notoriously difficult to debug. For instance, JavaScript is a dynamically typed language which makes static code analysis difficult. Therefore, existing techniques that can statically determine type errors cannot be applied. Another reason why debugging web applications is hard is that—despite existing standards—there are subtle implementation differences across browsers. As a result, code that works in one browser may not work in other browsers. Overall, testing web applications requires a lot of manual effort. As software release cycles are getting shorter and shorter, implementing effective quality assurance is difficult and therefore often ignored. As a consequence, users are faced with bad software that sometimes only fails to work correctly, but

D. Winkler, S. Biffl, and J. Bergsmann (Eds.): SWQD 2013, LNBIP 133, pp. 55–69, 2013.

sometimes also inadvertently leaks private data as witnessed by recent security breaches of popular web pages.

One way to alleviate this problem is to use *automated quality assurance*. As illustrated above, due to the complexity of the technology mix we cannot use static analysis or approaches like symbolic verification. Hence, the only technique that remains is *testing*. The technique of choice to verify that a web application is correct is *system testing*, which is able to check functional and non-functional requirements. However, manually creating and maintaining such tests again requires a lot of effort.

In the last years, we have seen a number of tremendously successful approaches that *automatically generate tests*. The majority of these techniques are being developed for individual programming languages, such as Java. In this paper, we investigate how existing approaches to test case generation can be applied in the context of Web 2.0 applications. Our work makes the following contributions:

1. We identify and discuss the main challenges when generating test cases for Web 2.0 applications (Sections 2 and 3).
2. We present WEBMATE, a tool that systematically explores web applications (Section 4). WEBMATE works fully automatically—it will only need credentials if parts of the web application are protected by a login.
3. We evaluate the effectiveness of WEBMATE and compare its performance to existing crawlers[1] (Section 5). While exploring the application, WEBMATE learns a *usage model* that describes all different functions of the web application. In one instance, our prototype is able to achieve up to 40 % code coverage.
4. We present an application where WEBMATE generates test cases to automatically test the compatibility of a web application in different browsers (Section 6).

We discuss related work in Section 7 and close the paper with concluding remarks and future work in Section 8.

2   Background: Test Case Generation

Automatic test case generation derives test cases from the program's code, its behavior, or other artifacts like a formal specification. The majority of these approaches generates tests for individual components of a program, such as methods or classes—so-called *unit tests*. On the other hand, *system tests* check the whole program at once by generating inputs for the user interface.

Existing approaches differ mainly in the concrete test generation approach and the resulting requirements:

---

[1] A crawler is a tool that systematically visits all pages of a web site and a web application, respectively.

- **Randomized testing** uses simple *randomized algorithms* to generate tests based on structural properties of the program. The work by Ciupa et al. [5] implements random testing for EIFFEL programs and uses invariants specified in the code to validate the test result.
- **Constraint-based testing** uses *symbolic execution* to simulate the execution of the program with symbolic values. From these executions, the techniques derive formulas that describe conditions on the program's input such that specific code regions are being exercised. With the help of a constraint solver, these formulas are solved to find valid input values. The scalability of these approaches is usually limited by the constraint solver. New approaches try to leverage this problem by combining concrete and symbolic execution [11].
- **Search-based testing** uses *machine learning algorithms* to efficiently navigate the search space for test inputs. The advantage of using genetic algorithms over constraint-based approaches is their ability to achieve maximum code coverage also for system tests, for example when generating inputs for user interfaces [9].
- **Model-based testing** requires a *model* that specifies the expected behavior of the program. The model is then used to derive test cases that cover as much of the specification as possible. One instance of such a tool is SPEC-EXPLORER from Microsoft. It allows to generate tests from specifications written in SPEC# [2] in order to verify that the code complies to the model.

With the exception of model-based testing, all of the above approaches cannot verify the correctness of the test outputs. An authority that decides whether a given test output is correct is called a *test oracle*. The lack of proper oracles for testing purposes is usually referred to as the *oracle problem*. This problem is one of the biggest challenges for automatic test case generation. Many approaches therefore only look for runtime exceptions when executing generated tests and disregard the program output.

Another issue for *unit test generation* is that many generated tests use test inputs that would never occur in reality. To circumvent this problem, we can generate tests on the system level rather than on the unit level; on the system level, inputs are no longer under the control of the program and therefore the program should be able to handle any input without raising an exception.

In the past few years, test case generation has made significant advances. Modern search-based approaches are able to achieve high coverage quickly by generating tests on the unit level [8] as well as on the GUI level [9].

3   Generating Tests for Web 2.0 Applications

In the scope of this work, we define the term *web application* to denote a program that requires a browser to be accessed by the user, and that is executed on a central server or, alternatively, in the cloud. Hence, web applications consist of two parts: a client-side part and a server-side part: on the client side, the web application uses HTML, CSS and JavaScript to implement the user interface; on the server side, a wide variety of different programming languages and techniques is used. Thus, while the technology mix on the client side is fixed, there is a large number of different platforms and languages on the server side.

Can we transfer existing test generation approaches to web applications? Due to the technology mix and the distributed nature of web applications, generating tests on the unit level is difficult. Since unit test case generation is typically very close to the code, it has to be re-implemented for every language and platform on the server side. This causes a considerable effort which in turn makes the approach difficult to implement for a large number of applications. To alleviate this problem, we can restrict the test generation to system tests for an interface that consists of HTML, CSS and JavaScript. Our approach analyses *only those parts of the application that are executed in the browser* (black-box approach). Starting from the application's landing page, our approach systematically analyses all elements of the user interface on the current web page and continues exploration until no new elements and new web pages, respectively, are found.

This approach has the advantage that it avoids the heterogeneity on the server side. However, it also comes with a number of new challenges:

Recognize the user interface. In order to generate system tests, we need to identify all elements of the user interface. In traditional web applications, this only includes buttons, links and forms. However, in modern Web 2.0 applications, arbitrary elements can be associated with a JavaScript snippet that will be executed, for instance, when the user clicks on the element. With JavaScript, these so-called *handlers* can be added dynamically, which makes identifying user interface elements difficult

Distinguish similar states of the user interface. In order to generate test cases efficiently, we have to be able to identify *similar application states*. Otherwise, thousands of tests would be generated for one and the same function. Rather than generating tests for the whole data-set of the application (for instance, a social graph in a database), we would like to generate tests for all functions. In traditional web applications, it is possible to distinguish application states based on the URL of the browser only. In Web 2.0 applications, however, this is no longer possible since many JavaScript handlers change the state of the page in the background; thus, without modifying the URL.

Hidden state. To generate tests, we only use those parts of the application state that are visible to the browser. Since virtually all web applications also *store information at the server*, parts of the application state may change at any point in time. For example, in an email application, a new email may pop up at any time. Such state changes often also change the state of the user interface and the testing tool has to be able to cope with these changes.

Since the test case generation is restricted to those parts of the state that are visible to the browser, it may be unable to reach all of the web application's functions. On the other hand, this approach has the advantage that it does not require access to the code that runs on the server and is therefore easily applicable to a large number of projects.

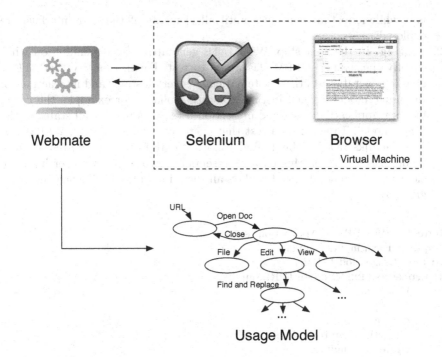

Fig. 1. WEBMATE employs Selenium to remote control the browser and learns a *usage model* that captures all possible ways to interact with the application. For security reasons, Selenium and the browser are sand-boxed in a virtual machine.

4 WebMate: A Test Case Generator for Web 2.0 Applications

WEBMATE is a prototype that implements the above approach to generate test cases for web applications. The main parts of WEBMATE are depicted in Figure 1: WEBMATE uses Selenium [6] to remote control the browser and extract the state of the user interface. In this setting, the state of the user interface comprises all elements that can be used to interact with the application. Using these techniques, WEBMATE is able to generate tests in two steps:

1. **Exploration.** In the first step, WEBMATE systematically tests all elements of the user interface in all different states of the application and derives a so-called *usage model*. This model captures the logical order of all possible ways to interact with the application. In essence, the usage model is a finite state automaton where states map to different states of the user interface and transitions between states are triggered by interacting with the application. Exploration ends as soon as WEBMATE is unable to find new states and all user interface elements have been explored. Figure 2 shows a pseudocode representation of the exploration algorithm. The main part of the procedure

is a while-loop that continues until all elements of the user interface are explored.

2. **Testing.** In the next step, WEBMATE generates tests depending on what exactly the user of WEBMATE wants to test. For instance, WEBMATE is able to generate tests that systematically cover all states and interactions of the usage model learned in the exploration phase. For example, the cross-browser application described in Section 6 requires to visit all states of the usage model. To generate a test that exercises a target state t, WEBMATE uses the dijkstra algorithm to find a shortest path from $start$ to t in the usage model. Each edge on this path represents an invocation of a user interface element. The generated test replays all these invocations following the order given by the path.

Require: Start URL of Application (startURL)
Require: Form inputs (inputs)
Ensure: Usage Model (V, E)
```
 1: procedure EXPLORE(startURL, inputs)
 2:     V = {start}
 3:     E = {}
 4:     s = start
 5:     e = getElementToExplore(s, V, E);
 6:     while e ! = null do
 7:         i = getInputs(e, inputs);
 8:         t = testElement(e, s, i);
 9:         if t ∉ V then
10:             V = V ∪ t
11:         end if
12:         E = E ∪ (s, t, e, i)
13:         s = t
14:         e = getElementToExplore(s, V, E);
15:     end while
16:     return(V, E)
17: end procedure
```

Fig. 2. Pseudocode algorithm for exploring a web application. In lines 5 and 14, method *getElementToExplore* uses the dijkstra algorithm to find the closest unexplored ui element. Method *testElement* executes the element and applies state abstraction to extract the new state of the application.

Since mouse clicks (and other movements like hovering) are the dominant way to interact with a web application, WEBMATE is able to trigger almost all user interface elements on its own. A problem, however, occurs with forms: in order to submit a form, all of its input fields must contain valid values. WEBMATE employs a set of heuristics to guess the range of values for an input field. Still, these heuristics fail as soon as a form requires complex input such as a pair of user name and passwords. For these cases, WEBMATE provides a way to specify input data for individual forms.

WEBMATE implements the following solutions for the challenges described in Section 3:

Recognize the user interface. WEBMATE recognizes all statically specified elements of the user interface by analyzing the HTML source code of the application. Dynamically added JavaScript handlers are also supported if they are added using one of the popular JavaScript libraries JQUERY or PROTOTYPE. If a web application uses other means to dynamically attach event handlers, WEBMATE will be unable to identify these elements as part of the user interface and therefore cannot include them in the analysis.[2]

Distinguish similar states of the user interface. To identify similar states of the user interface, WEBMATE uses an abstraction over all elements in the user interface. This abstraction characterizes the state of the application based on what functions are currently available to the user. Since WEBMATE is a testing tool, this abstraction makes sure that *two pages with the same functionality are mapped to the same state* and WEBMATE will visit each state only once. As any abstraction, this method also leads to a loss of information. In some cases, WEBMATE is therefore unable to explore all functions of the application.

Hidden state. The server-side part of the state is invisible to WEBMATE. If the state on the server changes, some states in the usage model may no longer be available to WEBMATE and the user interface would become non-deterministic from WEBMATE's point of view. As this problem is unavoidable, WEBMATE will tolerate these issues when exploring the application and will report errors when generating tests in the test phase.

In essence, WEBMATE is a tool to systematically explore all ways to interact with a web application and thus covers as much of the application as possible. Hence, WEBMATE basically generates *executions*. When combined with generic oracles such as cross-browser compatibility checks (see Section 6 below), WEBMATE is able to fully automatically detect errors in web applications.

5   Evaluation: How Does WEBMATE Improve Test Coverage?

To evaluate WEBMATE's effectiveness when analyzing Web 2.0 applications, we compare the coverage achieved by WEBMATE to that achieved by a traditional crawler for a set of subjects. From the point of view of the test case generator, we would like to achieve as much coverage as possible to test all parts of the program.

WEBMATE provides a first implementation of solutions to the challenges for Web 2.0 test case generation as described in Section 3. Since WEBMATE is still

---

[2] In JavaScript, there is no official, uniformly way to retrieve a dynamically attached event handler. However, all major JavaScript libraries offer their own way to retrieve attached handlers. Therefore, for the time being, WEBMATE has to specifically support each library.

Table 1. Subjects for the experimental evaluation. Project size is determined as the sum of the lines in all classes that are loaded at runtime.

Name	Homepage	Domain	Project Size (lines of code)
DMS	dmsnew1.sourceforge.net	document management	13,513
HippoCMS	www.onehippo.com	content management	65,692
iTracker	www.itracker.org	document management	15,086
JTrac	www.jtrac.info	task management	6,940
ScrumIt	scrum-it-demo.bsgroupti.ch	project management	1,448

an academic prototype, we cannot expect it to achieve full coverage (i.e., 100 %). It is also difficult to measure how much coverage the tool could possibly achieve. Since WEBMATE generates tests on the system level, the tests can only reach those parts of the code that are reachable via the user interface. In this setting, full coverage would only be possible if all parts of the program are actually reachable by the user interface, which is hardly feasible for most applications. Hence, in this evaluation, we focus on the *relative* improvement of the coverage and *not on absolute* values.

5.1 Experimental Setup

For this experiment we use five open-source subjects. Table 1 lists the names and project sizes for all subjects. We chose our subjects to cover a variety of project sizes and domains. Our subjects range from small projects (1,448 lines of code) to fully blown web applications (65,692 lines of code). To facilitate our setup, we restrict the evaluation to subjects implemented in Java.

For our experiments we chose SCRAPY (http://scrapy.org) as a representative for traditional crawlers. SCRAPY is a popular tool that extracts data from web sites and is also used to provide load tests for web applications. In contrast to other crawlers, SCRAPY also allows to specify credentials. Since all our test programs require a login, this is a crucial feature to provide meaningful results in our evaluation.

To compare the coverage achieved by WEBMATE and SCRAPY, we measure the amount of lines covered. To get line coverage, we use Cobertura [14] to instrument each subject before it is executed. At runtime, the instrumented program logs all executed lines and calculates coverage at the end of the program run.

Both SCRAPY and WEBMATE get as inputs the landing page of each subject and credentials for a user account. To evaluate a single subject, we first run SCRAPY to collect coverage, reset the database of the subject to the state before SCRAPY was run, and then run WEBMATE to again collect coverage. Both crawlers are configured to only analyse pages that are part of the application.

Table 2. Results of the experimental evaluation. WEBMATE achieves up to seven times better coverage than SCRAPY.

Name	Coverage (percent)	
	WEBMATE	SCRAPY
DMS	19.3	10.8
HippoCMS	42.0	11.1
iTracker	33.2	7.2
JTrac	28.6	18.6
ScrumIt	38.5	5.5

5.2 Results

Table 2 lists the results of our experiments. Each line shows the coverage achieved by WEBMATE and SCRAPY for one subject. For all the subjects in this experiment, WEBMATE is able to achieve a higher coverage than SCRAPY. Thus, we can conclude that WEBMATE is more effective when generating tests for Web 2.0 applications than SCRAPY. The approach implemented in WEBMATE can significantly increase the coverage of generated tests: For ScrumIt, WEBMATE is able to achieve seven times as much coverage as SCRAPY. For HippoCMS and iTracker, coverage is still four times as high. Both applications make heavy use of JavaScript and dynamic HTML, which is why SCRAPY fails to achieve good coverage values.

Absolutely speaking, WEBMATE achieves between twenty (DMS) and forty (HippoCMS) percent coverage. For an automated testing tool these values are acceptable, but they are still not good enough for the tool to be of practical value. When analyzing the results of this experiment, we had several insights that lead to new ideas how to further improve WEBMATE. Some of these ideas are discussed in Section 8.

5.3 Threats to Validity

As any experimental study, the results of our experiments are subject to threats to validity. When discussing those threats, we distinguish between threats to internal, external and construct validity:

Threats to external validity concern our ability to transfer our results to other programs. As our study only includes five subjects, we cannot claim that the results generalize to arbitrary applications. In our experiments, the degree of coverage achieved by WEBMATE differs strongly between subjects, so we cannot make any predictions as to how WEBMATE would perform for other applications. Nevertheless, our results show that modern web applications need new approaches to test case generation in order to achieve acceptable coverage values.

Threats to internal validity concern the validity of the connections between independent and dependent variables in our setting. Since the selection process for the subjects in this study was not randomized, our sample is not independent. The authors of this study may have unintentionally preferred applications that make uncharacteristically strong use of JavaScript and hence are difficult for SCRAPY to analyze. However, in order to succeed in the web today, a web application has to provide a good user experience and therefore has to make heavy use of dynamic techniques. On the long run we expect the vast majority of web applications to employ a high degree of dynamic techniques.

Threats to construct validity concern the adequacy of our measures for capturing dependent variables. In our setting, the only dependent variable is coverage which is measured as the set of lines executed when running the program. The number of executed lines is directly connected to the control flow of the program and is the industry standard of measuring coverage. To measure this value, we use an open-source tool that is used by many other projects and hence can be expected to provide correct results. Overall it is safe to say that our measures for capturing dependent variables are adequate.

6   Application: Cross-Browser Compatibility

Besides generating tests, a testing tool needs to generate oracles (see Section 2) in order to classify the outcome of each test. The oracle decides if the behavior of the program is correct or not. For semantic tests, oracles typically check the correctness of return values, for example "If there are three items in the shopping cart, the total sum is the sum of the individual prices for all three items." Without further information it is not possible to generate such oracles automatically. However, there is a number of problems for which *automatic oracles* can be generated. In this section, we present an application of WEBMATE where it is possible to provide such an automated oracle.

For the success of a web application it is vital that the application works correctly in all major browsers. A web application is said to be *cross-browser compatible* if it is rendered identically and works correctly in all browsers. In practice, maintaining cross-browser compatibility is a real challenge. In total, there are five major browser vendors; for almost all browsers, there is more than one version available and some browsers are provided for different platforms. The distribution of market shares in Table 3 shows that for many browsers more than one version is actively used. As a consequence, in order to support 95 % of the customers, the developers of a web application have to test 22 different browsers. These tests are necessary because different browsers (and also different versions of the same browser) behave differently despite the fact that there are existing standards for the most important technologies. For quality assurance, this has serious consequences: For instance, to test a small web application with just 10 pages, a tester would have to manually compare 220 pages. Moreover, to avoid regression errors, these tests would have to be carried out after each change to the application.

Table 3. Market shares of the major browsers first quarter 2012 [13]

Version	Market share [%]	Total [%]
IE 8.0	27.02	27.02
IE 9.0	12.82	39.84
Chrome 16.0	9.88	49.72
IE 6.0	7.38	57.10
Chrome 17.0	6.18	63.28
Firefox 9.0	5.54	68.82
IE 7.0	4.73	73.55
Firefox 10	4.43	77.98
Safari 5.1	3.37	81.35
Firefox 3.6	3.22	84.57
Firefox 8.0	2.82	87.40
Opera 11.x	1.45	88.85
Firefox 11	1.19	90.04
Safari 5.0	1.08	91.12
Firefox 4.0	0.64	91.76
Firefox 6.0	0.63	92.39
Firefox 7.0	0.56	92.95
Firefox 3.0	0.55	93.50
Firefox 5.0	0.51	94.02
Firefox 3.5	0.48	94.50
Chrome 14.0	0.47	94.97
Chrome 15.0	0.39	95.36

By using WEBMATE, we are able to fully automate these tests as follows. In practice, developers of web applications normally use a fixed browser to run tests while implementing the application. Hence, for this so-called *reference browser*, the application can be expected to work correctly. WEBMATE uses the reference browser to check the rendering of all *test browsers* (those browsers for which cross-browser compatibility is to be tested). If an element is rendered by a test browser at a different position than in the reference browser, WEBMATE will report this problem to the user. Besides the challenges for test generation described in Section 3, there are a number of additional problems when implementing an automated cross-browser compatibility oracle:

Recognize layout problems. To detect layout problems, WEBMATE has to compare positions and sizes for each element on the web page. A simple comparison of screen shots is insufficient as dynamic content such as ads may cause large visual differences even though all relevant elements are rendered the same. Also, in practice it is often tolerable for elements to be a few pixels off, but a screen shot based comparison would not tolerate such minor deviations.

Browser specific code. To avoid incompatibilities between browsers, some web applications deploy different code based on which browser is used. Since

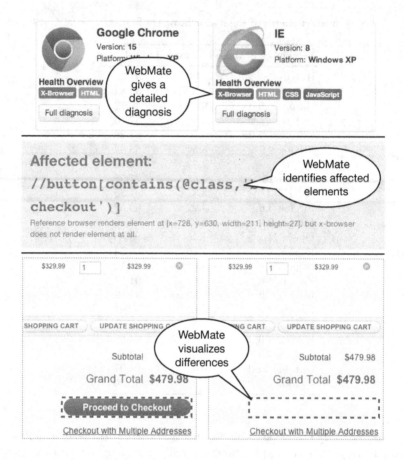

Fig. 3. Example of a diagnosis produced by WEBMATE. In Internet Explorer 8, the checkout button is missing. WEBMATE identifies the missing element and visualizes the problem using screen shots.

the state abstraction of WEBMATE is based on identifying elements of the user interface, it may happen that WEBMATE inadvertently considers the same page in different browsers to be different pages. In these cases, WEBMATE is unable to match pages across browsers and therefore cannot provide a cross-browser test.

Besides layout problems, WEBMATE is also able to recognize cases where functions are present in the reference browser, but are missing in one or more test browsers. WEBMATE compares the usage model (Section 4) of the reference browser with those extracted for the test browsers. For example, if a test browser does not display the button to remove an article from a shopping cart in a web shop, the user will be unable to remove accidentally added items and therefore will likely choose another web shop. For the maintainer of the web shop, this problem is only visible in the number of aborted transactions, which could also have a variety of other causes and is difficult to investigate. For the success of a web application, it can be vital to detect such missing functionalities in a test browser. To support developers in finding such errors, WEBMATE generates a report that visualizes all deviations found in the cross-browser analysis (Figure 3).

7 Related Work

The related work for this paper can be grouped into general approaches to test case generation and testing of web applications. A summary of the most important generic test case generation approaches was already given in Section 2.

The VeriWeb project by Benedikt et al. [3] is one of the first approaches to test dynamic web applications. In contrast to WEBMATE, VeriWeb does not use state abstraction and is therefore unable to systematically explore a web application. VeriWeb uses fixed time limits to restrict analysis time, whereas WEBMATE automatically finishes the exploration as soon as all states and interactions are explored.

Mesbah et al. [12] present *CRAWLJAX*, a tool for analysing web applications implemented with AJAX. Similar to WEBMATE, Crawljax also extracts a finite state automaton that describes different states of the application. However, in contrast to WEBMATE, Crawljax does not use state abstraction but employs tree comparison algorithms to identify user interface elements that were changed by AJAX operations. Since the recursion depth for this algorithm is limited, Crawljax is also not able to detect when all states and interactions are explored. Also, Crawljax requires the user to manually identify all active elements of the user interface, whereas WEBMATE is able to automatically identify them and can thus be used for arbitrary applications without further configuration.

In the area of cross-browser testing, Choudhary et al. [4] present their tool named Webdiff. In contrast to WEBMATE, Webdiff applies a screen-shot based comparison approach which has a number of problems in the presence of dynamic elements such as ads (see above). Also, Webdiff is not able to systematically explore a web application, which is one of the key features of WEBMATE.

Artzi et al. present APOLLO [1], a tool that analyses both the client-side and the server-side parts of a web application. APOLLO employs symbolic execution [10] and user inputs to systematically generate tests that reach previously uncovered code. Currently, APOLLO is only implemented for PHP and cannot be applied to other projects.

In earlier work on WEBMATE [7], we present initial ideas and an early evaluation. This paper extends our previous work with a discussion of general issues for test case generation in modern web applications. In the current paper, we study the effectiveness of specialized test case generation techniques compared to traditional crawlers.

8 Conclusions and Future Work

The technical complexity of modern web applications poses completely new challenges for automated test case generation. On the other hand, systematic quality assurance is even more important to guarantee dependable and secure systems. In this work, we identify the most important challenges when generating tests for modern web applications and discuss possible solutions. Our prototype WEB-MATE implements several of these solutions. In a controlled experiment, we investigate the effectiveness of the solutions built into WEBMATE in terms of the coverage achieved on a set of test subjects. Compared to traditional crawlers, WEBMATE is able to achieve up to seven times as much coverage and is therefore much more effective in generating tests.

Despite the promising results of our evaluation, the quality of the tests generated by WEBMATE is still not good enough to be useful in practice. In the future, we will investigate the following ideas to further improve the effectiveness of WEBMATE:

Server-side code analysis. The work of Artzi on APOLLO [1] shows that test case generation can benefit from analyzing server-side code. We plan to use code instrumentation on the server to provide feedback that allows WEB-MATE to specifically generate tests for uncovered areas of the program.

Test data provisioning. To improve the generation of input data for forms, we plan to use search-based testing techniques such as genetic algorithms. As a source of information, we would also like to use the content of the web site, which often already specifies valid values for input fields.

More information about WEBMATE can be found at

http://www.st.cs.uni-saarland.de/webmate/

References

[1] Artzi, S., et al.: A framework for automated testing of javascript web applications. In: ICSE, pp. 571–580 (2011)
[2] Barnett, M., et al.: The Spec# programming system: Challenges and directions, pp. 144–152 (2008), doi: http://dx.doi.org/10.1007/978-3-540-69149-5_16
[3] Benedikt, M., Freire, J., Godefroid, P.: Veriweb: Automatically testing dynamic web sites. In: Proceedings of 11th International World Wide Web Conference, WWW 2002 (2002)
[4] Choudhary, S.R., Versee, H., Orso, A.: WEBDIFF: Automated identification of cross-browser issues in web applications. In: ICSM, pp. 1–10 (2010)
[5] Ciupa, I., et al.: Experimental assessment of random testing for object-oriented software. In: ISSTA 2007: Proceedings of the 2007 International Symposium on Software Testing and Analysis, pp. 84–94. ACM Press, London (2007), doi: http://doi.acm.org/10.1145/1273463.1273476, ISBN: 978-1-59593-734-6
[6] Google Code. Selenium, http://code.google.com/p/selenium/
[7] Dallmeier, V., et al.: Webmate: A tool for testing web 2.0 applications. In: JsTools (To appear, 2012)

[8] Fraser, G., Zeller, A.: Generating parameterized unit tests. In: Proceedings of the 2011 International Symposium on Software Testing and Analysis, ISSTA 2011, pp. 364–374. ACM Press, Toronto (2011),
http://doi.acm.org/10.1145/2001420.2001464, doi:10.1145/2001420.2001464, ISBN: 978-1-4503-0562-4

[9] Gross, F., Fraser, G., Zeller, A.: Search-Based System Testing: High Coverage, No False Alarms. In: ISSTA (To appear, 2012)

[10] King, J.C.: Symbolic execution and program testing. Commun. ACM 19(7), 385–394 (1976), doi: http://doi.acm.org/10.1145/360248.360252, ISSN: 0001-0782

[11] Majumdar, R., Sen, K.: Hybrid Concolic Testing. In: ICSE 2007: Proceedings of the 29th International Conference on Software Engineering, pp. 416–426. IEEE Computer Society, Washington, DC (2007),
doi: http://dx.doi.org/10.1109/ICSE.2007.41, ISBN: 0-7695-2828-7

[12] Mesbah, A., van Deursen, A.: Invariant-based automatic testing of AJAX user interfaces. In: ICSE 2009: Proceedings of the 2009 IEEE 31st International Conference on Software Engineering, pp. 210–220. IEEE Computer Society, Washington, DC (2009), doi: http://dx.doi.org/10.1109/ICSE.2009.5070522, ISBN: 978-1-4244-3453-4

[13] NetMarketShare: Desktop browser version market share

[14] Sourceforge. Cobertura, http://sourceforge.net

Testing Web Services in the Cloud

Harry M. Sneed

ANECON GmbH, Vienna, Austria
Fachhochschule Hagenberg, Upper Austria
Harry.Sneed@T-Online.de

Abstract. This paper describes a tool supported process to test web services offered in the cloud against a service level agreement. After defining the goals of cloud service testing and reviewing previous approaches to testing web services, it goes on to define the particular problem of testing publically offered cloud services. The test is not directed at locating errors, but to evaluating the suitability of the service for a given application. To this end the requirements of the application, both functional und non-functional, have to be laid down in a service level agreement. The testing agent must extract the test criteria from that document to create a set of test cases. These requirement-based test cases are then matched to the cloud service interface definition to generate service test scripts. From the preconditions specified in the test script representative service requests are generated to be forwarded to the service under test in asynchronous modus. The responses from the service are collected in an output buffer to later be validated against the service post-conditions. Deviations between the expected and the actual results are reported. In the end a metric-based evaluation report is prepared to assist the user in deciding whether to use the service are not.

Keywords: Cloud Computing, Web Services, Service Testing, SLAs, WSDL, Interface-based Testing, Test specification, Test data generation, test result validation, Cloud Service Evaluation.

1 Introduction

Many enterprises are planning to modernize their IT landscape and would like to take advantage of cloud services – according to a recent survey by Forrester it is now about 45% - if only they knew that they could rely on those services. It is a problem of trust [1]. Cloud services are offered at many different levels of granularity. Some are elementary business or technical functions for computing specific results, others are complete business applications. The scope of the web services offered is extremely wide. With the help of the UDDI registration of a service together with the posted web service interface definition, it is possible to infer what the service proposes to do but there is no way to know if the service really does that or how it does it. The only way to find out is by testing it [2].

The testing of web services in the cloud is anything but easy. The user, who wants to try it, must have the proper testing environment, trained personnel and automated

D. Winkler, S. Biffl, and J. Bergsmann (Eds.): SWQD 2013, LNBIP 133, pp. 70–88, 2013.

test tools which allow the services to be tested quickly and effectively. The tools, now available on the market or from the open source community, require skills and knowledge to use them. Since few users have the knowledge and skills required to really test web services, they keep postponing their decision to deploy them. In doing so, they are losing a tremendous business opportunity. They have to go living with their old legacy applications and sustaining a staff of old legacy developers, while the new business process models remain an unfulfilled dream and the cloud computing providers remain sitting on their promising new services. There is a deadlock situation.

Many IT users would be more than willing to accept external help in testing out the perspective services, if only they could know what they get for their money. Like all customers of a service they want to know what a service entails and what they have to pay for it. If they have no trust in the cloud then they must at least be able to trust those who test it. They expect from the cloud testers documented, concrete evidence that the selected services are really reliable and usable, and that they fulfill their requirements. Besides they want to know what it will cost to provide that evidence. Then they must have the possibility of comparing offers. If the costs are too high, they may decide to test the services themselves or to go on without them. In no case is it advisable to employ foreign cloud services without having first tested them. For this reason, unlike agile testing which is done on a time and material basis, cloud service testing must be offered on a fixed price basis. The user should get a complete breakdown of the test results down to the lowest level with a price tag for each result. As such the user can then decide which of the test results he would like to have. There should be enough for him to determine if the service offered is suitable for his purposes.

The only way to provide such fixed price test services is with test automation. The testing process has to be automated to a high degree. Not only the testing itself but, also the test preparation and the subsequent test evaluation have to be automated. This is the motivation for this paper which handles the following issues:

- Goals and means of web service testing
- Existing tools for testing web services
- An automated process for testing web services
  - o Specifying the service test cases
  - o Generating service test scripts
  - o Editing and compiling service test scripts
  - o Generating web service requests
  - o Executing the service test
  - o Validating web service responses
  - o Evaluating web services
- Experience in testing web services with WebsTest

2   Goals and Means of Web Service Testing

To understand the purpose of a web service testing tool, one has to first understand the purpose of web services. Web services are ready make, pretested off the shelf software components which are accessed via the internet. In contrast to the earlier subroutines, class libraries and standard products, which had to be purchased by the user and physically built into his local environment, web services do not have to be physically available. They only have to be accessible via the web which means physically they would be anywhere in cyberspace. The user does not need to possess them; he only needs to use them on demand. To access them he has to go thru a web service interface made available by the service provider.

Building software means putting together thousands of atomic, elementary functions. A significant portion of those functions, according to Capers Jones well over 80% [3] can be reused in many different applications. In fact, they most could be reused in applications throughout the world. There is no rational reason for writing one's own version of these functions when they are available everywhere to everyone. The task of software development has taken on a different nature. Instead of conceiving and coding his own elementary functions or methods, today's developer should be concerned with how to put together the proper ready-made functions to serve his functions. A service-oriented architecture is intended to present the developers of individual software applications with a wide range of ready-made services to use within their applications. Not only will this result in a significant reduction of code volume. It also reduces the effort and time required to get to a working solution. The best method of increasing software productivity is to reduce the amount of software that has to be produced. A really agile project is one in which a minimum amount of code is newly written and in which a maximum amount is reused. That is the surest way to deliver working software on time and in budget. The problem of software development shifts from developing software to integrating and testing it. The question that comes up is where to find the appropriate service and how to confirm that it is suitable for the task at hand.

To find the proper service developers must know where to look, i.e. in what UDDI directories and how to filter out those services which come closest to their requirements. Genetic search algorithms can be helpful in this respect. The second question as to the suitability of the services has to be answered by testing. Only by testing the service can users be sure that a selected service serves their purpose. Since developers have many other things to do, this is something that can be delegated to others, who are specialists in this field. They need a broker to find and test web services for them. That should be the role of the tester. Rather than working after the developer to discover faults in his product, the tester should be working before the developer to provide him with the building blocks he needs to make his work.

This switch in roles is best illustrated by a service-oriented architecture. Before the first application project is started, the architecture should be in place with enough ready-made services available to significantly reduce the development effort. At first this may only be 40 to 50 %, but later it should be at least 80%. These services provided should of course be pre-tested and proven to comply with the demands placed on them. The users, i.e. the application developers should know beforehand whether they can rely on the services [4].

The role of the testers is changing here from a reactive to a pre-active one. The required services have to be tested before they are used. That requires new skills on the part of the tester and put new demands on the tools he uses. Web service testing is a new form of unit testing performed by specialists who test for all potential usages of a service instead of just testing it for one single purpose as is often done by developers in testing the modules or classes they are writing. The ultimate purpose of web service testing is to confirm that selected web services can be used without risk in pending application projects [5].

Web services in the cloud, like other software modules, require a test driver to be tested independently of their clients. It is possible to create a client, e.g. a BPEL Process or a Java script application to invoke the services, thus testing them indirectly via their client, but it is more efficient and more effective to test a service directly from a driver. The test driver gives the tester more control over the test object. He can determine what test data goes in and he can more easily check the results that come out. If an error occurs he can be sure that the error is in the service and not in the client. When testing thru a client, the tester cannot control the interaction between the client and the service, and should an error occur, he cannot be sure of whether the error is in the client, in the service or in the interaction between the two.

A web service testing tool serves the same purpose for services as JUnit or NUnit do for objects. It gives the tester control over the test object and allows him to observe its behavior by simulating the environment in which the object is operating. The difference is that the testing of objects is a white-box test, i.e. the tester has insight into the code and can derive his test cases from the structure of the code. He can also trace the flow of control as well as the data flow within the code. With web services that is not possible. The tester will most likely never see the source code of the service he is testing. It belongs to the person or the organization offering the service. If it happens to be an open source service, he may get access to it, but it is not his job to know how the service functions internally and it is better if he does not know. His job is to determine if the service satisfies the requirements of the application he represents. Therefore, the service test is by definition a black-box test. The test of a web service is aimed at validating the results of the service and at assuring that the performance criteria laid down in the service level agreement are met [6].

Every test is a test against something. That something is referred to as the test oracle. In a unit test the developer tests the module or the object under test against a module or object specification. In an integration test the integration tester tests the interaction of several modules or objects against the interface specifications. In a system test, the system tester tests the system as a whole against the requirement specification. In the unit test, the test cases are derived from the code. In the integration test, the test cases are taken from the interface definition. In the system test, the test cases are extracted from the requirements. The test of a web service is similar to an integration test. It is a test against the web service interface definition, but also a test against the service level agreement. The service level agreement supplements the interface definition by the requirements of the application under development, in particular the non-functional requirements such as time constraints, precision of results and transaction loads. In is the task of a tester to determine

a) if the service under consideration fulfills the requirements of the potential user, and

b) if the service under consideration satisfies the constraints defined in the service level agreement

The goal of a web service test is, as opposed to conventional testing, not to uncover errors to be corrected in the service, but to determine whether the service can be used or not. If a service is too faulty, too fragile or too slow it should be discarded and another service used in its place. It is the task of the tester to find this out for the developers who do not themselves have the time to deal with testing the suitability of potential services for their application. They rely on the tester to answer this question for them.

The purpose of a web service testing tool is to support the tester in this endeavor. It should enable him to set up and conduct the test of any web service with a minimum of effort while gathering a maximum of information for determining the suitability of the service. It should use both the web service interface definition and the service level agreement as a basis for generating the requests and for validating the correctness of the service responses. It should also measure the performance of the service and determine if the non-functional requirements are met. Finally, it should execute the test fully automatically in batch mode, even without the presence of the tester. The test should be as automated as possible to allow the tester to achieve his goal of evaluating a given service within a short time and at a low cost and still be able to judge the suitability of the service.

The time needed to evaluate a web service depends on the size of that service and the width of its interface, but it should never take more than a couple of days. The users and developers are working more and more in agile projects which require them to solve problems rapidly. They have no time to wait weeks on an answer if the service they desire to use is suitable or not. They need to know within a few days or maybe even within hours if they can rely on a given service or not. That means testers must react immediately.

Besides being fast and inexpensive the web service test must also present the test results in a compact graphical form which is easy to understand by developers and users. Within minutes it should be possible for them to interpret the results and to decide whether the service meets their requirements. The presentation of test metrics is yet another demand on web service testing. Not only should it be fully automated and easy to use, it should also provide the test results in a compact, easily interpretable format.

The demands placed on a web service testing tool can be summarized as follows:

- it should support the test in specifying service test cases
- it should automatically generate web requests from the web service interface definition
- it should automatically invoke the web service independently of the client
- it should automatically validate web responses against the web service specification
- it should automatically evaluate the web service according to the service level agreement.

3   Existing Tools for Testing Web Services

Web Services have been around for quite awhile so there is no lack of tools for testing them. Any search through the Internet will come up with hundreds. The question is whether they really suit to the goals outlined above. In a survey from the year 2007 made by researchers at Kings College in London, the authors refer to the gap between what is needed for evaluating web services and what is offered on the commercial market. They point to such tools as ParaSoft , SOATest, SOAPSmar, HP's Service Test and Oracle's Application Testing Suite as being representative of what is offered on the commercial market. The authors claim that "even although these tools do help to reduce the manual labor required for test case generation and reporting, they do not come close to automating the testing process. In all of the tools mentioned there is a facility for generating SOAP requests for each test case, but it is up to the tester to specify the test cases and fill in the test data. In some tools even the verification of the test results has to be performed manually. From the provided functionality of all tools, one can assume that automation is far from the desired level" [7].

Such was the state of service testing tools in 2007. Since then four years have passed and the situation has improved. Not only have the existing tools become better, but there are more of them to choose from, especially in the open source community. Representative of these newer tools is ASTRAR from Tsai and his associates. ASTRAR supports a form of n-version testing where multiple web services with similar business logic are tested together in the same test suite. Although the main goal of this cluster testing approach is to test multiple services at one time to reduce the cost of testing, it also achieves the purpose of establishing a test base line. The tool can be applied both to the testing of single services – unit testing – as well as to the testing of service sequences – integration testing [8].

Another tool of this type is SOA-Cleaner. It reads the web service interface definition (WSDL) and automatically generates a graphical user interface for composing requests to be sent to the service in a native and intuitive way. The input arguments, HTTP headers, URLs, attachments, etc., are edited though the generated GUI. The tool can be used to emulate a complete business process by defining sequences of service calls in a BPEL notation. The responses returned from the web services are verified by defining assertions, or by using them as an input to subsequent services. SOA-Cleaner is a MicroSoft based product implemented with .Net. It is therefore compliant with MicroSoft WCF without losing its high level of interoperability with Java-based service frameworks [9].

SOAPUI is yet another web service testing tool offered on the open source market. It does not require the user to write anything. Every step is supported by darg and drop techniques. The form editor creates a form from the user web service interface definition which allows him to select values to be used as input arguments. The tool has a hierarchical menu which steers the tester through the test from one request to the other, displaying the responses to him as they come and allowing him to change the sequence of the test at any time. Furthermore, the tester is allowed to enter assertions during the test, so that the test scenario can be altered on the fly at run time [10].

WebInject is another freeware tool for automated testing of web services. It can be used to test individual system components with HTTP interfaces as well as to create a suite of HTTP level automated functional, acceptance and regression tests. The test harness allows the tester to start a number of test cases at one time and to collect the results in report files for which the tool offers a real-time display of the web service responses. In addition, WebInject can be used for monitoring service performance.

As a test framework, Webinject can be used optionally as a standalone test engine or it can be bound together with other test frameworks or applications to be used as an extended test service. For this purpose it has an API interface which allows it to be called dynamically to dispatch web requests. The loading and defining of test cases is made via an XML-WSDL like interface. The test cases are stored in XML files. From there they are passed to the Webinject engine for executing the service under test via the current WSDL interface. This way, the internal implementation is hidden from the non-technical user while the technical user has the possibility of customizing the open architecture to his specific testing needs. The test results are generated in HTML for viewing and in XML for interpretation by user specific display tools. The reported results include the pass/fail status, error messages and response times [11].

In their survey of web service testing tools from 2007, Bozkurt and Harman also mention the original version of the first WebsTest tool – WSDLTest - which was reported on by Sneed and Huang in the Wiley Journal of Software Maintenance and Evolution in that year. They cite that the tool is capable of generating random service requests from the WSDL schemas and of validating the service responses against the post conditions formulated in a test script. To formulate those conditions, the tester must be familiar with the service under test [12]. The tool set described in this paper is the result of the evolution of that original prototype product.

4   An Automated Process for Testing Web Services

The two main purposes of a Web Service Testing Tool are 1) to find out whether a web service can be trusted and 2) to see if it is suitable for the purpose of the user as stated in the service level agreement. All other functions are subordinate to these two, the generation and editing of test scripts, the generation of test requests, the execution of the service under test, the validation of the service responses and the evaluation of the service test results. All of these sub functions contribute to the goals of gaining trust and assessing the suitability of the service in question.

To test any piece of software, test cases are required which represent productive use. Since the testers have no access to the source code, the test cases have to be taken either out of their heads or out of the web service description. This description may include a specification and/or a service level agreement. In any case it will include an interface definition – WSDL – and one or more data schemas. It is up to the tester to collect these documents and to analyze them.

The next step after defining the test cases is to generate data which can be used to test the cases. This has to be real data with numbers, codes and alphabetical strings embedded in a formal XML syntax; so it can be interpreted by the web service. Since the number of data combinations is practically unlimited, there has to be some kind of artificial limit imposed, which means the data combinations selected should be representative of the possible data combinations. This requires a combination of controlled data assignment and random data generation. Here it is recommended to use boundary analysis and equivalence classes.

With the web service requests generated, it should be possible to execute the target service by sending off messages to its internet address. For that the service request has to be packed into a transmission envelope, i.e. a SOAP protocol, for transmission. When an answer comes back, that response has to be unpacked and made available. Packing, sending, receiving and unpacking internet messages are the functions of a web service test driver.

It is not enough to confirm that the web service under test functions, and that it returns some response. The responses must also be validated to ensure that they contain the proper return values. The proper return values are those output data values specified in the post conditions of that particular request. That means the responses have to be matched to the requests and they have to be compared with the expected responses. This again implies that the expected results are defined and can be automatically verified.

The ultimate task of a web service tester is to assess the suitability of a particular web service. He has to judge whether the service is adequate for the task at hand or not. For this decision he needs information on the performance, the functionality, the reliability and the security of the service in question. The testing tool should provide this information in form of reports and graphics which can be easily interpreted by the tester. This requires an extra post processing component.

In summarizing, there are five principle sub functions to be carried out by a web service testing tool. These are:

- to aid the tester in specifying service test cases
- to generate representative web service requests
- to execute the target service with valid messages
- to validate the correctness of the returned responses
- to provide information for evaluating the tested services.

Thus, the WebsTest automated test process consists of seven well defined and tool supported steps.

- Step 1 is to extract a table of test cases from the service level agreement
- Step 2 is to generate a text script from the test case table and the web service interface schema
- Step 3 is to edit and compile the test script
- Step 4 is to generate the web service requests
- Step 5 is to execute the service test
- Step 6 is to validate the web service responses
- Step 7 is to evaluate the web service

4.1   Specifying Service Test Cases

The first step in the WebsTest automated test process is to analyze the service level agreement text and to extract logical test cases from it. A web service can be specified through a requirements document and/or a service level agreement. If both are available, both should be analyzed. If only one is available then at least that should be analyzed. If none are available, it is questionable whether the web service should be used at all.

Both types of documents are texts written in a natural language. To be analyzed the text should be in a certain format. There should be key words or tags to identify the function and quality attributes. For instance, a function may be identified by the keyword "Function:" followed by a function name and a statement of what that function does. A quality attribute should also be identified by a keyword such as "Response Time" followed by a number denoting the time in milliseconds. Both functions and quality attributes can be conditional or non conditional. Conditions are recognizable by the predicates they use, words like "if", "when", "should", "in so far as" etc.

Attribute	Description
Label:	processCustomerOrder
Requirements:	FREQ-01, FREQ-02, FREQ-03.
Rules:	BR-01, BR-02, BR-03, BR-04, BR-05, BR-06.
Functions:	FUNC-01, FUNC-02, FUNC-03, FUNC-04.
Inputs:	INPUT-01, INPUT-02, INPUT-03, INPUT-04.
Outputs:	OUTPUT-01, OUTPUT-02, OUTPUT-03, OUTPUT-04.
Objects:	BO-01, BO-02, BO-05, BO-06, BO-07, BO-09, BO-11, BO-13.
Trigger:	Menu_Selection
Actor:	Customer
Frequency:	Continuous
ResponseTime	3 Sec
PreConditions:	Ordered article must be on stock. Customer must be authorized to purchase articles. Customer must be credible.
PostConditions:	Article amount is reduced by the order and Dispatch order exits for each fulfilled order item and Billing item exits for each fulfilled order item Or back order exits for not fulfilled order item. A supply order item exits if the article amount falls below the minimum order amount required.

MainPath:	1) GetArticleTypes Customer requests article types.
	    Service returns a list of article types.
	2) ArticleQuery Customer selects an article type.
	    Service returns a list of articles and prices.
	3) CustomerOrder Customer orders an article.
	    Service checks customer credit.
	    Service checks if article on stock.
	    Service checks if amount on stock is sufficient.
	    If not sufficient, service creates a back order.
	    If sufficient, service subtracts amount ordered from amount on stock, creates a dispatch order item and creates a billing item .
	    If amount on stock falls below the minimum amount, the service creates a resupply order.

The text parsing tool will identify the functions and the quality criteria to be fulfilled and will create one or more test cases for each of them. If a function is conditional, there will be a test case for each outcome of the decision. If a function is compound, i.e. it contains several sub clauses connected by "and" or "or", the text analyzer will generate a test case for each one of them. There will also be a test case generated for each state specified. Thus in the end, there should be one test case for every specified action, state and condition. From the following business rule a test case will be generated to confirm that a back order exists for the current article whose amount on stock is less than the amount ordered.

BR-04: If the article amount on stock is less than the amount ordered, a back order should be created and the customer informed that delivery will be delayed.

PreCondition:	Article.Amount < Order.Amount;
PostCondition:	BackOrder.ArticleNo = Article.ArticleNo &
	CustomerMessage = "Delivery delayed";

Besides containing the business rules, the business objects and the use cases, the service specification should contain the service interface definition. Here the functions are identified together with their input and output interfaces as depicted below. It is not mandatory but useful to use the same parameter names as are used in the WSDL interface schema. In this way the test data can be matched to the test case table making it possible to generate a more complete test script. If the service specification is done properly it is possible to automate all of the subsequent test steps and to test the service within one working day.

FUNC-02: QueryAvailableProducts.

INPUT-02: QueryAvailableProducts2Request.

The article query request should contain:

> # CustNo = "009999".

> # ArtType = "BOOK".

OUTPUT-02: QueryAvailableProducts2Response.

The article query response should contain:

> # item[1].

>> # ResponseArtNo[1] = "004711".

>> # ResponseArtType[1] = "BOOK".

>> # ResponseArtName[1] = "My sex life" .

>> # ResponseArtPrice[1] = "40.50".

The test cases are stored in an Excel table, where they can be viewed and edited by the tester when he is preparing the test. Among the entities identified in the test case table are the functions and objects to be tested. By displaying the structure of the WSDL next to the test case table the tool enables the tester to match the functions and objects specified in the SLA with the operations and parameters defined in the WSDL. This association is very important to bridging the gap between the logical view of the service as depicted in the SLA and the physical view of the service as depicted in the WSDL [13].

Generated Test Case Table

TestCase	Operation	Parameter	Type	Ind	Value
Orders02	GetTypes	GetTypes1Request	Parameter		?
	GetTypes	item	Return	1	MAGA
	GetTypes	item	Return	2	NEWS
	GetTypes	item	Return	3	BOOK
	QueryAvail	CustNo	Parameter		009999
	QueryAvail	ArtType	Parameter		BOOK
	QueryAvail	Item	Return	1	Struc
	QueryAvail	ResponseArtNo	Return	1	4711
	QueryAvail	ResponseArtType	Return	1	BOOK
	QueryAvail	ResponseArtName	Return	1	MeinKampf
	QueryAvail	ResponseArtPrice	Return	1	40.50

4.2 Generating Service Test Scripts

The second step in the WebsTest automated test process is to generate a test script from a union of the test case table with the service interface definition. This is actually a merge operation. Each test case in the test case table refers to one or more operations in the web service. The tool takes one test case at a time and merges it with those operations and objects it refers to in the WSDL schema. Since any one test case may contain one or more operations, the requirement statement being tested is included as a comment to the test case. The tester may delete them but they are there to remind him what he should test. They also provide a link from the test to the requirements document, something which is very important when it comes to maintenance and tracing test cases to change requests. In the evaluation phase the test cases taken from the specification will be compared with those actually tested to measure the degree of test coverage. Since there is no code to measure, testers can only measure test coverage in respect to the tested requirements, the tested operations and the tested data parameters.

For any one service there can be any number of tests. A test here is equal to a test scenario. A test scenario is a sequence of test cases. The test cases are given in the test script. They are denoted by a if testcase = (..........) statement and marked by a comment line.

```
if (testcase = "WareHouseOrders_002");
// Test Customer Order with an invalid article number
```

A test case is a sequence of one or more requests, each followed by a response. Each request invokes an operation with a set of one or more parameters. The parameters may be elementary or complex data types. Complex data types are defined as objects. A request or response may contain any number of objects.

```
if ( operation =   "BuySomething");
      if ( request  =   "BuySomething4Request");
          if ( object = "AnOrder" );
```

If a test case applies to only a single operation then the test case will have only have one request. Normally, a test case will refer to a chain of related operations. In that case, the test case will have as many requests as there are operations to invoke. Often the tester will want to repeat the chain of operations several times to test them with different data combinations. For this the initial test case will be duplicated with different parameter values for each additional test of the selected operations. In this way the test cases make up a test loop.

4.3   Editing and Compiling Service Test Scripts

The third step in the WebsTest automated test process is to compile a test from the test script. The generated test script is already compilable but the data may not be complete. Normally the tester will want to vary that data, which he can do by editing the script. The script language offers the tester the possibility of specifying different combinations of data for the service requests and with which he can specify the expected contents of the service responses. The data inputs are specified as preconditions – assert inp, the data outputs as post conditions – assert out.

```
assert inp.OrderArtAmount = "5";
assert out.ResponseArtName  = "Newsweek";
```

The script language contains assertion statements for boundary analysis – the range-statement - as well as for defining representative values of equivalence classes – the set statement. It also allows for computations, concatenations and alterations. The assertions can be both data assignments as well as data checks. If the tester is specifying a request the assertion statements are data assignments in which the target data names have the prefix inp. If he is specifying a response, the statements are data checks whereby the result names have the prefix out.

The test script language is structured in accordance with the hierarchy of web service definitions. At the top level the service is defined. There is a separate test script for each service. One can say that the test script corresponds to a test scenario. Within the service the test cases are inserted. A test case may trigger one or more operations in a sequence of related operations, similar to a use case or a transaction. Each of the invoked operations has a request and a response. The request contains the input parameters for that particular operation or method. The response contains the expected return values. Request and Responses contain assertion statements which generate or validate data values. The contents of a request are generated. The content of a response are validated. A sample test script obtaining the day of the week is given below.

```
service: IWareHouseWebServiceservice;
  if (testcase = "WareHouseOrders_001");
// First Request to Frontend to order Articles
    if ( operation =  "GetTypes");
      if ( request  =  "GetTypes1Request");
        assert inp.GetTypes1Request_DummyParam  = "?";
      endRequest ;
      if ( response  =  "GetTypes1Response");
        assert out.$ResponseTime < "1000";
        if ( object = "return" occurs = "2");
          assert out.item[1]  = old.item[1];
          assert out.item[2]  = old.item[2];
        endObject;
      endResponse ;
    endOperation;
    if ( operation =  "QueryAvailableProducts");
      if ( request  =  "QueryAvailableProducts2Request");
        assert inp.CustNo  = "009999";
        assert inp.ArtType  = "BOOK";
      endRequest ;
      if ( response  =  "QueryAvailableProducts2Response");
        assert out.$ResponseTime < "1000";
        if ( object = "return" occurs = "1");
          if ( object = "item[1]");
            assert out.ResponseArtNo  = "4711";
            assert out.ResponseArtType  = "BOOK";
            assert out.ResponseArtName  = "MeinKampf";
            assert out.ResponseArtPrice = "40.50";
          endObject;
```

As seen in this script, the tester can also specify the minimum response time for each request. Should it take longer, an exception will be reported.

4.4   Generating Web Service Requests

The fourth step in the WebsTest automated test process is to generate a service request. When compiling the test script a table of test data objects is created. These objects are identified by test case, request or response name and by a qualified data name. The elementary data items are qualified by the data structures to which they belong. The request generator merges these data objects with a framework request structure taken from the WSDL schema. Thus the interface structure is supplemented by the physical test data contained in the test script. The result is an executable request.

For every operation specified at least one request is generated. A chain of requests makes up a test case. There will be *n* test cases generated for each service with *n* requests per test case. Thus, the same request will be repeated many times, as many times as there are test cases. Each request will have another combination of data values to ensure that all representative request states are covered. The data generation is aimed at generating various combinations of requests with varying data states. The goal is to achieve the highest possible test coverage with the lowest possible number of test cases. This is the essence of value driven testing.

4.5   Executing the Service Test

The fifth step in the WebsTest automated test process is to execute the service test. Once the test request has been generated, the target service can be executed. The user needs only to select the test he wants to run. He may also select specific test cases. The possible test cases are displayed on the screen for selection.

The test driver processes the selected test requests sequentially from beginning to end. Each individual request is taken and packed into a standard SOAP envelope to be sent out to the target service. The service specific attributes of the envelope are taken from the service WSDL definition. The envelope is then dispatched to the operation specified therein by placing it in the output message queue.

Parallel to the dispatching of requests, the test driver is also receiving responses from requests it has already sent. To that end, it is continually polling its input message queue. Messages that come back from the server are unpacked, i.e. extracted from the SOAP envelope and placed in a response file for validation.

In this manner the service execution can be repeated many times, as many times as the tester desires. The number of tests is a parameter to the tool which can be set by the tester. The default is one. Should an error occur in executing a request, the test will continue with the next request. If, however, two requests in sequence return an error response, the test will be interrupted since there is obviously a problem with the service.

4.6   Validating Web Service Responses

The sixth step in the WebsTest automated test process is to validate the service responses. Upon return the web service responses are stored by the test driver in a log file for further processing. This further processing is the function of response validation. Here the contents of the responses, i.e. the returned values are compared with the values specified in the service script. Those that do not match are reported as discrepancies. The discrepancy report is the result of the validation process.

The validation process is started by the tester after each service test. In the first step the script for that service is read in and a table of valid output values and value ranges created. Then the returned responses for the last test are sorted by the response-id. The response-id should correspond to the request-id. Based on the response-id the return responses are matched to the requests specified in the assertion script. The return values are then matched b name to the post assertions for that request.

Values can be compared with a specific value - a number, a code or a string, they can be compared with a set of values to check if they are a member of that set, they can be compared with the result of an arithmetic operation, or they can be checked to see if they are equal, less or greater than another value. The comparisons always apply to the selected response or to the previous version of that response. For the sake of that comparison all previous responses are kept. This way, it is possible to compare the response of the current test with the response of the last test.

Response Validation Report

```
+-----------------------------------------------------------------------+
|                 WSDL Response Validation Report                        |
| Tester: IWareHouseWebService                      Date: 11.07.12      |
| TestName: WSDL-Response     TestCase: 001         System: Orders      |
+---------------------------------------+-------------------------------+
| Non-Matching Params                   | Non-Matching Values           |
+---------------------------------------+-------------------------------+
| Resp-Id: GetTypes1Response_001        |                               |
| Ist: $ResponseTime                    | 24131                         |
| Soll:Asserted_Value                   | <1000                         |
+---------------------------------------+-------------------------------+
| Resp-Id: GetTypes1Response_001_return|                               |
| Ist: item[1]                          | MAGI                          |
| Soll:item[1]                          | =MAGA                         |
| Ist: item[2]                          | BUCH                          |
| Soll:item[2]                          | =BOOK                         |
+---------------------------------------+-------------------------------+
```

An assertion violation occurs, when an actual return value does not match to the asserted return value or values. In this case a deviation is logged in the discrepancy report, where also statistics are kept on the relation of deviations recorded to the number of return values checked. The proportion of correct responses to all responses is also reported there. It is then up to the tester to verify the reported discrepancies and to produce the necessary problem reports for the error tracking system.

4.7   Evaluating Web Services

The ultimate goal of a web service test is to evaluate the suitability of that service for the user. The user wants to know if he can trust the service and it is the job of the tester to provide an answer to that question. In this respect the tester is fulfilling the role of a rating agency. He is rating the service in the name of the prospective user.

There are a number of ways to rate a service:

- by functionality
- by reliability
- by efficiency
- by security
- by performance [14].

4.7.1 Rating Service Functionality

To rate a service by functionality the tester must compare the operations offered by the service with the functions required by the user. The tool can help by extracting the functions contained in the service level agreement with those defined in the service interface. There is an extra component in WebsTest for making this comparison. It reports which functions specified in the SLA are missing in the WSDL. The rating metric is

$$Functionality = \frac{operations\_defined}{functions\_specified}$$

4.7.2 Rating Service Reliability

To rate the reliability of a service, first each operation defined has to have been tested. This is the functional test coverage. WebsTest record every operation tested and gives the relation of all operations defined

$$coverage = \frac{operations\_tested}{operations\_defined}$$

This in itself is not enough. Also the error rate has to be considered

$$error\ rate = \frac{invalid\_return\_values}{return\_values\_checked}$$

$$* \frac{return\_values\_checked}{all\_return\_values}$$

$$* \frac{correct\_responses}{all\_responses}$$

The error rate needs to be adjusted by the test coverage to give the final reliability rate.

$$reliability = error\_rate * test\_coverage$$

4.7.3 Rating Service Efficiency

To rate the efficiency of the web service two response time metrics have to be considered:

- maximum response time and
- median response time

Each are measured by WebsTest and both are to be compared with the required values in the service level agreement:

$$maximum\_efficiency\_rate = \frac{specified\_maximum\_time}{actual\_maximum\_time}$$

$$median\_efficiency\_rate = \frac{specified\_median\_time}{actual\_median\_time}$$

4.7.4 Rating Service Security

To rate security test cases must be devised to gain unauthorized access to the service, i.e. they either violate the authentication and authorization checks or they circumvent them. In addition to that, there should be some test cases running over corrupted data to the service. There should be enough such test cases to warrant making assumptions about the security of the service, i.e. at least as many as there are operations defined. It is expected that the service will reject them. If not, this is considered a security violation.

The measure for rating security is

$$security\_rating = \frac{security\_threats\_rejected}{security\_threats\_tested}$$

4.7.5 Rating Service Conformity

The rating of conformity is a byproduct of the WSDL static analyzer. It checks the WSDL code against a set of standard rules for compliance. Every interface rule violation is recorded as a major, medium or minor deficiency. The major deficiencies are weighted by 2, the medium by 1 and the minor by 0,5. The conformance rating is calculated as the

$$Confomity = \frac{weighted\_deficiency\_count}{number\ of\ WSDL\ statements}$$

The result is the degree to which the web service interfaces conforms to the interface rules. Since the testers will normally not have access to the web service source they can rate such internal qualities as conformance solely on the basis of the interface description.

4.7.6 Rating Overall Service Quality

To rate the service as a whole the tool WebsTest offers a function which aggregates the individual ratings and computes for the tester an aggregate rating. The individual ratings are adjusted by the weights assigned to them by the tester. It is then up to the tester to present the compound rating report produced by the tool to the user for deciding on the suitability of the service.

There will be many services whose rating is so low, i.e. below 75%, that they can be immediately eliminated. A few services may attain a rating well over 90%. These are the services which come closest to fulfilling the requirements of the user. In between will be services which fulfill 75-90% of the user requirements. They can be considered for use if there are no better alternatives, but the user may have to wrap them to compensate for their deficiencies. In the end the user may decide to employ no foreign service at all but to develop a service of his own.

5   Experience in Testing Web Services with WebsTest

The wide spread use of cloud services in industrial applications is yet to come. IT users are still somewhat cautious to take this step away from developing everything themselves to using ready-made services from the cloud. So the experience gained in testing such services with Webstest is limited to research projects. Several smaller services such as calendar and currency conversion services have been tested, however the largest service tested so far is an order entry system containing seven operations, three for ordering articles, one for dispatching, one for billing, one for resupplying and one for handling back orders. The three ordering operations were implemented in Java, the four backend operations in COBOL. This application was also intended to prove the feasibility of wrapping legacy COBOL programs. These programs had previously been implemented to run in batch mode on an IBM mainframe. After wrapping them in a WSDL shell they could be run anywhere, even on a PC work station. The Java components were developed on an Eclipse workbench for execution under MS-Windows. So for this test the Java and COBOL server components were bound together behind a common server interface on an Apache server.

The WebsTest tool set itself runs under a Windows-XT operating system with a Delphi user interface. It was used by students of Software Engineering at the University of Regensburg to test the order entry service. Some 122 test cases were extracted automatically from the service level agreement in English language. Of these half were eliminated as being either redundant or irrelevant. In the end only 59 test cases remained. These were merged with the WSDL interface definition to generate 59 requests. The greatest effort was spent in editing and compiling the test scripts. This required an average of seven hours to prepare the test. The test itself could be conducted within 1,5 hours. All 59 requests could be dispatched and their results captured. The response validation report revealed 11 errors in the 59 requests that had gone unnoticed before, errors such as to the creation of duplicate resupply orders and the selection of the cheapest supplier. Also uncovered were simple arithmetic errors in calculating the amount due. On top of that it was discovered that many requests, in particular the backend requests, required more time than the 2000 milliseconds specified. This was mainly due to the wrapping.

6   Conclusion and Projection

Testing cloud services will present a new challenge to software testers, one which will change their current way of working. Testers now run after the developers, testing their software to make sure that most errors are found before the software is released.

As such, it is important to maintain a close relationship to the developers. The sooner the errors are found the better. The main job of the testers today is to find errors before the users do. This can be referred to as reactive testing.

With cloud computing this will change. Rather than being the lackeys of the developers, testers on the user side will become the judges of the developers. The test of the potential services will be made before the development is begun. The task is to find out what services are best suitable for the planned application. So the goal of testing services is not to find errors in them but to judge their quality. The user must know if he can rely on the services selected. For that tools are needed which can make a quick and through test. WebsTest is intended to be such a tool. It automatically extracts test cases from the service level agreement or service requirements and combines them with the data taken from the service interface definition to generate artificial requests. It then submits the test requests and checks the corresponding responses against the assertions specified by the tester. At the end it summarizes the test metrics and presents the tester with an assessment of the service quality. All of this can be done in a minimum of time with a minimum of effort.

Of course there are still many improvements to be made, but WebsTest sets a benchmark for other commercial testing tools to consider. It is certain there will be many other tools of this type in the near future, as the use of cloud services comes to be a common practice in constructing IT applications.

References

1. Yau, S., Ho, G.: Software Engineering meets Services and Cloud Computing. IEEE Computer Magazine, 47 (October 2011)
2. Sinivasan, S., Getov, V.: Navigating the Cloud Computing Landscape – Technologies, Services and Adopters. IEEE Computer Magazine, 22 (March 2011)
3. Jones, C.: Software Engineering Best Practices. McGraw-Hill, New York (2010)
4. Baresi, L., Di Nitto, E.: Test and Analysis of Web Services. Springer Pub., Berlin (2007)
5. Shull, F.: A brave new World of Testing – an Interview with Google's James Whittaker. IEEE Software Magazine, 4 (March 2012)
6. Sneed, H.: Certification of Web Services. In: Workshop on Service-oriented Architecture Maintenance-SOAM, CSMR 2008, Athens, p. 336 (2008)
7. Bozkurt, M., Harman, M., Hassoun, Y.: Testing Web Services – A Survey. Softw. Test. Verif. Reliab., 1–7 (2007), doi:10.1002/000
8. Tsai, W.T., Zhou, X., Chen, Y., Bai, X.: On Testing and Evaluating service-oriented Software. IEEE Computer Magazine, 40 (August 2008)
9. http://Supersareware.com/info/SOA-Cleaner (2010)
10. Riungu-Kalliosaari, L., Taipale, O., Smolander, K.: Testing in the Cloud – Exploring the Practice. IEEE Software Magazine, 46 (March 2012)
11. World Wide Web Consortium 2, http://WWW.Webinject.org
12. Sneed, H., Huang, S.: The Design and Use of WSDLTest – a Tool for testing web services. Journal of Software Maintenance and Evolution 19(5), 297 (2007)
13. Sneed, H.: Bridging the Concept to Implementation Gap in Software Testing. In: 8th Int. Conference on Software Quality (QSIC 2008), Oxford (2008)
14. Sneed, H.: Measuring Web Service Interfaces. In: IEEE Proc. of Workshop on Website Evolution – WSE 2010, Timesvar, Ro., p. 41 (2010)

Model-Based Strategies for Reducing the Complexity of Statistically Generated Test Suites

Winfried Dulz

FAU University of Erlangen-Nuremberg,
Department of Computer Science, Erlangen, Germany
dulz@cs.fau.de
http://www7.informatik.uni-erlangen.de/~dulz/

Abstract. The main purpose of this paper is to show how model-based techniques are used to efficiently control the generation of less complex test suites. By directed adjusting specific probability values in the usage profile of a Markov chain usage model it is relatively easy to generate abstract test suites for different user classes and test purposes in an automated approach. A stepwise refinement process for hierarchical Markov chain usage models and choosing appropriate test generation, respectively selection strategies can reduce the complexity of the resulting test suite significantly. By using proper tools, like the TestUS Testplayer even less experienced test engineers will be able to efficiently generate abstract test cases and to graphically assess quality characteristics of different test suites.

Keywords: model-based testing, Markov chain usage model, statistical test suite generation, test suite assessment.

1 Introduction

Implementing a software system usually consists of many different phases. Starting from requirements definition the development process is divided into a number of design, specification, programming and testing steps. Each software engineering step is guided by an appropriate method and generally supported by a dedicated tool.

1.1 Model-Based Test Case Generation

An approach, where the test cases are generated in parts or completely from a model is called *Model-based Testing*. Model-driven testing techniques [1], [2] make use of models of either the SUT (*system under test*) or the expected usage of the users of the SUT. In general, a distinction is made between

- *System specifications*, which model the functional behavior of the SUT and
- *Usage models* that model the usage behavior of the future users of the system.

D. Winkler, S. Biffl, and J. Bergsmann (Eds.): SWQD 2013, LNBIP 133, pp. 89–103, 2013.
© Springer-Verlag Berlin Heidelberg 2013

Test cases, which are generated from a system specification [3] are often used in the so-called component or unit test. Usage models are mostly applied for the generation of test cases for the system or acceptance test. The widespread *V-Model* [4] clarifies this relation by distinguishing between the development and the test of a system.

1.2 Statistical Test Case Generation

Because exhaustive testing of real systems is infeasible in practice an appropriate set of test cases is derived for accomplishing a given test goal. With the help of statistical usage models, so-called *Markov chains* [5], [6], individual test cases or complete test suites are automatically derived by simple push button operations. Markov chains are graphical models and represent

- usage states for modeling the user behavior during the interaction with the system, as well as
- state transitions to specify the reaction of the system on a user's interaction.

Usually there are many alternatives to reach possible successor states from a given usage state. The probability that a particular action can be executed is called *transition probability* between the usage states. By adjusting the operational profile [7], i.e. the probability values of the usage distribution it is very easy to specify varying usage behavior for different *user classes*. In this way, the test engineer can automatically create distinct test cases for different system users. Test cases are derived by traversing the Markov chain between two specific **start** and **end** states by considering the probabilities of the selected *usage profile*. How to derive the usage distribution for a Markov chain usage model in a more systematic way is discussed in [5], [8], [9], [10] and [11].

1.3 Automatic Test Case Generation

The TestUS[1] *TestPlayer*© is a versatile tool for the automatic generation of test cases and enables the user-friendly analysis, evaluation and visualization of the resulting test suites [12].

Using the TestPlayer the test engineer will assess the quality of the generated test cases on the basis of graphical representations at an early stage and even before the actual test suite execution. The TestPlayer reveals in an convenient way the basic characteristics of the generated test suite, such as the mean and maximum length of the test cases in a test suite, the accordance between the usage profile of the Markov chain and the usage frequencies of the generated test suite, the coverage of all usage states, respectively transitions after having executed the test suite.

The concept of the TestPlayer is very general and independent of specific application domains. In this way, test models are created that can be used in any domain. Our expertise and experience from various national and international

---

[1] http://www.testus.eu/

projects show that statistical usage models based on Markov chains are very well suited for the testing of applications in different domains, such as Information and communication technology, Medical technology, Automotive, as well as Automation technology.

To our knowledge only two further tools are available that support statistical usage testing at the moment. JUMBL[2] [13] developed at SQRL (Software Quality Research Laboratory, University of Knoxville Tennessee) and MaTeLo [14] licensed from ALL4TEC[3]. Because both tools lack in the graphical assistance for analyzing and comparing different generation strategies for statistical usage testing the versatile TestPlayer was developed in cooperation with the TestUS company. Using the TestPlayer, it is easy to perform a tool-driven assessment of intra and inter test suite characteristics. It is also possible to decide very fast, which and how many test cases are needed to reach a given test objective [12]. Another technique, which focuses on optimizing the number of test cases that are generated from a given usage model is discussed in [15].

In the next sections we take a closer look on the underlying test case generation processes. By applying a concrete usage model that was published in [16] we demonstrate how to perform typical tasks in the test case generation, analyzing and selection process. We will also discuss different measures that allows us to evaluate the test suite selection process, when we have to decide, which test cases are the best choice in order to fulfill a certain test criteria.

2 TestPlayer - A Tool for Automatic Test Case Generation

At the beginning of the test generation process a concrete usage model must be provided. For this purpose we decided to edit and visualize the model diagrams by means of the yED graph editor from yWorks[4].

Fig. 1 shows the visualization of a Markov chain usage model that was discussed by Poore and Trammell [16] and which will serve as a running example. Start and end states of the hierarchical NAS usage model have labels S_1 and S_{17}, respectively. Labels e_i and p_i that are attached to the edges represent events and the associated probabilities for the state transition. There also exist two hierarchical states *Mode-1* and *Mode-2* that contain inner states S_4 to S_9, respectively S_5 to S_{16} that allow to generate test cases of lower complexity as discussed in section 3.

The TestPlayer can be executed in any modern web browser via a graphical user interface that provides HTML5[5] and AJAX[6] web technologies. Specific elements of the graphical user interface enable a comfortable and user-friendly control of different tasks when statistical usage testing is performed.

---

[2] http://sqrl.eecs.utk.edu/esp/jumbl.html

[3] http://www.all4tec.net/

[4] http://www.yworks.com/

[5] http://www.w3schools.com/html5/77

[6] http://www.w3schools.com/ajax/

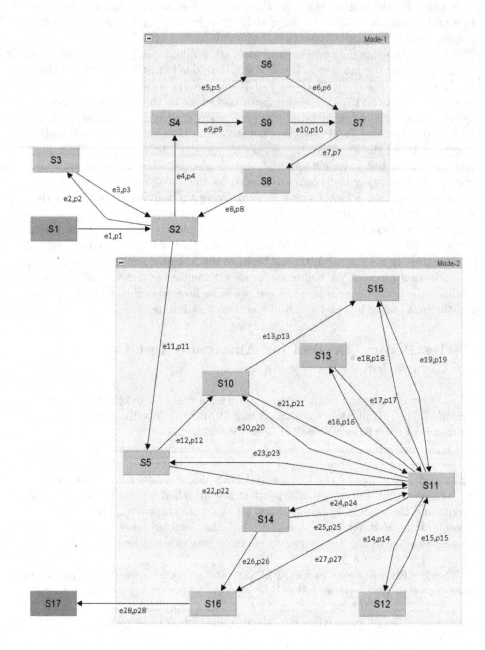

Fig. 1. The NAS [16] Markov chain usage model

2.1 Global Definitions for the Test Case Generation

In the global section, all essential definitions for the automatic generation of test cases using the TestUS TestPlayer can be specified (Fig. 2). These include

- `Model`: file name of the usage model
- `Number of test cases`: target number of test cases that have to be provided
- `Model start state`: name of the start state of the usage model
- `Model end state`: name of the final state of the usage model
- `Profile usage`: declaration, whether a statistical usage profile (clicked) or a uniform distribution (unclicked) will be employed for the generation algorithm of the test cases
- `Profile file name`: file name of the statistical usage profile if the button has been clicked before.

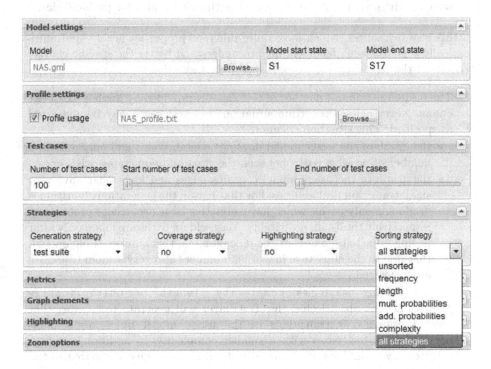

Fig. 2. TestPlayer User Interface

2.2 Automatic Generation of Test Cases

If a complete usage model is given test cases can be generated and sorted by using predefined sorting strategies:

- **unsorted**: individuell test cases are generated either from a selected usage profile or randomly from a uniform distribution; the output order of the test case list is unsorted
- **frequency**: the output list is sorted by the relative frequency of the test cases, i.e. common test cases appear first, seldom test cases appear at the end of the list
- **length**: the output list is sorted by the length of the test cases, i.e. shorter test cases appear first, longer test cases appear at the end of the list
- **multiplicative probabilities**: the output list is sorted by the occurrence probability of the test cases, i.e. test cases with a higher probability appear first, test cases with a small probability appear at the end of the list
- **additive probabilities**: the output list is sorted by the additive probabilities of all test steps, i.e. test cases with a higher total probability appear first, test cases with a small total probability appear at the end of the list
- **complexity**: the output list is sorted by the complexity of the test cases, which is the product of the test case length and its additive probabilities.

In this way test suites, which have quite different properties are created automatically. The following facts will help to understand better the specific characteristics of the resulting test cases, respectively test suites:

- The desired maximum number of test cases is provided by **Number of test cases**. Nevertheless, in certain situations less test cases may be generated as specified. This situation occurs if
  - the graph of the usage model does not contain loops and only a limited number of possible paths between the start and end states exist, or
  - the graph of the usage model contains edges and loops that have very small transition probabilities. For that reason the generation algorithm is producing only paths, which have a relative large occurrence probability, respectively total sum probability. Very seldom paths are found only after having adjusted **Number of test cases**, i.e. this number is big enough that due to the statistical law of big numbers also very seldom test cases are generated.
- If the sorting strategies **complexity**, **length** or **multiplicative probabilities** are selected the TestPlayer will generate test suites that cover the nodes or transitions of the usage model by a larger number of shorter test cases with a smaller complexity. In addition, strategy **complexity** is minimizing the total test suite complexity, compared to the other strategies.
- By choosing sorting strategies **unsorted** or **multiplicative probabilities** the TestPlayer will generate test suites that cover the nodes or transitions of the usage model by a smaller number of longer test cases and that result in a greater total test suite complexity.

How to assess the resulting test suites is discussed in section 3 and summarized in Table 1.

2.3   Textual Output of Test Suite Metrics

After having automatically generated the test cases, a first analysis of the test suite is recommended. For this purpose the TestPlayer produces two files in the selected test suite directories:

- `testsuite_name.tsm`: the *test suite repository* that contains all details in a binary representation format to be retrieved later for further explorations
- `statistics.txt`: relevant analysis results for the generated test suite in a human readable textual representation format.

Among others, the following information is contained in the statistics file:

- *Number of relevant nodes/transitions*: number of usage states/transitions, i.e. nodes/edges in the usage model that may be visited at least once during the test.
- *Source entropy of the profile*: measure of uncertainty of the usage model. The larger the entropy for a given usage model the more uncertain is the forecast, which path is chosen when the test cases are generated [17]. Small values of the entropy reduce the possible number of paths while traversing the usage model.
- *Number of unique test cases in the test suite*: number of distinct test cases. In the normal case this number should be equal to the provided Number of test cases but it may be smaller under certain circumstances, as discussed in the previous subsection.
- *Mean length of a test case for the profile*: mean number of single test steps a test case is composed of with respect to a given usage model.
- *Mean length of a test case in the test suite*: mean number of single test steps a test case is composed of with respect to a generated test suite. The more accurate the compliance of both numbers for the usage model and the test suite is, the better is the approximation of the predicted usage behavior during the test suite execution.
- *Kullback/Leibler divergence between MCUM and test suite*: this metric is comparing the probability distribution of the usage model and the frequencies of the generated test suite [17]. The closer this number is to the value 0, the more accurate is the approximation.
- *Number of test cases needed to cover all nodes / transitions*: number of necessary test cases to visit all usage states/transitions (nodes/edges of the usage model) at least once during the test execution.

2.4   Graphical Output of Test Suite Metrics

After having generated a test suite specific metrics are used visualize the quality of the test suite graphically. Again, we apply the NAS example [16] for discussing some details:

- SSP: comparison of the *steady state probabilities* of the usage model and the *relative frequencies* of the corresponding states in the generated test suite.

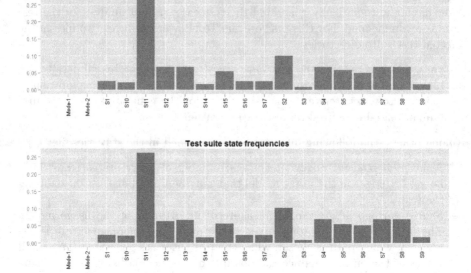

Fig. 3. Steady state probabilities vs. relative frequencies

Fig. 3 shows that states S_2, respectively S_{11} have probabilities 0.0998, respectively 0.2662 for the usage model and 0.1018, respectively 0.2631 for the relative frequencies inside a test suite that consists of 100 test cases. The concrete numbers are contained in the file SSP.txt, which is provided by the TestPlayer for textual documentations. Because we didn't use hierarchical states *Mode-1* and *Mode-2* for generating higher level test cases both states have probability values of zero. It should also be mentioned that the steady state results are in accordance with the values that are published in Table 4 of [16].

If no usage profile is provided by the test engineer a *uniform distribution* is automatically calculated during the test generation procedure. As a result the SSP diagram (Fig. 4) and the corresponding file SSP.txt show different values for usage states S_2, respectively S_{11} in a test suite consisting of 100 test cases. Again, the results for the long run steady state probabilities are in accordance with the values that are published in Table 3 of [16].

- SSV: comparison of the mean number of test cases needed to visit a certain usage state once in the usage model and during the test execution.
- KL: visualization of the Kullback/Leibler divergence [17] and the mean weighted deviation [12] between the usage model and the test suite.
- SSP.N, SSV.N, KL.N: corresponding values for test suites that cover all nodes of the usage model.
- SSP.T, SSV.T, KL.T: corresponding values for test suites that covers all transitions of the usage model.

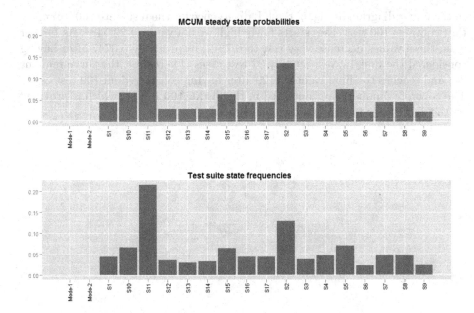

Fig. 4. Steady state probabilities vs. relative frequencies (uniform case)

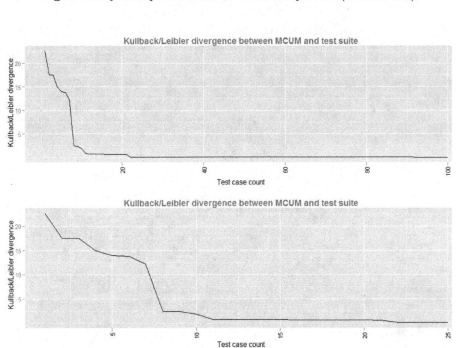

Fig. 5. Kullback/Leibler divergence for a test suite of 100 test cases

In the upper diagram of Fig. 5, the KL divergence for the test suite 100_sort_c_p that contains 100 test cases starts fairly high with a value of 22.5488. As further seen, these values decrease very fast to 0.7812, respectively 0.0747 after having considered the first 11, respectively 22 test cases. Thereafter, the curve remains flat and reaches the final value 0.1129 after having considered all 100 test cases. The concrete numbers are contained in the file KL_100_0.txt, which is provided by the TestPlayer for textual documentations.

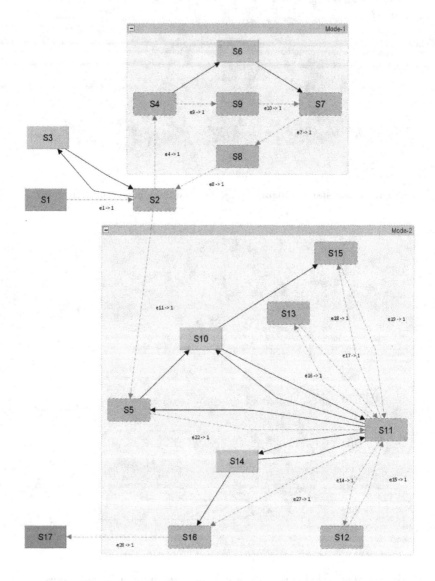

Fig. 6. Last test case for strategy **single test case**

The lower diagram of Fig. 5 shows a zoom of the first 25 test cases. After the interpretation of these figures a test engineer may conclude that 22 test cases are sufficient for testing the SUT.

2.5 Graphical Visualization of Test Cases

The TestPlayer offers a variety of ways to visualize individual test cases, groups of test cases or a complete test suite. The `Highlighting strategy` determines whether test cases are labeled as a group (`accumulated`) or if each test case (`single test case`) is labeled individually. This means in detail

- `single test case`: labels of nodes and edges are carried out for all test cases independently and individually.
- `accumulated`: usage states (nodes) that are already labeled in the previous test cases keep their labels; in addition new labels are added for those nodes that appear for the first time in a test case.
- *Node labels* are modifications in shape and color and have the meaning that a usage state is visited during the test case. In this way, test cases change successive usage models on and on, until finally all nodes except the start and end states are labeled, provided that a sufficient number of test cases is selected or the coverage strategy `node coverage` was chosen.
- State transitions (edges) also have labels that can be changed. *Edge labels* are individually markings for each test case and contain the *event* and the *frequency* that counts how often the individual edges are traversed during the test case.

In Fig. 6 the last test case for covering all nodes in the NAS usage model is highlighted by using the highlighting strategy `single test case`.

3 Hierarchical Usage Models

The application of hierarchical usage states enables the modeling and test case generation for arbitrary complex software systems. By using progressive refinement steps for top-down design processes or stepwise coarsening for a bottom-up design approach usage models for generating less complex test suites are developed. We demonstrate the principle approach by defining two hierarchical usage states in the NAS usage model (see Fig. 1):

- *Mode-1* consisting of atomic usage states S_4, S_6, S_7, S_8 and S_9
- *Mode-2* consisting of atomic usage states S_5, S_{10}, S_{11}, S_{12}, S_{13}, S_{14}, S_{15} and S_{16}.

Atomic usage states in this context are elementary, not further decomposable states. If one ore both of the two hierarchical usage states *Mode-1* and *Mode-1* are closed, all internal atomic states are no longer visible and should not be considered during the test suite generation.

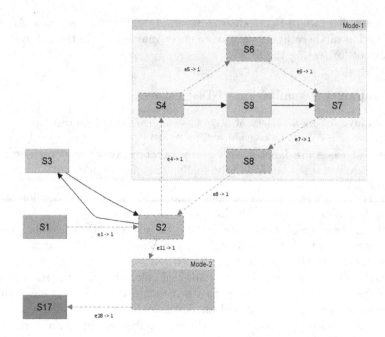

Fig. 7. Highlighted test case after pruning inner states of usage state Mode-2

After pruning inner states the TestPlayer will generate test suites that consist of less complex test cases. The result of closing and pruning hierarchical usage state *Mode-2* is shown in Fig. 7, where the last test case for covering all states is displayed by applying the highlighting strategy `single test case`.

Table 1 compares the complexity of test suites that are generated by the different generation strategies introduced in section 2.3. Each test suite consists of a subset out of 100 test cases that covers all transitions of one of the four underlying usage models:

- *NAS*: complete, unchanged usage model published in [16]
- *NAS_pruned (Mode-1)*: reduced usage model, where all inner states of the hierarchical usage state *Mode-1* have been pruned
- *NAS_pruned (Mode-2)*: reduced usage model, where all inner states of the hierarchical usage state *Mode-2* have been pruned
- *NAS_pruned (Mode-1 and Mode-2)*: reduced usage model, where all inner states of the hierarchical usage states *Mode-1* and *Mode-2* have been pruned

Each entry in Table 1 is a pair of (number of test cases/complexity of the test suite). Each row in the table contains the results for a specific generation strategy, e.g. `Complexity` that is chosen for the test case generation procedure.

The entries in the first row for sorting strategy `Complexity` show that no other strategy will produce a test suite with a lower value for the complexity.

Table 1. Complexity of test suites that cover all transitions

	NAS	NAS_pruned (Mode-1)	NAS_pruned (Mode-2)	NAS_pruned (Mode-1 and Mode-2)
Complexity	10/1039	11/879	4/126	3/43
Length	11/1129	12/1100	4/126	3/43
Mult. Prob.	13/2317	11/970	4/126	3/43
Frequency	8/8941	5/3506	4/126	3/86
Add. Prob.	3/15915	2/11559	1/7774	1/1343
Unsorted	6/8835	4/8029	4/790	3/624

On the other hand sorting strategy Additive Probabilities generates test suites with the smallest number of test cases, which have a very high complexity value.

If the test engineer is interested in extensively testing of hierarchical usage state Mode-1 the test focus of test suite NAS_pruned (Mode-2) provides sufficient insight in the SUT and the complexity of the resulting test cases is significantly lower compared to NAS.

Another technique to focus only on specific parts of a given usage model is based on the probability profile, which is discussed in the next section. For that reason the probabilities in the profile are changed in order to visit only those states of special interest.

4   Test Focusing by Means of Adapted Usage Profiles

Of particular importance for the validation of the SUT are customized usage profiles that focus the test execution on selected usage states, respectively sets of usage states. This can be done either by

- *avoiding* a transition (S_i, S_j) that is starting in usage state S_i and ending in usage state S_j by setting the corresponding probability value $p(S_i, S_j)$ to zero, i.e. $p(S_i, S_j) = 0$ or by
- *forcing* a transition (S_i, S_j) by setting the corresponding probability value $p(S_i, S_j)$ to one, i.e. $p(S_i, S_j) = 1$.

The result is an *adopted usage profile* that will serve for the test case generation process. A test case that has to be performed by all means during the test execution due to special security requirements is often referred to as the *happy path*. The implementation of a happy path can easily be achieved with the concept of adapted usage profiles as well.

An adopted usage profile for the NAS usage model (Fig. 1) that focuses on the hierarchical usage state Mode-1 is is given by the following set of modified probability values: $p(S_2, S_3)=0$, $p(S_5, S_{10})=0$, $p(S_5, S_{11})=1$, $p(S_{11}, S_5)=0$, $p(S_{11}, S_{10})=0$, $p(S_{11}, S_{12})=0$, $p(S_{11}, S_{13})=0$, $p(S_{11}, S_{14})=0$, $p(S_{11}, S_{15})=0$ and $p(S_{11}, S_{16})=1$.

The test suite for covering all transitions by using the sorting strategy **Complexity** consists of 3 test cases and has the complexity value 190 compared to 126 of the *NAS_pruned (Mode-2)* of Table 1.

Note that the inner usage states S_5, S_{11} and S_{16} of the hierarchical usage state *Mode-2* cannot be avoided, because they are a part of the path to reach the final state S_{17}. This is the reason why the complexity is higher than in the case of pruning inner states of *Mode-2*.

5   Main Findings and Final Remarks

In this paper we discussed different techniques for reducing the complexity of automatically generated test cases by using the versatile TestPlayer© tool for the generation, analysis and evaluation of abstract test suites.

A small running example published in [16] was used to explain the major steps of our approach. Using the TestPlayer, it is easy to perform a tool-driven assessment of intra and inter test suite characteristics. It is also possible to decide very fast, which and how many test cases are needed to reach a given test objective. The main findings of our paper are the following:

- Model-based techniques that provide and use *graphical representations of usage models* yield in a good acceptance also for unexperienced test engineers.

  By using a *graphical user interface* it is very easy to set the test focus on specific regions that shall be tested. Based on diagrams that *visualize test suite characterists*, e.g. deviation of steady state probabilities and usage frequencies the decision, which test suite should be chosen is more easily done then only by analyzing columns of numbers.

  If the resulting test cases are displayed in a clear, highlighted format test engineers and customers can better understand certain test steps that will influence the outcome of the test.

- The application of *hierarchical usage states* supports the clarity of bigger real-life applications and the resulting usage models at one side. On the other side, directed focusing on the interesting parts of the usage model by closing of hierarchical states and *pruning the inner states*, as discussed in section 3, will result in more manageable test suites of lower complexity.

- *Adopted probability profiles* support the selective generation of special test cases that are necessary to test specific parts of the SUT. Sometimes a concrete *happy path* has to be executed during the test due to special security or other non-functional requirements.

  Based on adopted probability profiles different user groups that interact with the SUT can be distinguished by different test suites that result from different adopted probability profiles. How to systematically derive an adopted profile is published in [11].

- The *complexity of a test suite* is a main criteria for comparing and selecting different test suites, as shown in section 3.

When no other selection criteria will overrule the decision the test suite with the smallest number of test cases and the lowest complexity shall be chosen.
- Based on graphical representations it is more easy to find a good criteria for *stopping the test execution*. The Kullback/Leibler divergence (Fig. 5) discussed in subsection 2.5 will help the test engineer to determine the best value for selecting an optimal subset of the test cases during the test execution.

References

1. El-Far, I.K., Whittaker, J.A.: Model-based Software Testing. In: Marciniak, J.J. (ed.) Encyclopedia on Software Engineering. Wiley (2001)
2. Legeard, B., Utting, M.: Practical Model-Based Testing. Elsevier (2007)
3. Rosaria, S., Robinson, H.: Applying models in your testing process. Information and Software Technology 42, 815–824 (2000)
4. Tian, J.: Software Quality Engineering. John Wiley&Sons (2005)
5. Whittaker, J.A., Poore, J.H.: Markov Analysis of Software Specifications. ACM Transactions on Software Engineering and Methodology 2(1), 93–106 (1993)
6. Walton, G.H., Poore, J.H., Trammell, C.J.: Statistical Testing of Software Based on a Usage Model. Software - Practice and Experience 25(1), 97–108 (1995)
7. Musa, J.D.: The operational profile. NATO ASI Series F, Computer and System Sciences 154, 333–344 (1996)
8. Walton, G., Poore, J.: Generating transition probabilities to support model-based software testing. Software Practice and Experience 30(10), 1095–1106 (2000)
9. Poore, J., Walton, G., Whittaker, J.: A constraint-based approach to the representation of software usage models. Information & Software Technology 42(12), 825–833 (2000)
10. Takagi, T., Furukawa, Z.: Constructing a Usage Model for Statistical Testing with Source Code Generation Methods. In: Proceedings of the 11th Asia-Pacific Software Engineering Conference, APSEC 2004 (2004)
11. Dulz, W., Holpp, S., German, R.: A Polyhedron Approach to Calculate Probability Distributions for Markov Chain Usage Models. Electronic Notes in Theoretical Computer Science 264(3), 19–35 (2010)
12. Dulz, W.: A Comfortable Test Player for Analyzing Statistical Usage Testing Strategies. In: ICSE Workshop on Automation of Software Test (AST 2011), Honolulu, Hawaii (2011)
13. Prowell, S.J.: Jumbl: A tool for model-based statistical testing. In: HICSS, p. 337 (2003)
14. Dulz, W., Zhen, F.: MaTeLo - Statistical Usage Testing by Annotated Sequence Diagrams, Markov Chains and TTCN-3. In: IEEE International Conference on Quality Software (QSIC 2003), pp. 336–342 (2003)
15. Barade, S., Srivastava, P.R., Jose, N., Ghosh, D.: Optimized Test Sequence Generation from Usage Models using Ant Colony Optimization. International Journal of Software Engineering & Applications (IJSEA) 1(2), 14–28 (2010)
16. Poore, J.H., Trammell, C.J.: Application of statistical science to testing and evaluating software intensive systems. In: Statistics, Testing, and Defense Acquisition. National Academy Press, Washington, D.C. (1998)
17. Prowell, S.: Computations for Markov Chain Usage Models. Technical report, Software Engineering Institute, Carnegie-Mellon University, Pittsburgh, USA, UT-CS-03-505 (2000)

Hazard Analysis for Technical Systems

Mario Gleirscher

Institut für Informatik, Technische Universität München, Germany
Mario.Gleirscher@TUM.de

Abstract. Hazard analysis is an indispensable task during the specification and development of safety-critical, technical systems, particularly, their software-intensive control parts. There is a lack of methods supporting an effective and integrated way to carry through such analyses for these systems in the context of software quality assurance. Crucial issues are to properly (i) encode safety-relevant domain knowledge, (ii) identify and assess all relevant hazards as well as (iii) preprocess this information and make it easily accessible for adjacent safety and systems engineering activities. This work contributes a framework for qualitative modelling and hazard analysis. The approach is exemplified by the investigation of a commercial road vehicle in its operational context.

Keywords: Safety risks, hazard analysis, system modelling, safety engineering, requirements specification, interdisciplinary control design.

1 Safety of Technical Systems

Modern plants, machines or vehicles are equipped with a high proportion of software mastering complex control problems to ultimately provide sophisticated usage functions. As such functions strongly affect the physical environment, *safety*—the degree of freedom from *hazards* —is a critical quality attribute of these systems. The more necessary the human or societal needs are they have to fulfill, the higher are the user expectations on vendor responsibility or warranty. Moreover, their vendors face the pressure of competition in safety innovations [45]. This is mirrored by national laws, standards such as, e.g., EN 61508 or ISO 26262, EU directives or guidelines of the vendors themselves.

Safety Engineers' Tasks and Problems. Following the mentioned circumstances, a systems engineering process includes requirements engineering (RE) for proper specification of the system's interface and functionality, architecture design (AD) for technically mature planning of realisation, and interdisciplinary realisation and integration (RI). During RE, a safety engineer has to gain understanding of *candidate hazards* [22] and to perform safety-oriented validation of the specification. She identifies and characterises hazards using various sources of information such as, e.g., insurance models, human error classifications [47], injury severity scorings, accident databases[1], driving situation registers, the international

---

[1] E.g., at the AOPA Air Safety Institute: www.aopa.org/asf/accident_data or the Institut für Unfallanalysen: http://unfallforensik.maindev.de.

D. Winkler, S. Biffl, and J. Bergsmann (Eds.): SWQD 2013, LNBIP 133, pp. 104–124, 2013.
© Springer-Verlag Berlin Heidelberg 2013

nuclear event scale [56], expert discussions. By consulting design documents during AD, she has to relate possible weaknesses or faults to hazards at the system interface. This enables her to recommend measures to avoid or mitigate *relevant hazards*, their causative weaknesses or other causal factors. To properly finish RI, she needs to prepare information for safety-oriented verification or testing. Her responsibility is to assure that the software-intensive control mechanisms at the heart of a technical system are safe because they do exactly what is needed to *reliably avoid or mitigate* relevant hazards.

State of the Art. Safety analysis aims at understanding the relationship between software, electronic or mechanical hardware faults and their impact in terms of hazardous system failures. Safety is inherently interdisciplinary and as such a core systems engineering issue. But the relationship between system safety goals and component safety and reliability requirements is often not formally captured. This makes it difficult to relate software, electronic or mechanical component weaknesses to hazards at the system level. The system is mainly modelled as a glass-box to tie defects and their propagation to its edificial structure and to support detailed design for reliability. This detracts from the investigation of system behaviour before and after critical events and the consideration of weaknesses to be temporally distant or even external causal factors.

Hazard knowledge has hardly ever[2] been systematically transferred to interdisciplinary, qualitative behavioural system models describing interaction between the system and its environment. [45] already pointed out this issue in accident analysis and interdisciplinary risk management. Available approaches (as surveyed in Section 7) do not consider such models already used in projects applying model-based RE [53]. They are suitable to be checked for correctness, completeness and consistency w.r.t. the tasks of safety engineering. Commercial reliability and safety tools[3] also still lack support for this kind of models. While misoperation of the environment or misbehaviour of users are improperly analysed [46] or even neglected, the development of fault-tolerant (i.e., fail-operational or fail-silent) functions is well supported. These and further problems are considered relevant by [6,38]. For safety as a critical software quality attribute, we might then ask:

How can the judgement of a software's safety be significantly improved?

To address this cumulative problem, the work at hand takes a human-centric qualitative perspective of the whole physical system to be analysed. The framework and a procedure (Figure 1) suggested for this are described in Section 2, demonstrated and discussed in Section 3. An overview of related work is given in Section 4. Section 5 provides concluding remarks and hints further work.

---

[2] The author interviewed nine experienced safety practitioners to conclude this.

[3] E.g., Isograph FaultTree+/Hazop+ (www.isograph-software.com), APIS IQ-FMEA (www.apis.de), ReliaSoft Xfmea (www.reliasoft.de), medini analyze (www.ikv.de).

2   A Framework for Hazard Modelling and Analysis

The *framework* comprises a model of both, the system's and the environment's functionality, suited for alignment with RE and testing. This requires the consideration of two primary *artefacts*: A *specification* $\mathcal{S}$ and a *realisation* $\mathcal{W}$.

2.1   Safety-Oriented System Modelling

Concepts. $\mathcal{S}$ is described in two complements: A *qualitative behaviour (or black-box) model* $\mathcal{M}$ of the world consisting of the system $\mathcal{M}_\mathcal{I}$ to be controlled and the operational environment $\mathcal{M}_\mathcal{E}$ as this system's context, and a set of *property assertions* $\mathcal{S}_p$ for $\mathcal{M}$. $\mathcal{M}$ takes the role of an *operational functional specification* [11] which a realisation $\mathcal{W}$ encompassing the *system* $\mathcal{I}$ and the *environment* $\mathcal{E}$ has to be aligned with. $\mathcal{M}$ results from the *parallel composition* $\mathcal{M}_\mathcal{E} \| \mathcal{M}_\mathcal{I}$ of these two components. For hazard analysis, $\mathcal{M}$ abstracts from the boundary between the control software and its sensors and actuators to the boundary between $\mathcal{I}$ and $\mathcal{E}$ [43]. This *machine boundary* is described by *interface phenomena* [30] In $\mathcal{M}_*$, where $* \in \{\mathcal{I}, \mathcal{E}\}$, three *functional aspects* are separated:

- *Usage functionality* $\mathsf{f}^*_{\mathsf{use}}$ (also called *nominal* functionality),
- *defective functionality* $\mathsf{f}^*_{\mathsf{fail}}$ (for explicit modelling of defects, e.g., failures), and
- *safety functionality* $\mathsf{f}^*_{\mathsf{save}}$ as an enhancement of $\mathsf{f}^*_{\mathsf{use}}$ to avoid or mitigate $\mathsf{f}^*_{\mathsf{fail}}$.

Each aspect can consist of hierarchically composed *functional fragments*. A *function* of $\mathcal{M}_\mathcal{I}$ resp. a *tactic* of $\mathcal{M}_\mathcal{E}$ is a merger of matching fragments of all three aspects of $\mathcal{M}_\mathcal{I}$ resp. $\mathcal{M}_\mathcal{E}$. $\mathcal{S}_p$ takes the role of a *descriptive functional specification* of, e.g., safety goals. The setting of $\mathcal{S}_p$ and $\mathcal{M}$ is suited to apply formal methodology as described in [2]. A *local situation* σ of $\mathcal{M}$ is any coherent and distinguished class of value tuples over $\mathcal{M}$'s interface phenomena. σ_0 denotes an *initial* situation.

Semantics. A behaviour is an observable execution trace of a system [34]. $\mathcal{W} \models \mathcal{S}$ resp. $\mathcal{W} \not\models \mathcal{S}$ (spoken "$\mathcal{W}$ satisfies resp. violates $\mathcal{S}$") means that all behaviours in $\mathcal{W}$ are allowed resp. some are prohibited by $\mathcal{S}$. The behaviours allowed by $\mathcal{S}$ equal the cutting set of possible behaviours of $\mathcal{M}$ and $\mathcal{S}_p$. Here, the satisfaction relation $\models$ corresponds to the subset relation $\subseteq$ on behaviours.

2.2   Step 1: Specify the Usage Functionality $\mathsf{f}^*_{\mathsf{use}}$

Under the assumption that a proper initial, informal set of goals or requirements $\mathcal{R}$ is available from RE and that the current step achieves or maintains $\mathsf{f}^\mathcal{I}_{\mathsf{use}} \| \mathsf{f}^\mathcal{E}_{\mathsf{use}} \models \mathcal{S}_p$, set up $\mathcal{S}_p$ and $\mathsf{f}^*_{\mathsf{use}}$ by adopting or redoing the following RE tasks:

1.1 Transform the informal function definitions $\mathcal{R}_f$ into *use cases (UC)* according to, e.g., [15] and the set of informal property assertions $\mathcal{R}_p$ into $\mathcal{S}_p$ according to, e.g., [21].

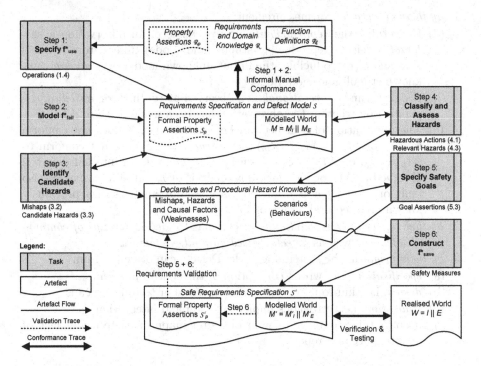

Fig. 1. A procedure in six steps for using the framework

1.2 To capture possibilities of interaction, determine the machine boundary and its interface phenomena from the preliminary system interface concept.

1.3 Transform the UCs into a *multi-level hierarchy of usage functions* [10] by extracting and arranging their independent, concurrent and common parts.

1.4 Identify *modes of operation* and *operations* of $\mathcal{I}$ and $\mathcal{E}$ at all non-leaf levels.

1.5 Model the *interaction* of $\mathcal{I}$ and $\mathcal{E}$ via *usage functions* in $\mathfrak{f}_{use}^{\mathcal{I}}$ and *environment tactics* in $\mathfrak{f}_{use}^{\mathcal{E}}$. For each leaf function of the hierarchy, identify *actions*, their repetition and order by the help of *modes*.

2.3 Taxonomy and Representation of Safety-Related Defects

Taxonomy. A *defect* is an observable and unacceptable *lack of behavioural conformance* between two artefacts, for example, $\mathcal{S} \neq \mathcal{S}'$[4], $\mathcal{M}_{\mathcal{I}} \not\models \mathcal{S}'_p$ or $\mathcal{W} \not\models \mathcal{M}'$. Behaviours deviating from $\mathfrak{f}_{use}^{\mathcal{I}}$ or $\mathcal{S}_p$ represent *currently unacceptable*[5] *executions or suppressions* of actions or operations and allow to explicitly differentiate between their *allowed* and *forbidden performance*. I distinguish defects

---

[4] x' denotes that the intended level of *safety* has been achieved for the artefact x.

[5] Unwanted, unintended or unexpected, but not yet validated w.r.t. safety.

1. *by their observation* or measurement:
   (a) Concerning the *reproducibility or recurrence* of an observation a *systematic* defect (reproducible stimuli and mode) differs from a *semi-systematic* (reproducible stimuli but unknown mode) or a *random* (unknown stimuli and mode) one.
   (b) A defect can be *operational*, i.e., observed at runtime, or *modelled*, depending on whether the observation has been made in $\mathcal{W}$ or $\mathcal{M}$.
   (c) The observation of a defect can be *internal* (i.e., $\mathcal{I}$ does not conform to $\mathcal{M_I}$ or $\mathcal{S}_p$, or $\mathcal{M_I} \not\models \mathcal{S}_p$) or *external* (i.e., $\mathcal{E}$ does not conform to $\mathcal{M_E}$ or $\mathcal{S}_p$, or $\mathcal{M_E} \not\models \mathcal{S}_p$). I speak of a *failure* if an internal defect is observed in $\mathcal{M_I}$ or via black-box analysis of $\mathcal{I}$ and of a *weakness* (also fault or error) if it is observed via glass-box analysis of a previously known architectural design of $\mathcal{I}$.
2. *by their effect-to-cause multiplicity*: One has to identify *groups of common cause defects* as well as *defects caused by multiple factors*.
3. *by their origin* in the system life cycle: Defects can originate from
   (a) *specification*, i.e., wrong conception of the control problem,
   (b) *design*, i.e., improper choice of architectural or technical means,
   (c) *realisation*, i.e., erroneous implementation and integration, or
   (d) *operation*, i.e., damage or wear out after inapproperiate use or lack of maintenance and repair.

Representation of Defects by $\mathsf{f}^*_{\mathsf{fail}}$. The mentioned kinds of defects are expressible by $\mathcal{M}$ and $\mathcal{S}_p$, for example, hazardous specification defects as a lack of conformance $\mathcal{M} \neq \mathcal{M}'$ or $\mathcal{M} \not\models \mathcal{S}'_p$. By using *mode transition systems*[6] for $\mathcal{M}$, I encode such defects as nondeterministic or probabilistic, *defective transitions* (i.e., erroneous, inconsistent or ill-timed guard or trigger conditions or effects) as well as *failure modes* and *faulty states*. By using *temporal logic* interface assertions in $\mathcal{S}_p$, I encode more subtle interface defects like *misperception of responsibility*: *Violable assumptions* of $\mathcal{I}$ about $\mathcal{E}$ may lead to a justification of defects $\mathsf{f}^{\mathcal{I}}_{\mathsf{fail}}$ as an acceptable addition to $\mathsf{f}^{\mathcal{I}}_{\mathsf{use}}$. These assumptions may turn out to be too strong or the system's guarantees too weak. This style of specification [9] relates external to internal defects.

Two kinds of *specification defects* (3.a) getting tangible when applying the mentioned techniques for $\mathcal{M}$ and $\mathcal{S}_p$ are those of *wrong type abstraction* and *disregarded physical phenomena*. Thereafter, $\mathcal{M_I}$ could be defective in terms of violable assumptions about

- the type and interpretation of monitored phenomena or of dependencies of physical quantities to be effectively controlled (*independence assumptions* violable by $\mathcal{E}$ may disclose invalid function signatures in $\mathcal{M_I}$),
- single observations of monitored events (*domain maintenance assumptions* violable by $\mathcal{E}$ may disclose invalid function ranges in $\mathcal{M_I}$) or, in general,

---

[6] A hierarchical, concurrent, probabilistic state machine model built on Markov chains and qualitative abstraction of physical interface phenomena.

- histories of event observations (*trace conformance assumptions* violable by $\mathcal{E}$ may disclose invalid function behaviour in $\mathcal{M_I}$).

These classes of violable assumptions have to be made explicit in $\mathcal{S}'_p$.

2.4 Step 2: Model the Defective Functionality f^*_{fail}

Provided the concepts from Section 2.3, set up f^*_{fail} using three strategies:

2.1 Use incompleteness in a) f^*_{use} and introduce indeterminacy to derive explicit hypotheses about possible defects, cf. [7, 18, 44], b) f^*_{use} combined with f^*_{fail} for guessing implicit defects. This incompleteness is understood as implicit assumptions on monitored interface phenomena.

2.2 Add *physically relevant* side effects of f^*_{use} as part of f^*_{fail}.

2.3 Apply *reliability and failure analysis* techniques to the architectural design of $\mathcal{I}$ to answer the questions: *How do weaknesses identified in $\mathcal{I}$ cause failures? Which are the minimal cut sequences, i.e., the shortest sequences of weaknesses to occurr resulting in a failure?*[7] Qualitatively abstract from this knowledge to identify failure transitions and modes in $f^{\mathcal{I}}_{fail}$. This confirms and improves the guesses about $f^{\mathcal{I}}_{fail}$ in steps 2.1 and 2.2.

2.5 Hazards, Their Identification and Classification

Hazard Conception and Modelling. Early reliability engineering perceived a hazard as a conditional failure rate, i.e., as a risk solely induced by system failure [55]. The broader concept of *hazard* as discussed in [22] combines a hazardous element with an initiating mechanism[8] to threaten a target. The *risk* consists in a potential negative outcome from this mechanism's performance, i.e., a *mishap* for the target.

In $\mathcal{M}$, the hazardous element as a part of $\mathcal{I}$ and the target as a part of $\mathcal{E}$ are connected to interface phenomena, $\mathcal{I}$ and $\mathcal{E}$ share with each other. The initiating mechanism corresponds to actions of $\mathcal{I}$ and $\mathcal{E}$. A mishap or harming event for $\mathcal{E}$ is a condition μ on these phenomena reachable by performing these actions. A hazard—understood as a set of hazardous states or interaction events—is a condition χ constraining [45] these phenomena. This way, χ declares hazardous *performance*, i.e., execution or suppression of these actions following a local situation σ and potentially leading to μ. χ, σ and f^*_{fail} as possible deviations from f^*_{use} or $\mathcal{S}_p$ can be combined to investigate potential progression towards μ.

Candidate Hazard Identification. In $\mathcal{M}$, the identification of potential threats to safety can be accomplished by taking two complementary *viewpoints*:
The *(H)azard Viewpoint: Which hazards are possible? How does $\mathcal{I}$ endanger $\mathcal{E}$? Which actions could be performed in an unsafe manner?*

---

[7] Techniques for these two questions are out of scope of this article.

[8] Concerning $\mathcal{S}$, hazards can be related to nominal or defective behaviours.

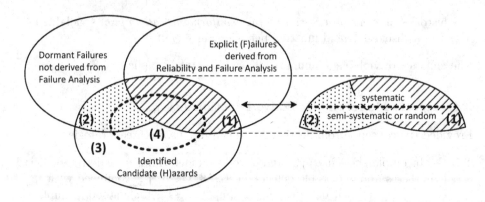

Fig. 2. H vs. F: Hazard analysis determines (4), safety engineering builds on this

Table 1. Combinations ($\oplus$) of f_{use}^* with f_{fail}^* or f_{save}^* for hazard analysis: Nominal (CN), explicitly defective (CD), with safety functions (CS); I ... agent interaction

I	Component / Agent	Functional Aspect	CN	CD				CS						
			1	2	3	4	5	6	7	8	9	10	11
$\|$	$\mathcal{M_I} = f_{use}^{\mathcal{I}} \oplus \ldots$	$f_{fail}^{\mathcal{I}}$		×		×	×		×	×		×	×
		$f_{save}^{\mathcal{I}}$				×	×	×					×
	$\mathcal{M_E} = f_{use}^{\mathcal{E}} \oplus \ldots$	$f_{fail}^{\mathcal{E}}$		×	×		×	×		×	×	×	
		$f_{save}^{\mathcal{E}}$							×	×	×	×	

The *Reliability and (F)ailure Viewpoint*: *Which failures are possible? How could $\mathcal{I}$ violate $\mathcal{S}$? Which actions could be performed in an unexpected manner?*
Beyond the taxonomy for F in Section 2.3, [45] has already stated demand and a proposal for a taxonomy to characterise typical hazard sources.

Hazard Classification. As the title suggests, I will pay more attention to H, but both viewpoints are needed to address the following problems (Figure 2):

(1) *Which explicit failures (w.r.t. $\mathcal{S}$ and derived in F) are hazards?*
(2) *Which hazards are dormant failures (w.r.t. $\mathcal{S}$ and not derived in F)?*
(3) *Which hazards are no failures (w.r.t. $\mathcal{S}$) at all?*
(4) *Which hazards are relevant to be treated by $\mathcal{S}'$ and, thus, $\mathcal{W}'$?*

There are eleven[9] *combinations* ($\oplus$) of $\mathcal{M_E}\|\mathcal{M_I}$, f_{use}^* and f_{fail}^* (Table 1). The combinations 1–4 help answer the above questions to *classify hazards*:

1. Nominal behaviours at both sides, i.e., $f_{use}^{\mathcal{E}}\|f_{use}^{\mathcal{I}} \models \mathcal{S}_p$
2. Machine failures, i.e., $f_{use}^{\mathcal{E}}\|(f_{use}^{\mathcal{I}} \oplus f_{fail}^{\mathcal{I}}) \not\models \mathcal{S}_p$

---

[9] I do not regard all of the 16 possible combinations based on f_{use}^* as I consider f_{save}^* as meaningful only if $\mathcal{M}$ already contains f_{fail}^*.

3. Defects of the environment, i.e., $(f^{\mathcal{E}}_{use} \oplus f^{\mathcal{E}}_{fail}) \| f^{\mathcal{I}}_{use} \not\models \mathcal{S}_p$
4. Defects of both agents, i.e., $(f^{\mathcal{E}}_{use} \oplus f^{\mathcal{E}}_{fail}) \| (f^{\mathcal{I}}_{use} \oplus f^{\mathcal{I}}_{fail}) \not\models \mathcal{S}_p$

Explicit failures (1) violate guarantees in $\mathcal{S}$. The difference between (2) and (3) stems from the fact that dormant failures are defined as violations of implicit assumptions in $\mathcal{S}$. The *relevant hazards* (4) represent *safety validity defects* (systematic, originating from specification or design) and *safety integrity defects* (semi-systematic or random, any origin) w.r.t. an $\mathcal{S}'$ to be derived (Figure 2).

2.6 Step 3: Identify Candidate Hazards

For all operations o (step 1.4) descending top-down the hierarchy (step 1.3):

3.1 Determine whether o is *physically relevant*, i.e., whether physical interface phenomena from steps 1.2 and 2.2 are affected.
3.2 Identify *conditions of harming events*[10] μ based on o's interface phenomena, e.g., areas which could get *contaminated* or where objects *collide*, get *sounded*, *glared* or *shot*; places where objects could get *clamped*, *sheared*, *scraped* or *cut*; surfaces where objects could get *burned*, *vibrated*, *electrically shocked* or *dissolved*. Combine mishap guidewords such as, e.g., "too fast, close, hot, much, many" [5, 49], to derive μ from o.
3.3 Derive *candidate hazards* $\tilde{\chi}$ which indicate *hazardous executions* or *suppressions* of o and separate *hazardous* from *safe performance*. Use hazard guidewords such as, e.g., "unattended, unintended, unexpected, unwanted or denied start, stop or change of o." $\tilde{\chi}$ uses o as predicate on modes, actions and interface phenomena missing, being active or combined in an unforeseen manner. A default $\tilde{\chi}$ would be "Hazardous performance of o."
3.4 Define situations σ by clustering conditions on $\mathcal{M}$'s interface phenomena.

2.7 Quantitative Hazard Assessment

Risks are usually quantified by severity and probability values. To derive safety goals, standards like, e.g., DIN 19250 [5] characterise a hazard χ by

a. the *severity* S of χ's potential, harming events or consequences μ,
b. the *probability* W or H of χ's occurrence without the measures of f^*_{save},
c. the *exposure* A of $\mathcal{E}$'s vulnerable assets to χ (part of W in ISO 26262), and
d. the *detectability* D and *controllability* C in $\mathcal{E}$ or $\mathcal{I}$ in case of χ's occurrence (here, modelled as f^*_{save} and aggregated as G).

To estimate S using $\mathcal{M}$, the assertion for a harming event μ can be manually assessed by accident analysts (Section 1). For W, the probability of χ can be calculated (cf. [23]) from the probabilistic model underlying $\mathcal{M}$ without f^*_{save}. To extract A, the environment parts of μ or χ have to assessed based on $\mathcal{M}_{\mathcal{E}}$ regarding all phenomena consituting σ. For G, the probability has to be calculated from the probabilistic model underlying $\mathcal{M}$ with f^*_{save}, particularly $f^{\mathcal{E}}_{save}$. Thresholds and tables to act on these parameters are discussed in, e.g., [5].

---

[10] An *event condition* is a behavioural property, e.g., a condition of a failure event circumscribes unwanted deviations from f_{use} or $\mathcal{S}_p$, a condition of a harming event circumscribes behaviours including physical harms of humans or the environment.

2.8   Step 4: Refine, Classify and Assess Hazards

How and when is a candidate hazard $\tilde{\chi}$ possible in f_{use}^*? Which defects in f_{fail}^* can be causal factors? Investigate hazards and their relationship to defects and nominal operation of $\mathcal{W}$. For all combinations $c \in \{1..4\}$ (steps 1 and 2, Table 1), harming events μ (step 3.2) and local situations σ (step 3.4):

4.1 Consider behaviours b exhibiting μ (Figure 2, H). For each b, determine the *actions* and *modes* of the leaf *usage functions* or *environment tactics* involved in executing or suppressing the *operations* o related to μ. Identify *regions* of b where $\tilde{\chi}$ holds. Derive *refined (H)azards* χ and *classify* them based on the taxonomy in Section 2.3 and according to Figure 2 by refining $\tilde{\chi}$ for each region, where b
   - makes explicit use of f_{fail}^* or $f_{fail}^{\mathcal{I}}$ (step 2.1a), and put it into the set (1) of known hazardous defects or (F)ailures.
   - violates implicit assumptions in $\mathcal{S}$, i.e., b has been guessed as implicit defect hypothesis (step 2.1b), and put it into the set (2) of dormant hazardous defects or (F)ailures.
   - neither violates implicit assumptions nor guarantees in $\mathcal{S}$, and put it into the set (3) of hazardous nominal behaviours, i.e., potential specification defects such as misperception of responsibility.
4.2 To quantify and determine *relevant hazards* (4), *assess* all χs w.r.t. the parameters and thresholds mentioned in Section 2.7.

2.9   Step 5: Specify Safety Goals in $\mathcal{S}_p'$

Transform the set (4) into a specification $\mathcal{S}_p'$ of *unaccepted behaviours*:

5.1 Derive a *safety goal assertion* $\tilde{\gamma}$ by negation of μ or transforming χ, cf. [21].
5.2 *Assign* $\tilde{\gamma}$ to the usage functions of $\mathcal{M}_{\mathcal{I}}$ and environment tactics of $\mathcal{M}_{\mathcal{E}}$ which are related to o as identified in step 4.1.
5.3 Enhance γ by the risk at which it is allowed to be violated. This corresponds to specifying *integrity classes* (IC)—i.e., SIL, ASIL, DAL, AK, Cat or PL— for functions and tactics as well as their modes and transitions.

2.10   Hazard Mitigation or Avoidance

The more that has to be done to identify relevant unknown (combinations 1–4) and untreated (combinations 5–11) hazards χ, the stronger it can be stated that $\mathcal{S}$ is safe ($\mathcal{S} = \mathcal{S}'$). A non-empty set (4) means, that $\mathcal{S}$ is not safe ($\mathcal{S} \neq \mathcal{S}'$) and not valid ($\mathcal{M} \not\models \mathcal{S}_p'$). Hence, if there are relevant hazards, $\mathcal{M}_{\mathcal{I}}$ or $\mathcal{M}_{\mathcal{E}}$

   - is not safe enough, i.e., too severe systematic defects, or
   - shows unacceptable safety integrity, i.e., too many or too early random defects.

Strategies for hazard mitigation deal with the question of how $\mathcal{W}$ can be equipped to detect hazards and take over the control to avoid or mitigate mishaps. Concerning $f_{save}^{\mathcal{I}}$, this results in the introduction of

1. *fail-safe transitions* such as *fail-operational* or *fail-silent* transitions in case an internal weakness is detected (corresponds to set (1) ∩ (4) in Figure 2),
2. *passive* or *preventive transitions* independent of whether an internal weakness is detected or not (corresponds to set ((2) ∪ (3)) ∩ (4) in Figure 2).

The implementation of such transitions in $\mathcal{I}$ depends on the defect type and usually amounts to the *state observation or runtime diagnosis* of

1. weaknesses appearing in $\mathcal{I}$ for the achievement of fault-tolerance or
2. hazardous situations occurring in $\mathcal{E}$ for passive/preventive functions in $f_{save}^{'\mathcal{I}}$.

Concerning $f_{save}^{'\mathcal{E}}$, external measures usually consist of training, guidance, warning signs and signals or technical protection mechanisms like in $f_{save}^{'\mathcal{I}}$.

2.11 Step 6: Design the Safety Functionality f_{save}^{*}

Develop $\mathcal{S}'$ to reduce hazards, to assess and to mitigate hazardous weaknesses. Starting from the results on f_{fail}^{*} and having safety goals in $\mathcal{S}'_p$, construct valid and reliable safety functions in $f_{save}^{'\mathcal{I}}$ or properly assign responsibilities by assuming $f_{save}^{'\mathcal{E}}$ on top of $f_{use}^{'*}$. The ICs from step 5 are assigned to the superpositions of the linked fragments to be implemented. The enhancement of $\mathcal{S}_p$ and $\mathcal{M}$ towards $\mathcal{S}'$, where $\mathcal{M}' \models \mathcal{S}'_p$, should represent sufficient evidence to declare $\mathcal{S} = \mathcal{S}'$ as safe for inclusion into further design activities.

3 Application to Commercial Road Vehicle Safety

The procedure of Figure 1 as explained in Sections 2.2–2.11 is now exemplified.

3.1 Demonstration

I interpret $\mathcal{I}$ to be a commercial road vehicle ("truck" for short) and $\mathcal{E}$ the part of the world including the driver, a truck is usually performing in.

Step 1. (1.1) The *driving missions* of a truck[11] and possible tactics of its driver are provided as use cases, e.g., #27 use truck (Table 2), #5 park at steep hill (Table 3), #10 use brakes (Table 4). Some of the formal assertions for $\mathcal{S}_p$ could be derived from the preconditions, the minimal or success guarantees of the UCs. However, I do not need them for the current example. (1.2) Consider the simplified entities **area**, $\mathcal{I}$ and **other objects** (*oo*) located in **area**. As physical phenomena, consider two vectors for speed, $v_{\mathcal{I}}$ and v_{oo}, and two for position, $pos_{\mathcal{I}}$ and pos_{oo}. (1.3) Figure 3 shows the $\mathcal{M}_{\mathcal{I}}$ part of the function hierarchy of a truck. The tactics in $\mathcal{M}_{\mathcal{E}}$ are constructed similarly from the UCs but are not focused in this example. (1.4) The upper levels of the hierarchy help identify complex operations observable at the interface of a truck by co-executing its functions and the environment's tactics, e.g., it can be moved or driven, loaded or unloaded. Let **move** be operations of both, $f_{use.Drive/Move}^{\mathcal{I}}$ and $f_{use.ooMove}^{\mathcal{E}}$. (1.5) For example, Figure 4a shows the nominal specification of the function $f_{use.StopBrake}^{\mathcal{I}}$.

---

[11] The data used in this example is an abstract from a larger case study focusing the drive chain of a truck and performed in collaboration with a partner from industry.

Table 2. Use case #27 "Use truck"

UC #27	Use truck (usage goal #27, $f^{\mathcal{E}}_{Missions} \| f^{\mathcal{I}}_{Truck}$)
Scope	$\mathcal{I}$; level: primary task in f^*_{use}; primary actor: $\mathcal{E}$
Preconditions	Enough fuel, battery on, etc.
Minimal Guarantees	Neither the trucker, his goods, nor the environment will be harmed.
Success Guarantees	The trucker accomplishes his mission by using the truck.
Trigger	The trucker activates the vehicle by applying the key.
Description (list of interaction descriptions)	1. The trucker activates the vehicle by applying the key. 2. She performs, e.g., UC #5,10 to accomplish her missions. 3. The vehicle reacts properly to her commands. 4. The trucker deactivates the vehicle.

Table 3. Use case #5 "Park at steep hill"

UC #5	Park at steep hill (usage goal #5, $f^{\mathcal{E}}_{use.Park} \| f^{\mathcal{I}}_{use.Drive/Move}$)
Scope	$\mathcal{I}$; level: primary task in f^*_{use}; primary actor: $\mathcal{E}$
Preconditions	The truck is driving near a free and proper parking lot.
Minimal Guarantees	
Success Guarantees	The truck is parked in a parking lot at a steep hill compatible to the current mission goal.
Trigger	The trucker stops in front of a parking lot at a steep hill.
Description (list of interaction descriptions)	1. The trucker stops in front of a parking lot at a steep hill. 2. She uses gas pedal, steering wheel, clutch, gears, brakes (UC#10) and rear mirrors to place the truck into the lot.

Step 2. (2.1, 2.2) Figure 4b shows failure possibilities as fragment $f^{\mathcal{I}}_{fail.StopBrake}$. (2.3) For sake of brevity, I assume that failure analysis confirms the aspect $f^{\mathcal{I}}_{fail}$.

Step 3. I look for risks steming from truck operations from step 1.4. (3.1) move is physically relevant because it affects $\boldsymbol{v}_{\mathcal{I}}$ and $\boldsymbol{pos}_{\mathcal{I}}$. (3.2) A mishap or harming event for move is a *collision* defined as a combination of *too small distances* and *too high relative velocities* and, thus, represented by an approximating condition

$$\mu_3 \equiv |\boldsymbol{v}_{\mathcal{I}} - \boldsymbol{v}_{oo}| \geq v_{ok} \wedge |\boldsymbol{pos}_{\mathcal{I}} - \boldsymbol{pos}_{oo}| \leq max_{x \in \{oo, \mathcal{I}\}} \{diameter_x\} \quad (1)$$

(3.3) The candidate hazard as a condition $\tilde{\chi}$ for hazardous performance of move would be tied to situations, such as, e.g., move triggered or altered without foreseen user operation (Table 5). For example, $\tilde{\chi}_7 \equiv$ *"Unattended start of movement"* formalised in terms of the hazard assertion

$$\tilde{\chi}_7 \equiv \neg(move \vee userOperation) \, \mathbf{U} \, move \quad (2)$$

(3.4) From UC #5 we know a relevant local situation $\sigma \equiv$ *"The truck is standing in a steep parking lot and the stop brake is activated."* σ should be formalised by

Table 4. Use case #10 "Use brakes" always included by UC#5

UC #10	Use brakes (usage goal #10, $f_{\text{Missions}}^{\mathcal{E}} \| f_{\text{use.Accelerate/Brake}}^{\mathcal{I}}$)
Scope	$\mathcal{I}$; level: primary task in f_{use}^*; primary actor: $\mathcal{E}$
Preconditions	None.
Minimal Guarantees	The truck is slowing down.
Success Guarantees	The truck is properly slowing down or coming to a stable halt.
Trigger	The trucker actuates the brake pedal.
Description (list of interaction descriptions)	1. The trucker actuates the brake pedal. 2. The truck decreases its speed accordingly. 3. Optional: When the truck comes to a halt, the trucker decides to activate the stop brake.

Table 5. Hazard assessment after DIN 19250 as adopted by EN 61508 and ISO 26262

Step 1			Step 3	Step 4				Step 5
o	μ	$\tilde{\chi}$	**Short Description of Hazard**	**S**	**A**	**G**	**W**	**IC**
move	3	7	Unattended driveaway or start of movement	2	2	1	1	ASIL D
move	3	8	Unattended leaving of lane or change of direction	2	2	1	1	ASIL D

parameters like, e.g., constitution of the road surface (temperature, ice, water) or the environment (wind, gravity, nearby objects, road down-grade and route section), physical or control state of vehicle (load, age/maintenance).

Step 4. (4.1) Assertion 2 is refined by $move \equiv v_{\mathcal{I}} \neq 0$ and $userOperation \equiv \neg idle$. $\neg idle$ is determined by $\mathcal{M}_{\mathcal{E}}$ and contains, e.g., $gasPedal = pressed$ and $\exists x.(\bullet gearLever = x) \to gearLever \neq x$. I consider $move$ without f_{save}^* (page 110) and derive refined hazards, i.e., possibilities of how and when $move$ is performable in a hazardous manner (Figure 5). The decomposition of the usage function containing $move$ into actions at the leaf level of the function hierarchy shows that, e.g., the mode **active** and the action **brake** of $f_{\text{use.StopBrake}}^{\mathcal{I}}$ are physically relevant, because in this mode, this action is responsible to maintain $v_{\mathcal{I}} = 0$ or to contribute to the operation **park**. Automated analysis offers a trace b where the failure transition **suppressBrake** of $f_{\text{fail.StopBrake}}^{\mathcal{I}}$ (Figure 4) contributes to $\tilde{\chi}_7$ and potentially to mishap μ_3, e.g., because of gravity in σ and no input from the driver is needed to reach **move**. This analysis leads to the assertion

$$\chi_{7.1} \equiv (\neg move \wedge mode(f_{\text{StopBrake}}^{\mathcal{I}}) = active) \ \mathbf{U} \ move \qquad (3)$$

where $\chi_{7.1} \to \tilde{\chi}_7$. As this failure, identified and confirmed in step 2.3, contributes to $\tilde{\chi}_7$, $\chi_{7.1} \in (1)$ (Figure 2). (4.2) Whether $\chi_{7.1}$ is in set (4) (Figure 2) can be determined by automated probabilistic reasoning to estimate the hazard characteristics as mentioned in Section 2.7. As I do not provide automation for this preliminary example, let us assume, $\chi_{7.1} \in (4)$. Finally, Table 5 shows the results for $\tilde{\chi}_7$.

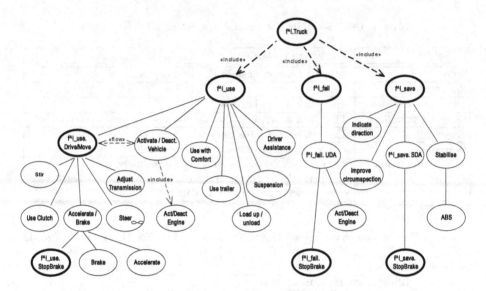

Fig. 3. Excerpt of a truck function hierarchy representing $\mathcal{M}_{\mathcal{I}}$

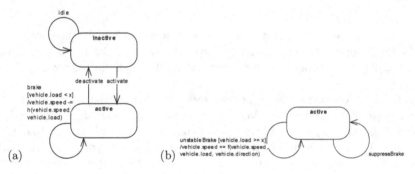

Fig. 4. The usage function $f^{\mathcal{I}}_{\text{use.StopBrake}}$ (a) and possible defects $f^{\mathcal{I}}_{\text{fail.StopBrake}}$ (b)

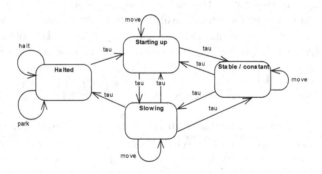

Fig. 5. The usage function $f^{\mathcal{I}}_{\text{use.Drive/Move}}$

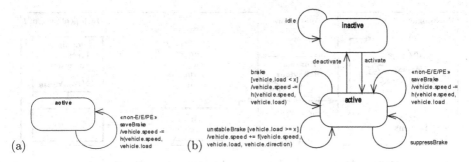

Fig. 6. The safety fragment $f^{\mathcal{I}}_{\text{save.StopBrake}}$ (a) and the overall function $f^{\mathcal{I}}_{\text{StopBrake}}$ (b)

Step 5. (5.1) The safety goal for the truck as already embedded into UC #27 asserts "not to harm any persons, goods or the environment" is broken down. This implies $\neg\mu_3 \equiv$ "no collision". More specifically, this goal is broken down and constrained by hazards like, e.g., $\tilde{\chi}_7$:

$$\tilde{\gamma}_7 \equiv \Box(\neg move \rightarrow (\neg move \ \mathbf{U} \ (userOperation \land \neg move))) \tag{4}$$

(5.2) $\tilde{\gamma}_7$ is assigned to $f^{\mathcal{I}}_{\text{Drive/Move}}$. (5.3) From the list of relevant hazards like $\chi_{7.1}$ (step 4.2), safety requirements for $f^{\mathcal{I}}_{\text{StopBrake}}$ have been derived by assigning the high integrity class ASIL D according to ISO 26262.

$$\gamma_7 \equiv \Box_{Pr \geq 99.99\%}(\neg move \rightarrow (\neg move \ \mathbf{U} \ (userOperation \land \neg move))) \tag{5}$$

Step 6. I assume that reliability or failure analyses, e.g., [50], provide characteristics of the physical action **suppressBrake**. To realise ASIL D for $f^{\mathcal{I}}_{\text{StopBrake}}$, it has to be designed to mitigate or avoid the hazards $\chi_{7.1} \rightarrow \tilde{\chi}_7$. The fail-safe transition in $f^{\mathcal{I}}_{\text{save.StopBrake}}$ (Figure 6a) could incorporate a fail-silent mechanism suited to quickly mask potential **suppressBrake** transitions. This results in a safer—i.e., ASIL D compatible—version of $f^{\mathcal{I}}_{\text{StopBrake}}$ (Figure 6b).

3.2   Discussion

General Notes. The example is small and simple but should give enough insight to the presented framework's capabilities. It allows *a-posteriori or empirical modelling* of known hazards, as done in some accident analysis approaches [27], as well as *a-priori, predictive or constructive modelling* of $\mathcal{W}$ to elicit candidate hazards from guessing potential mishaps. However, the problem of *improper abstractions* causes too many safety goals and usage functions to be considered. The set-up of $\mathcal{M}$ in steps 1 and 2 has to be done careful. Moreover, the problem of *overlooked or wrongly assessed candidate hazards* still exists. The method only incorporates heuristics to elicit potential mishaps from the knowledge of physical truck or environment operations and parameters encoded in $\mathcal{M}$. An incomplete or improper model may not provide access to relevant hazards.

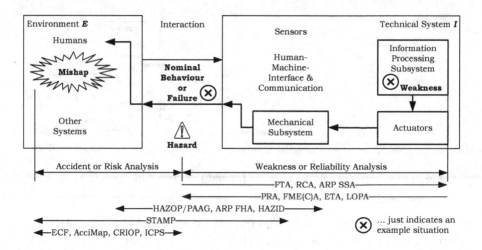

Fig. 7. Approaches to hazard analysis for system safety assessment

Detectability of hazardous, operational Defects. As long as $\mathcal{S} \neq \mathcal{S}'$, the remaining lack of observability and safety knowledge during verification and testing entails threats to validity in the framework, i.e., a defect

a. stays *undetected*: $\mathcal{M_I}$ is unknowingly defective and $\mathcal{I}$ conforms to it. Thus, $\mathcal{I}$ unknowingly differs from $\mathcal{M'_I}$.
b. is a *false positive*: $\mathcal{M_I}$ is unknowingly defective but $\mathcal{I}$ unknowingly conforms to $\mathcal{M'_I}$. Tests based on the current $\mathcal{M_I}$ do not unfold this.
c. is certainly *detected*: $\mathcal{I}$ is knowingly defective because it neither conforms to $\mathcal{M_I}$ nor, unknowingly, to $\mathcal{M'_I}$.

Raising the Limits of Safety-oriented Verification or Testing. Safety-oriented verification confirms the hypotheses represented by $\mathcal{S}$ and intentionally imposed on $\mathcal{W}$, by checking or testing $\mathcal{W}$. Verification and testing shall provide sufficient evidence for $\mathcal{W} \models \mathcal{S}$. $\mathcal{S}'$, which compensates f^*_{fail}, increases the *level of trust* into $\mathcal{W}$ and strengthens the argument for declaring $\mathcal{W} = \mathcal{W}'$.

Verification and testing often require $\mathcal{W}$ for validation of $\mathcal{M}$ and for definition of test stop and coverage criteria. So, test execution and monitoring or similar dynamic abstractions will produce essential feedback to facilitate this task.

4   Related Work

Early ideas for this paper have been published in [24]. The way of modelling as chosen in Section 3 has been investigated in a former case study [25]. This section discusses related approaches w.r.t. the fields of contribution, i.e., (i) defect modelling, (ii) causation reasoning, and (iii) engineering guidance. Figure 7 lists approaches to *hazard analysis* for system safety assessment [22] according to their direction towards effects or causal factors of hazards.

Defect Classification and Representation (i). Because of their variety of perception, defects are categorised along technology and task specific, non-standard
criteria. [29] classifies defects to compare system testing approaches. General
defect classifications [3, 14] are rare, vague or difficult to use in practice [54].
Defect models are purpose specific, ranging from abstractions for fault-tolerance
or reliability analysis [19, 50] to sophisticated mutation or fault-injection techniques for programme diagnosis or bug localisation [18, 28, 57]. Defect models
based on foreseen architectural designs are vital to many reliability and hazard
analysis techniques. However, [7, 8] and [44] discuss defect modelling by transforming nominal functional specifications. The taxonomy presented in Section
2.3 coheres with this and [36,37,39] and claims to be effective for hazard analysis.

Top-Down from Hazard to Weakness (ii). This direction can be carried out
using deductive techniques like, e.g., static or dynamic fault tree (FTA) [19]
or root cause (RCA) [35] analysis. [13, 40, 42] focus on reliability analysis of
safety functions based on electronic control. Their tool HiP-HOPS [41] allows
automated FTA via synthesis of fault trees based on fault-to-failure propagation
through a design model. [4] shows how early safety analysis based on models of
embedded control software fosters efficient safety-oriented redesign. Their defect
model is based on the dataflow architecture of the system.

[16, 17] sketch computer-supported verification based on a state machine
model[12] extended with fault variables and ports for each software component.
The faulty state machine undergoes reachability checks for hazard assertions to
generate fault trees for FTA. Their concept reduces overapproximation, i.e., too
pessimistic fault trees, but is restricted to software and electronic hardware. It
is formally elaborate but lacks methodical guidance.

Bottom-Up from Weakness to Hazard (ii). This direction can be addressed by inductive methods like, e.g., failure mode, effect and criticality analysis (FMECA)
[26,52,59], event tree analysis (ETA) after DIN 25419 or, similarly, layer of protection analysis (LOPA). Hazard and operability analysis (HAZOP or PAAG)
according to IEC 61882 [5] takes particular account of controllability by humans.
There are elaborate approaches like probabilistic risk assessment (PRA) [33] or
informal, early-stage methods like hazard identification (HAZID) or preliminary
hazard lists [22].

[39] identifies hazard types capturing ways of physical component interaction
and applies SysML—a standard notation for system modelling—to HAZOP.
[60] describes hazard analysis on data flow models of automotive embedded
control software. [48] discusses automated abstraction of programme code to
perform such analyses. [50] proposes inductive diagnosis by constraint solving
to automatically predict the propagation of local component faults (i.e., value
and time deviations of effect quantities) through a model of the physical system.
[44] combines interface behaviour with FMECA, but does not consider hazard
analysis in an interdisciplinary way.

---

[12] IBM Rational Statemate http://www.ibm.com.

Between Hazard and Mishap (ii). To understand mishaps and their risks, methods like, e.g., events and causal factors (ECF) [12] or AcciMap [45, 51] consider causal factors of all, environment, user and system. This includes system operations or use cases (e.g., driving missions and situations), operational incidents or damage scenarios (e.g., car accidents) as well as the physical system interface. Event chains between mishaps and hazards are chronologically traced forward or backward. Some methods use detailed physical models, some are specific to a domain. For example, crisis intervention in offshore production (CRIOP) [31] assesses the interface between human operators and technical systems within offshore control rooms to uncover obstacles for accident response. The international classification for patient safety (ICPS) [58] identifies potential clinical incidents to properly establish patient safety concepts in processes of health-care systems.

Inspired by [45], system-theoretic accident model and processes (STAMP) [36] perceives safety as a control problem in a socio-technical system, i.e., a collaboration of humans and technical systems. Accidents and hazards are explained by a *non-linear model of causation*, where interactions within this collaboration violate safety constraints and lead to unsafe states. STAMP classifies human errors, identifies *inadequate control* beyond system failures and derives required constraints. Instead of just preventing failures and technical root causes, these constraints shall be enforced by the collaboration. [20] applies system dynamics, i.e., qualitative cause analysis, to STAMP. [49] extends it using HAZOP-like guidewords to identify inadequate actions of humans and organisations.

While these approaches discuss system safety in a wider organisational and societal context, the work at hand focuses on preparing a precise theoretic basis for the development of engineering tools.

Safety Engineering Guidance and Standards (iii). Beyond these techniques, [32] investigates the concept of *safety cases*, their development, maintenance and reuse, based on a tree structure of arguments built on evidence using single techniques or measures to finally confirm safety goals. The author shows how FMECA can be embedded into his method but does not consider behavioural system models directly to make arguments more precise and reusable, as opposed to [1, 36]. [1] applies formal methodology in train control development by modelling the rail environment to precisely understand the control problem. The author derives model refinements to fulfill formalised safety requirements. However, defect modelling and hazard analysis have not been focused.

Hazard analysis is a vital early step recommended by general or domain-specific safety standards, e.g., IEC 65108 for general mechatronics, ISO 26262 for automotive control, EN 50128 for train control or DoD MIL-STD-882D [22] for technical systems. They consider the whole safety process for the regarded kinds of systems to avoid unwanted relationships between system safety goals and subsystem or component requirements. IEC 65108 speaks of preliminary hazard and risk analysis (PHA). The SAE aircraft recommended practices (ARP) 4754 and 4761 advise the steps of functional hazard assessment (FHA) based on a function list regarding failures and crew actions, followed by preliminary and final system safety/reliability assessment (SSA), which among FTA requires a mixture of techniques. Standards and their terminology are intentionally general, solely providing some references to applicable methods.

5   Summary and Conclusion

The work at hand contributes a framework and procedure for hazard modelling and analysis. It uses formal methodology for behavioural modelling of the world under consideration, particularly, the interface between the system and its environment in terms of a specification S. The qualitative abstraction applied in S makes it possible to treat the system in an interdisciplinary way, largely independent from technology. The framework supports the capture of candidate hazards and relates this knowledge to the task of defect modelling. A defect model classifies and encodes consequences or effects of technology-specific weaknesses to understand how they are related to hazards. Reliability and failure analysis based on a glass-box model of the system justifies the defect model. Like [36], the procedure shall elucidate cases where hazards have been caused by past events or long-term deviations from safe behaviour of both, the system and its environment. S enables the assessment of hazards that arise from the co-existence of usage functions and their unknown but unwanted interactions. To understand intentional or unconscious misbehaviour of the user or the rest of the environment, hazard analysis benefits from S including a defect model. Precise and justified knowledge of all these classes of defects leverages the installation of measures to avoid or mitigate hazards. This includes the development of passive (e.g., airbag) or active (e.g., crash avoidance) safety functions.

By applying the framework, a transition to the use of prevalent system models can be made much more easily to achieve (i) a proper encoding of domain, risk and defect knowledge, (ii) a comprehensive assessment of hazards based on that and (iii) profound and justified results to effectively carry through subsequent safety and systems engineering tasks. As important next steps, I envisage the detailed choice of modelling concepts, the corresponding adoption of reasoning algorithms such as, e.g., [23], and tool support for both of these. Among this, a more detailed case study of the presented example will be elaborated.

Acknowledgements. I specially thank professor Manfred Broy for his inspiring and helpful feedback. Sincere thanks go to several of my colleagues at his chair for the many stimulating discussions about this topic or its context as well as to the interviewed project partners and safety professionals from industry providing valuable insight into their daily challenges.

References

1. Abrial, J.-R.: Train Systems. In: Butler, M., Jones, C.B., Romanovsky, A., Troubitsyna, E. (eds.) Fault-Tolerant Systems. LNCS, vol. 4157, pp. 1–36. Springer, Heidelberg (2006)

2. Baier, C., Katoen, J.-P.: Principles of Model Checking. The MIT Press (May 2008)
3. Beizer, B.: Software Testing Techniques, 2nd edn. Thomson (1990)
4. Biehl, M., DeJiu, C., Törngren, M.: Integrating safety analysis into the model-based development tool chain of automotive embedded systems. In: LCTES 2010, Stockholm, Sweden (April 2010)
5. Börcsök, J.: Funktionale Sicherheit: Grundzüge sicherheitstechnischer Systeme, 3rd edn. VDE-Verlag (May 2011)
6. Braun, P., Phillips, J., Schätz, B., Wagner, S.: Model-based safety cases for software-intensive systems. Position paper (2008)
7. Breitling, M.: Modellierung und Beschreibung von Soll/Ist-Abweichungen. In: Spies, K., Schätz, B. (eds.) FBT, pp. 35–44. Herbert Utz Verlag (1999)
8. Breitling, M.: Formale Fehlermodellierung für verteilte reaktive Systeme. Dissertation, Technische Universität München (2001)
9. Broy, M.: A functional rephrasing of the assumption/commitment specification style. Formal Methods in System Design 13(1), 87–119 (1998)
10. Broy, M.: Service-oriented Systems Engineering: Specification and Design of Services and Layered Architectures – The JANUS Approach. In: Broy, M. (ed.) Engineering Theories of Software Intensive Systems, pp. 47–81. Springer (2005)
11. Broy, M., Stølen, K.: Specification and Development of Interactive Systems: Focus on Streams, Interfaces, and Refinement. Springer (2001)
12. Buys, J., Clark, J.: Events and Causal Factors (ECF) Analysis. Technical Research and Analysis Center, SCIENTECH Inc. (1995)
13. Chen, D., Johansson, R., Lönn, H., Papadopoulos, Y., Sandberg, A., Törner, F., Törngren, M.: Modelling Support for Design of Safety-Critical Automotive Embedded Systems. In: Harrison, M.D., Sujan, M.-A. (eds.) SAFECOMP 2008. LNCS, vol. 5219, pp. 72–85. Springer, Heidelberg (2008)
14. Chillarege, R., Bhandari, I., Chaar, J., Halliday, M., Moebus, D., Ray, B., Wong, M.: Orthogonal defect classification – a concept for in-process measurements. IEEE Transactions on Software Engineering 18(11), 943–956 (1992)
15. Cockburn, A.: Writing Effective Use Cases. Crystal Series for Software Development. Addison-Wesley Longman, Amsterdam (2000)
16. Damm, W., Peikenkamp, T.: Model-based safety analysis. Presentation Slides. Lecture series for "Model-based Development" at HU Berlin (July 2004)
17. Damm, W., Pnueli, A., Ruah, S.: Herbrand Automata for Hardware Verification. In: Sangiorgi, D., de Simone, R. (eds.) CONCUR 1998. LNCS, vol. 1466, pp. 67–83. Springer, Heidelberg (1998)
18. Das, S., Banerjee, A., Dasgupta, P.: Early analysis of critical faults: An approach to test generation from formal specifications. IEEE Trans. on CAD of Integrated Circuits and Systems 31(3), 447–451 (2012)
19. Dugan, J., Bavuso, S., Boyd, M.: Dynamic fault-tree models for fault-tolerant computer systems. IEEE Transactions on Reliability 41(3), 363–377 (1992)
20. Dulac, N.: A Framework for Dynamic Safety and Risk Management Modeling in Complex Engineering Systems. PhD thesis, Massachusetts Institute of Technology, Cambridge, MA (2007)
21. Dwyer, M.B., Avrunin, G.S., Corbett, J.C.: Patterns in property specifications for finite-state verification. In: ICSE 1999, pp. 411–420 (1999), http://patterns.projects.cis.ksu.edu/documentation/patterns/ctl.shtml
22. Ericson, C.A.: Hazard Analysis Techniques for System Safety. John Wiley and Sons, Hoboken (2005)

23. Forejt, V., Kwiatkowska, M., Norman, G., Parker, D.: Automated Verification Techniques for Probabilistic Systems. In: Bernardo, M., Issarny, V. (eds.) SFM 2011. LNCS, vol. 6659, pp. 53–113. Springer, Heidelberg (2011)
24. Gleirscher, M.: Hazard-based Selection of Test Cases. In: Proc. 6th ICSE Workshop on Automation of Software Test, AST 2011 (May 2011)
25. Gleirscher, M.: Ein Kaffeevollautomat – Fallstudie für modellbasierte Spezifikation zur Vorlesung "Requirements Engineering" im Sommersemester 2011. Technical Report I-125, Technische Universität München (May 2012) (in German)
26. Goddard, P.L.: Software FMEA Techniques. In: Proc. Ann. Reliability and Maintainability Symposium (RAMS), pp. 118–123. IEEE (2000)
27. Hopkins, A.: Lessons from Longford: The Esso Gas Plant Explosion. CCH, Sydney (2000)
28. Howden, W.: Weak mutation testing and completeness of test sets. IEEE Transactions on Software Engineering (4), 371–379 (1982)
29. Illes, T., Paech, B.: An analysis of use case based testing approaches based on a defect taxonomy. Software Engineering Techniques: Design for Quality, 211–222 (2007)
30. Jackson, M.: Problem Frames: Analysing & Structuring Software Development Problems. Addison-Wesley (2001)
31. Johnsen, S.O., Bjørkli, C., Steiro, T., Fartum, H., Haukenes, H., Ramberg, J., Skriver, J.: CRIOP: A scenario method for Crisis Intervention and Operability analysis. Technical Report A4312, SINTEF, Trondheim, Norway (March 2011)
32. Kelly, T.P.: Arguing Safety – A Systematic Approach to Safety Case Management. PhD thesis, University of York, Dept. of Computer Science (1998)
33. Kumamoto, H., Henley, E.J.: Probabilistic risk assessment and management for engineers and scientists, 2nd edn. John Wiley and Sons, New York (2000)
34. Lamport, L.: Specifying Systems. Addison Wesley (2002)
35. Leszak, M., Perry, D., Stoll, D.: A case study in root cause defect analysis. In: Proc. International Conference on Software Engineering (ICSE), pp. 428–437. IEEE (2000)
36. Leveson, N.: A new accident model for engineering safer systems. Safety Science 42(4), 237–270 (2004)
37. Leveson, N.G.: Engineering a Safer World: Systems Thinking Applied to Safety. Engineering Systems. MIT Press (January 2012)
38. McDermid, J.: Software Safety: Where's the Evidence?. In: Australian Workshop on Industrial Experience with Safety Critical Systems and Software (2001)
39. Mehrpouyan, H.: Model-based hazard analysis of undesirable environmental and components interaction. Master's thesis, Linköpings universitet (2011)
40. Papadopoulos, Y., Maruhn, M.: Model-based synthesis of fault trees from matlab-simulink models. In: International Conference on Dependable Systems and Networks (DSN), pp. 77–82 (2001)
41. Papadopoulos, Y., McDermid, J.A.: Hierarchically Performed Hazard Origin and Propagation Studies. In: Felici, M., Kanoun, K., Pasquini, A. (eds.) SAFECOMP 1999. LNCS, vol. 1698, pp. 139–152. Springer, Heidelberg (1999)
42. Papadopoulos, Y., McDermid, J.A., Sasse, R., Heiner, G.: Analysis and synthesis of the behaviour of complex programmable electronic systems in conditions of failure. Reliability Engineering and System Safety 71(3), 229–247 (2001)
43. Parnas, D., Madey, J.: Functional Documentation for Computer Systems. Science of Computer Programming 25, 41–61 (1995)
44. Pister, M.: Integration formaler Fehlereinflussanalyse in die Funktionsentwicklung bei der Automobilindustrie. Dissertation, Technische Universität München (2008)

45. Rasmussen, J.: Risk management in a dynamic society: a modelling problem. Safety Science 27(23), 183–213 (1997)
46. Rasmussen, J.: The concept of human error: Is it useful for the design of safe systems? Safety Science Monitor 3 (Special Edition), 1–3 (1999)
47. Shappell, S., Wiegmann, D.: The human factors analysis and classification system – HFACS. Technical Report DOT/FAA/AM-00/7, Office of Aviation Medicine, Civil Aeromedical Institute, Oklahoma City, OK (2000)
48. Snooke, N., Price, C.: Model-driven Automated Software FMEA. In: Ann. Proc. Reliability and Maintainability Symp. (RAMS), pp. 1–6. IEEE (2011)
49. Stringfellow, M.V.: Accident Analysis And Hazard Analysis For Human And Organizational Factors. PhD thesis, Massachusetts Institute of Technology (2010)
50. Struss, P., Fraracci, A.: FMEA of a Braking System – A Kingdom for a Qualitative Valve Model. In: 25th Intl. Workshop on Qualitative Reasoning, Barcelona, Spain (2011)
51. Svedung, I., Rasmussen, J.: Graphic representation of accident scenarios: Mapping system structure and the causation of accidents. Safety Science 40, 397–417 (2002)
52. Tietjen, T., Müller, D.H.: FMEA Praxis: Das Komplettpaket für Training und Anwendung, 3rd edn. Hanser (2011)
53. Van Lamsweerde, A.: Requirements Engineering: From System Goals to UML Models to Software Specifications. Wiley (2009)
54. Wagner, S.: Defect classification and defect types revisited. In: Proc. Workshop on Defects in Large Software Systems (DEFECTS 2008), pp. 39–40. ACM, New York (2008)
55. Watson, G.S., Leadbetter, M.R.: Hazard analysis. I. Biometrika 51(1-2), 175 (1964)
56. Wikipedia. Internationale Bewertungsskala für nukleare Ereignisse — Wikipedia, Die freie Enzyklopädie (June 27, 2012)
57. Winter, S., Winter, S., Sârbu, C., Suri, N., Murphy, B.: The impact of fault models on software robustness evaluations. In: Taylor, R.N., Gall, H., Medvidovic, N. (eds.) ICSE, pp. 51–60. ACM Press, New York (2011)
58. World Health Organization (WHO). International Classification for Patient Safety (ICPS) (June 27, 2012),
    http://www.who.int/patientsafety/implementation/taxonomy
59. Wu, B.-G., Tang, R.-Z.: Study on Software FMEA Techniques. Mechanical & Electrical Engineering Magazine 21(3) (March 2004)
60. Zhang, H., Li, W., Chen, W.: Model-based hazard analysis method on automotive programmable electronic system. In: 3rd Intl. Conf. on Biomedical Engineering and Informatics, BMEI (2010)

Using Defect Taxonomies to Improve the Maturity of the System Test Process: Results from an Industrial Case Study

Michael Felderer[1] and Armin Beer[2]

[1] Institute of Computer Science University of Innsbruck, Austria
michael.felderer@uibk.ac.at
[2] Beer Test Consulting, Baden, Austria
info@arminbeer.at

Abstract. Defect taxonomies collect and organize the domain knowledge and project experience of experts and are a valuable instrument of system testing for several reasons. They provide systematic backup for the design of tests, support decisions for the allocation of testing resources and are a suitable basis for measuring the product and test quality. In this paper, we propose a method of system testing based on defect taxonomies and investigate how these can systematically improve the efficiency and effectiveness, i.e. the maturity of requirements-based testing. The method is evaluated via an industrial case study based on two projects from a public health insurance institution by comparing one project with defect taxonomy-supported testing and one without. Empirical data confirm that system testing supported by defect taxonomies (1) reduces the number of test cases, and (2) increases of the number of identified failures per test case.

Keywords: System testing, test management, test design, defect taxonomy, case study research.

1 Introduction

Systematic defect management based on bug tracking systems like Bugzilla [1] is well established and successfully used in many software organizations. Defect management weights the classification of failures observed during the execution of tests according to their severity and is the basis for the implementation of effective defect taxonomies.

A *defect taxonomy* is a system of (hierarchical) categories designed to be a useful aid for reproducibly classifying faults and failures [2]. Such a classification is concerned with removing the subjectivity of the classifier and creating distinct categories with the goal to better control the number of defects reaching the customer [3]. Defect taxonomies provide information about the distribution of faults and failures in a project and are valuable for learning about the kinds of errors being made in the development process. Thus, defect taxonomies can be applied to control the

D. Winkler, S. Biffl, and J. Bergsmann (Eds.): SWQD 2013, LNBIP 133, pp. 125–146, 2013.

design of tests and quality of releases to keep testing manageable although time and resources in projects are limited.

In practice, most defect taxonomies are only used for the a-posteriori allocation of testing resources to prioritize failures for debugging purposes. But the full potential of these taxonomies to control the overall test process and to improve its maturity is not exploited. This is especially the case when testing the user requirements of a system, as system-level defect taxonomies improve the design of requirements-based tests, the tracing of defects to requirements and the control of the relevant defect management. Prioritized requirements, defect categories and failures enable system testing to be improved by using defect taxonomies. We therefore consider priority values assigned to requirements and severity values assigned to defect categories and failures.

In the organization where the case study was performed, the standardized test process of the *International Software Testing Qualifications Board* (ISTQB) [2] is mandatory for all projects. While the introduction of this process has its benefits in promoting systematic testing, we also observed some of its weaknesses as regards the consideration of defect data:

— The experience documented in defect management systems is not used for testing.
— System test cases are designed without taking specific defect types into account.
— The manual assignment of severity levels to failures stored in a defect management system is often unreliable.

In this paper, we propose a novel process of system testing with defect taxonomies and investigate how this process can systematically improve the maturity compared to the standard ISTQB test process. According to the ISTQB, the *maturity* of a test process is defined by its *efficiency* validating the testing resources used to perform a particular function and its *effectiveness* judging the effect of the test process on the application [2]. The presented work is conducted in the context of an industrial case study based on two projects from a public health insurance institution where we study and interpret the following two research questions to indicate an improvement of the ISTQB test process maturity by the integration of defect taxonomy-supported testing. (1) We study the reduction of the number of system test cases to improve the efficiency of system testing. (2) We study the increase of the number of identified failures per test case to improve the effectiveness of system testing supported by defect taxonomies.

Our contribution defines and empirically evaluates how to improve system testing by systematically using traceable and prioritized defect taxonomies where defect categories with assigned severity values are linked to prioritized requirements and failures. Bach [4] highlights the important role of requirements prioritization for system testing. In our approach the requirements prioritization is refined by assigning requirements to defect categories which enables more specific test design techniques to be applied. Our results are relevant for practice and research. On the one hand, we derive advice that can be applied by test designers and managers in industrial projects. On the other hand, we empirically evaluate the role of defect taxonomies for system testing via an industrial case study and raise further research questions.

In our case study, we adopt the Beizer taxonomy defined by Boris Beizer in his book on software testing techniques [5]. This taxonomy offers a comprehensive means of hierarchically classifying defects. The classification is generic, well established in system testing and has been adopted by other authors, e.g. Black [6]. Based on the statistics of various software projects, the Beizer taxonomy subdivides the causes of defects in the major categories of requirements, features and functionality, structure, data, implementation and coding, integration, system and software architecture, testing, and unspecified. Although we use this taxonomy as a starting point to define our product-specific defect taxonomy, this approach is not bound to a specific classification schema, and other defect taxonomies (see Section 2 for an overview) can also be applied. Even Beizer states that it is more important to adopt any taxonomy and use it as a statistical framework on which to base the testing strategy than to adopt the 'right' taxonomy [5].

This paper is structured as follows. In the next section we give an overview of related work. We then present our defect taxonomy-supported test process in Section 3, and the design and results of our case study in Section 4. Finally, in Section 5 we conclude and present future work.

2   Related Work

Our approach is related to previous work on defect taxonomies in general, the application of defect taxonomies to software testing, and empirical studies in these fields.

Taxonomies are applied in several software engineering domains, e.g. for identifying risks in risk management [7], for quality specifications in requirements engineering [8], in inspection [9], or as defect taxonomies in software [10].

Several generic and application-specific defect taxonomies with various objectives have been listed by Vijayaraghavan and Kaner [10]. The most influential generic defect taxonomies in the software testing literature have been defined by Beizer [5], as applied in this paper, and Kaner [11]. The defect taxonomy proposed by Kaner distinguishes defects related to the user interface, error handling, boundaries, calculation, race conditions, load conditions, hardware, version control, and testing. The IEEE Standard 1044-1993 on test classification provides a classification scheme of anomalies [12]. It defines an anomaly as any condition that deviates from expectations based on requirements specifications, design documents, user documents, standards, etc. or from someone's perceptions or experience. McDonald [3] organizes his defect taxonomy around the stages of a defect, i.e. occurrence stage, contributing cause(s) stage, change stage, detection stage, and mitigation stage.

Additionally, there are various application-specific defect taxonomies, e.g. for component-based applications [13], safety critical systems [14], web services [15], or web applications [16].

The purpose of software testing is not just to detect failures but also to increase trust in a software product by demonstrating the absence of pre-specified defects. The latter is the main motivation for defect-based testing [17], which identifies those defects that cannot be present in software on the basis that if they were present the test execution would have been different. Defect taxonomies as applied in our approach are the basis for defect-based testing supporting the systematic definition of test strategies.

Although many defect distribution statistics are based on defect taxonomies, for instance in Beizer [5], there are relatively few empirical studies of their properties. Marchetto et al. [16] investigate exclusiveness, ambiguity, classifiability, distribution, specifity, and stability of web-defect taxonomies based on several hundred bugs from 68 web applications. The results are used to define a defect taxonomy for web applications in an iterative way.

Vallespir et al. [18] define a framework to evaluate and compare different defect taxonomies based on a meta taxonomy including attributes, structure type and properties. The comparison in their paper considers several taxonomies, including those of Beizer and Kaner. The *orthogonal defect classification* (ODC) scheme [19] defining attributes for the classification of failures is also introduced in the framework of Vallespir et al. [18]. ODC can be used for fault detection in static analysis [20] and for inspection [9]. The reliability of ODC has been investigated in several publications [21,22,23]. The approaches of Marchetto and Vallespir are orthogonal to our own and can be used to define a suitable taxonomy to adapt our approach to a specific domain.

Besides defect distribution statistics based on defect taxonomies [5], other publications such as Fenton and Ohlsson [21], Basili et al. [25] or Andersson and Runeson [26] empirically investigate the distribution of defects and failures in systems. These publications found evidence that a small number of modules contain most of the defects and confirm the presence of similar defect densities in similar testing and operational phases in broadly similar environments. However, the role of defect taxonomies in comparable projects or environments with respect to the distribution of defects and the application of defect taxonomies to testing has been investigated only to some extent.

Marchetto et al. [16] have defined a web-defect taxonomy based on several web applications and use it to perform taxonomy-based testing of a web application: First, specific defect categories are selected. Then, at least one usage scenario is defined for each selected categories. Finally, for each scenario a test case is defined and executed. For a sample address book web application Marchetto et al. indicate a reduction of test cases compared to use case-based testing. Compared to Marchetto et al., our defect taxonomy-based testing approach additionally considers traceability between requirements and defect categories, and weighting (priority of requirements, severity of defect categories severity of defects). This supports more accurate methods for test design and release quality assessment. Furthermore, our approach is empirically evaluated via an industrial case study.

3 Defect Taxonomy-Supported Testing

In this section we define our defect taxonomy supported testing approach and its integration into the ISTQB test process.

3.1   Basic Concepts

In this section, we discuss the main concepts underlying the case study. For this purpose, we give an overview of the main artifacts and their relationships within the context of the case study. The artifacts for system testing with defect taxonomies and their relationships are shown in Figure 1.

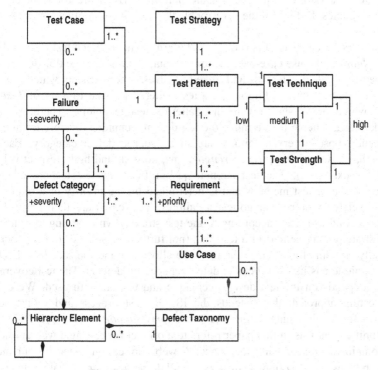

Fig. 1. Basic Artefacts and their relationship

A *Defect Taxonomy* consists of a tree of *Hierarchy Element*s. Its leaves are formed by *Defect Category* (DC) elements. Each defect category has a *severity* (SDC) which defines the degree of impact that a defect in that category has on the development or operation of the system. In our approach, the defect categories are defined on the basis of the categories in the Beizer taxonomy and the potential faults of the system. Table 1 shows an example for a defect taxonomy.

A *Requirement* defines a functional capability of the system. A requirement has a *priority* (PR) defining its level of business importance, which may be high, normal, or low. A requirement can be assigned to defect categories such that failures occurring when testing a specific requirement fall into one of the assigned defect categories. Each requirement is assigned *Use Cases* that define its behavior and are the main source for the design of test cases. The test case design may additionally be refined by *graphical user interface* (GUI) descriptions attached to use cases.

Failures, i.e. malfunctions identified during the testing of requirements, are assigned to defect categories. Each failure also has a *severity* (SF) reflecting its potential impact. The possible values for the severity of defect categories and failures follow Bugzilla [1], and may be blocker, critical, major, normal, minor, or trivial. Therefore the value *blocker* means that the software version cannot be tested or used, *critical* a very limited testing is possible, *major*, the usage is still very limited, *normal* the damage of a failure is not significant, *minor* or *trivial* are for instance minor layout deficiencies. Defects of the severity blocker or critical imply a high risk for the project.

A *Test Strategy* consists of several *Test Pattern* elements. Each test pattern defines a *Test Technique* like use case-based testing, syntax testing or state transition testing, is assigned to a defect category, and linked to several requirements which are tested based on the test pattern. Additionally, a test pattern is linked to a set of *Test Case* elements which are designed with the pattern's test technique. Therefore, a test pattern defines a scheme to determine the test design technique to apply for a specific requirement whose observed failures are in a specific defect category. Each test technique has assigned three *Test Strength*s low, normal, and high, respectively (see Table 2 for examples). The test strength [27] refines the test technique, e.g. by coverage criteria or test methods and is determined by the priority of a requirement and the severity of defect categories or failures. Test cases are then derived from requirements and use cases according to the test strategy with varying test strengths. The test strategy may be part of a test plan (not further considered in this paper) that additionally contains for instance the resource allocation and the schedule. Each test design technique has its own focus in detecting specific defects. The test coverage of a domain depends on the test design technique and test strength used. We call our system testing approach that extends the ISTQB test process and utilizes defect taxonomies for requirements testing *defect taxonomy-supported testing* (DTST).

Each unit of analysis in this paper refers to a project for testing a web application in the domain of public health insurance. A web application tested by our method uses a web browser as a client to display the GUI and a server for data management and program control. The architecture is service oriented, and various applications support the different business processes. The services communicate via an *Enterprise Service Bus* (ESB) running on a flexible infrastructure (virtualization). The users have role-specific access to the various applications. External internet services are connected through a portal of the central IT department. For these types of applications, the highest priority is not assigned to freedom from errors such as in embedded systems but to an optimal number of test cases supported by the use of defect taxonomies.

The requirements and the attached use cases are defined by domain experts and analysts. The defect taxonomy and test strategy are defined by a test manager. The requirements tests are systematically designed and executed by testers based on the test patterns. Note that the requirements and defect taxonomy are defined by different persons, and are consequently also prioritized independently of each other.

The relationships between defect categories, failures and requirements have been defined and maintained by a test manager who analyzed the defect entries in the defect management tool (Bugzilla in our case) with the aim of creating and optimizing the product-specific defect taxonomy.

3.2   Test Process

In the organization where the case study was implemented, the ISTQB test [2] was already in place. The ISTQB test process shown in Figure 2 consists of the steps (1) test planning and control, (2) test analysis and design, (3) test implementation and execution, (4) test evaluation and reporting, and (5) test closure activities.

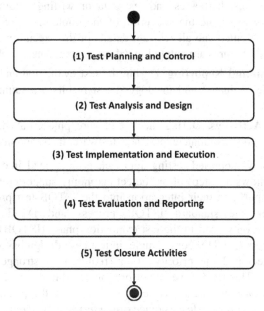

Fig. 2. ISTQB Test Process

In the subsequent paragraphs we explain the particular steps of the ISTQB test process following the ISTQB standard glossary of terms used in software testing [2].

(1) Test Planning and Control. Test planning is the activity of establishing or updating a test plan. A test plan is a document describing the scope, approach, resources, and schedule of intended test activities. It identifies, amongst others, the features to be tested, the test design techniques, and exit criteria to be used and the rationale of their choice. In the analytical ISTQB test process, test planning occurs at the beginning. Ideally, it proceeds in parallel with overall project planning. Templates for test plans and their content are specific to the domain or to the architecture of a product. For example, a test plan for a business-oriented web application contains test design techniques and exit criteria, which may not be relevant for embedded systems in the automotive domain and vice versa. Once the test plan has been established, test control begins. Test control is an ongoing activity (which is not reflected in the abstract process representation of Figure 2). In test control, the actual progress is compared against the plan which often results in concrete measures.

(2) Test Analysis and Design. During the test analysis and design phase the general testing objectives defined in the test plan are transformed into tangible test conditions and test cases. Based on a test design specification which contains test design techniques and coverage criteria, high-level test cases with logical operators and without concrete data are derived. In case of system testing common coverage criteria are for example 100% coverage of requirements or use case branches. The high-level test cases are then refined to low-level test cases with actual values.

(3) Test Implementation and Execution. Test implementation contains remaining tasks like preparing test harnesses and test data or writing automated test scripts which are necessary to enable the execution of the implementation-level test cases. The tests are then executed and all relevant details of the execution are recorded in a test log. The detected failures are entered in a defect management tool.

(4) Test Evaluation and Reporting. During the test evaluation and reporting phase the exit criteria are evaluated and the logged test results are summarized in a test report.

(5) Test Closure Activities. During the test closure phase, data is collected from completed activities to consolidate experience, testware, facts, and numbers.

Our defect taxonomy-supported testing approach is integrated into the ISTQB test process. Figure 3 shows the steps of our defect taxonomy-supported testing approach, their input and output, and their integration into the ISTQB test process. The main difference between the standard ISTQB process and DTST is that defect categorization is not only used in the test evaluation phase (ISTQB), but throughout the whole test process (DTST). For example, in test case design based on the severity of a potential defect and the priority of the requirement stronger or lighter test techniques are used. This saves time and effort compared to the goal of creating a test case pool with 100% coverage of use case branches. In the phase evaluation and reporting the arguments for a release advice of the test management are recognized by the other stakeholders, because the outstanding product risks are assessed taking also a long-term impact of an error into account.

The steps 1 to 4 (Analysis and Prioritization of Requirements, Creation of a Defect Taxonomy, Linkage of Requirements and Defect Categories, Definition and Assignment of Test Patterns) (see Figure 3) are integrated into the ISTQB process step (1) Test Planning and Control. The ISTQB steps (2) Test Analysis and Design and (3) Test Implementation and Execution take the DTST specific guidelines of the test strategy into account, but the procedures of (2) and (3) are not changed. However, ISTQB step (4) Test Evaluation and Reporting has to be adapted to the procedure of DTST step 5 (Analysis of Failures after a Test Cycle). ISTQB step (5) Test Closure Activities will be performed according the ISTQB standard. In the following paragraphs we explain the steps 1 to 5 of our defect taxonomy-supported testing approach in more detail.

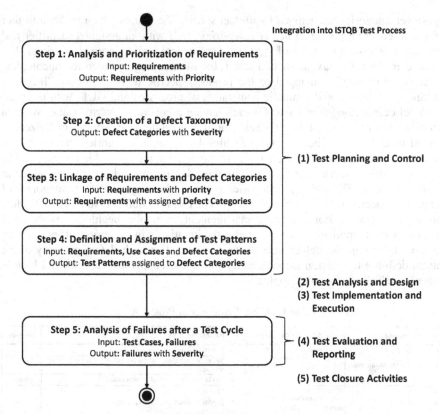

Fig. 3. Defect Taxonomy-Supported Test Process and Integration in ISTQB Test Process

Step 1: Analysis and Prioritization of Requirements

The analysts create the requirements in cooperation with the domain experts. A priority (high, normal, low) is then assigned to the requirements taking the impact of malfunctioning into account. Thus a high priority is assigned if a potential failure has a great impact, e.g. erroneous credit transfer. The attribute normal is assigned to requirements taking the usability of the application in the implementation of a user task into account. For example, low priority is assigned to 'nice-to-have' features. After a review by the stakeholders, the requirements are ready for analysis of the use cases.

Step 2: Creation of a Defect Taxonomy

When the analysis of the first iteration is completed, a defect taxonomy is created by test managers on the basis of the Beizer taxonomy [5], because of its suitability for black-box-testing and user-oriented systems. The taxonomy has three levels of abstraction, starting with selected high-level defect categories from the top-level categories of Beizer, i.e. (1) requirements (2) features and functionality, (4) data, (6) integration, and (9) unclassified defects. The Beizer categories (3) structural defects, (5) implementation and coding, (7) system, software architecture, and (8) test definition and execution are not relevant for system testing in our context. The high-level categories are mapped to product specific categories which are then further refined to concrete low-level *defect categories* (DC) with an assigned identifier and severity. The severity can be of type blocker, critical, major, normal or trivial. For instance, in the defect taxonomy of Table 1, the Beizer category "incorrect/incomplete feature/functionality" is mapped to the product specific defect category "Incorrect handling of syntactic and semantic constraints of processes and GUI" with assigned low-level defect categories F1 to F9 each having a concrete severity value. When a defect taxonomy is created, first the relevant high-level defect categories of Beizer are entered in Column 1. Then the mapped high-level defect categories specific to the product, i.e. web applications with a GUI in our respect, are entered in Column 2. The product specific defect categories DC with their description and severity are added in Columns 3 to 5. These defect categories partition the original defect categories of Beizer to a specific domain and technology. The example defect taxonomy of Table 1 considers a specific domain (case management in public health insurance) and technology (web application) and was adjusted iteratively in the course of interpreting the new defects in the defect management system. For each defect category a test pattern defining test design techniques for the test strengths low, normal and high is created (see Table 2 for an example).

Table 1. Defect Taxonomy of Project A

Defect Category of Beizer	Product-Specific Category	DC	Description of DC	Severity
1xx . . Requirements	Unsuitability of the system taking the organizational processes and procedures into account.	R1	Client not identified correctly	critical
11xx . . Requirements incorrect		R2	Goals and measures of case manager are not processed correctly	normal
16xx . . Requirement changes		R3	Update and termination of case incorrect	normal
12xx . . Logic 13xx . . Completeness	Incorrect handling of the syntactic or semantic constraints of GUI.	R4	GUI-layout Syntactic specifications of input fields Error massages	major
2xx . . Functionality as implemented	Incorrect handling of the syntactic or semantic constraints of processes and GUI.	F1	Client not identified correctly	critical
21xx . . Correctness 22xx . . Completeness, features		F2	Goals and measures of case manager, e.g. case termination, are not processed correctly	normal
		F3	Check of termination of case not correct	critical
		F4	Erroneous identification of client: Wrong / missing error messages	normal
		F5	Wrong / missing error message: Save-button etc.	critical
		F6	GUI behaviour; Wrong / missing error message: status, domain limitations	major
		F7	Display of incorrect data on screen/report	normal
		F8	Incorrect behaviour of GUI: disable/ enable of controls navigation; default values	normal
		F9	Display of syntactic incorrect data, minor errors in Layout	minor
4xx . Data 42xx . . Data access and handling		D1	Incorrect access / update of client information, states etc.	normal
		D2	Erroneous save of critical data	critical
62xx . . External interfaces and timing 623x . . . I/O timing or throughput	Interface to external components	I1	Data are incorrect or incomplete because of error in service call	normal
		I2	Data of clients are not available because partner application is not available	critical
9xx . . Unclassified bugs		U1	e.g.sporadic failures during performance testing	normal

Step 3: Linkage of Requirements and Defect Categories

Still in the test planning phase, the tester annotates the list of requirements with the defect categories taking the project experience of experts into account. For example, in the project A of the case study (see Section 4.2 for more details) the requirement "Identification of a client by the case manager" has the priority value high and is linked to category F1 which has critical severity. Other requirements describe properties of the user interface and are linked to F5 with severity value critical or F6 with severity value major, for example.

Step 4: Definition and Assignment of Test Patterns

Black-box tests are derived from requirements in two steps. First, high-level test cases defining the test objective and test condition are created, followed by the implementation of low-level test cases. Test analysis and best design practices are used to create effective test cases. The challenge here is to find a balance between the number of test cases and the depth of testing or test strength [14]. The test strength refines the testing technique of the test pattern, e.g. by coverage criteria or test methods and is determined by the priority of requirements and the severity of defect categories or failures. The test design techniques to be applied for the design of test cases depend on the object to be modeled. For the purpose of the recommendation of test design methods taking its own focus in finding specific types of defects into account. De Grood [27] defines the usefulness of some practical test design techniques. He points out that defects found with one technique are not necessarily found by another technique. In our approach we go a step further. The specific defect detection capability of each test technique is related to the defect categories of the product specific taxonomy. The generated test cases are goal-oriented in respect to detect specific categories of defects with a coverage taking the severity of an expected failure into account. In Table 2 the test design techniques used in project A are listed.

Table 2. Test Design Techniques for Various Defect Categories and Test Strengths

	Id	Test Design Technique	Defect Categories	Test Strength 1 (low)	Test Strength 2 (normal)	Test Strength 3 (high)
S: Sequence oriented	S1	Use case-based testing; process cycle tests	R1, R2, R3, F1,F2, F3	Main paths	Branch coverage	Loop coverage
	S3	State transition testing	I1, I2, F7, F8, F9	State coverage	State transition coverage	Path coverage
D: Data oriented	D1	CRUD (Create, Read, Update and Delete)	D1, D2		Data cycle tests	Data cycle tests
	D3	EP: Equivalence partitioning	F3, F5, F6	EP valid	EP valid+invalid	EP valid+invalid
	D4	BVA: Boundary value analysis	F3, F5, F6	BVA valid	BVA valid+invalid	BVA r values at boundaries
	D6	CE: Cause-effect graphing	F2, F3, F4		CE	CE
	D8	Syntax testing	R4, F6	Syntax valid	Syntax valid + invalid	Syntax valid + invalid
	D10	Condition testing	F3	Simple condition coverage	modified condition/decision coverage	modified condition/decision coverage
H:Heuristic and fault oriented methods	H1	HT: Heuristic (experience-based) testing	U1	Experience-based criteria	Experience-based criteria	Experience-based criteria
	H7	Load/performance testing	U1	Experience-based criteria	Experience-based criteria	Experience-based criteria
	H8	Stress testing	U1	Experience-based criteria	Experience-based criteria	Experience-based criteria

For example, the test pattern state transition testing with Id S3 has three test strengths, i.e. (low) state coverage, (normal) state transition coverage, and (high) path coverage. The defect category F9 of Table 1 is assigned to the test pattern state transition testing which is applied to design tests for all requirements linked to DC F9.

Test design techniques allow the variation of the test strength based on the risk of a failure. Due to a positive correlation between the priority of the requirements and the severity of the defect categories the test strength can be determined in a very specific and goal oriented way as shown in Table 3.

Table 3. Determination of the Test Strength

PR	SDC, SF	Test strength
high	blocker, critical, major	3
normal	blocker, critical	3
normal	major, normal, minor, trivial	2
low	minor, trivial	1

The assignment of the test strength 1,2 or 3 to the combination of PR and SDC/SF is similar to various standards in safety-critical systems like IEC 61508 [28], where a specific test technique is defined as recommended, highly recommended or mandatory depending on the *safety integrity level* (SIL).

For example, the requirement "An insurant should be identified and his profile displayed on the GUI" has the priority high. The requirement is related to use cases (see Figure 1) specified as activity diagram with a main path and alternative paths. The defect categories R1 (severity critical), F1 (severity critical), and the defect categories I1 (severity normal), I2 (severity critical) have to be taken into account. The recommended test techniques are S1 (use case-based testing) with test strength 3 (loop coverage which is in our respect defined as passing each loop zero, exactly one and more than one time) and S3 (state transition testing) with test strength 2 (state transition coverage). The number of test cases is calculated from the number of branches and loops specified in the activity diagram and the transitions of the message sequence chart of the external interface.

After a test design technique has been selected for a specific severity of a defect category (SDC) and priority of a requirement (PR) based on test pattern and the test strength determination (see Table 2 and Table 3), tests for this requirement are systematically designed by testers on the basis of the requirements specification and the assigned use cases.

With the test pattern concept we manage to relate the specific defect detection capability of each testing technique as pointed out by de Grood [27] to defect categories and to optimize the coverage level and therefore also the number of test cases by varying the test strength which takes the requirement's priority and the defect category's severity into account. Besides the testing techniques of de Grood [27], also the characterization schema of Vegas and Basili [29] and the experience of previous projects have been considered for the definition and assignment of test patterns.

Step 5: Analysis of Failures after a Test Cycle

After the execution of a system test, the test exit criteria have to be evaluated by the test management. To check the quality of the system and the test progress not only the ratio of the passed test cases to the overall number of executed test cases but also the defects and their severity (stored in a defect management tool) have to be considered. If the test management then decides that the quality of a release is low and that an additional iteration to integrate hotfixes and perform specific testing is needed, arguments to convince the project management that additional resources and time are essential have to be collected. In this situation, the test management has to evaluate the failures in the defect management system, linked to the test cases and the prioritized requirements, taking the severity and the defect categories into account. To prevent a defect becoming a risk for the quality of the system, the following issues have to be resolved: (1) assignment of competent members of the development team to analyze the defect, (2) selection of the defects to be corrected in the next version, and (3) adaptation of iteration and release plans.

Experience gained during the system test of several releases and data from the defect management tool Bugzilla are used to improve the defect taxonomy. If defect taxonomies are applied in projects using the same technology, for example, a service-oriented architecture reuse and organization-wide deployment are to be recommended.

As soon as defect taxonomy supported testing has been introduced in an organization by providing a description of the procedure, respective templates, and training for the testers, the effort for applying the method in a concrete project is due to our experience marginal. We therefore focus on the benefits of the method itself, and do not further consider return on investment calculations in this paper.

4   Case Study

The case study design follows the guidelines of case study research in software engineering according to Runeson and Höst [30]. In this section, therefore, we present the research questions, the case and subject selection as well as the data collection, analysis and validity procedures, and the results.

4.1   Research Questions

In this paper the following research questions are investigated to identify whether defect taxonomy supported testing improves test design compared to the standard ISTQB test process.

(RQ1) **Defect taxonomy-supported testing reduces the number of system test cases.**

(RQ2) **Defect taxonomy-supported testing increases the number of identified system failures per system test case.**

4.2   Case and Subjects Selection

We collected and analyzed data from two web-based health-insurance projects. The units of analysis were selected from a series of similar projects in the organization. All of them are using the same iterative development process and guidelines, a common GUI-style guide, a defined analysis procedure and a test process, which are mandatory for all projects in the organization. In both projects, the company's employees, provide the domain knowledge and external personnel the know-how about the applied technologies, software engineering methods and tools.

Project A is an application developed for case managers of the public health insurance institution. It supports the tasks of the employees of the public health insurance institution in caring for handicapped people and managing these cases. Project B, an application for mastering client data with interfaces to other applications via an ESB, is similar to project A, and has the same complexity. For instance, the address of residence of insurants between one insurance company and the data, administered by the main association of the national social security institutions are mapped and synchronized automatically.

In the first product, subsequently called project A, the defect taxonomy supported testing approach based on the ISTQB test process was applied. In the second one, project B, the ISTQB test process was already in place, but no defect taxonomy guided test case design was used. Table 4 gives an overview of both projects comparing the characteristics area, staff, duration, number of iterations, size, ratio of system testing, and test process. Both projects have similar characteristics mainly differing in the application of defect taxonomy-supported testing in project A.

Table 4. Overview of the Studied Projects

	Project A	Project B
Area	Application for case managers	Administration of clients of the public health insurance institution.
Staff	About 7	Up to 10
Duration	9 month development, now under maintenance	9 month development, now under maintenance
Number of iterations	4	3
SIZE: NOR + NUC	41+14	28+20
Ratio of system testing	27% of overall project effort	28% of overall project effort
Test Process	ISTQB process + defect taxonomy-supported testing Manual regression testing	ISTQB process Manual regression testing

In both projects the *number of requirements* (NOR) plus the *number of use cases* (NUC) are used to estimate the *system size* (SIZE) which is 55 in project A and 48 in project B.

4.3   Data Collection Procedure

In this section we focus on the collection of data in the framework of iterative software development in a public health insurance institution. Referring to Runeson and Höst [30] we consider data collection techniques of three degrees.

— First degree (direct methods) means that the researcher is in direct contact with the stakeholders and collects data in real time.
— Second degree (indirect methods) means that the researcher directly collects raw data without actually interacting with the subjects during the data collection.
— Third degree means that independent analysis of work artifacts where already available or compiled data is used.

The data were collected following the steps of defect taxonomy-supported testing (see Section 3.2):

Step 1: The requirements were retrieved from the repositories of projects A and B and stored in an Excel table. The analysts defined the requirements in the tool Enterprise Architect. The priority of requirements was assigned in cooperation with domain experts taking the business value and the impact of a failure into account.

Step 2: The defect taxonomies were created in Excel. Before the testers started to design test cases for project A, they were trained to apply defect taxonomy-supported testing. The general guideline for all projects was that test cases have to be designed on the basis of the use case descriptions with 100% branch coverage. In project A however the testers were advised to reduce the coverage of test cases taking priority of requirements and defect categories into account.

Step 3 and 4: To each requirement in the exported Excel table, a defect category was assigned. Then all test cases were implemented in the test management tool SiTEMPPO [31]. The test case pool was interpreted by the test management to validate the correct application of DTST and to give feedback in regular test team meetings.

Step 5: The correct analysis of failures after a system test was crucial, because stakeholders expect information about release quality and outstanding risks. In project A, defect entries (defect identifier, severity and short description) of the defect management system were exported into a csv file using specific queries of Bugzilla. Finally, the defect entries are assigned to the defect categories via the traceable test case identifiers and requirements.

The central test management group responsible for the application of best practices in software testing to all projects of the organization integrated the methodology into the framework of an improvement project. Qualitative data were additionally collected by interviewing project managers, testers with good domain knowledge and testing skills, and analysts. To analyze the effectiveness of the improvement measure, the stakeholders, i.e. analysts, testers, test managers, and project managers were interviewed. Test cases were reviewed with respect to their test strength and test technique used. During and after system testing, the defect entries of Bugzilla were analyzed and linked to the defect categories of the product. Issues such as, efficiency of the test cases, quality of a release and severity and impact of a defect were discussed with project management, system testers, analysts and development staff. As a result a smart decision about the allocation of resources to solve open issues and to plan the next versions and deployments of the software could be made.

Indirect methods were used to collect data taking the regular reports of the project manager created for the organization's steering board, minutes of regular project meetings, thematic queries to the test management and the defect tracking tool into account.

For third degree methods the test management collected archival data having access to the repositories of the studied projects. The main sources were documents of the project management for example project and test plans, controlling data, milestones and defect reporting metrics.

Only defect data on integration/system level were taken into account. The approach guarantees traceability from the requirements to the test cases and the defect entries, which is a precondition for an objective assessment of the product quality on the system level.

4.4   Analysis Procedure

To answer the two research questions we measure the *system size* (SIZE), i.e. the sum of the *number of requirements* (NOR) and *use cases* (NUC), the *number of test cases* (NOT), and the *number of failures* (NOF) in project A and B. To decide whether the number of test cases decreases by the application of DTST in an ISTQB test process (RQ1), we compare the ratio NOT/SIZE of projects A and B, i.e. the number of test cases of projects A and B relative to their project size. To decide whether the number of identified system failures per system test case increases by the application of DTST in an ISTQB test process (RQ2), we compare the ratio NOF/NOT of projects A and B, i.e. the number of failures of projects A and B divided by their number of test cases. NOF/NOT is an established measure for test effectiveness [32] measuring the effect of the test cases on the system under test. The reduction of the number of test cases by the application of defect taxonomy-supported testing in RQ1 is additionally shown by comparing the number of test cases per module with DTST to the estimated number of test cases with standard ISTQB in project A. To show the significance of the test case reduction in project A compared to the estimation, a paired two-sample t-test [33] is applied.

4.5   Validity Procedure

In this section we present the applied measures to guarantee validity of our results. Referring to Runeson and Höst [30] we discuss threats to the construct validity, internal validity, external validity, and reliability of the case study along with countermeasures taken to reduce the threats.

Construct Validity. This type of validity reflects to what extent the studied operational measures represent what is investigated according to the research questions. To answer the research questions, where the number of test cases and the ratio of failures per test case of two projects have to be compared, we selected the projects A and B which have similar characteristics. The projects A and B are both in the public health insurance domain and were performed by the same development and test organization which has standardized guidelines for all its projects. Additionally, as the project overview in Section 4.2 shows, they have similar duration, number of iterations, size, and ratio of system testing. Finally, both projects are based on the ISTQB test process, only differing in the application of defect taxonomy-supported testing in project A. Although the number of requirements of project A (41) and project B (28) differ significantly (see Table 5), the results are comparable. First, NOT is normalized by SIZE, i.e. the sum of the number of requirements and use cases, and therefore independent of NOR. Second, the distribution of failures per top-level defect category is independent of the number of requirements which has therefore no side effect on the ratio NOF/NOT. The source of data was the defect management tool and the test management tool including all test reports of projects A and B. Data quality has been assured and maintained throughout the study, e.g. starting with a selection of the projects and iterated consistency, correctness and completeness checks of the data. The descriptions of failures of severity blocker or critical and the change requests tracked in the defect management tool were additionally reviewed by the test management aligned with domain experts and analysts during and after system testing. To better understand the exact nature of the failures and to perform their assignment to defect categories, the test cases, test plans and change control board protocols were also analyzed. Additionally, we have informally collected feedback concerning defect taxonomy-supported testing from testers and test managers involved in projects A and B to validate the results.

Internal Validity. This type of validity is of concern when causal relations are examined where one factor affects another factor and the influence of additional factors is not considered. We investigate a causal relation between the application of *defect taxonomy-supported testing* (DTST) in an ISTQB system test process, and both the *number of system test cases* (NOT) and the *number of failures* (NOF). The obtained dependency between DTST and NOT might have been influenced by several additional factors. Such factors are the test budget, the experience of the involved test designers, the used technologies, or the quality of the initial defect categorization, requirements definition and the code quality [34]. As the same test and development organization was involved in both projects A and B, and because of the fact that the projects where selected according to their duration, number of iterations, size, the code quality, ratio of system testing, technological space and the applied test process in order to be comparable (see Section 4.2), the presumable influence of the mentioned additional factors is small. Additionally, the data for answering RQ2 is triangulated as NOT, NOF, and SIZE of projects A and B but also the estimated NOT in project A and the qualitative feedback of testers are considered.

External Validity. This type of validity is concerned with to what extent it is possible to generalize the findings. Our case study has been performed in the domain of public health insurance based on the defect taxonomy of Beizer and the standardized ISTQB test process. As our defect taxonomy-supported testing approach is independent of a specific domain and defect taxonomy, we expect similar results in other contexts where an ISTQB-based test process is established but have to show this as future work.

Reliability. The reliability is concerned with to what extent the data and the analysis are dependent on the specific researchers. Our defect taxonomy-supported testing approach is well-defined, and the data collection, analysis, and validity procedures are completely documented. Additionally, the underlying data is available in Bugzilla and a test management tool.

4.6   Results

Table 5 shows the basic and derived metrics of project A and project B to answer the research questions RQ1 and RQ2.

Table 5. Metrics for Project A and Project B

Metrics	Project A	Project B
NOR	41	28
NUC	14	20
SIZE (NUC+NOR)	55	48
NOT	148	170
NOF	169	114
NOT/SIZE	2.69	3.54
NOF/NOT	1.14	0.67

The *system size* (SIZE) determined by the sum of the *number of requirements* (NOR) and *use cases* (NUC) is 55 in project A and 48 in project B. The *number of tests* (NOT) is 148 in project A and 170 in project B. For both projects, the number of test cases has been extracted from the test management tool SiTEMPPO. The test cases in project A have been defined with DTST as defined in Section 3.2. In project B the test cases have been defined with the ISTQB based test design procedure established in the institution where the case study has been conducted, i.e. suitable standard test design techniques for use cases and requirements were selected, and applied to reach 100% coverage. For instance, if a use case is defined by an activity diagram, branch coverage as recommended by the ISTQB has been applied. The *number of failures* (NOF) is 169 in project A and 114 in project B. For both projects, the number of failures has been extracted from the defect management tool Bugzilla.

(RQ1). The number of test cases related to the project size is smaller for project A than for project B, as NOT/SIZE is 2.69 in project A but 3.54 in project A (see Table

5). This fact indicates that defect taxonomy-supported test design reduces the number of system test cases and therefore also the resources needed for implementing executing and evaluating them which helps to increases the efficiency of the ISTQB test process.

The reduction of the number of test cases by the application of DTST in an ISTQB test process is confirmed by comparing the actual and estimated number of test cases in project A. Table 6 shows the *estimated number of tests without considering defect taxonomy-supported testing in the ISTQB test process* (NOT Estimated) and the *actual number of tests with defect taxonomy-supported testing* (NOT DTST) for each module of project A. NOT Estimated is determined by estimating the number of test cases in project A with the same procedure as applied in project B, i.e. selecting suitable standard test design techniques for use cases and defining test cases to reach 100% coverage according to the respective test design techniques.

Table 6. Number of Test Cases in Project A

Module	NOT Estimated	NOT DTST	Reduction
GUI	32	29	9%
M1	9	8	11%
M2	58	41	29%
M3	43	34	21%
M4	14	13	7%
M5	26	23	12%
Total	182	148	19%

As the column Reduction, i.e. the percentage reduction of test cases from NOT Estimated to NOT DTST, in Table 6 indicates, NOT is absolutely reduced for each module and the average reduction is 19%. The test case reduction by defect taxonomy-supported test design in project A is even significant as a paired two-sample t-test based on the data of Table 6 shows (T=2.209, df=5, p=0.039).

(RQ2). Table 5 shows that the test effectiveness measure NOF/NOT, i.e. the average number of failures found by a test case. NOF/NOT is greater for project A (1.14) where DTST has been applied than for project B (0.67) where DTST has not been applied. Thus, each test case designed with DTST is more effective than without DTST. The reduced number of test cases and the greater test effectiveness indicates that the application of defect taxonomies as indicated in this paper improves system test design in the ISTQB test process as the defined tests are more goal-oriented. The generated test case set is more focused on the detection of defects and avoids redundant test cases.

These quantitative results of our case study are validated qualitatively by feedback of the testers which emphasized that defect taxonomy-supported testing helps them to improve their test cases to find more defects of severity major, critical or blocker. Differing from project A, we observed that in project B hot fixes and unplanned releases were needed to remove failures of type major, critical or blocker which confirms the statement of the testers. The reduction of test cases and the availability of a stable defect classification and its impact on budgeting and resource allocation caused additional discussion amongst the stakeholders in project A. For instance, the effort for test design and execution was reduced as the number of test cases decreased compared to the originally estimated number of test cases covering 100% of the use case branches in project A. The testers accepted the reduction of test cases and their feedback confirmed that DTST guarantees quality of the product and allows realistic statements about the release quality although the number of test cases is reduced. Also the feedback of the test management confirms more precise statements about the quality of a release in our approach. The test management emphasizes that the severity value of a failure is more realistic and as a consequence the number of unplanned releases was reduced and the test management process went more smoothly.

5   Conclusion and Future Work

In this paper, we presented a method of system testing based on defect taxonomies and investigated via an industrial case study how it can improve the maturity, i.e. efficiency and effectiveness of the ISTQB test process. We defined a relevant defect taxonomy-supported test process considering traceability between prioritized requirements, defect categories, and failures. We then studied two research questions based on the data of two representative projects of a public health insurance institution with the following results. Defect taxonomy-supported testing (1) reduces the number of system test cases and (2) increases the number of identified failures per test case.

Thus, enhancing the ISTQB test process by defect taxonomy-supported testing has several benefits. The design and execution of system tests is goal-oriented increasing the efficiency and effectiveness of the test process. The number of unplanned releases and hot fixes can be reduced significantly during maintenance. The effort required for defining and maintaining the defect taxonomies is manageable.

The results have been applied to improve design of system tests and statements on release quality. This approach is already being successfully applied to the system testing of applications in the health insurance domain. So far, it has only been applied to system testing based on the defect taxonomy of Beizer and the standardized ISTQB test process. But as the Beizer taxonomy can also be adapted to the integration and unit levels, this approach can be extended to manage testing on these levels. Also the underlying ISTQB test process does not restrict the applicability of defect taxonomy-supported testing in practice, as most industrial test processes can be subsumed under the generic ISTQB test process.

In future, we investigate the role of defect taxonomies in our approach in more detail. On the one hand we empirically investigate how our approach scales for different defect taxonomies such as the Kaner or IEEE taxonomies. On the other hand we study the evolution of taxonomies in the maintenance phase and its consequences for regression testing. We also intend to integrate defect taxonomies into system risk assessment in order to define a risk-based testing approach and to compare it to other system test prioritization approaches. Furthermore, we investigate the value contribution of defect taxonomy-supported testing, e.g. reduced release planning uncertainty, and its relationship to value-based software testing approaches [35]. In this respect, we also perform a detailed return on investment study of defect taxonomy-supported testing based on the ongoing application in several projects.

Acknowledgments. This work has been supported by the project QE LaB – Living Models for Open Systems (FFG 822740).

References

1. Serrano, N., Ciordia, I.: Bugzilla, ITracker, and other bug trackers. IEEE Software 22(2), 11–13 (2005)
2. ISTQB: Standard glossary of terms used in software testing. Version 2.1 (2010)
3. McDonald, R., Musson, R., Smith, R.: The practical guide to defect prevention - techniques to meet the demand for more reliable software. Microsoft Press (2008)
4. Bach, J.: Risk and Requirements-Based Testing. IEEE Computer 32(6), 113–114 (1999)
5. Beizer, B.: Software testing techniques. Thomson Computer Press (1990)
6. Black, R.: Advanced Software Testing. Guide to the ISTQB Advanced Certification as an Advanced Test Analyst, vol. 1. Rocky Nook (2008)
7. Carr, M.J., Konda, S.L., Monarch, I., Ulrich, F.C., Walker, C.F.: Taxonomy-based risk identification, Software Engineering Institute, Carnegie-Mellon University, Pittsburgh (1993)
8. ISO/IEC: ISO/IEC 9126-1:2001 Software engineering - Product quality - Part 1: Quality model (2001)
9. Kelly, D., Shepard, T.: A case study in the use of defect classification in inspections. In: Proceedings of the 2001 Conference of the Centre for Advanced Studies on Collaborative Research (2001)
10. Vijayaraghavan, G., Kaner, C.: Bug taxonomies: Use them to generate better tests. STAR EAST (2003)
11. Kaner, C., Falk, J., Nguyen, H.Q.: Testing computer software. Van Nostrand Reinhold (1993)
12. IEEE: IEEE Std 1044-1993: IEEE Standard Classification for Software Anomalies (1993)
13. Mariani, L.: A fault taxonomy for component-based software. Electronic Notes in Theoretical Computer Science 82(6), 55–65 (2003)
14. Beer, A., Peischl, B.: Testing of Safety-Critical Systems – a Structural Approach to Test Case Design. In: Safety-Critical Systems Symposium, SSS 2011 (2011)
15. Looker, N., Munro, M., Xu, J.: Simulating errors in web services. International Journal of Simulation Systems, Science & Technology 5, 29–37 (2004)
16. Marchetto, A., Ricca, F., Tonella, P.: An empirical validation of a web fault taxonomy and its usage for web testing. Journal of Web Engineering 8(4), 316–345 (2009)
17. Morell, L.J.: A theory of fault-based testing. IEEE Transactions on Software Engineering, 844–857 (1990)
18. Vallespir, D., Grazioli, F., Herbert, J.: A framework to evaluate defect taxonomies. In: Argentine Congress on Computer Science (2009)

19. Chillarege, R., Bhandari, I.S., Chaar, J.K., Halliday, M.J., Moebus, D.S., Ray, B.K., Wong, M.Y.: Orthogonal defect classification-a concept for in-process measurements. IEEE Transactions on Software Engineering 18(11), 943–956 (1992)
20. Zheng, J., Williams, L., Nagappan, N., Snipes, W., Hudepohl, J.M.: On the value of static analysis for fault detection in software. IEEE Transactions on Software Engineering, 240–286 (2006)
21. El Emam, K., Wieczorek, I.: The repeatability of code defect classifications. IEEE (1998)
22. Henningsson, K., Wohlin, C.: Assuring fault classification agreement-an empirical evaluation. IEEE (2004)
23. Falessi, D., Cantone, G.: Exploring feasibility of software defects orthogonal classification. Software and Data Technologies, 136–152 (2008)
24. Fenton, N.E., Ohlsson, N.: Quantitative analysis of faults and failures in a complex software system. IEEE Transactions on Software Engineering 26(8), 797–814 (2000)
25. Basili, V., Briand, L.C., Melo, W.L.: A validation of object-oriented design metrics as quality indicators. IEEE Transactions on Software Engineering 22(10), 751–761 (1996)
26. Andersson, C., Runeson, P.: A replicated quantitative analysis of fault distributions in complex software systems. IEEE Transactions on Software Engineering, 273–286 (2007)
27. de Grood, D.J.: TestGoal – Result-Driven Testing. Springer (2008)
28. IEC: S+ IEC 61508 Commented version (2010)
29. Vegas, S., Basili, V.: A characterisation schema for software testing techniques. Empirical Software Engineering 10(4), 437–466 (2005)
30. Runeson, P., Höst, M.: Guidelines for conducting and reporting case study research in software engineering. Empirical Software Engineering 14(2), 131–164 (2009)
31. Atos: SiTEMPPO, http://at.atos.net/de-at/solutions/sitemppo/ (accessed: June 10, 2012)
32. Spillner, A., Rossner, T., Winter, M., Linz, T.: Software Testing Practice: Test Management. Rocky Nook (2007)
33. Argyrous, G.: Statistics for research: with a guide to SPSS. Sage (2011)
34. Ramler, R., Klammer, C., Natschläger, T.: The Usual Suspects: A Case Study on Delivered Defects per Developer. In: ESEM 2010 (2010)
35. Ramler, R., Biffl, S., Grünbacher, P.: Value-Based Management of Software Testing. In: Value-Based Software Engineering, pp. 225–244 (2006)

A Transformation of Business Process Models into Software-Executable Models Using MDA[*]

Nuno Santos[1], Francisco J. Duarte[2],
Ricardo J. Machado[2], and João M. Fernandes[2]

[1] CCG - Centro de Computação Gráfica, Guimarães, Portugal
[2] Centro Algoritmi – Universidade do Minho, Braga/Guimarães, Portugal

Abstract. Traditional software development projects for process-oriented organizations are time consuming and do not always guarantee the fulfillment of the functional requirements of the client organization, and thus the quality of the resulting software product. To reduce the time spent for developing software and improve its quality, we adopt the inclusion of automation in some parts of the software development process. Thus, in this paper, we propose a model transformation approach to derive an executable model for the business processes of a given organization. We execute a mapping between processes (described with a business process execution language) and software components. We also propose a supporting software architecture based on an Enterprise Service Bus and on Java Business Integration, and we use an already defined methodology to execute the model transformation project.

Keywords: business process, JBI, model-driven architecture, MDA, enterprise service bus, ESB.

1   Introduction

Business Process Management (BPM) [1] is a discipline followed by organizations where business processes are required to exist, either by quality norms or by internal directives. Additionally, to cope with the requirements of the business processes, the software development process must properly support them [2,3].

In every organization, it is desirable to reduce the time and the cost to implement business processes in software systems. An aggravating factor during the development of software to support business processes is the diversity of applications used in a real-world business context, which causes integration problems.

We base our approach on the Model-Driven Architecture (MDA) [4] initiative from the OMG. We use two types of models: a Platform-Independent Model (PIM), representing the business process, and a Platform-Specific Model (PSM), allowing the PIM to be executed in software. With our business process-based

---

[*] This work is financed by Fundos FEDER through Programa Operacional Fatores de Competitividade – COMPETE e por Fundos Nacionais através da FCT – Fundação para a Ciência e Tecnologia no âmbito do Projeto: FCOMP-01-0124-FEDER-022674.

D. Winkler, S. Biffl, and J. Bergsmann (Eds.): SWQD 2013, LNBIP 133, pp. 147–167, 2013.
© Springer-Verlag Berlin Heidelberg 2013

approach, the complexity to implement in software the functional requirements derived from business processes is reduced because, among others, of the automation used in model transformations.

The effort to improve the quality of the resulting software product results in a better fulfillment of the functional requirements expressed in the business processes because of the diminishing gaps between business process models and software that our approach facilitates. In projects that adopt model-driven techniques, the model transformations are crucial for the overall success of the project, because they allow moving features from abstract models into software-executable ones, without loosing quality.

We use an Enterprise Service Bus (ESB), the Apache ServiceMix[1], for the PSM implementation. Typically, software solutions based on ESBs are loose-coupled, use reliable messaging mechanisms, and integrate different software technologies.

In this paper, we present a model-driven transformation approach for implementing business process models into software. The considered approach reduces the complexity to implement the business models into software, thus improving the overall quality of the information system. Our transformation approach is part of the Business Implementation Methodology (BIM) [5], which adopts reference models of business processes to provide business best practices to the client organization. However, it is important to note that the approach is sufficiently generic to be adopted in different methodological contexts.

In section 2, we present the state of art, namely the phases and states of the BIM, the MDA based model transformations, and the Apache ServiceMix ESB. In section 3, we propose a quantitative method to select the most appropriate language for modeling the business processes of a software development organization, including explicitly considering the specific staffing environment of a project. Section 3 also describes a case study, executed at Bosch Car Multimedia Portugal. Section 4 presents the business process model transformations, according to the MDA principles. We claim the adequateness of this approach to move from a business process model into a software-executable model, following BIM. First, we establish a correlation between the four states that business process models pass through in BIM, and the states of the PIM and the PSM defined in MDA. A business process model at the PIM level, ready to be transformed into software, is then established. The transformation process is completed by mapping platform-independent elements of the business process model into platform-specific ones. The resulting business process model at the PSM level is presented in section 5. In section 6, the conclusions of the work and proposals for future work are discussed.

2   Model-Driven Implementation of Business Processes

2.1   BIM

BIM is a methodology specially targeted for implementing in software the business processes of a given organization. This methodology proposes the use of

---

[1] http://servicemix.apache.org

best practices in the business domains and allows the customization of a business process according to the specific needs of the organization. It also promotes the building of a software solution with components of different technologies. BIM is composed of four phases (Fig. 1): the 'Selection' of the adequate generic business processes; the 'Definition' of the business processes to use; the 'Concretization' of the business processes into the software system; and the 'Implementation' in software of the various elements that compose the process.

Fig. 1. The four phases of the BIM ([5])

For each phase, BIM describes a corresponding state of the process framework (PF) (Fig. 2). The PF is an artifact of the BIM methodology representing the business processes at different implementation phases. Once the necessary requirements to complete each phase are fulfilled, a new state is assigned to the PF. The state of the PF is mainly defined by the state of the business process model. The four states defined in the methodology are 'Generic', 'Instantiated', 'Runnable' and 'Software Implemented'.

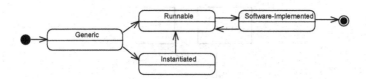

Fig. 2. The Process Framework states in BIM ([5])

The bi-directional state transformations from 'Runnable' and 'Software-Implemented' are possible by having latent runnable business processes moved into a software-implemented state and vice versa.

2.2 Model-Driven Architecture

In an MDA-guided project, after modeling the business processes, one can obtain a software-executable business process model; this is basically a transformation from a PIM into a PSM. For these kinds of transformations, the commonly accepted standard is OMG MOF Query/View/Transformation (MOF QVT) language [6]. It allows the creation of relations between models based in transformation rules. A transformation of PIM business processes, modeled by UML 2 Activity Diagrams, into a PSM in BPEL, through Regular Expression Language (REL) is demonstrated in [7]. The same kind of transformation is described in [8], using the ATLAS Transformation Language (ATL) [9]. A similar transformation is described using the Object Constraint Language (OCL) rules in [10].

Another kind of approach is proposed in [11], which begins by designing a CIM business process model in EPC, then continues by transforming the CIM business process model into a platform-independent one in BPMN, and finally obtains the platform-specific business process model in BPEL. Another approach is presented in [12], which describes a transformation of a CIM modeled in BPMN into a PIM modeled in UML, using either use case or class diagrams.

One of the characteristics of an MDA project is the clear separation between the specification of the system functionalities and the description of how the platform resources are used. An MDA project suggests the following:

- both the environment and the requirements of the system are specified (CIM);
- the system is specified independently from the platform that supports it (PIM);
- the platform is specified;
- a platform is chosen for the system;
- the specification of the system is transformed into specifications containing details of a specific platform (PSM).

The PSM is obtained from the transformation process that takes the PIM as the input. The transformation of the PIM into the PSM is accomplished by combining the PIM with specific details of the platform (Fig. 3).

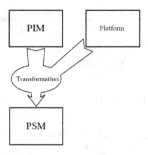

Fig. 3. Transformation from PIM into PSM [13]

Model marking (represented by the activities inside the circle of Fig. 4) is an approach, proposed by OMG for model transformations, that is performed by indicating the PIM elements that are transformed into PSM elements. In the mapping task, relationships between the PIM elements and the PSM one are established. For example, one can create a mapping that relates classes in the model with Java classes. Mappings must comply with the characteristics of both the business models and the programming language.

A PIM element can be related to several PSM elements, and, similarly, a PSM element can be related to several PIM elements. Once a mapping is defined, the execution of the transformation results in code generation.

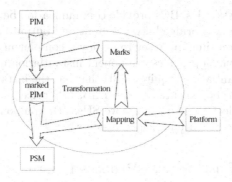

Fig. 4. Model transformation in MDA [13]

2.3 Apache ServiceMix

After model transformations, the resulting PSM model is a software-executable solution. This solution may require the integration with other applications. The integration can be achieved by using hubs or brokers as a middleware between applications. There are some commonly used approaches for enterprise application integration, like the Spring framework [14]. Spring provides a supporting software platform to facilitate the development and execution of business processes by using, among other capabilities, the inversion of control software pattern. Spring can support all the three common layers of a distributed application: user interface, business rules and entities, and the persistence of data. Integration can also be achieved by using ESB-based software frameworks, which allow developing distributed software in a loose-coupled manner. ESBs suggest the usage of a bus, instead of several brokers. Normally, ESBs contain normalized message routers to extract orchestrations from the different software components and place them in a central repository. Orchestrations can be edited without changing the different software components. ESB also include some others handy features, like reliable message buses to guarantee message exchange, or clustering to allow scalability. The core functionalities of an ESB are defined in [15] as being location transparency, transport protocol conversion, message transformation, message routing, message enhancement, security, monitoring, and management. A set of usage patterns for ESBs is presented in [16].

In this work, we use the Apache ServiceMix 4, which is a widely accepted, open source and open standards based ESB solution. ServiceMix may bring benefits to software development projects, like low cost and high quality of the resulting product. It is based on OSGi technology [17] and includes support to the Java Business Integration (JBI) specification [18]. JBI defines a framework for integrating applications, based in added components that interoperate through a method of normalized message exchanges. This method is based in the WSDL 2.0 specification of Message Exchange Patterns (MEPs) [19]. JBI defines two types of components: Service Engines (SEs) and Binding Components (BCs). SEs provide business and processing logic, for instance for processing data or to implementing business rules. BCs provide communication between the ESB and its exterior, working as a bridge between input and output data.

During compilation time, in order to deploy a component into ServiceMix, a Service Unit (SU), which provides component instantiation to the ESB, is used. Each SE or BC instantiation requires a SU that has the instantiated component definition. A SU can be executed in the ESB, if Service Assemblies (SAs) are used. A SA is a collection of one or more SUs. JBI components are unable to interpret SUs, unless SUs are packaged inside a SA.

3   Selection of a Business Process Language

To assure the quality of the software resulting from a business processes implementation project, it is advisable to select a business process language compatible with the organization where processes will run. To achieve that purpose, we include in this section a comparison between five business process modeling languages: BPMN [20], BPEL [21], XPDL [22], YAWL [23], and Coloured Petri Nets (CPNs) [24].

Several languages are reviewed in [25], namely by describing their technological characteristics and their strengths and weaknesses. Twelve business process languages are compared in [26], according to a representation model proposed in [27], to establish differences to their representational capabilities in the information system domain. The most common approach to compare the modeling capabilities of the business process languages is the set of workflow patterns defined in [28], which shows if the representation of a business process workflow is directly supported by the language.

The process of selecting a business process language should not be restricted to the comparison of the workflow patterns. An organization should not just be concerned with technological issues. Thus, based in [29], we propose that the selection process should be enlarged, being based on the three strategies of the triangle shown in Fig. 5: information systems, organizational, business.

The triangle relates the business strategy with the information system (IS) strategy and the organizational strategy. The selection process for the adopted business process language took into account the information systems strategic triangle. Since IS strategy is related to the definition of the implementation of the business processes in the IS solution, we base our comparison analysis on the workflows that each language supports. Regarding the organizational strategy, we base the comparison on the preferences of the development team. In what concerns the business strategy, our comparison takes into account a set of important aspects related with the alignment of the business process and the business strategy.

3.1   Information Systems Strategy

To compare the business process modeling languages by their added-value in the design and execution of the business processes, a study was performed based

Fig. 5. The information systems strategic triangle (adapted from [29])

in the language functionality, using the workflow patterns defined in [28]. The results of this comparison are described in Table 1. The table derives from a collection of previous comparisons, which can be seen in [30,23,31,32]. If the language supports directly the pattern, it is represented in the table by a "+". If it is supported indirectly, it is represented by a "0". Finally, if it is not supported at all, it is represented by a "-". The workflow patterns descriptions are not detailed in this paper.

Table 1. Workflow Patterns based Comparison

Nr.	Workflow Patterns	BPML	BPEL	XPDL	YAWL	CPN
1	Sequence	+	+	+	+	+
2	Parallel split	+	+	+	+	+
3	Syncronization	+	+	+	+	+
4	Exclusive choice	+	+	+	+	+
5	Simple merge	+	+	+	+	+
6	Multi-choice	-	+	+	+	+
7	Syncronizing merge	-	+	+	+	-
8	Multi-merge	0	-	-	+	+
9	Discriminator	-	-	+	+	-
10	Arbitrary cycles	-	-	+	+	+
11	Implicit termination	+	+	+	-	-
12	Multiple instance without syncronization	+	+	+	+	+
13	Multiple instances with a priori design time knowledge	+	+	-	+	+
14	Multiple instances with a priori runtime knowledge	-	-	-	+	-
15	Multiple instances without a priori runtime knowledge	-	-	-	+	-
16	Deferred choice	+	+	-	+	+
17	Interleaved parallel routing	-	0	-	+	+
18	Milestone	-	-	-	+	+
19	Cancel activity	+	+	-	+	0
20	Cancel case	+	+	-	+	-

3.2 Organizational Strategy

The need for this comparison lies in the fact that the organization's software development team members will be the users of the chosen business process language. It is then necessary to conclude which business process language is the best identified with the profile and skills of its users.

Surveys were performed at Bosch Car Multimedia Portugal to assess the technological skills of the development team, concerning the business process implementation. The aim was to establish a language comparison which can be considered as the most subjective part of our work. In our case, we have based the structure of the survey on a collection of key characteristics of the business process language. We have questioned the development team on their confidence on the following characteristics: workflow modeling, graph-based modeling, XML, Petri nets, pi-calculus, business process modeling languages and notations, service-oriented architecture (SOA), web services, protocols, brokers, ESBs, and threading. Additionally, the team was questioned about BPM issues. This complementary study was helpful to characterize the team regarding its knowledge on the business process to be implemented. Thus, the survey has included questions related to the knowledge and confidence of the team on:

- business processes, activities, key performance indicators, and strategic goals;
- BPM-based tools (e.g., BPM systems, EAI, ERP, CRM);
- business quality management (Total Quality Management, Six Sigma, Balanced ScoreCards);

The answers were given with a level of knowledge about the presented standards, valued from a minimum knowledge of 1 and ending with a maximum of 5. The presented values are relative results obtained by each of the languages in each of the surveys, resulting then the addition of all the surveys classification for each language. The results of the surveys are represented in Table 2 and allow to represent the confidence of the user on using each language (for instance, survey #1 is 76% confident on using BPML, 76% on using BPEL, etc.).

Table 2. Results of the conducted surveys

Survey	BPML	BPEL	XPDL	YAWL	CPN
#1	0.76	0.76	0.76	0.65	0.84
#2	0.70	0.80	0.79	0.94	0.99
#3	0.64	0.74	0.79	0.83	0.78
#4	0.59	0.60	0.79	0.57	0.59
#5	0.62	0.72	0.79	0.70	0.76
#6	0.67	0.88	0.87	0.90	0.95
#7	0.15	0.38	0.35	0.34	0.30
#8	0.34	0.53	0.59	0.49	0.48
#9	0.78	0.79	0.92	0.69	0.75
Total	**5.26**	**6.20**	**6.65**	**6.11**	**6.43**

3.3   Business Strategy

The last comparison relates to the specific aspects of the business environment, in this case referring to the software development industry. Some of these aspects were suggested by [33] as a basis for language supporting tools comparison. Other aspects are generally relevant concepts for using a language in a business process implementation projects (e.g., language maturity and implementation costs) with the goal of determining the added-value in using one of these languages in the organization. In Table 3 it is represented a set of characteristics, namely: language maturity, usability, existing language implementation tools, online tutorials available, if the language is translatable to another one, the language learning effort, transformability in object-oriented code, implementation costs, portability, interoperability, security, efficiency and data management, and the integration of the language in a ERP (e.g., SAP). In Table 3, for each language a set of business aspects was graded in a scale from 1 to 5. The value for each business aspect was given based on technical specifications and discussion forums. The classification was totally based on our subjective judgement after analyzing the information for each language.

Table 3. Relevant Business Aspects Considered for Comparison

Nr	Business Aspects	BPML	BPEL	XPDL	YAWL	CPN
1	Maturity	4	4	4	3	5
2	Usability	4	4	4	3	3
3	Existing Tools	4	5	3	2	5
4	Online Tutorials	5	5	3	3	5
5	Translatability	5	5	3	4	4
6	Learning Effort	4	4	4	3	3
7	Transformation to OO-code	2	5	3	2	2
8	Implementation costs	5	5	3	5	4
9	Portability	3	5	3	5	5
10	Interoperability	5	5	4	5	3
11	Security	5	5	3	5	3
12	Efficiency	4	5	2	5	5
13	Data Management	4	4	5	4	5
14	Integration in ERP SAP	5	5	3	4	3

After the comparisons of the three dimensions of the information system strategic triangle, the final results were collected in Table 4, where it shows the ordered level of suitability obtained by the languages, and the final result of each language is an overall value of all the executed comparisons.

The language with the best overall result was BPEL, because it was considered the most adequate in the business strategy and also with good classifications in information systems and organization strategies. For the #1 ranking of BPEL should be kept in mind the good result obtained for the particular software development team answering the survey. With different software development teams, the order of business strategies may vary.

Table 4. Final Comparison of the Business Process Languages

Strategy	BPML	BPEL	XPDL	YAWL	CPN
Information System	4	2	5	1	2
Organization	5	3	1	4	2
Business	2	1	5	4	3
Final	4	1	4	3	2

4 Transformation of Business Process Models

4.1 Correlation between BIM States and MDA Models

During a BIM-based business implementation project, it is possible to establish a correlation between the four states of BIM and the states of the PIM and the PSM models. The main characteristics of a business process model that is in the 'Generic', 'Instantiated' or 'Runnable' state are similar to the characteristics of a PIM, because the PF in these states do not include any reference to any platform. During the first three BIM phases ('Selection', 'Definition' and 'Concretisation'), it is not yet decided if the process will be software-executed or not. In fact, BIM suggests that, at the end of the 'Concretisation' phase, a process should be defined to be software implemented in the next phase of the methodology. However, it is also advisable to consider other alternatives, and at least one of the business processes may not require any software implementation. The 'Software-implemented' state corresponds to the PSM, since the process is executed using software, so it must obey specifications of the technological platform.

4.2 Business Process Model at the PIM Level

The third phase of BIM, 'Concretisation', defines a set of requirements the PF must respond in order to conclude that phase. The state of the PF at the end of the 'Concretisation' phase assures that the modeled PIM is ready to be transformed into a PSM. To reach that final state, we first adopt a business process reference model, as proposed in the 'Selection' phase. The use of process reference models in organizations assures adequately modeled business process, responding this way to concerns about business improvement and the quality of the resulting software system.

To exemplify the transformations across the BIM phases, we adopted a business process at the lowest representation level contained in UBK-RM (Unternehmensbereich Kraftfahrzeugausrüstung - Reference Model). UBK-RM is a reference model of the automotive divisions of the Bosch Group. One of the several second-level business processes that are part of the supply-chain process is chosen for the example. This second level process is decomposed hierarchically into some third-level business processes, before the representation at a more detailed level containing activities. We choose the product stock quantities record business process to exemplify our transformation technique due to its simplicity.

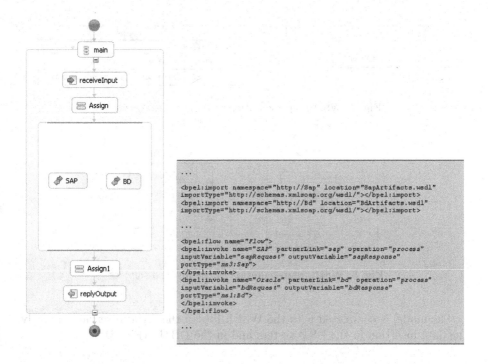

Fig. 6. The runnable Process Framework in BPEL

UBK-RM describes this process with the task that updates the product quantities in stock.

In the 'Definition' phase of BIM, the client describes his/her requirements for this process that has to update the stock of the new product and the stock of the consumed materials for the production of the new product. Thus, the business process has two activities. In the 'Concretisation' phase, the business process model is designed to fit in the information system of the organization. In this particular case, the business process inserts data into an ERP and into a Database Management System (DBMS). The business process was modeled in BPEL, as represented in Fig. 6.

The platform-independent business process illustrated in Fig 6 already embodies the characteristics described in BIM to allow their transformation into a PSM. In our modeled business process, the data received from the client is sent to two components of the information system in a parallel flow: to the ERP system and to the DBMS. The BPEL representation of the business process requires a corresponding WSDL code (Fig. 7) in order to execute correctly.

For this kind of approach, the relevant parts from the WSDL code are the data referring to the service ("lancQuantService"), the port ("LancQuantPort"), the port type ("LancQuant"), the operations ("process"), the input elements ("LancQuantRequest"), and the output elements ("LancQuantResponse").

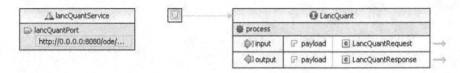

Fig. 7. WSDL representation of the business process

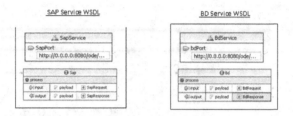

Fig. 8. WSDL representation of the invoked services

The model is completed with the WSDL files of the invoked services, namely the data insertion in the ERP system and in the DBMS (Fig. 8).

4.3 Description of the Platform

One of the required elements for a model transformation is the description of the platform. To define the required functionalities of the platform, BIM proposes the use of Orchestrated Business Objects (OBOs) [5]. For our business process, four OBOs are identified:

- the client component, which gives the command to initiate the process through its invocation;
- the BPEL component, with the process orchestration role, which defines the sequence of service invocations;
- the ERP component, which interfaces with the ERP to execute transactions;
- the DBMS component, which executes the record of the stock quantities.

Based on the ServiceMix JBI-based behavior, three BCs and three SEs are needed to execute the considered business process (Fig. 9). The need for the BCs is justified in order to have connections to the ERP system, to the DBMS, and the request from and the response to the client.

An adequate BC is one that allows the use of Web Services, because the characteristics of the SOAP protocol are more appropriate to send requests to and receive responses from a client. Regarding the connections to the ERP system and the DBMS, the implementation choice is based on the nonexistence of a SE with ERP functions and providing Java Database Connectivity (JDBC) [34]. For the latter two, the execution of the Web Service is made through SEs, a

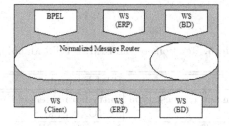

Fig. 9. Platform components to execute the process

"SAP SE" and a "DB SE". It is also required a BPEL execution engine SE. For that, we use the Apache Orchestration Director Engine (ODE) to execute the process workflow and to orchestrate the services. Apache ODE can be used as a SE inside ServiceMix.

4.4 PIM-to-PSM Mapping

In this subsection, we present the required mappings to achieve the PSM in the case study presented in the previous section. We show a set of simple transformation mappings, which can be implemented using a transformation language (e.g., MOF QVT or ATL) or a general-purpose language (e.g., Java or XSLT). For the composition of the transformation mappings, we use elements from the BPEL and the WSDL, the identified OBOs, and the typical JBI-based behavior of the ESB.

In what concerns the required transformations, the WSDL file that composes the PIM is the most used for the transformation, because in the BPEL file only few elements are marked for being transformed. In the BPEL file, the invoked activities, the imported namespaces, and the WSDL files are the elements to be transformed. Regarding the WSDL file, the elements to be transformed are the namespaces, portType, services, and ports. These elements, both from the BPEL and the WSDL files, derive the elements required by the JBI-based model, i.e., they are mapped into elements related to BCs, SEs, BPEL engine (Apache ODE), POJO classes, Java and BPEL and WSDL files.

The invoked BPEL activities expect the response of a service to a request. Therefore, the ESB component that provides this characteristic is the Service Engine. The namespaces, as well as the service data from the WSDL code - portType, service and port -, correspond to the identification data of the created SUs. The PIM-to-PSM mapping is accomplished by relating (SAP) invocations with the "SAP SE" OBO, and "BD" invocations with "BD SE" OBO. For better understanding, the relations are shown and described in Table 5, where each element of the PIM, related with the BPEL and the WSDL files, gives origin to at least one PSM element. In this architecture, PSM elements are a set of JBI-based ESB files (e.g., Java, XML, BPEL, WSDL). The marking of the elements is made from the relationships identified in the mapping (Fig. 10). Its purpose is to assist in the transformation task.

Table 5. Relations of the PIM to PSM Mapping

PIM Elements	PSM Elements
WSDL - Elements from the Request type	Entry parameters of the POJO class of the SU (CXF SEs)
WSDL - Service name ("LancQuantService", "SapService" e "BdService")	Name of the Web Service in the Java file belonging to the SU (CXF SEs)
	targetService of the SU (CXF BCs)
	Name of the service of the respective partnerLink in the SU (BPEL SE "ODE")
WSDL - Port type of the service ("LancQuant", "Sap" e "Bd")	targetInterface of the SU (CXF BCs)
WSDL - Port name of the service ("LancQuantPort", "SapPort" e "BdPort")	targetEndpoint of the SU (CXF BCs)
	Port name of the service of the respective partnerLink in the SU (BPEL SE "ODE")
BPEL - namespaces of the imported services	namespaces in the xbean.xml files and targetNamespace in the JAVA file of the SU (CXF SEs)
	namespaces of the WSDL files which are PartnerLinks in the BPEL file
BPEL - Imported WSDL files	wsdl of the SU (CXF BC), generated by the CXF SE
BPEL - "input" variable and WSDL - Request element	Entry parameters of the client Web Service
	"input" element from the Request of the WSDL
	"input" variable of the BPEL
BPEL - Invoke activity "SAP"	BPEL invoke activity "SAP SE"
BPEL - WSDL file which is "Sap" PartnerLink	Generated WSDL file from the CXF SE
BPEL - Invoke activity "BD"	BPEL invoke activity "BD SE"
BPEL - WSDL file which is "Bd" PartnerLink	Generated WSDL file from the CXF SE
BPEL - "output" variable and WSDL - Response element	Return parameters of the client Web Service
	"output" element from the Response of the WSDL
	"output" variable of the BPEL

PIM

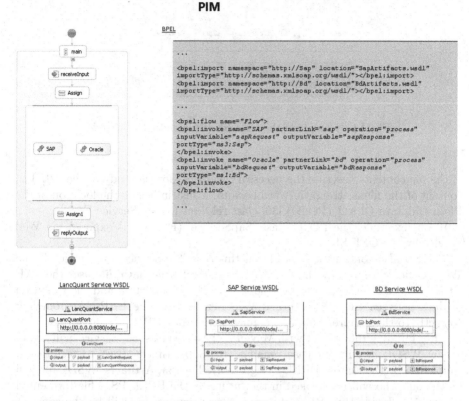

Fig. 10. Representation of the marked PIM elements to be transformed

5   Software-Executable Models at PSM Level

This section presents the technological implementation in the ServiceMix ESB of the model mapping described in the Section 4. We now detail the component deployment to assure that the ESB executes correctly.

5.1   Service Engines

The first step is to define SUs that, after being deployed into ServiceMix, are responsible for creating SEs. The choosen SE type is Apache CXF [35]. It is worthwhile to mention that this choice is related with the absence of a SE directly supporting the ERP functions. Our choice to overcome the absence is to use an interface based on Web Services as a solution. The behavior of the SU is described in a file, called 'xbean.xml', generated from a Maven[2] specific archetype for ServiceMix. The definition of the SU as a SE component is made in the first line of the file, where the namespace is defined (xmlns:cxfse=...), while the rest

---

[2] http://maven.apache.org

```
...
<bean class="pt.bosch.com.teste_cxfse_su.SapService" />
```

```
...
<bean class="pt.bosch.com.teste_cxfse_su.BdService" />
```

Fig. 11. Excerpts of the CXF SE (SAP and DB) SU code

of the file contents describe the necessary elements for the body of the SU. The content of the file is straightforward because it just indicates the location of the Plain Old Java Object (POJO) [36] class relevant for the Service Engine.

In our example, the POJO class 'SapService' (Fig. 11) is exposed via Web Service by the CXF SE.

The SU also contains a Java file, in this case 'SapService.java', which is the Web Service executed by the CXF SE. The 'SapService.java' file uses the SAP Java Connector (JCo) [37] to be able to execute the insertion and the reception of data between the CXF-exposed Web Service and the ERP SAP, obeying correctly to the requirements of a connection to an ERP.

After building the project with Maven 2, the Java class 'SapService' will create a new WSDL file, in our case renamed to 'SapArtifacts' (just to facilitate a simple use by the Eclipse BPEL Design tool). The 'SapArtifacts' WSDL file will be the one who will be invoked in the future by the BPEL PSM file (presented in Fig. 13). Inside that BPEL file, the chosen namespace will be the same as provided by the mapping.

Similarly to the implementation of the interface to the ERP recurring to a CXF SE with a Web Services, the definition of the SU containing the interface to the DB is accomplished in the same manner. The main difference of this SU to the ERP SU is just the definition of the POJO class, which will refer now to the 'BdService' class, the Web Service exposed by the CXF SE. The file 'BdService.java' will contain the code for the JDBC connection, and thus allowing the communication with the database. Also, in this case the WSDL file is generated by a Maven 2 build.

5.2   Binding Components

The configuration of a SU, originating a BC, is similar to the one originating an SE (see Section 5.1). The type of component is defined in the first line of the file 'xbean.xml' (xmlns:cfxbc=...). In this case, the component is a CXF BC, which communicates with the CXF SE, sending and receiving values from a Web Service. The element data that defines the BC must be filled in with the data from the PIMs BPEL and WSDL files, according to Table 5. This correct identification of the component endpoints required by the ESB is then the basis

```
...
<beans xmlns:cxfbc="http://servicemix.apache.org/cxfbc/1.0"
       ...
       xmlns:lq="http://LancQuant"
       ...
   <cxfbc:consumer wsdl="LancQuantArtifacts.wsdl"
                   targetEndpoint="lq:LancQuantPort"
                   targetService="lq:LancQuantService"
                   targetInterface="lq:LancQuant"/>
</beans>
```

```
...
<beans xmlns:cxfbc="http://servicemix.apache.org/cxfbc/1.0"
       ...
       xmlns:sap="http://Sap"
       ...
   <cxfbc:consumer wsdl="classpath:SapArtifacts.wsdl"
                   targetEndpoint="sap:SapPort"
                   targetService="sap:SapService"
                   targetInterface="sap:Sap"/>
</beans>
```

```
...
<beans xmlns:cxfbc="http://servicemix.apache.org/cxfbc/1.0"
       ...
       xmlns:bd="http://Bd"
       ...
   <cxfbc:consumer wsdl="classpath:BdArtifacts.wsdl"
                   targetEndpoint="bd:BdPort"
                   targetService="bd:BdService"
                   targetInterface="bd:Bd"/>
</beans>
```

Fig. 12. Excerpts of the CXF BC (Client, ERP, and DB) SU code

for a proper data routing inside the ESB. In Fig. 12 excerpts of the SU code for the client and the ERP BCs are presented.

Now that the transformation is completed, we present the implemented PSM. Fig. 13 shows the PSM representation in BPEL. In terms of visual notation, it does not suffer modifications related with the PIM represented in Fig. 6, due to the fact that the mapping 'SAP" to 'SAP SE' and 'BD' to 'BD SE' does not require any addition or removal of BPEL activities. An excerpt of the BPEL code containing the transformations suggested in Table 5 is also presented in Fig. 13.

The BPEL business process, to be interpreted by ODE, requires a XML file that describes the connections to the process 'PartnerLinks' so the process can be executable after deployment. In opposition to what happens with the other SUs, in which the 'xbean.xml' file defines its execution, the behavior of ODE is configured by a 'deploy.xml' file. After being correctly defined, the ODE SU is ready to be implemented in the framework. When all SUs are created, they are ready to be packaged in a SA and deployed into the ESB. Each SUs must be compiled and each one originates a compiled file. The definition of the SUs that are part of an SA is described in a 'pom.xml' file. The POM file, generated by a Maven 2 archetype, contains the general information of the project, like its name and location, as well as the identification of the components which will be used in the ESB. After being deployed into ServiceMix, the SUs contained in the

Fig. 13. Platform-specific business process in BPEL

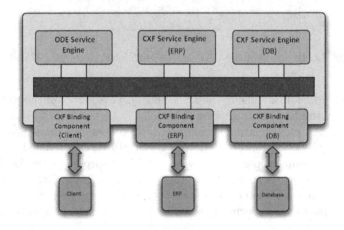

Fig. 14. PSM Final Model in ServiceMix according to JBI

SA will be used as JBI components. Depending of each 'xbean.xml' file, each SU originates either a SE or a BC. ServiceMix ESB is capable of identifying, by using the 'xbean.xml' files, what kind of component is defined in the SU. So, after their deployment, ODE SU becomes ODE SE, CXFSE SU becomes CXF SE and CXFBC SU becomes CXF BC.

The whole PSM, correctly deployed in ServiceMix, is presented in Fig. 14.

6   Conclusions and Future Work

In this paper we showed a set of techniques to use the OMG Model Driven Architecture approach in order to map business process descriptions into software systems. We proposed a mapping between the MDA platform-independent and platform-specific models, and business process models expressed by BPEL. The MDA Service Engines and Binding Components data are effectively obtained from the model transformation.

BPEL is directly executable in software, and can be used during all phases of a software development process for process-oriented organizations. These characteristics can reduce the time to implement a project, as well as the value that an organization receives from using BPEL due to the reduction of functional requirements misunderstandings and losses occurring during normal software development projects. We used a case study to better clarify these perceptions.

We also proposed an holistic technique to properly choose a business process modeling language supporting technology, business, and information systems strategies of an organization. As a result from our work, we defined also a mapping of the business process model states in order to define a correct passage from the third to the last phase of BIM.

The implementation of business process models recurring to ESBs software architectures provides an easy and sound composition of business process that require applications external to the ESB, in a standardized way.

A limitation of BPEL is that it only allows designing fully automatic business processes, i.e., business processes where all activity is executed in the computing domain. In many organizations, most of the business processes - eventually some core business processes - are not fully automatic, requiring human intervention to proceed with its flow of activities. BPEL4People [38], yet with little tool support, allows the addition of the representation of human tasks in BPEL process providing a basis to further develop the proposed techniques, now also interfacing humans. Additionally, we intend to further use the technique to choose an adequate business process modeling language in different organizations and project contexts in order to have a broader quantitative evaluation of the adequateness of each business process modeling language to the current organizations developing software.

References

1. Smith, H., Fingar, P.: Business Process Management – The Third Wave. Meghan-Kiffer Press (2002)
2. Fernandes, J., Duarte, F.: A reference framework for process-oriented software development organizations. Software and Systems Modeling 4(1), 94–105 (2005), doi:10.1007/s10270-004-0063-0
3. Fernandes, J.M., Duarte, F.J.: Using RUP for Process-Oriented Organisations. In: Bomarius, F., Iida, H. (eds.) PROFES 2004. LNCS, vol. 3009, pp. 348–362. Springer, Heidelberg (2004)
4. Kleppe, A., Warmer, J., Bast, W.: MDA Explained: The Model Driven Architecture – Practice and Promise. Addison-Wesley (2003)

5. Duarte, F.J., Machado, R.J., Fernandes, J.M.: BIM: A Methodology to Transform Business Processes into Software Systems. In: Biffl, S., Winkler, D., Bergsmann, J. (eds.) SWQD 2012. LNBIP, vol. 94, pp. 39–58. Springer, Heidelberg (2012)
6. OMG, Meta Object Facility (MOF) 2.0 Query/View/Transformation Specification, version 1.1. OMG Document Number, formal/2011-01-01 (2011)
7. Zhao, W., Hauser, R., Battacharya, K., Bryant, B., Cao, F.: Compiling business processes: untangling unstructured loops in irreducible flow graphs. International Journal on Web and Grid Services 2(1), 68–91 (2006), doi:10.1504/IJWGS.2006.008880
8. Bezivin, J., Hammoudi, S., Lopes, D., Jouault, F.: Applying MDA approach to B2B applications: a road map. In: Workshop on Model Driven Development (WMDD 2004), within the 18th European Conference on Object-Oriented Programming, ECOOP 2004 (2004)
9. Bezivin, J., Dupe, G., Jouault, F., Pitette, G., Rougui, J.: First experiments with the ATL model transformation language: Transforming XSLT into XQuery. In: 2nd OOPSLA Workshop on Generative Techniques in the Context of Model Driven Architecture (2003)
10. Koehler, J., Hauser, R., Sendall, S., Wahler, M.: Declarative techniques for model-driven business process integration. IBM Systems Journal 44(1), 47–65 (2005)
11. Lezoche, M., Missikoff, M., Tininini, L.: Business process evolution: a rule-based approach. In: 9th Workshop on Business Process Modeling, Development and Support, BPMDS 2008 (2008)
12. Rungworawut, W., Senivongse, T.: Using ontology search in the design of class diagram from business process model. In: Proc. International Conference on Computer Science (ICCS 2006), Vienna, Austria, pp. 165–170 (2006)
13. MDA Guide Version 1.0.1, OMG Std.
14. Johnson, R., Hoeller, J., Arendsen, A., Risberg, T., Sampaleanu, C.: Professional Java Development using the Spring Framework. John Wiley & Sons (2005)
15. Rademakers, T., Dirksen, J.: Open-Source ESBs in Action. Manning (2008)
16. Schmidt, M.-T., Hutchison, B., Lambros, P., Phippen, R.: The enterprise service bus: making service-oriented architecture real. IBM Systems Journal 44(4), 781–797 (2005), doi:10.1147/sj.444.0781
17. Alliance, T.O.: OSGi Service Platform Core Specification 4.2, The OSGi Alliance Std. 4, Rev. 4.2 (June 2009), http://www.osgi.org
18. Ten-Hove, R., Walker, P.: Java Business Integration (JBI) 1.0, Final release, Technical report, JSR 208 (2005)
19. Web Service Description Language (WSDL), W3C Std., http://www.w3.org/TR/wsdl
20. OMG, Business Process Modeling Notation (BPMN) 1.2, Object Management Group Std. OMG Document Number: formal/2009-01-03, Rev. 1.2 (January 2009), http://www.omg.org/spec/BPMN/1.2
21. Juric, M., Mathew, B., Sarang, P.: Business Process Execution Language for Web Services, 2nd edn. Packt Publishing (2006)
22. Shapiro, R.: XPDL 2.0: Integrating process interchange and BPMN. In: Workflow Handbook, pp. 183–194 (2006)
23. van der Aalst, W., ter Hofstede, A.: YAWL: yet another workflow language. Information Systems 30(4), 245–275 (2005), doi:10.1016/j.is.2004.02.002
24. Jensen, K., Kristensen, L.: Coloured Petri Nets - Modelling and Validation of Concurrent Systems. Springer (2009)

25. Ko, R., Lee, S., Lee, E.: Business process management (BPM) standards: a survey. Business Process Management Journal 15(5), 744–791 (2009), doi:10.1108/14637150910987937

26. Recker, J., Indulska, M., Rosemann, M., Green, P.: Business process modeling - a comparative analysis. Journal of the Association of Information Systems 10(4) (2009)

27. Wand, Y., Weber, R.: An ontological model of an information system. IEEE Transaction on Software Engineering 16(11), 1282–1292 (1990), doi:10.1109/32.60316

28. van der Aalst, W., ter Hofstede, A., Kiepuszewski, B., Barros, A.: Workflow patterns. QUT Technical report, FIT-TR-2002-02 (2002)

29. Pearlson, K., Saunders, C.: Managing and Using Information Systems, 4th edn. Wiley Publishing (2009)

30. van der Aalst, W., Dumas, M., ter Hofstede, A., Wohed, P.: Pattern-based analysis of BPML (and WSCI). QUT Technical report, FIT-TR-2002-05 (2002)

31. van der Aalst, W.: Patterns and XPDL: A critical evaluation of the XML process definition language. QUT Technical report FIT-TR-2003-06 (2003)

32. Mendling, J., Moser, M., Neumann, G.: Transformation of yEPC business process models to YAWL. In: ACM Symposium on Applied Computing (SAC 2006), pp. 1262–1266. ACM (2006), doi:10.1145/1141277.1141572

33. Helkiö, P., Seppälä, A., Syd, O.: Evaluation of Intalio BPM tool. Special Course in Information System Integration (2006)

34. van Haecke, B.: JDBC: Java Database Connectivity. John Wiley & Sons (1997)

35. A. CXF, Apache CXF: An open-source services framework (2012), http://cxf.apache.org

36. Fowler, M., Parsons, R., MacKenzie, J.: Pojo, an acronym for: Plain old java object (2000), http://www.martinfowler.com/bliki/POJO.html

37. Schuessler, T.: Developing applications with the SAP Java Connector (JCo). AraSoft, vol. 1 (2002), http://ARAsoft.de/

38. Kloppmann, M., Koenig, D., Leymann, F., Pfau, G., Rickayzen, A., von Riegen, C., Schmidt, P., Trickovic, I.: WS-BPEL extension for people – BPEL4people, Joint white paper, IBM and SAP (2005)

Aligning Domain-Related Models for Creating Context for Software Product Design*

Nuno Ferreira[1], Nuno Santos[2], Ricardo J. Machado[3], and Dragan Gašević[4]

[1] I2S Informática, Sistemas e Serviços S.A., Porto, Portugal
nuno.ferreira@i2s.pt
[2] CCG - Centro de Computação Gráfica, Campus de Azurém, Guimarães, Portugal
nuno.santos@ccg.pt
[3] Centro ALGORITMI, Escola de Engenharia, Universidade do Minho, Guimarães, Portugal
rmac@dsi.uminho.pt
[4] School of Computing and Information Systems, Athabasca University, Canada
dgasevic@acm.org

Abstract. A typical software product is developed so that it can fulfill the specific needs (problem that needs to be solved) within a given business domain, based on a proper product design context. Although, assuring an alignment between the technological developments with the business domain is a demanding task. With the purpose of clarifying the relations between the models that support the business and the software representations, we present in this paper a V-Model based approach to align the business domain requirements with the context for product design. This V-Model encompasses the models that support the initial definition of the project goals, expressed through organizational configurations, and the analysis and design of models that result in a process-level perspective of the system's logical architecture. Our approach adopts a process-level perspective with the intent to create context for product-level requirement elicitation. We present a case study as a demonstration and assessment of the applicability of our approach. Since the case study is extremely complex, we illustrate how to use the ARID method to evaluate the obtained process-level architecture.

Keywords: Software Engineering, Requirements Engineering, Model Alignment, Logical Architectures.

1 Introduction

One of the top concerns of information technologies (IT) managers for almost thirty years relates to software and the business domain alignment [1]. The importance of aligning the software with domain specific needs for the purpose of attaining synergies and visible success is a long-running problem with no visible or deterministic solution.

* This work is financed by project ISOFIN (QREN 2010/013837), Fundos FEDER through Programa Operacional Fatores de Competitividade – COMPETE and Fundos Nacionais though FCT – Fundação para a Ciência e Tecnologia (FCOMP-01-0124-FEDER-022674).

D. Winkler, S. Biffl, and J. Bergsmann (Eds.): SWQD 2013, LNBIP 133, pp. 168–190, 2013.
© Springer-Verlag Berlin Heidelberg 2013

There are many questions concerning this subject, going from how to align several strategic components of an organization with the necessary maturity or how specific domain needs and software that supports the domain are aligned with each other. The perspective on domain specific needs with software alignment has changed along the years. Initially, alignment meant relating specific domain needs with supporting software plans. Later, the concept evolved to include business and software strategies, business needs and information system priorities. This created the need for aligning business models (as a rationale for how the organizations create, deliver and capture value for a given business) with the underlying information system (people and software solutions) that is designed to support part or whole of the business model.

One of the possible representations of a software solution is its logical architecture, resulting from a process of transforming business-level and technological-level (of any given domain) decisions and requirements into a representation (model). A model can be seen as a simplified view of reality, and possesses five key characteristics: abstraction, understandability, accuracy, predictiveness, and inexpensiveness [2]. This representation is fundamental and mandatory to analyze and validate a system but is not enough for achieving a full transformation of the requirements into a model able to implement stakeholders' decisions. It is necessary to promote an alignment between the logical architecture and other supporting models, like organizational configurations, products, processes, or behaviors.

An organization is about people. Stakeholders are responsible for the decision-making processes that influence the organization's strategy at any given level under analysis [3]. At the same time, the stakeholders also influence the organization's software architecture and systems. Aligning domain specific needs with the way that software solutions are organized is a task that must be accounted for and whose results are not easily, or at all, measurable.

Our approach is based on the premise that there is no clearly defined context for eliciting product requirements within a given specific domain. As an example for a situation where there is no clearly defined context, we present the ISOFIN project [4]. This project is executed in a consortium comprising eight entities (private companies, public research centers and universities), making the requirements elicitation and the definition of a development roadmap difficult to agree. The initial request for the project requirements resulted in mixed and confusing sets of misaligned information. Even when a requirement found a consensus in the consortium, all the stakeholders did not easily understand the intended behavior or its definition. Our proposal of adopting a process-level perspective was agreed on and, based on the knowledge that each consortium member had of the intended project results, the major processes were elicited and a first approach to a logical (process-level) architecture was made. After execution of the process-level perspective, it was possible to gather a set of information that the consortium is sustainably using to evolve to the traditional (product-level) development scenario. Elicited requirements in a process-level perspective describe the processes in a higher level of abstraction, making them understandable by the consortium key decision-taking members (business stakeholders). At the same time, by defining the major activities, their relations and flows, the definitions and intended behavior of the system, expressed in the architecture that results from the process-level 4SRS method, describe the system to the consortium key technological developers (technological stakeholders).

Our approach results in a "Vee" Model-based adaptation (V Model) [5], which suggests a roadmap for product design based on domain specific needs. The model requires the identification of those domain specific needs and then, by successive models derivation, it is possible to transit from a domain level perspective to a software (IT) level perspective and at the same time, aligns the requirements with the derived models, reducing the gap between business and technological stakeholders.

This paper is structured as follows: section 2 presents the related work associated with our work; section 3 presents our V-Model representation to promote domain and software; section 4 includes a case study and details the pertinence of using the chosen presented models for creating context to product design. It also explains how to proceed from one model to another and includes discussions, comparison with the related work and an assessment overview of the presented approach and its validation through ARID; section 6 presents our conclusions and future work.

2   Related Work

A typical software development project is coordinated so that the resulting product properly aligns with the domain-specific (business) model intended by the leading stakeholders. As an economical plan for the organization or for a given project, the business model contributes for eliciting the requirements by providing the product's required needs in terms of definitions and objectives. By "product" we mean applications that must be computationally supported. In situations where organizations focused on software development are not capable of properly eliciting requirements for the software product, due to insufficient stakeholder inputs or some uncertainty in defining a proper business model, a process-level requirements elicitation is an alternative approach. The process-level requirements assure that organization's business needs are fulfilled. However, it is absolutely necessary to assure that product-level (software-related) requirements are perfectly aligned with process-level requirements, and hence, are aligned with the organization's domain-specific requirements. In this section, we chose to refer to other author's work related to ours in the diverse topics that integrate our approach: business and IT alignment, governance, alignment of requirements with system specifications, the process-level perspective, process architectures and the models that can be used to describe requirements and help build the context for product elicitation.

An approach that enacts the alignment between domain-specific needs and software solutions, is the goal oriented approach GQM+Strategies (Goal/Question/Metric + Strategies) [6]. The GQM+Strategies approach uses measurement to link goals and strategies on all organizational levels. This approach explicitly links goals at different levels, from business objectives to project operations, which is critical to strategic measurement. Applying GQM+Strategies makes easier to identify goal relationships and conflicts and facilitates communication for organizational segments. Another goal-oriented approach is the Balanced Scorecard (BSC) [7]. BSC links strategic objectives and measures through a scorecard in four perspectives: financial, customer, internal business processes, and learning and growth. It is a tool for defining strategic goals from multiple perspectives beyond a purely financial focus.

Another approach, COBIT [8], is a framework for governing and managing enterprise IT. It provides a comprehensive framework that assists enterprises in achieving their objectives for the governance and management of enterprise IT. It is based on five key principles: (1) meeting stakeholder needs; (2) covering the enterprise end-to-end; (3) applying a single, integrated framework; (4) enabling a holistic approach; and (5) separating governance from management. These five principles enable the enterprise to build an effective governance and management framework that optimizes information and technology investment and use for the benefit of stakeholders.

In order to represent the intended aligned system specification we use models. It is recognized in software engineering that a complete system architecture cannot be represented using a single perspective or model [9, 10]. Using multiple viewpoints, like logical diagrams, sequence diagrams or other artifacts, contributes to a better representation of the system and, as a consequence, to a better understanding of the system. Some architecture views can be seen in the works of Clements *et al.* [11], Hofmeister *et al.* [12] and Krutchen [10]. Krutchen's work refers that the description of the architecture can be represented into four views: logical, development, process and physical. The fifth view is represented by selected use cases or scenarios. Zou and Pavlovski [13] add another extra view, the control case view, that complements the use case view to complete requirements across the collective system lifecycle views.

Since the term *process* has different meanings depending on the context, in our process-level approach we acknowledge that (1) real-world activities of a software production process are the context for the problem under analysis and, (2) in relation to a software model context [14], a software process is composed of a set of activities related to software development, maintenance, project management and quality assurance. For scope definition of our work, and according to the previously exposed acknowledgments, we characterize the process-level perspective by (1) being related to real world activities, including business, and when related to software (2) those activities encompass the typical software development lifecycle. Typically, product-level approaches promote the functional decomposition of systems models. Our approach is characterized by using refinement (as one kind of functional decomposition) and integration of system models. Activities and their interface in a process can be structured or arranged in a process architecture [15].

The process architecture represents a fundamental organization of service development, service creation, and service distribution in the relevant enterprise context [16]. Designing a software architecture provides a more accurate definition of the requirements. There are several approaches to supporting the proper design of software architectures, like FAST [17], FORM [18] or KobrA [19]. These all relate to the product-level perspective. In a process-level perspective, Tropos [20] is a methodology that uses notions of actor, goal and (actor) dependency as a foundation to model early and late requirements, architectural and detailed design. Machado *et al.* present the 4SRS (Four-Step-Rule-Set) method for architecture design based on requirements. 4SRS is usually used in a product-level perspective [21], but it also supports a process-level perspective [22, 23]. The result of the application of the 4SRS method is a logical architecture. Logical architectures can be faced as a view of a system composed by a set of problem-specific abstractions supporting functional requirements [10].

The defined and derived models suggested by our approach, used alone and un-aligned with each other, are of a lesser use to organizations and stakeholders. Our approach begins in a domain-specific perspective, by defining the organizational configurations that represent major interactions, at a very high-level, in the chosen domain, and ends with a technological view of the system. From one perspective to the other, alignment must be assured. The alignment we refer to relates to domain-specific and software alignment [24], and in our case, where the domain-specific needs must be instantiated into the creation of context for proper product design.

A possible point of failure in achieving the intended alignment relates to the lack of representativeness of the necessary requirements for expressing domain-specific needs. According to Campbell *et al.* [3], the activities that support the necessary information for creating context for requirements elicitation are not explicitly defined or even promoted. Also, existing approaches to designing software architecture do not support any specific technique for requirements elicitation in a process-level perspective; rather, they use the information delivered by an adopted elicitation technique. Typical (product-oriented) elicitation techniques may not be able to properly identify the necessary requirements within a given context creating an opportunity for our approach to define the process that support the derivation of models with the purpose of creating context for product design. With the case study described in this paper we demonstrate that firstly adopting a process-level perspective allows for better understanding of the project scope and then support the creation of context for the elicitation of requirements of the product to be developed.

3   An Approach to Domain and Software Models Alignment

In this section, we present our approach, based on successive and specific models generation. As models, we use Organizational Configurations (OC) [25], *A-Type* and *B-Type* Sequence Diagrams [26], use cases and process-level logical architecture diagrams. All these models are briefly described in this section and properly exemplified in the case study section of this paper, where more detail is given on how to derive a model from the previous models.

Traditional development processes can be referenced using the Royce's waterfall model [27] that includes five typical phases in its lifetime: Analysis, Design, Implementation, Test and Deployment. Defining a simplified macro-process for supporting the requirement elicitation in a process-level approach must take into account the waterfall model lifecycle for a project. We frame our proposed V-Model approach in the Analysis phase of the lifecycle model, as depicted in Fig. 1.This simplified development macro-process based on the waterfall model uses the V-Model generated artifacts for eliciting requirements that, in a process-level approach, are used as input for the traditional 4SRS usage (product level) [21]. The product-level 4SRS promotes the transition from the Analysis to the Design phase.

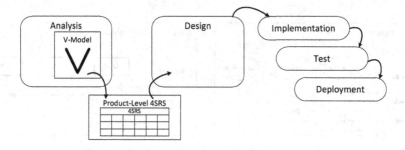

Fig. 1. Framing the V-Model representation in the development macro-process

The OC model is a high-level representation of the activities (interactions) that exist between the business-level entities of a given domain. Fig. 2 shows an example of the aspect of an OC, with two activity types, each with a role and two interactions.

The set of interactions are based on domain-specific requirements (such as business) and, in conjunction with the entities and the stakeholders, are represented with the intention of describing a feasible scenario that fulfills a domain-specific business vision. In what concerns OCs characterization for the purpose of our work, each configuration must contain information on the performed activities (economical [22] or non-economical [28]), the several professional profiles (actors and skills) that participate in the activity execution and also the exchange of information or artifacts. There must be defined as much OCs as the ones required to express all the major interactions defined by the business stakeholders that relate to the intended system.

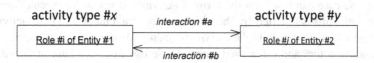

Fig. 2. Organizational Configuration

Our approach uses a UML stereotyped sequence diagram representation to describe interactions in early analysis phase of system development. These diagrams are presented in this paper as *A-Type* Sequence Diagrams. Another stereotyped sequence diagram, called *B-Type* Sequence Diagrams, allows for deriving process sequences represented by the sequence flows between the logical parts depicted in the logical architecture. One must assure that a process' sequences modeled in *B-Type* Sequence Diagrams depict the same flows as the ones modeled in *A-Type* Sequence Diagrams, as well as being in conformity with the interactions between architectural elements (AEs) depicted in the logical architecture associations. An AE is a representation of the pieces from which the final logical architecture can be built. This term is used to distinguish those artifacts from the components, objects or modules used in other contexts, like in the UML structure diagrams. An example of *A-Type* and *B-Type* Sequence Diagrams can be found in Fig. 3.

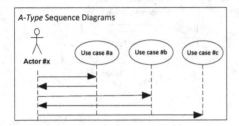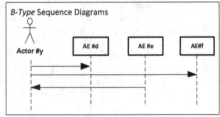

Fig. 3. A- and *B-Type* Sequence Diagrams

The generated models and the alignment between the domain specific needs and the context for product design can be represented by a V-Model as seen on Fig. 5. The V-Model representation [5] provides a balanced process representation and, simultaneously, ensures that each step is verified before moving to the next. In this V-Model, the models that assemble it are generated based on the rationale and in the information existing in previously defined models, i.e., *A-Type* diagrams are based on OCs, use cases are based on *A-Type* diagrams, the logical architecture is based on the use case model, and *B-Type* diagrams comply with the logical architecture.

A-Type Sequence Diagrams can be gathered and afterwards used as an elicitation technique for modeling the use cases. It can be counterintuitive to consider that use case diagrams can be refinements of sequence diagrams. It is possible if we take into consideration that the scenarios expressed in the *A-Type* Sequence Diagrams are built using the use-case candidates in the form of activities that will be executed and must be computationally supported by the system to be implemented. These activities in form of use cases are placed in the *A-Type* Sequence Diagram and associated with the corresponding actors and other used cases. These use cases are later arranged in use case diagrams after redundancy is eliminated and proper naming is given. The flow expressed by the sequences creates the rationale for discovering the necessary use cases to complete the process.

Use cases are modeled and textually described and used as input for the 4SRS. The execution of the 4SRS [23] results in a logical architecture with a direct relation between the process-level use cases assured by the method's execution. Due to that, the logical architecture is derived, in a process- or in a product-level perspective, using the use case information to create AEs and their associations, in a properly aligned approach. The product level perspective is described in [21] and the process-level perspective in [22, 23]. The process-level perspective imposes a different rationale to the method's execution. It is not our intention to describe the 4SRS method application. That is thoroughly done in the literature [21-23] and we use it as described in those works. For the sake of understandability, we only present a brief paragraph of the method's structure and application.

Step 1 - architectural element creation		Step 2 - architectural element elimination				2v - architectural element					Step 3 - packaging & aggregation	Step 4 - architectural element association	
		2i - use case classification	2ii - local elimination	2iii - architectural element naming	2iv - architectural element description	represented by	represent	2vi - global elimination	2vii - architectural element renaming	2viii - architectural element specification		4i - Direct Associations	4ii - UC Associations
{U2.1.}		cd											
{AE2.1.c}	Generated AE		T	IBS Analysis Pre-Start Decision	Browse the IBS and SBS Catalogs searching already existing IBS and SBS information with the intent of analyzing if the current business need isn't already fulfilled and if the ISOFIN Platform infrastructure supports the new implementation. ...	{AE2.1.c}	{AE1.11.i} {AE2.2.c} {AE2.5.c}	T	Access Remote Catalogs	Allows browsing the available catalogs in the ISOFIN Platform (ISOFIN Application, IBS, and SBS). The user (Business User or the IBS Business Analyst) is allowed to search for information regarding the desired artifact and to select artifacts to use on his purposes.	{P2.2} IBS Analysis Decisions	{AE1.11.d1} {AE1.11.d2} {AE2.1.d}	{AE2.3.1.i} {AE2.3.2.i} {AE2.10.i} {AE2.11.i} {AE3.3.i} {AE3.7.1.i}
{AE2.1.d}	Generated AE		T	ISOFIN Functionalities Requirements List	Set of functional and non-functional requirements needed to fulfil identified business needs, intended system functionalities and all the constraints that may restrict design and implementation.	{AE2.1.d}		T	ISOFIN Functionalities Requirements List		{P2.1} IBS Requirements	{AE2.1.c}	
{AE2.1.i}		F											

Fig. 4. Tabular Transformation of the 4SRS Method

The 4SRS method is organized in four steps to transform use cases into architecture elements: Step 1 (architectural element creation) creates automatically three kinds of AEs for each use case: an *i-type* (interface), *c-type* (control) and *d-type* (data); Step 2 (architectural element elimination) removes redundancy automatically create architectural elements, redundancy in the requirements passed by the use cases, and promotes the discovery of hidden requirements; Step 3 (architectural element packaging & aggregation) semantically groups architectural elements in packages and also allows to represent aggregations (of, for instance, existing legacy systems); and Step 4 (architectural element association) whose goal is to represent associations between the remaining architectural elements.

According with the previously described, the 4SRS method takes use cases representations (and corresponding textual descriptions) as input and (by recurring to tabular transformations) creates a logical architectural representation of the system. We present a subset of the tabular transformations in Fig. 4. These tabular transformations are supported by a spreadsheet and each column has its own meaning and rules. Some of the steps have micro-steps; some micro-steps can be completely automatized. Tabular transformations assure traceability between the derived logical architecture diagram and the initial use case representations. At the same time it makes possible to adjust the results of the transformation to changing requirements. Tabular transformations are thoroughly described in [23, 29].

As suggested by the V-Model represented in Fig. 5, the models placed on the left hand side of the path representation are properly aligned with the models placed on the right side, i.e., *B-Type* Sequence Diagrams are aligned with *A-Type* Sequence Diagrams, and the logical architecture is aligned with the use case model. Alignment between the use case model and the logical architecture is assured by the correct application of the 4SRS method. The resulting sets of transformations along our V-Model path provide artifacts properly aligned with the organization's business needs (which are formalized through Organization Configurations).

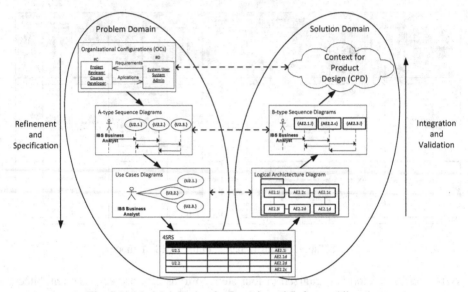

Fig. 5. V-Model Adaption for Domain and Software Alignment

The V-Model representation promotes the alignment between the models on the problem domain and the models on the solution domain. The presented models are created in succession, by manipulating the information that results from one to make decisions on how to create the other. In the descending side of the V-Model (left side of the V), models created in succession represent the refinement of requirements and the creation of system specifications. In the ascending side (right side of the V), models represent the integration of the discovered logical parts and their involvement in a cross-side oriented validating effort.

To assess the V-Model approach, we present a process regarding our real case study, the ISOFIN project, as an example. The process under analysis, called "Create IBS", deals with the creation of a new Interconnected Business Service (IBS). The inter-organizational relations required to create a new IBS are described under a new OC. The definition of activities and actors required to create a new IBS are described in an *A-Type* Sequence Diagram. This diagram provides detail on required functionalities in order to create an IBS, formally modeled in use cases. Use cases are used as input for a transformation method and the process-level logical architecture is derived. A *B-Type* Sequence Diagram allows for validation of the logical architecture required to create an IBS and also validates the requirement expressed in the corresponding *A-Type* Sequence Diagram. After the generation of these models, we assure that the "Create IBS" process is aligned with the stakeholder's needs.

4   Case Study: The ISOFIN Project

We assess the applicability of the proposed approach with a case study that resulted from the process-level requirements elicitation in a real industrial case: the ISOFIN project (Interoperability in Financial Software) [4]. This project aims to deliver a set of coordinating services in a centralized infrastructure, enacting the coordination of independent services relying on separate infrastructures. The resulting ISOFIN platform, allows for the semantic and application interoperability between enrolled financial institutions (Banks, Insurance Companies and others), as depicted in Fig. 6.

The ISOFIN project encompasses eight institutions, ranging from universities, research centers and private software development companies for the bank and insurance domains. The stakeholders of this group had different backgrounds and expectations regarding the project outcome. These differences resulted in the lack of definitions for the requirements that the project's applications would support and even to a proper definition of a business model that the organizations that participate in the project would pursue.

If there is no agreed or even a defined business model, it is not possible to define the context for the requirements elicitation of the products (applications) to be developed. There is, however, communality in the speech of the stakeholders. They all contain hints on the kind of activities that the intended products would have to support – that is, they got beforehand an idea of the processes that the ISOFIN platform applications were required to computationally support.

The authors of this paper proposed a process-level approach to tackle the problem of not having a defined context for product design and researched on the models that the stakeholders agreed on to support the knowledge they had of the process-level requirements – Organizational Configurations, *A-Type* Sequence Diagrams and Use Cases. After executing the 4SRS method, properly adjusted to handle the process-level perspective we were able to deliver a process-level logical architecture representation of the processes that are intended to be computationally supported by the applications to be developed. This approach created the context for product design, since the authors were able to identify the primary constructors that would support the processes. *B-Type* Sequence Diagrams appeared seamlessly in the process. They represented the scenarios depicted in the *A-Type* Sequence Diagrams and also contributed to the validation of the process-level logical architecture diagram. These two aspects will be detailed later.

The primary constructors that were identified correspond to the two main service types that the global ISOFIN architecture relies on: Interconnected Business Service (IBS) and Supplier Business Service (SBS). IBSs concern a set of functionalities that are exposed from the ISOFIN core platform to ISOFIN Customers. An IBS interconnects one or more SBSs and/or IBSs exposing functionalities that relate directly to business needs. SBSs are a set of functionalities that are exposed from the ISOFIN Suppliers production infrastructure. Fig. 6 encompasses the primary constructors related to the execution of the platform (IBS, SBS and the ISOFIN Platform) available in the logical representations of the system: in the bottom layer there are SBSs that connect to IBSs in the ISOFIN Platform layer and the later are connected to ISOFIN Customers.

There are other constructors that were identified by using the V-Model approach and that support the operations for the execution of the ISOFIN Platform. These other constructors are, for instance, Editors, Code Generators, Subscriptions Management

Systems, and Security Management Systems. These constructors support the creation and the operation of the primary constructors (IBS, SBS and ISOFIN Platform). The process-level architecture, later presented, depicts their interactions, major elements and organization.

By adopting the process-level perspective we were able to create a system's representation that supports the elicitation of the process-level requirements from the stakeholders. This approach also allowed creating the context for product design by representing the processes that must be supported by the applications to be developed. The next sections detail the V-Model process and exemplify the construction of the adopted models in real case study situations.

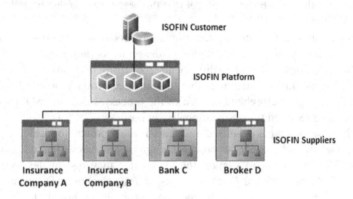

Fig. 6. Desirable Interoperability in ISOFIN

4.1   Alignment between Organizational Configurations and Interactions

In a process-level approach, in opposition to the product-level approach, the characterization of the intended system gives a different perspective on the organizational relations and interactions. When defining a specific domain context, we consider that interactions between actors and processes constitute an important issue to be dealt. This section focuses on characterizing those interactions by using three different levels of abstraction, as depicted in Fig. 7: OCs represents the first level; different types of Stereotyped UML Sequence Diagrams, presented as *A-Type* and *B-Type* Diagrams (later described) represent the other two.

Today's business is based on inter-organizational relations [25], having an impact on an organization's business and software strategy [30]. We model a set of OCs to describe inter-organizational relations as a starting point to the definition of the domain-specific context. An OC models a possible inter-organizational relation, at a very high-level of abstraction and not considering lower-level processes and/or actors involved in the relation. For better deriving the domain-specific context, it is advisable to model as many OCs as required to describe, at least, the main relations as depicted by the stakeholders' domain-specific needs.

We present an example of an OC, for the purpose of assessing our approach, which has been characterized and applied in our case study (the ISOFIN project). Firstly, it is necessary to define the types of activities performed in the domain-specific context. By analyzing the types of activities, the execution of an IBS within a domain activity regards #A activities, while the creation of a new IBS regards #B activities:

(1) #A Activities – Financial Domain Business Activities: these are the delivered domain business activities regarding the financial institutions.

(2) #B Activities – ISOFIN Platform Services Integration: these are the activities that relate to the integration of supplier services.

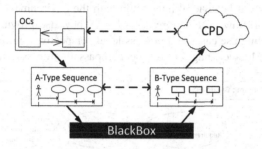

Fig. 7. Organizational Configurations and Interactions Alignment

In order to characterize an organization, it is required to relate a set of roles to the performed activity type. Finally, the interactions between organizations are specified. In Fig. 8, it is possible to depict the required relations between organizations in order to create an IBS and providing it to ISOFIN Customers. The professional profiles and the exchange of information between organizations are not relevant in this paper, so only brief and simple examples are presented and only the types of activities are described.

Fig. 8. Organizational Configuration Example

In an early analysis phase, we need to define the relations between activities and actors, defined through interactions in our approach. Interactions are used during the more detailed design phase where the precise inter-process communication must be set up according to formal protocols [31]. An interaction can be displayed in a UML sequence diagram.

Traditional sequence diagrams involve system objects in the interaction. Since modeling structural elements of the system is beyond the scope of the user requirements, Machado *et al.* propose the usage of a stereotyped version of UML sequence diagrams that only includes actors and use cases to validate the elicited requirements at the analysis phase of system development [26]. We create *A-Type* Sequence Diagrams, as shown in Fig. 9. In the example, we present some of the activities and actors required to create a new IBS. *A-Type* Sequence Diagrams also models the message exchange among the external actors and use cases (later depicted in Fig. 13).

In Fig. 9 we depict sequential flows of process-level use cases that refer to the required activities for creating an IBS. These activities are executed within #B activities, after receiving domain-specific requirements from ISOFIN Customers and before delivering IBS (interactions depicted in the OC of Fig. 8).

The usage of *A-Type* Sequence Diagrams is required to gather and formalize the main stakeholder's intentions, which provide an orchestration and a sequence of some proposed activities. *A-Type* sequence diagrams realize the roles presented within an OC and instantiates them into activities. *A-Type* Sequence diagrams allow a pure functional representation of behavioral interaction with the environment and are appropriate to illustrate workflow user requirements [26]. They also provide information for defining and modeling use cases at a process-level perspective and frame the activities execution in time. Modeled diagrams must encompass all processes and actors.

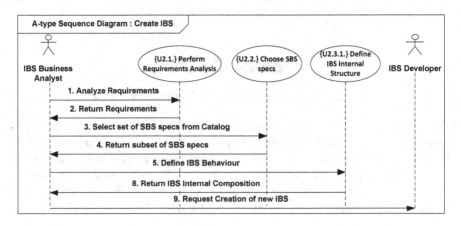

Fig. 9. A-Type Sequence Diagram

One of the purposes of creating a software logical architecture is to support the system's functional requirements [10]. It must be assured that the derived logical architecture is aligned with the domain-specific needs. On the one hand, the execution of a software architecture design method (e.g., 4SRS) provides an alignment of the logical architecture with user requirements (presented in section 4.3). On the other hand, it is necessary to validate if the behavior of the logical architecture is as expected. So, in a later stage, after deriving a logical architecture, to analyze the sequential process flow of AEs (as shown in Fig. 10), we adopt different stereotype of UML sequence diagrams, where AEs (presented in the logical architecture), actors and packages (if justifiable) interactions are modeled. In Fig. 10, we present the same activities concerning creating an IBS but in a lower level of abstraction, closer to product design. *B-Type* Sequence Diagrams differ from the traditional ones, since they model the exchange of information between actors and logical AEs, thus they are still modeled at the system level.

Sequence flows between AEs are only possible if such a path is allowed within the logical architecture. *B-Type* Sequence Diagrams are used to validate the derived logical architecture, through the detection of missing architecture elements and/or associations to execute a given process within the derived logical architecture.

B-Type Sequence Diagrams can also be used to validate sequences in the previously modeled *A-Type* Sequence Diagrams, since the sequence flows between use cases must comply with the related sequence flows between AEs in *B-Type* diagrams. This validation is considered essential in our V-Model process. There must be modeled as many *A-Type* sequence diagrams as necessary to fully represent the business context detail. *B-Type* sequence diagrams must be modeled to match corresponding business requirements given in *A-Type* sequence diagrams and there must be enough *B-Type* sequence diagrams to ensure that all AEs of the logical architecture are used.

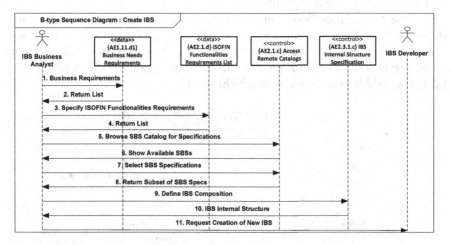

Fig. 10. B-Type Sequence Diagram

4.2 An UML Metamodel Extension for *A-Type* and *B-Type* Sequence Diagrams

The usage of *A-Type* and *B-Type* sequence diagrams in our approach is perfectly harmonized with UML sequence diagram's original semantics, as described in the UML Superstructure [31]. We present in the left side of Fig. 11 some of the classes of the UML metamodel regarding sequence diagrams (in the *Interactions* context of the UML Superstructure). As *A-Type* and *B-Type* sequence diagrams differ from typical sequence diagrams in the participants of the interactions, the usage of these diagrams regards the *Lifeline* class. A lifeline represents an individual participant in the *Interaction*. The *Lifeline* notation description presented in the UML Superstructure details that the lifeline is described by its <connectable-element-name> and <class_name>, where <class_name> is the type referenced by the represented *ConnectableElement*, and its symbol consists in a "head" followed by a vertical line (straight or dashed). A *ConnectableElement* (from *InternalStructures*) is an abstract metaclass representing a set of instances that play roles of a classifier. The *Lifeline* "head" has a shape that is based on the classifier for the part that this lifeline represents.

The participants in the interactions in *A-Type* sequence diagrams are use cases and in *B-Type* sequence diagrams are architectural elements. Regarding *A-Type* sequence diagrams, the UML Superstructure clearly defines a class for use cases. However, regarding *B-Type* sequence diagrams, architectural elements are not considered in any class of the UML metamodel and, despite some similarities in semantics, are different from UML components. Such situation leads to the necessity of defining a stereotype «*Architectural Element*» for the *NamedElement* class (depicted in the right side of Fig. 11). AEs refer to the pieces from which the final logical architecture can be built and currently relate to generated artifacts and not to their connections or containers. The nature of architectural elements varies according to the type of system under study and the context where it is applied.

Like the *ConnectableElement* class, *UseCase* class is also generalized by *NamedElement* class. The information regarding abstract syntax, concrete syntax, well-formedness and semantics [32] of *UseCase* class and the context in which we defined the stereotype «*Architecture Element*» does not express any condition that restricts them of being able to act as a *ConnectableElement*.

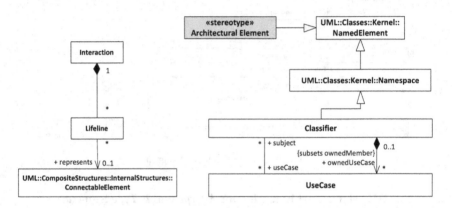

Fig. 11. The Proposed Extension to the UML Metamodel for Representing *A-Type* and *B-Type* Sequence Diagrams [29]

4.3   Derivation of Process-Oriented Logical Architectures

In this section, we present the process-level logical architecture derived using the 4SRS method. The process-level application of the 4SRS method used in this example is detailed in [23], and so detailing it is not in the scope of this work, being, as such, treated like a black box in the V-Model description as represented in Fig. 12. The method takes use cases as input, since they reflect elicited requirements and functionalities. Use cases are derived from *A-Type* Sequence Diagrams and from the OCs.

Gathering *A-Type* Sequence Diagrams can be used as an elicitation technique for modeling use cases, after eliminating redundancy and give a proper name to the use cases used in the sequences. All use cases defined in the *A-Type* Sequence Diagrams must be modeled and textually described in the use case model in order to be used in the 4SRS method.

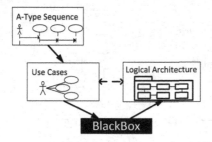

Fig. 12. Derivation of Process-Oriented Logical Architectures

The use case model specifies the required usages of the ISOFIN Platform. In Fig. 13, we present a subset of such usages, regarding the development of functionalities to be accessed by ISOFIN Customers. These use cases intent to capture the requirements of the system that where initially expressed through OCs in the business perspective and later represented using *A-Type* sequence diagrams.

Use cases, in the process-level perspective, portray the activities (processes) executed by persons or machines in the scope of the system, instead of the characteristics (requirements) of the intended products to be developed. It is essential for use case modeling to include textual descriptions that contain information regarding the process execution, preconditions and actions, as well as their relations and dependencies.

The 4SRS method execution results in a logical architecture diagram, presented in Fig. 14. This logical architecture diagram represents the architectural elements, from which the constructors can be retrieved, their associations and packaging. The architectural elements derive from the use case model by the execution of the 4SRS method. In this representation, there are packages that represent, for example, subscription activities in *{P6} ISOFIN Platform Subscriptions Management*, and the SBS and IBS development in *{P1.} SBS Development* and *{P2} IBS Development* respectively. Inside both *{P1}* and *{P2}* it can be found the requirements activities, the analysis decisions and the generators for the major constructors (IBS and SBS). It is also possible to observe that each SBS (in *{P1.4} SBS*) and IBS (in *{P2.4} IBS*) result from activities able to generate their code. This process-level logical architecture shows how activities are arranged so the major constructors are made available to ISOFIN Customers within the intended IT solution.

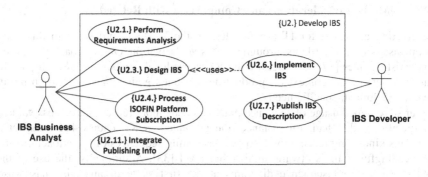

Fig. 13. Subset of the Use Case Model from the ISOFIN Project

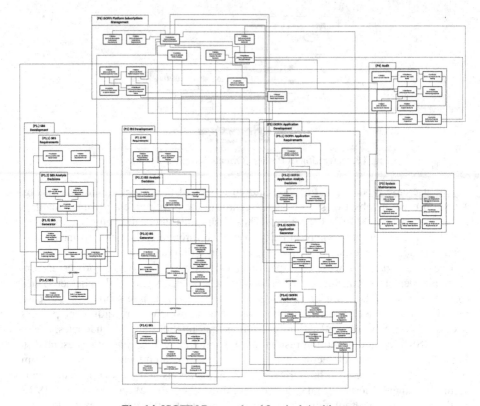

Fig. 14. ISOFIN Process-level Logical Architecture

Fig. 14 depicts the process-level logical architecture for the ISOFIN project and contains nearly eighty architectural elements. This figure is intentionally not zoomed in (and thus not readable), just to show the complexity of the ISOFIN project that has justified the adoption of process-level techniques to support the elicitation efforts. A proper zoom of the architecture can be found in Fig. 15, detailing some of its constructors.

4.4   V-Model Considerations and Comparison with Related Work

For creating a context for IT product design, the V-Model presented in this paper encompasses a set of artifacts through successive derivation. Our approach is different from existing ones [17-19], since we use a process-level perspective. Not only do we manage to create the context for product design, but we also manage to align it with the elicited domain-specific needs.

Our stereotyped usage of sequence diagrams adds more representativeness value to the specific model than, for instance, the presented in Krutchen's 4+1 perspective [10]. This kind of representation also enables testing sequences of system actions that are meaningful at the software architecture level [33]. Additionally, the use of this kind of stereotyped sequence diagrams at the first stage of analysis phase (user

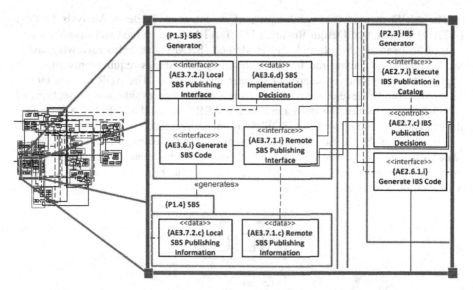

Fig. 15. Subset of the ISOFIN Process-level Logical Architecture

requirements modeling and validation) provides a friendlier perspective to most stake-holders, easing them to establish a direct correspondence between what they initially stated as functional requirements and what the model already describes.

In the ISOFIN project the usage of *A-Type* Sequence Diagrams also contributed to creating a standard representation for the scenarios that are intended to be supported. The *B-Type* Sequence Diagrams that derived from the *A-Type* Sequence Diagrams allowed designers to validate the logical architecture against the given scenarios and at the same time represent the process flow depicted in the architectural elements.

Regarding alignment approaches that use set of models (like GQM+Strategies [6], Balanced Scorecards [7] or COBIT [8]), all relate to aligning the domain-specific concerns with software solutions. As far as the authors of this paper are concerned, none of the previous approaches encompasses processes for deriving a logical representation of the intended system processes with the purpose of creating context for eliciting product-level requirements. Those approaches have a broader specification concerning risk analysis, auditing, measurement, or best practices in the overall alignment strategy.

4.5   Assessment of the V-Model

Having a structured method makes the analysis repeatable and at the same time helps ensuring that the same set of validation questions are placed in early development stages. With the purpose of assuring the attained logical architecture representation is tenable, we chose to validate it and the underlying V-Model, using the Active Reviews for Intermediate Designs (ARID) method [34].

Our concerns relate to discovering errors as soon as possible, inconsistencies in the logical architecture or even inadequacies with the elicited requirements, expressed through the *A-Type* Sequence Diagrams (scenario requirements) and use case models (specific process-level requirements).

The ARID method is a combination of Architecture Tradeoff Analysis Method (ATAM) with Active Design Review (ADR). ATAM is a refined and improved version of Software Architecture Analysis Method (SAAM) that helps reviewing architectural decisions having the focus on the quality attributes requirements and their alignment and satisfaction degree of specific quality goals. The ADR method targets incomplete (under development) architectures, performing evaluations on sections of the global architecture. Those features made ARID our method of choice regarding the evaluation of the in-progress ISOFIN logical architecture.

The focus of this section is not to present the ARID adaptation to our V-Model, which will be addressed in a future publication. Instead, we present a simplified diagram that encompasses major ARID representations required to align with our V-Model models, as seen on Fig. 16.

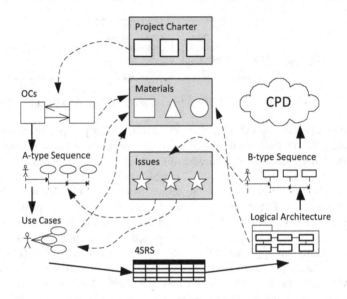

Fig. 16. ARID and the V-Model Intertwining

We present our adapted ARID specific models like *Project Charter*, *Materials* and *Issues*. ARID requires that a project context is defined, containing information regarding the identification of the design reviewers. We have represented such information using the *Project Charter* box as used in project management [35] terminology. The *Materials* box represents the supporting documentation, like presentation that needs to be done to stakeholders, seed scenarios and meeting agenda. *Issues* relates to a checklist that includes but is not limited to notes concerning the presentation, the presented logical architecture, newly created scenarios and validation scenarios. The *issues* representation is used to identify flaws in the logical architecture diagram and therefore promoting a new iteration of the 4SRS method.

ARID was used in the ISOFIN project to assess the process-level logical diagram as a result of the V-Model approach. The *Project Charter* was created with the initial requirements the project, the stakeholders, the teams, budget, timings, intended context and others, that influence directly or indirectly the project's execution. Having this in mind, it is possible to represent the Organizational Configurations (high-level interactions in the domain of analysis). The intended context described in the *Project Charter* gives hints on the domain interactions and the stakeholders are able to provide more information about the roles and activity types that must be supported.

The *Materials* model stores information regarding the created Organizational Configurations, *A-Type* Sequence Diagrams, Use Case models and the derived Logical Architecture. This information is useful for presenting the project, the rationale that sustained the creation of the used models and the scenarios that are used as basis for the requirements elicitation.

Using the information of the *Materials* model a presentation is made to the stakeholders with the intention of assuring that all the initial requirements are met, in the form of scenarios. A scenario is represented by an *A-Type* Sequence Diagram and, for each, is discussed and presented the path that must be followed in the Logical Architecture diagram to accomplish that given scenario. This path is represented using *B-Type* Sequence Diagrams. Any problem with the path (architectural elements missing, associations not possible to accomplish, bad routes, etc.) are stored in the *Issues* model and a new iteration of the 4SRS method is executed. This iteration can be promoted by changing the initial scenarios (*A-Type* Sequence Diagrams) or the initial requirements (use cases).

5 Conclusions and Outlook

In this paper, we have presented a process-level approach to creating context for product design based on successive derivation of models in a V-Model representation. We use *A-Type* sequence diagrams as a bridge from domain-specific needs to the first system requirements representation, *B-Type* sequence diagrams are used as validation for *A-Type* sequence diagrams and the logical architecture diagram. The used models represent the system in its behavior, structure and expected functionalities.

The approach assures that validation tasks are performed continuously along the modeling process. It allows for validating: (i) the final software solution according to the initial expressed requirements; (ii) the *B-Type* sequence diagrams according to *A-Type* sequence diagrams; (iii) the logical diagram by traversing it with *B-Type* sequence diagrams.

Due to the use of a process-level perspective instead of the typical product-level perspective, our approach might be considered to delay the delivery of usable results to technological teams. Although, we are formalizing a model called process-level architecture that is the basis for the domain-specific and software alignment, assuring the existence of one effective return on the investment put into action during that so-called delay, decreasing, namely, the probability of project failure or the need for post-deployment product rework. These advantages were well appreciated by the designers and developers that used the process-level logical architecture artifacts in their work. Also, they were presented with the rationale that was made, in terms of processes that must be supported by the applications they developed.

The presented approach compels the designers and developers to provide a set of models that allow the requirements to be sustainably specified. Also, using multiple viewpoints, like logical diagrams, sequence diagrams or other artifacts, contributes to a better representation and understanding of the system. Each created model in the V-Model takes knowledge from the previously created model as input. Since they are created in succession, the time required to derive a given model, for the same degree of representativeness, is smaller than the previous one. For example, *A-Type* Sequence Diagrams take as input information from the OC model. This means that the context for building *A-Type* Sequence Diagrams is created by the OC model.

In the left-side of the process, the OC model represents processes at a very high-level. The refinement of requirements lowers the abstraction level. In similar context to the one presented in our case study (not having a defined context for product design), this approach is capable of starting with very high-level models and end with low-level information. Also, deriving the models allows uncovering requirements that weren't initially elicited.

As recommended by the ARID method, the V-Model is able to conduct reviews regarding architectural decisions, namely on the quality attributes requirements and their alignment and satisfaction degree of specific quality goals that are imposed to the created scenarios (*A-Type* Sequence Diagrams). These quality attributes reviews were not explicitly done in the ISOFIN project. Instead, those requirements were imbued in design decisions related to the logical architecture.

Unfortunately, our approach could not be compared with other approaches within the same case study. It was also not possible to add a fresh team on the project just to perform other approach for comparison reasons.

It is a common fact that domain-specific needs, namely business needs, are a fast changing concern that must be tackled. Process-level architectures must be in a way that potentially changing domain-specific needs are local in the architecture representation. Our proposed V-Model process encompasses the derivation of a logical architecture representation that is aligned with domain-specific needs and any change made to those domain-specific needs is reflected in the logical architectural model through successive derivation of the supporting models (OCs, *A-* and *B-Type* Sequence Diagrams, and Use cases). In addition, traceability between those models is built-in by construction, and intrinsically integrated in our V-Model process.

As future work, we plan to study the derivation of the current process-level architecture into product-level models, maintaining business alignment.

Acknowledgments. This work has been supported by project ISOFIN (QREN 2010/013837).

References

1. Luftman, J., Ben-Zvi, T.: Key issues for IT executives 2010: judicious IT investments continue post-recession. MIS Quarterly Executive 9, 263–273 (2010)
2. Selic, B.: The pragmatics of model-driven development. IEEE Software 25, 19–25 (2003)
3. Campbell, B., Kay, R., Avison, D.: Strategic alignment: a practitioner's perspective. Journal of Enterprise Information Management 18, 653–664 (2005)
4. ISOFIN Research Project, http://isofincloud.i2s.pt

5. Haskins, C., Forsberg, K.: Systems Engineering Handbook: A Guide for System Life Cycle Processes and Activities; INCOSE-TP-2003-002-03.2. 1. INCOSE (2011)
6. Basili, V.R., Lindvall, M., Regardie, M., Seaman, C., Heidrich, J., Munch, J., Rombach, D., Trendowicz, A.: Linking Software Development and Business Strategy Through Measurement. Computer 43, 57–65 (2010)
7. Kaplan, R.S., Norton, D.P.: The balanced scorecard–measures that drive performance. Harvard Business Review 70, 71–79 (1992)
8. Information Technology Governance Institute (ITGI): COBIT v5 - A Business Framework for the Governance and Management of Enterprise IT. ISACA (2012)
9. Sungwon, K., Yoonseok, C.: Designing logical architectures of software systems. In: Sixth International Conference on Software Engineering, Artificial Intelligence, Networking and Parallel/Distributed Computing, 2005 and First ACIS International Workshop on Self-Assembling Wireless Networks. SNPD/SAWN 2005, pp. 330–337 (2005)
10. Kruchten, P.: The 4+1 View Model of Architecture. IEEE Softw. 12, 42–50 (1995)
11. Clements, P., Garlan, D., Little, R., Nord, R., Stafford, J.: Documenting software architectures: views and beyond, pp. 740–741. IEEE (2003)
12. Hofmeister, C., Nord, R., Soni, D.: Applied software architecture. Addison-Wesley Professional (2000)
13. Zou, J., Pavlovski, C.J.: Modeling Architectural Non Functional Requirements: From Use Case to Control Case. e-Business Engineering. In: IEEE International Conference on ICEBE 2006, pp. 315–322 (2006)
14. Conradi, R., Jaccheri, M.L.: Process Modelling Languages. In: Derniame, J.-C., Kaba, B.A., Wastell, D. (eds.) Software Process. LNCS, vol. 1500, p. 27. Springer, Heidelberg (1999)
15. Browning, T.R., Eppinger, S.D.: Modeling impacts of process architecture on cost and schedule risk in product development. IEEE Trans. on Engineering Management 49, 428–442 (2002)
16. Winter, R., Fischer, R.: Essential Layers, Artifacts, and Dependencies of Enterprise Architecture. In: 10th IEEE International Enterprise Distributed Object Computing Conference Workshops (EDOCW), p. 30 (2006)
17. Weiss, D.M., Lai, C.T.R.: Software Product-Line Engineering: A Family-Based Software Development Process. Addison-Wesley Professional (1999)
18. Kang, K.C., Kim, S., Lee, J., Kim, K., Shin, E., Huh, M.: FORM: A feature-oriented reuse method with domain-specific reference architectures. Annals of Sw. Engineering (1998)
19. Bayer, J., Muthig, D., Göpfert, B.: The library system product line. A KobrA case study. Fraunhofer IESE (2001)
20. Castro, J., Kolp, M., Mylopoulos, J.: Towards requirements-driven information systems engineering: the Tropos project. Information Systems (2002)
21. Machado, R.J., Fernandes, J.M., Monteiro, P., Rodrigues, H.: Refinement of Software Architectures by Recursive Model Transformations. In: Münch, J., Vierimaa, M. (eds.) PROFES 2006. LNCS, vol. 4034, pp. 422–428. Springer, Heidelberg (2006)
22. Machado, R.J., Fernandes, J.M.: Heterogeneous Information Systems Integration: Organizations and Methodologies. In: Oivo, M., Komi-Sirviö, S. (eds.) PROFES 2002. LNCS, vol. 2559, pp. 629–643. Springer, Heidelberg (2002)
23. Ferreira, N., Santos, N., Soares, P., Machado, R.J., Gasevic, D.: Transition from Process-to Product-level Perspective for Business Software. In: 6th International Conference on Research and Practical Issues of Enterprise Information Systems (CONFENIS 2012), Ghent, Belgium (accepted for publication, 2012)
24. Campbell, B.: Alignment: Resolving ambiguity within bounded choices (2005)

25. Evan, W.M.: Toward a theory of inter-organizational relations. Management Science, 217–230 (1965)
26. Machado, R., Lassen, K., Oliveira, S., Couto, M., Pinto, P.: Requirements Validation: Execution of UML Models with CPN Tools. International Journal on Software Tools for Technology Transfer (STTT) 9, 353–369 (2007)
27. Ruparelia, N.B.: Software Development Lifecycle Models. SIGSOFT Softw. Eng. Notes 35, 8–13 (2010)
28. Bensaou, M., Venkatraman, N.: Interorganizational relationships and information technology: A conceptual synthesis and a research framework. European Journal of Information Systems 5, 84–91 (1993)
29. Machado, R.J., Fernandes, J.M., Monteiro, P., Rodrigues, H.: Transformation of UML Models for Service-Oriented Software Architectures. In: Proceedings of the 12th IEEE International Conference and Workshops on Engineering of Computer-Based Systems, pp. 173–182. IEEE Computer Society (2005)
30. Barrett, S., Konsynski, B.: Inter-Organization Information Sharing Systems. MIS Quarterly 6, 93–105 (1982)
31. Open Management Group (OMG), http://www.omg.org/spec/UML/2.4.1/
32. Atkinson, C., Kuhne, T.: Model-Driven Development: A Metamodeling Foundation. IEEE Softw. 20, 36–41 (2003)
33. Bertolino, A., Inverardi, P., Muccini, H.: An explorative journey from architectural tests definition down to code tests execution. In: Proceedings of the 23rd International Conference on Software Engineering, pp. 211–220. IEEE Computer Society, Toronto (2001)
34. Clements, P.C.: Active Reviews for Intermediate Designs, Technical Note CMU/SEI-2000-TN-009 (2000)
35. Project Management Institute: A Guide to the Project Management Body of Knowledge (PMBOK® Guide) (2008)

Mapping CMMI and RUP Process Frameworks for the Context of Elaborating Software Project Proposals[*]

Paula Monteiro[1], Ricardo J. Machado[2,4], Rick Kazman[3], Ana Lima[1],
Cláudia Simões[4], and Pedro Ribeiro[2,4]

[1] CCG-Centro de Computação Gráfica,
Guimarães, Portugal
[2] Centro ALGORITMI, Escola de Engenharia,
Universidade do Minho,
Guimarães, Portugal
[3] University of Hawaii,
Honolulu, USA
[4] Departamento de Sistemas de Informação,
Universidade do Minho,
Guimarães, Portugal

Abstract. To improve quality, organizations are widely using Software Process Improvement (SPI) models and in particular CMMI. Nevertheless, Small and Medium Enterprises (SMEs) are reluctant in adopting CMMI since the complexity and size of the framework discourage its adoption. RUP is presented as a disciplined approach for assigning tasks and responsibilities within a software organization, with the aim of ensuring the production of software meeting the users' needs and in strict compliance with a predictable timetable and budget. CMMI and RUP can be used together since CMMI defines "what to do" and RUP defines "how to do". In this paper, we present the mappings between the CMMI Maturity Levels 2 and 3 process areas and the RUP activities, tasks, artifacts and roles. Our main contribution relates to the alignment of CMMI and RUP when adopted in the preliminary stage of every project: the elaboration of the project proposal. This paper also presents the assessment of the effectiveness of RUP support to the elaboration of the project proposals.

Keywords: RUP, CMMI ML 2 and ML3, RUP Roles, Project Proposal.

1 Introduction

The organizational world is ruled by reference models that influence and mold any organization, whichever its activity, size or organizational culture. Regarding

---

[*] This work has been supported by FEDER through Programa Operacional Fatores de Competitividade – COMPETE and by Fundos Nacionais through FCT – Fundação para a Ciência e Tecnologia in the scope of the project: FCOMP-01-0124-FEDER-022674.

D. Winkler, S. Biffl, and J. Bergsmann (Eds.): SWQD 2013, LNBIP 133, pp. 191–214, 2013.

software development organizations one must refer to reference models such as CMMI, SPICE (ISO/IEC 15504:1998), ISO/IEC 9000, RUP, PMBOK, BABOK, PSP, ISO/IEC 9126, SWEBOK [1-3], amongst many others. Although these reference models act in many different perspectives and sub-fields, their main purpose is to enhance the quality of the developed software according to the final users' needs [4]. Software is used on an everyday basis by organizations, supporting organizational processes and, consequently, helping them become more flexible and able to change. Software is ubiquitous and might be regarded as an organization's DNA.

Using reference models to assess software quality is nowadays not only a minimum requirement for an organization's survival [5] but also a business strategy [6]. The present work is focused on two reference models for software development processes: RUP [6] and CMMI [7, 8]. RUP and CMMI are used for different purposes, the first being focused on the necessary activity flow and responsibilities, and the later determining the maturity of the process in use. RUP is a generic and configurable software development process framework that recommends activities in order to convert the user's needs into software by attributing responsibilities and guidelines to the development team [2, 6, 9]. CMMI is a framework that provides principles and practices in order to achieve a certain maturity level for the software development process, improving these processes [7, 8, 10, 11] and, therefore, enhancing software quality [11]. RUP and CMMI have a common goal: improving software quality and increase customer satisfaction. They can be used together: with CMMI we understand what we have to do; with RUP we realize how we have to do.

The main purpose of this work is to discuss if RUP for small projects [12] is enough to elaborate project proposals in a CMMI ML2 (Maturity Level 2) organization. Usually, one project proposal is a response to a client request. However, it could be also required by an internal purpose of the company [13-16]. The project proposal document should be composed by the plan of action, the reasons for each action, the timeline to perform the project, the methodology that will be used and the budget required to perform (execute) the project. The ultimate goal of each project proposal is to describe and explain a detailed description of the actions and activities needed to solve a given problem (the problem that motivates the client to ask for a certain project).

We will start by presenting the mapping of CMMI ML2 and ML3 (Maturity Level 3) process areas (PAs) into RUP tasks, activities and roles. Since we are concerned with the elaboration of project proposals, we will focus mainly on the RUP Inception phase and the CMMI REQM (Requirements Management) and PP (Project Planning) process areas. The usefulness of CMMI-RUP mapping will be illustrated in two different case studies, where we interpret the obtained results in terms of the teams' performance to elaborate project proposals.

2   Related Work

CMMI was created in 2002 [7, 8, 10, 11] and enables an organization to coordinate its efforts in order to continuously improve development processes. CMMI evolved from CMM which was created in 1991 by the Software Engineering Institute (SEI) [7, 8, 10, 11], and is more engineering-focused. Although CMMI provides technical guidelines to achieve a certain level of process development quality, it cannot determine how to attain such a level [2]. CMMI-DEV v1.3 [8] was released in November 2010 and encloses generic goals and practices as well as specific goals and practices for each CMMI process areas.

An appraisal at ML2 guarantees that the organization's processes are performed and managed according to the plan [5]. Although ML2 contains engineering process areas [11], the engineering approach is only considered relevant at ML3 by several companies; due to the "level 2 syndrome" [17], they tend to skip ML2 and directly implement ML3, which is considered a dangerous practice and was never reported as viable. In Portugal, there are six ML2 organizations, nine ML3 and only one ML5 organization [18], which represents 0,3% of the CMMI appraised organizations.

RUP is a framework developed by Rational Software for software development that includes activities, artifacts, roles and responsibilities and the best practices recognized for software projects. RUP enables the development team to accomplish an iterative transformation of the user's requirements into software that suits the stakeholder's needs [2, 6, 9]. RUP also provides guidelines for "what", "who" and "when" [2], avoiding an ad-hoc approach [6] that is usually time consuming and costly [5]. RUP can be represented in a bi-dimensional plan where time and process dynamics are shown on the horizontal axis (presenting phases, iterations and milestones) and the vertical axis is static and corresponds to activities, paths and roles [6]. This phased division reduces the risk and enhances the overall management of the project [3].

Inception refers to the beginning of the project and has an estimated cost of 10% [6]. Its aim is to establish the scope and context of the project, identify stakeholders and success criteria, estimate the cost and risks and describe the main use cases in a consensual manner [6], for one or more iterations [2]. By the end of this stage, one should be able to decide upon the viability of the project. The case studies considered in this paper are framed within the efforts of RUP Inception phase.

There are some drawbacks related to the RUP framework, such as the partial absence of issues related to human resources management, communication management and contract management [2]. In addition, the team may get lost in details and excessive documentation when it is not able to determine valuable artifacts for its project [6].

The use of RUP in small projects [12] began in 2006 (Table 1). It is possible to conclude that 36 mandatory artifacts (optional artifacts excluded) were reduced to 18 when it comes to small projects. This will be retaken further on for the CMMI-RUP mapping analysis.

Table 1. Trimming RUP for mall Projects at Inception Phase [12, 19]

Main Change in RUP for small projects at inception phase (mandatory components)		
Activities	**Task**	**Status**
Assess Business Status	All	T
Develop Initial Vision	All	T
Develop Domain Model	All	T
Prepare Environment for Project	Develop Development Case	T
	Prepare Templates for the Project	T
	Prepare Guidelines for the Project	T
Create Project Configuration Management (CM) Environments	Create Integration Workspaces	T
Prepare Environment for an Iteration	Develop Development Case	T
	Prepare Guidelines for the Project	T
	Develop Manual Styleguide	T
	Prepare Templates for the Project	T
	Set Up Tools	T
	Verify Tool Configuration and Installation	T
Plan the Project	Develop Measurement Plan	T
	Develop Risk Management Plan	T
	Develop Product Acceptance Plan	T
	Develop Problem Resolution Plan	T
	Develop Quality Assurance Plan	T
	Define Monitoring & Control Processes	T
	Compile Software Development Plan	T
Monitor and Control Project	Monitor Project Status	T
	Handle Exceptions and Problems	T
	Project Review Authority (PRA) Project Review	T
Manage the Scope of the System	Manage Dependencies	T
	Develop Vision	P (Requirements Attributes artifact)
Define the System	Manage Dependencies	T
	Develop Vision	P (Requirements Attributes artifact)
	Find Actors and Use Cases	P (Requirements Attributes artifact)
	Develop Supplementary Specifications	P (Requirements Attributes artifact)
Perform Architectural Synthesis	Define System Context	T
Define Evaluation Mission	Identify Test Motivators	T
	Agree on the Mission	T
	Identify Targets of Test	T
	Define Assessment and Traceability Needs	T
	Define Test Approach	P (Test Plan artifact e Define Test Approach)
Manage Iteration	Iteration Acceptance Review	P (Test Plan artifact e Define Test Approach)
Artifacts		
Analysis Model, Architectural Proof-of-Concept, Business Case, Change Request, Deployment Model, Design Model, Development Process, Iteration Assessment, Project Repository, Review Record, Software Architecture Document, Software Development Plan, Stakeholder Requests, Status Assessment, Test Evaluation Summary, Test Strategy, Use Case Model, Work Order		

Legend: T (Totally Removed) P (Partially Removed)

CMMI and RUP intersect each other in regards to software quality and hence customer satisfaction. In addition, both models have been constantly updated so they do not become obsolete [6] and prevent an ad-hoc and chaotic software development environment [11]. While created by independent entities, they both counted with the participation of experts from the software industry and government [11]. There are many reasons why organizations should use these two frameworks: increased quality, productivity, customer and partners satisfaction; lower costs and time consumed; and better team communication [2, 5, 11]. CMMI-DEV may be used to evaluate an organization's maturity whether it uses or not RUP as a process model. Usually, the CMMI evaluation is managed by a technical report called SCAMPI (Standard CMMI

Appraisal Method for Process Improvement) [7, 8, 10, 11] that may only be performed by SEI authorized appraisers. There have been defined three classes for the SCAMPI appraisals; this allows the evaluation to have different goals, Class A being the only appraisal methodology that offers a rating and covers the 40 requirements of the evaluation procedure [7, 8, 10, 11].

Since its origins, some process areas of CMMI are supported by RUP tasks, namely REQM, PP. These two process areas are the ones that require most effort during Inception [6]. Our study is mainly based on PP and REQM process areas of the CMMI ML2. Thus, our study will allow the determination of the RUP practices that support these two process areas.

3   General CMMI-RUP Mapping for ML2 and ML3

As a first step to the main goal, we have performed an extension to the mapping described in [20-22] that relates "CMMI-DEV v1.2 ML2" and "RUP for large projects". We have extended the mapping to cover CMMI ML3. We had to map CMMI ML3 specific practices and subpractices into RUP activities or tasks and CMMI ML3 work products into RUP artifacts. This effort will also improve a previous work that maps the "CMMI-SE/SW v1.02" and the "Rational Unified Process 2000.02.10" [23] (these are older versions of CMMI and RUP). [23] presents a mapping between all CMMI PAs and RUP workflows, where only the mapping for one subpractice of each PA is detailed. The SPs and subpractices of CMMI-SE/SW v1.02 are quite different from the CMMI-DEV v1.2. RUP has also evolved and in the latest version, there are new artifacts, tasks and activities that better implement CMMI subpractices. For these reasons, [23] is quite dated and almost irrelevant for the results we are presenting in our manuscript.

It is important to clarify that one PA is composed by one or more specific goals (SGs); one SG is divided in one or more specific practices (SP); and one SP is divided in one or more subpractices. To implement one PA, we have to fully cover all the process area SPs, which means that we have to fully cover all the subpractices that compose the SPs.

When performing the initial CMMI-RUP gap analysis, we had to consider different coverage levels:

— *High coverage* (H): CMMI fully implemented with RUP elements, which means that there are no substantial weaknesses;
— *Medium-High coverage* (MH): CMMI nearly fully implemented with RUP elements, although some weaknesses can be identified;
— *Medium coverage* (M): CMMI mostly implemented with RUP elements, however additional effort is needed to fully implement this process area using RUP;
— *Low coverage* (L): CMMI is not directly supported using RUP elements, or there is a minimal RUP support;
— *Not covered* (N): CMMI is not covered by any RUP elements.

Table 2 presents the results of CMMI-RUP gap analysis for ML2 and ML3. Two tasks are needed to perform this gap analysis: (1) to identify all the RUP activities, tasks and artifacts needed to perform each one of the SPs, subpractices and work products for each process area; (2) to identify the RUP roles assigned to each RUP activities, tasks and artifacts of each process area. All process areas of CMMI ML2 are totally or, at least, partially covered by RUP. In the case of ML3, process areas belonging to the *process management* and *support* categories are not covered by RUP.

Table 2. CMMI-RUP Gap Analysis for ML2 and ML3

	Category	PA	Acronym		RUP Compliance
MATURITY LEVEL 2	Engineering	Requirements Management	{PA 1}	REQM	MH
	Project Management	Project Monitoring and Control	{PA 2}	PMC	H
	Project Management	Project Planning	{PA 3}	PP	MH
	Project Management	Supplier Agreement Management	{PA 4}	SAM	M
	Support	Measurement and Analysis	{PA 5}	MA	MH
	Support	Configuration Management	{PA 6}	CM	M
	Support	Process and Product Quality Assurance	{PA 7}	PPQA	H
MATURITY LEVEL 3	Engineering	Product Integration	{PA 8}	PI	H
	Engineering	Requirements Development	{PA 9}	RD	H
	Engineering	Technical Solution	{PA 10}	TS	M
	Engineering	Validation	{PA 11}	VAL	H
	Engineering	Verification	{PA 12}	VER	M
	Process Management	Organizational Process Definition	{PA 13}	OPD	N
	Process Management	Organizational Process Focus	{PA 14}	OPF	N
	Process Management	Organizational Training	{PA 15}	OT	N
	Project Management	Integrated Project Management	{PA 16}	IPM	M
	Project Management	Risk Management	{PA 17}	RSKM	MH
	Support	Decision Analysis and Resolution	{PA 18}	DAR	N

Table 3 and 4 present the CMMI-RUP mapping for ML2 originally performed by IBM [20-22]. Table 5 and 6 present our extension for ML3 (except for the Requirements Development process area, that was also analyzed by IBM). In the tables, we present the CMMI specific practices and the RUP artifacts, activities for each process area. For some CMMI process areas, we will next comment the results obtained from the coverage analysis.

The main purpose of the Technical Solution process area is to "*design, develop, and implement solutions to requirements. Solutions, designs, and implementations encompass products, product components, and product-related lifecycle processes either singly or in combination as appropriate*". This process area is divided into three SGs: *select product component solutions* (see SP1.1 and SP1.2 in Table 5), *develop the design* (see SP2.1 to SP2.4 in Table 5), and *implement the product design* (see SP3.1 and SP3.2 in Table 5). The RUP coverage for this process area is only

Table 3. CMMI-RUP ML2 Mappings (IBM [21-23]) – part I

Process Area	Specific Practices	RUP Compliance – Artifacts	RUP Compliance – Activities	RUP Compliance - Tasks
Requirements Management	SP1.1 Obtain an Understanding of Requirements SP1.2 Obtain Commitment to Requirements SP1.3 Manage Requirements Changes SP1.4 Maintain Bidirectional Traceability of Requirements SP1.5 Identify Inconsistencies Between Project Work and Requirements	Requirements Management Plan Vision Requirements Attributes Software Requirements Specification Requirements Attributes Software Development Plan Iteration Assessment Change Request	Manage Change Requests Manage Changing Requirements	Develop Requirements Management Plan Develop Vision Elicit Stakeholder Requests Detail the Software Requirements Review Requirements Manage Dependencies Review Change Requests Define Monitoring & Control Processes Assess Iteration Iteration Acceptance Review Project Planning Review Conduct Review Submit Change Request
Requirements Development	SP1.1 Monitor Project Planning Parameters SP1.2 Monitor Commitments SP1.3 Monitor Project Risks SP1.4 Monitor Data Management SP1.5 Monitor Stakeholder Involvement SP1.6 Conduct Progress Reviews SP1.7 Conduct Milestone Reviews SP2.1 Analyze Issues SP2.2 Take Corrective Action SP2.3 Manage Corrective Action	Project Repository Iteration Assessment Status Assessment Review Record Risk List Stakeholder Requests Issues List Problem Resolution Plan		Assess Iteration Monitor Project Status Identify and Assess Risks Project Review Authority (PRA) Project Review Report Status Lifecycle Milestone Review Handle Exceptions and Problems Conduct Review Report on Configuration Status Submit Change Request Review Change Requests Develop Problem Resolution Plan
Project Planning	SP1.1 Estimate the Scope of the Project SP1.2 Establish Estimates of Work Product and Task Attributes SP1.3 Define Project Lifecycle SP1.4 Determine Estimates of Effort and Cost SP2.1 Establish the Budget and Schedule SP2.2 Identify Project Risks SP2.3 Plan for Data SP2.4 Plan for Project Resources SP2.5 Plan for Needed Knowledge and Skills SP2.6 Plan Stakeholder Involvement SP2.7 Establish the Project Plan SP3.1 Review Plans that Affect the Project SP3.2 Reconcile Work and Resource Levels SP3.3 Obtain Commitment	Software Architecture Document Development Process Software Development Plan COTS Package Screening Criteria and Rationale Iteration Plan Business Case Risk Management Plan Risk List Compile Software Development Plan Development Case Vision Review Record Software Requirements Specification	Plan the Project Refine the Development Plan Plan for Next Iteration	Plan Phases and Iterations Iteration Evaluation Criteria Review Develop Iteration Plan Identify and Assess Risks Schedule and Assign Work Recommend Solution Incorporate Existing Design Elements Architectural Analysis Tailor the Development Process for the Project Develop Problem Resolution Plan Develop Risk Management Plan Risk Management Plan Risk List Report Status Monitor Project Status Assess Iteration Compile Software Development Plan Write Configuration Management (CM) Plan Develop Development Case Define Project Organization and Staffing Acquire Staff Project Planning Review Define Project Organization and Staffing Acquire Staff Project Planning Review Tailor the Development Process for the Project Select and Acquire Tools Iteration Plan Review Review Requirements

Medium because RUP does not give guidance on the selection of alternative solutions, as well on how to perform analyses to decide if it is better make, buy, or reuse components. RUP elements that partially implement this process area are presented in Table 5.

The Verification process area has the purpose to "*ensure that selected work products meet their specified requirements*". This process area is divided in three SGs: prepare for verification, perform peer reviews, and verify selected work products. This process area is mostly compliant with RUP, since almost all the subpractices are covered. The subpractices not covered by RUP are "*store the data for future reference and analysis*" and "*protect the data to ensure that peer review data are not used inappropriately*". RUP does not have any mechanism to allow the storage of the reviews or a mechanism to ensure the security of the peer reviews data. To use RUP as a guideline to implement the Verification process area we must extend RUP in order to cover those gaps. Table 6 presents the RUP elements that will cover the remaining Verification subpractices.

Table 4. CMMI-RUP ML2 Mappings (IBM [21-23]) – part I

Process Area	Specific Practices	RUP Compliance – Artifacts	RUP Compliance – Activities	RUP Compliance - Tasks
Supplier Agreement Management	SP1.1 Determine Acquisition Type SP1.2 Select Suppliers SP1.3 Establish Supplier Agreements SP2.1 Execute the Supplier Agreement SP2.2 Monitor Selected Supplier Processes SP2.3 Evaluate Selected Supplier Work Products SP2.4 Accept the Acquired Product SP2.5 Transition Products	Software Development Plan Iteration Plan Software Development Plan Iteration Assessment Status Assessment Development Process Test Evaluation Summary Product Acceptance Plan Test Results Issues List Development Case		Assess Iteration Tailor the Development Process for the Project Plan Phases and Iterations Develop Iteration Plan Monitor Project Status Organize Review Conduct Review Review the Architecture Review the Design Review Code Project Review Authority (PRA) Project Review Identify and Assess Risks Define Monitoring & Control Processes Identify Targets of Test Agree on the Mission Define Test Approach Define Test Details Implement Test Suite Execute Test Suite Determine Test Results Assess and Advocate Quality Report Status Develop Product Acceptance Plan Manage Acceptance Test Handle Exceptions and Problems
Measurements and Analysis	SP1.1 Establish Measurement Objectives SP1.2 Specify Measures SP1.3 Specify Data Collection and Storage Procedures SP1.4 Specify Analysis Procedures SP2.1 Collect Measurement Data SP2.2 Analyze Measurement Data SP2.3 Store Data and Results SP2.4 Communicate Results	Measurement Plan Project Measurements Status Assessment	Monitor & Control Project	Develop Measurement Plan Project Planning Review Assess Iteration Iteration Plan Review Report Status Monitor Project Status Report on Configuration Status Project Review Authority (PRA) Project Review
Configuration Management	SP1.1 Identify Configuration Items SP1.2 Establish a Configuration Management System SP1.3 Create or Release Baselines SP2.1 Track Change Requests SP2.2 Control Configuration Items SP3.1 Establish Configuration Management Records	Configuration Management Plan Project Repository Change Request Configuration Audit Findings	Manage Baselines & Releases Manage Change Requests	Establish Configuration Management (CM) Policies Write Configuration Management (CM) Plan Make Changes Develop Iteration Plan Establish Change Control Process Deliver Changes Create Baselines Perform Configuration Audit Assess Iteration Promote Baselines Submit Change Request Review Change Requests Report on Configuration Status Create Development Workspace Create Integration Workspaces Update Workspace Verify Changes in Build Monitor Project Status
Process and Product Quality Assurance	SP1.1 Objectively Evaluate Processes SP1.2 Objectively Evaluate Work Products and Services SP2.1 Communicate and Ensure Resolution of Noncompliance Issues SP2.2 Establish Records	Quality Assurance Plan Iteration Assessment Status Assessment Change Request Review Record Configuration Audit Findings Test Evaluation Summary Test Log Test Results Review Record		Assess Iteration Submit Change Request Develop Quality Assurance Plan Develop Development Case Tailor the Development Process for the Project Conduct Review Define Assessment and Traceability Needs Assess and Advocate Quality Determine Test Results Review Change Requests Update Change Request Report Status Project Review Authority (PRA) Project Review Identify and Assess Risks Assess and Improve Test Effort Report on Configuration Status

The main purpose of the Integrated Project Management process area is to "*establish and manage the project and the involvement of the relevant stakeholders according to an integrated and defined process that is tailored from the organization's set of standard processes*". This process area is divided in two SGs: *use the project's defined process* and *coordinate and collaborate with relevant*

Table 5. CMMI-RUP ML3 Mappings – part I

Process Area	Specific Practices	RUP Compliance – Artifacts	RUP Compliance – Activities	RUP Compliance - Tasks
Product Integration	SP1.1. Determine Integration Sequence SP1.2. Establish the Product Integration Environment SP1.3. Establish Product Integration Procedures and Criteria SP2.1. Review Interface Descriptions for Completeness SP2.2. Manage Interfaces SP3.1. Confirm Readiness of Product Components for Integration SP3.2. Assemble Product Components SP3.3. Evaluate Assembled Product Components SP3.4. Package and Deliver the Product or Product Components	Iteration Plan Integration Build Plan Design Model Test Log Build Implementation Subsystem Product Deployment Unit Release Notes	Integrate each Subsystem Integrate the System Package Product Provide Access to Download Site	Plan System Integration Set Up Configuration Management (CM) Environment Plan Subsystem Integration Structure the Implementation Model Implement Developer Test Execute Developer Tests Submit Change Request Integrate Subsystem Integrate System Write Release Notes Verify Manufactured Product
Requirements Development	SP1.1 Elicit Needs SP1.2 Develop the Customer Requirements SP2.1 Establish Product and Product Component Requirements SP2.2 Allocate Product Component Requirements SP2.3 Identify Interface Requirements SP3.1 Establish Operational Concepts and Scenarios SP3.2 Establish a Definition of Required Functionality SP3.3 Analyze Requirements SP3.4 Analyze Requirements to Achieve Balance SP3.5 Validate Requirements	Business Case Storyboard Architectural Proof-of-Concept Use Case Iteration Assessment Software Architecture Document Vision Stakeholder Requests Supplementary Specifications Product Acceptance Plan Software Requirement Software Requirements Specification Requirements Attributes Design Model Use-Case Realization		Elicit Stakeholder Requests Find Actors and Use Cases Manage Beta Test Manage Acceptance Test Business Use-Case Analysis Construct Business Architectural Proof-of-Concept Find Business Actors and Use Cases Elicit Stakeholder Requests Develop Vision Find Actors and Use Cases Capture a Common Vocabulary Construct Architectural Proof-of-Concept Prototype the User-Interface Iteration Acceptance Review Project Review Authority (PRA) Project Review (...) Data Model Analysis Design Testability Elements Design the User Interface Architectural Analysis Use-Case Analysis Use-Case Design Identify Design Elements Subsystem Design
Technical Solution	SP1.1. Develop Alternative Solutions and Selection Criteria SP1.2. Select Product Component Solutions SP2.1. Design the Product or Product Component SP2.2. Establish a Technical Data Package SP2.3. Design Interfaces Using Criteria SP2.4. Perform Make, Buy, or Reuse Analyses SP3.1. Implement the Design SP3.2. Develop Product Support Documentation	Business Case Service Component Software Architecture Document Design Model Supplementary Specifications Implementation Element Training Materials User Support Material Installation Artifacts	Define a Candidate Architecture Refine the Architecture Perform Architectural Synthesis Develop Support Material	Define System Context Implement Design Elements Review Code Analyze Runtime Behavior Implement Testability Elements Implement Developer Test Execute Developer Tests

stakeholders. To fulfill the IPM coverage by RUP we need extensions to support the integration of plans and managing the dependencies between them. Additionally, RUP does not support the majority of SP1.6 which requires the gathering of information for process assets. In Table 6 we can see the existent RUP elements that partially cover the IPM subpractices.

The main purpose of the Risk Management process area is to *"identify potential problems before they occur so that risk-handling activities can be planned and invoked as needed across the life of the product or project to mitigate adverse impacts on achieving objectives"*. This process area is divided in three SGs: *prepare for risk management*, *identify and analyze risks*, and *mitigate risks*. RUP covers almost all the Risk Management SPs. The main gap found in this process area is related with the definition of parameters to allow the risk analysis and categorization (SP1.2).

Table 6. CMMI-RUP ML3 Mappings – part II

Process Area	Specific Practices	RUP Compliance – Artifacts	RUP Compliance – Activities	RUP Compliance - Tasks
Validation	SP1.1. Select Products for Validation SP1.2. Establish the Validation Environment SP1.3. Establish Validation Procedures and Criteria SP2.1. Perform Validation SP2.2. Analyze Validation Results	Product Acceptance Plan Deployment Plan Test Environment Configuration Stakeholder Requests Test Suite Review Record Change Request	Manage Acceptance Test	Develop Product Acceptance Plan Manage Acceptance Test Manage Beta Test Project Acceptance
Verification	SP1.1. Select Work Products for Verification SP1.2. Establish the Verification Environment SP1.3. Establish Verification Procedures and Criteria SP2.1. Prepare for Peer Reviews SP2.2. Conduct Peer Reviews SP2.3. Analyze Peer Review Data SP3.1. Perform Verification SP3.2. Analyze Verification Results	Test Strategy Test Plan Test Environment Configuration Test Data Iteration Plan Development Project-Specific Guidelines Review Record Software Development Build Test Suite Test-Ideas List Test Log Test Results		Identify Targets of Test Identify Test Motivators Define Assessment and Traceability Needs Define Test Approach Structure the Test Implementation Define Testability Elements Determine Test Results Organize Review Conduct Review Execute Test Suite Analyze Test Failure
Integrated Project Management	SP1.1. Establish the Project's Defined Process SP1.2. Use Organizational Assets for Planning Project Activities SP1.3. Establish the Project's Work Environment SP1.4. Integrate Plans SP1.5. Manage the Project Using the Integrated Plans SP1.6. Contribute to the Organization's Process Assets SP2.1. Manage Stakeholder Involvement SP1.2. Manage Dependencies SP2.3. Resolve Coordination Issues	Development Case Project-Specific Templates Project-Specific Guidelines Development Process Software Development Plan Tools Development Project Measurements Review Record Iteration Plan Product Acceptance Plan	Support Environment During an Iteration Monitor & Control Project	Tailor the Development Process for the Project Prepare Templates for the Project Develop Development Case Prepare Guidelines for the Project Plan Phases and Iterations Select and Acquire Tools Set Up Tools Support Development Compile Software Development Plan Identify and Assess Risks Develop Risk Management Plan Develop Product Acceptance Plan Define Project Organization and Staffing Develop Problem Resolution Plan Monitor Project Status Iteration Evaluation Criteria Review Iteration Acceptance Review Project Review Authority (PRA) Project Review Conduct Review Organize Review
Risk Management	SP1.1. Determine Risk Sources and Categories SP1.2. Define Risk Parameters SP1.3. Establish a Risk Management Strategy SP2.1. Identify Risks SP2.2. Evaluate, Categorize, and Prioritize Risks SP3.1. Develop Risk Mitigation Plans SP3.2. Implement Risk Mitigation Plans	Risk List Risk Management Plan		Identify and Assess Risks Develop Risk Management Plan

The main purpose of the Organizational Process Definition process area is *"to establish and maintain a usable set of organizational process assets and work environment standards"*. There is any RUP element that fully implements this process area. RUP gives only general topics under the concept of implementing a process in an organization. In RUP, a "concept" addresses more general topics than guidelines and span across work products, tasks, or activities.

The main purpose of the Organizational Process Focus process area is to *"plan, implement, and deploy organizational process improvements based on a thorough understanding of the current strengths and weaknesses of the organization's processes and process assets"*. RUP tasks are targeted to project processes. This process area is concerned with organization processes. RUP does not support this process area.

The main purpose of the Organizational Training process area is to *"develop the skills and knowledge of people so they can perform their roles effectively and efficiently"*. The organizational training issues are out of the RUP's scope. The RUP task `acquire staff` refers in one of its steps the project staff training. This is the closest to organizational training issues that we can find in RUP.

The main purpose of the Decision Analysis and Resolution process area is *"to analyze possible decisions using a formal evaluation process that evaluates identified alternatives against established criteria"*. RUP scope does not cover the main issues of this process area.

4   RUP Reduced Model Roles

The described CMMI-RUP mappings are useful to understand what to expect in terms of CMMI coverage when adopting RUP as our development process framework. In terms of execution, it is important to additionally perceive who must be in charge to comply with each CMMI general goal, and to perform each CMMI specific practice. Here, we have considered the RUP Reduced Model presented in [24] as a first step towards the attribution of responsibilities in terms of CMMI implementation supported by RUP.

Table 7 summarizes the eight RUP Reduced Model roles (`project manager, integrator, project reviewer, process engineer, implementer, system administrator, test manager` and `system tester`). The remaining 29 roles are not discarded; their responsibilities are mapped into one of the eight Reduced Model roles. For instance, the `project manager` inherits the responsibilities of: `business-process analyst, change control manager, deployment manager, requirements specifier, review coordinator, test analyst, system analyst, business designer` and `use case specifier`. The complete analysis, justification, and implications of the Reduced Model responsibilities' accumulation can be found in [24].

Table 7. Roles Considered in RUP Reduced Model

Project Manager	Change Control Manager	Test Analyst	Review Coordinator	Requirements Specifier	Deployment Manager	Business-Process Analyst	System Analyst	Use Case Specifier	Business Designer
Integrator	Capsule Designer	Software Architect	Integration Tester	Database Designer	Design Reviewer	Code Reviewer	Course Developer		
Project Reviewer	Management Reviewer	Business Reviewer	Requirements Reviewer						
Process Engineer	Tool Specialist	Architecture Reviewer							
Implementer	Designer	Component Engineer	User-Interface Designer	Graphic Artist	Technical Writer				
System Administrator	Configuration Manager								
Test Manager	Test Designer	Use Case Engineer							
System Tester									

Table 8. Reduced Model Roles for ML2 and ML3 Process Areas

CMMI vs RUP	Requirements Management	Project Monitoring and Control	Project Planning	Supplier Agreement Management	Measurement and Analysis	Configuration Management	Process and Product Quality Assurance	Product Integration	Requirements Development	Technical Solution	Validation	Verification	Organizational Process Definition	Organizational Process Focus	Organizational Training	Integrated Project Management	Risk Management	Decision Analysis and Resolution
Implementer								X										
Technical Writer										X								
Graphic Artist																		
User-Interface Designer									X									
Component Engineer																		
Designer								X	X	X								
System Tester				X			X	X			X							
Test Manager				X			X			X		X						
Use Case Engineer																		
Test Designer				X							X	X						
Process Engineer			X	X	X		X				X					X		
Architecture Reviewer				X					X	X	X	X				X		
Tool Specialist				X												X		
Project Reviewer																		
Requirements Reviewer	X			X					X		X	X				X		
Business Reviewer											X	X				X		
Management Reviewer	X	X	X	X	X		X		X		X					X		
Integrator						X		X										
Course Developer											X							
Code Reviewer				X						X	X	X				X		
Design Reviewer				X					X		X	X				X		
Database Designer										X								
Integration Tester																		
Software Architect				X					X		X	X				X		
Capsule Designer										X								
Project Manager	X	X	X	X	X	X	X	X	X	X	X					X	X	
Business Designer									X									
Use Case Specifier																		
System Analyst	X	X	X						X		X	X						
Business-Process Analyst									X									
Deployment Manager				X					X	X	X							
Requirements Specifier	X		X						X									
Review Coordinator		X	X	X	X		X				X					X		
Test Analyst	X			X		X	X				X	X						
Change Control Manager	X	X				X	X				X							
System Administrator								X			X					X		
Configuration Manager		X	X			X	X	X								X		

In Table 8, the grey cells represent the Reduced Model roles and the white cells represent the additional responsibilities that each Reduced Model role inherits [24-26]. To state which role or responsibilities are required to achieve a given process area we mark in Table 8 the corresponding column with an "x".

As an example, to implement the Requirements Management process area we need the project manager role when it assumes its own responsibilities and, simultaneously, the responsibilities of the change control manager, test analyst, requirements specifier and system analyst role. The project reviewer role is also needed, but, in this case, when it only assumes the responsibilities of the management reviewer and the requirements reviewer role. The other Reduced Model roles are not needed to support the execution of the Requirements Management process area using RUP.

In what regards the Product Integration process area, as an example, the role responsible for implementing the artifact iteration plan is the project manager and the role responsible for the task plan system integration is the integrator. A similar effort was performed for all the artifacts, tasks and activities compliant with this process area.

The Validation process area is quite demanding, since it involves several roles, either by puting into pratice only their own direct responsibilities (such as the system administrator and the system tester), or by requiring the accumulation of several roles (such as the project manager and the process engineer roles, that, besides their own responsibilities, must perform the responsibilities of some other roles under their supervision).

Some process areas involve one single role, such as the project manager (performing its own responsibilities) that is capable of implementing completely the Risk Management process area.

5   Detailing CMMI-RUP Mappings for PP and REQM

Since our main goal is to understand what kind of support can we expect from RUP to elaborate project proposals in a CMMI-compliant perspective, it is extremely important to detail the previous analysis for both the Project Planning and Requirements Management process areas at the subpractices level.

Table 9 presents the detailed CMMI-RUP for the Project Planning process area. The table contains the required RUP tasks or activities to support each Project Planning subpractice. Artifacts were replaced by tasks of which they are output.

Project Planning process area has a good support from RUP (MH coverage); with a few recommendations and actions we can completely cover this process area using RUP tasks and activities.

We can highlight the subpractice SP1.4.1 (that can be nearly implemented with the RUP task plan phases and iterations) and the subpractice SP1.4.2 (that can be practically implemented with the RUP task schedule and assign work). However, these two subpractices do not cover the estimation process. Therefore, to achieve a high coverage, an estimation process should be added to RUP.

Subpractices SP2.3.1 could also be better supported if we upgrade the RUP task `write configuration management (CM) plan` with the capability of including privacy and security requirements the RUP artifact `configuration management plan`.

Subpractices SP2.4.3 could be better supported if we upgrade the RUP task `select and acquire tools` with the capability of identifying the facilities, equipment, and component requirements for all project activities.

Subpractice SP2.5.3 is not covered by RUP, since there are no RUP tasks or activities that impose the selection of mechanisms to provide the project needed knowledge and skills.

Subpractice SP2.6.1 requires the identification of the stakeholders' involvement in all phases of the project lifecycle. RUP task `develop vision` only suggests a general identification of the stakeholders, independently of the phases that justify their involvement.

With the RUP task `define project organization and staffing`, we achieve only a medium coverage for the subpractice SP3.3.1 because the negotiating commitments are not enclosed. Subpractice SP3.3.2 presents low coverage because the recording commitments demanded by CMMI are not guaranteed by RUP. A high coverage could be achieved if these recording commitments are added to the task.

We have considered two different contexts for the elaboration of project proposals: (1) the context where the team is completely focused to comply with CMMI recommendations, which means the team needs to perform all the subpractices referred in table 9; (2) the context where the team is being constricted to time or cost bounds, which means the team may not be able to perform all the subpractices referred in table 9. Teams framed in the context #2 should only get focused in what we have called P1 priority subpractices. Teams framed in the context #1 should perform both P1 and P2 priority subpractices (see the last column of table 9). P2 (lower priority) subpractices may also be skipped, either by the lack of information or of metrics to be completely covered in the project proposal phase. P1 (higher priority) subpractices are considered mandatory by us in all project proposals elaboration.

Even taking into account that some Requirements Management subpractices are not needed for the elaboration of project proposals, the adoption of RUP does not fully cover this process area. Additional actions must be performed to fully cover this process area.

Table 10 presents our detailed CMMI-RUP mapping for the Requirements Management process area. Subpractices marked with P2 should be considered of lower priority when the elaboration of project proposals is performed with insufficient time or cost limits, and subpractices marked with should be considered mandatory in any context. Next, we will analyze some situations where coverage is not satisfactory and present some recommendations and actions to completely cover this process area using RUP tasks and activities.

Subpractice SP1.1.1 demands to establish criteria for distinguishing appropriate requirements providers. With the tasks `develop requirements management plan` and `develop vision`, we can implement the majority of this subpractice

Table 9. Detailed CMMI-RUP Mapping for the Project Planning PA

Process Areas	Specific Goals (SG)	Specific Practices (SP)	Subpractices	Task: Develop Iteration Plan	Task: Identify and Assess Risks	Task: Schedule and Assign Work	Task: Plan Phases and Iterations	Task: Architectural Analysis	Task: Identify Relevant COTS Packages and Vendors	Task: Recommend Solution	Task: Define Solution	Task: Incorporate Existing Design Elements	Task: Tailor the Development Process for the Project	Task: Develop Problem Resolution Plan	Task: Report Status	Task: Monitor Project Status	Task: Assess Iteration	Task: Write Configuration Management (CM) Plan	Task: Develop Development Case	Task: Define Project Organization and Staffing	Task: Select and Acquire Tools	Task: Acquire Staff	Task: Project Planning Review	Task: Iteration Plan Review	Task: Review Requirements	Task: Lifecycle Milestone Review	Task: Project Review Authority (PRA) Project Review	Task: Compile Software Development Plan	Task: Develop Vision (Artifact: Vision)	Activity: Plan the Project	Activity: Refine the Development Plan	Activity: Plan for Next Iteration	Priority
PP (Category: Project Management)	SG 1	SP1.1 H	1	H	H		H																										P1
			2	H		H	H																									P1
			3					H	H	H	H																						P1
			4			H	H					H																					P1
		SP1.2 H	1				H						H																				P1
			2				H																										P1
			3				H																										P1
		SP1.3 H	1				H																										P1
		SP1.4 MH	1				M																										P1
			2			M																											P1
			3				H																										P1
	SG 2	SP2.1 H	1				H																										P1
			2				H																										P1
			3	H			H																										P1
			4	H			H																										P1
			5	H			H																										P1
			6											H																			P1
		SP2.2 H	1			H																											P1
			2			H																											P1
			3													H																	P1
			4												H	H																	P1
		SP2.3 MH	1															M															P1
			2															H															P2
			3																H														P2
		SP2.4 MH	1								H																						P2
			2																	H													P2
			3																		M												P1
		SP2.5 MH	1																	H													P1
			2																			H											P2
			3																														P1
			4	H			H																										P2
		SP2.6 M	1																											M			P1
		SP2.7 H	1																											H	H	H	P1
	SG 3	SP3.1 H	1																				H	H	H								P1
		SP3.2 H	1																					H		H	H						P2
		SP3.3 MH	1															M															P2
			2															L															P2
			3																									H					P2
			4																									H					P2
			5		H																							H					P2

H	High coverage	MH	High-Medium Coverage	M	Medium coverage	L	Low Coverage
	Not Covered	P1	Priority 1	P2	Priority 2		

Table 10. Detailed CMMI-RUP Mapping for the Requirements Management PA

Process Areas	Specific Goals (SG)	Specific Practices (SP)	Subpractices	Task: Review Requirements	Task: Manage Dependencies	Task: Balance Competing Stakeholder Priorities	Task: Develop Requirements Management Plan	Task: Elicit Stakeholder Requests	Task: Detail the Software Requirements	Task: Project Planning Review	Task: Conduct Review	Task: Submit Change Request	Task: Develop Vision	Task: Review Change Requests	Activity: Manage Change Requests	Activity: Manage Changing Requirements	Priority
REQM (Category: Engineering)	SG1	SP1.1 MH	1				M				M						P1
			2			H	H										P1
			3	H	H				H	H							P2
			4	H	H												P2
		SP1.2 H	1			H		H									P1
			2	H	H			H									P2
		SP1.3 H	1							H							P2
			2											H	H		P2
			3	H											H		P2
			4							H						H	P2
		SP1.4 H	1		H												P1
			2		H												P2
			3		H												P2
		SP1.5 MH	1	H						H	H						P2
			2	L											L		P2
			3	H	H												P2
			4											H			P2

H	High coverage	MH	High-Medium Coverage	M	Medium coverage	L	Low Coverage
	Not Covered	P1	Priority 1	P2	Priority 2		

since RUP does have a detailed process to determine how we select the stakeholders. However, to fully implement SP1.1.1 we need to include the criteria to select the appropriate stakeholders in the RUP artifact `requirements management plan` (output of the RUP task `develop requirements management plan`).

Subpractice SP1.5.2 presents low coverage because RUP does not consider in the review process any indication to investigate the source of requirements inconsistencies and the reason why they occurred. The inclusion of this indication in the review process will fully cover this subpractice.

6   Case Studies

Two case studies were developed to assess the usefulness of the CMMI-RUP mapping to support the execution of both the Project Planning and Requirements Management subpractices in the context of elaborating project proposals. The first case study was performed at an educational environment. The second case study was performed in an industrial setting.

The first case study involved 88 students enrolled in the course 8603N3 Software Processes and Methodologies (SPM) from the second year of the undergraduate degree in Information Systems and Technology in University of Minho (the first University to offer in Portugal DEng, MSc and PhD degrees in Computing). Students were divided in 19 development software teams, each one receiving a sequential identification number (Team 1, Team 2 ... Team 19).

The software project to be developed was requested by a real customer that provided all the information about the organization and interacted directly with the teams. The main goal of the teams was to elaborate a project proposal to solve the customer's problem, by producing one report. The report should address the following issues: the main features of the technical software solution and the cost and duration of the project. Control team 15 was randomly chosen to not follow the RUP guidelines (this team is referred as "control team"). The other teams are referred in this paper as "regular teams".

The assessment of the teams' performance adopted the following 7 steps: (1) A survey with 31 questions was developed based on REQM and PP subpractices; (2) The developed survey was assessed by 2 experts in SCAMPI model. The resulting suggestions were incorporated into the final version of the survey; (3) Survey was answered by each element of the 19 teams; (4) Each team element was characterized by mean of an online survey to collect information about age, sex, RUP role performed. The survey response was 100%; (5) The RUP work products generated by each team were assessed in terms of their existence. This has allowed the validation of the data obtained from step 3 by each one of the project managers; (6) Direct observation of the teams' work (during their regular meetings) to perceive their difficulties and doubts; (7) Analysis of the teams' academic performance based on the marks given by the SPM course instructors.

Table 11 shows the results obtained after the assessment. For each team, we present the coverage level observed for each subpractice, the corresponding average for each SP of REQM and PP process areas and the PA average. The coverage level was converted into numeric values: high coverage (H) corresponds to 100%; medium-high coverage (MH) corresponds to 75%; medium coverage (M) corresponds to 50%; low coverage (L) corresponds to 25%, and no coverage (N) corresponds to 0%. We have adopted a weighted average to calculate the coverage of each SP and PA. The subpractices weight was based in the level of priority: higher priority (P1) subpractices correspond to a weight of 1 and lower priority subpractices correspond to a weight of 0,5 (P2_weight=P1_weight/2). The SP weight was defined as the sum of its subpractices weight.

In general, teams implemented mainly the P1 subpractices. However, some teams have implemented also some P2 subpractices. In what considers the PP process area, we can observe similar results across the teams: averages with P1 and P2 subpractices are between 37,50% and 44,85%, and averages with only P1 subpractices are between 44,44% and 56,48%. Taking into account the results of the control team, we can conclude that PP process area was reasonably performed by the students. However, the results for the REQM process area were quite weak, which means that the teams

Table 11. Case study 1: Project Planning and Requirements Management Assessment

PP (Category: Project Management)

Specific Practices	SP weight	Subpractice	Subpractice weight	Team 1	Team 2	Team 3	Team 4	Team 5	Team 6	Team 7	Team 8	Team 9	Team 10	Team 11	Team 12	Team 13	Team 14	Control Team 15	Team 16	Team 17	Team 18	Team 19	Priority
SP1.1	4,0	1	1	H	H	H	H	H	H	H	H	H	H	H	H	H	H		H	H	H	H	P1
		2	1	H	H	H	M	M	H	M	H	H	M	H	H	H	H		H	MH	H	H	P1
		3	1																				P1
		4	1																				P1
SP1.1 Average				50,00	50,00	50,00	37,50	37,50	50,00	37,50	50,00	50,00	37,50	50,00	50,00	50,00	50,00	0,00	50,00	43,75	50,00	50,00	
SP1.2	3,0	1	1																			L	P1
		2	1	H	H	H	H	H	H	H	H	H	H	H	H	H	H		H	H	H	H	P1
		3	1	MH	M	MH	MH	MH	M	M	M	MH	MH	MH	MH	M	MH		MH	MH	MH	MH	P1
SP1.2 Average				58,33	50,00	58,33	58,33	58,33	50,00	50,00	50,00	58,33	58,33	58,33	58,33	50,00	58,33		58,33	58,33	66,67	58,33	
SP1.3	1,0	1	1	M	M	M	M	M	M	M	M	M	M	M	M	M	M		M	M	M	M	P1
SP1.3 Average				50,00	50,00	50,00	50,00	50,00	50,00	50,00	50,00	50,00	50,00	50,00	50,00	50,00	50,00	0,00	50,00	50,00	50,00	50,00	
SP1.4	3,0	1	1	M	M	M	M	M	M	M	M	M	M	M	M	M	M		M	M	M	M	P1
		2	1																				P1
		3	1	H	H	H	H	H	H	H	H	H	H	H	H	H	H		M	H	H	H	P1
SP1.4 Average				50,00	50,00	50,00	50,00	50,00	50,00	50,00	50,00	50,00	50,00	50,00	50,00	50,00	50,00	0,00	33,33	50,00	50,00	50,00	
SP2.1	6,0	1	1	H	H	H	H	H	H	H	H	H	H	H	H				M	M	MH	MH	P1
		2	1	H	H	H	H	H	H	H	H	H	H	H	H	H	H		H	H	MH	H	P1
		3	1			H			M			M	M			H			M	H	MH	H	P1
		4	1	H	H	H	H	H	H	H	H	H	H	H	H	H	L		H	H	H	H	P1
		5	1	H	H	H	H	H	H	H	H	H	H	H	H	H	MH		M	M	MH	H	P1
		6	1														MH			L		M	P1
SP2.1 Average				66,67	66,67	83,33	66,67	66,67	75,00	66,67	75,00	75,00	50,00	83,33	50,00	58,33	70,83	12,50	66,67	66,67	70,83	66,67	
SP2.2	4,0	1	1	H	H	H	H	H	H	H	H	H	H	H	H	H	H		H	H	H	H	P1
		2	1	H	H	H	H	H	H	H	H	H	H	H	H	H	H		H	H	H	H	P1
		3	1																				P1
		4	1																				P1
SP2.2 Average				50,00	50,00	50,00	50,00	50,00	50,00	50,00	50,00	50,00	50,00	50,00	50,00	50,00	50,00	50,00	50,00	50,00	50,00	50,00	
SP2.3	2,0	1	1											M					M	L	M	MH	P1
		2	0,5																				P2
		3	0,5																				P2
SP2.3 Average				0,00	0,00	0,00	0,00	0,00	0,00	0,00	0,00	0,00	0,00	25,00	0,00	0,00	0,00	25,00	0,00	12,50	25,00	37,50	
SP2.4	2,0	1	0,5																				P2
		2	0,5											M	L								P2
		3	1																				P1
SP2.4 Average				0,00	0,00	0,00	0,00	0,00	0,00	0,00	0,00	0,00	0,00	12,50	6,25	0,00	0,00	0,00	0,00	0,00	0,00	0,00	
SP2.5	3,0	1	1											L					M		L	M	P1
		2	0,5											L							MH	M	P2
		3	1	M	M	M	M	M	M	M	M	M	M	M	M	M	M		L	MH	M	M	P1
		4	0,5											L						MH			P2
SP2.5 Average				16,67	16,67	16,67	16,67	16,67	16,67	16,67	16,67	16,67	16,67	33,33	16,67	16,67	33,33	0,00	8,33	45,83	33,33	16,67	
SP2.6	1,0	1	1	MH	M	H	H	H	H	H	M	H	H	H	H	M	H		MH	MH	H	H	P1
SP2.6 Average				75,0	50,0	100,0	100,0	100,0	100,0	100,0	50,0	100,0	100,0	100,0	100,0	50,0	100,0	0,0	75,0	75,0	100,0	100,0	
SP2.7	1,0	1	1	MH	MH	MH	MH	MH	MH	MH	MH	MH	MH	MH	MH	MH	M		M	MH	M	MH	P1
SP2.7 Average				75,00	75,00	75,00	75,00	75,00	75,00	75,00	75,00	75,00	75,00	75,00	75,00	75,00	50,00	0,00	50,00	75,00	50,00	75,00	
SP3.1	1,0	1	1	0	0	0	0	0	0	0	0	0	0	0	0	0	0		0	0	0	0	P1
SP3.1 Average				0	0	0	0	0	0	0	0	0	0	0	0	0	0	0	0	0	0	0	
SP3.2	0,5	1	0,5																				P2
SP3.2 Average				0	0	0	0	0	0	0	0	0	0	0	0	0	0	0	0	0	0	0	
SP3.3	2,5	1	0,5																				P2
		2	0,5																				P2
		3	0,5																				P2
		4	0,5																				P2
		5	0,5																				P2
SP3.3 Average				0	0	0	0	0	0	0	0	0	0	0	0	0	0	0	0	0	0	0	
PP Average with P1				49,11	47,22	53,70	48,15	48,15	50,93	47,22	49,07	51,85	44,44	56,48	44,44	47,22	51,85	18,52	46,30	50,00	54,63	52,78	49,64
PP Average with P1 + P2				40,44	38,97	44,12	39,71	39,71	41,91	38,97	40,44	42,65	36,76	47,06	37,50	39,34	42,65	14,71	37,50	43,01	44,85	43,38	41,05

REQM (Category: Engineering)

Specific Practices	SP weight	Subpractice	Subpractice weight	Team 1	Team 2	Team 3	Team 4	Team 5	Team 6	Team 7	Team 8	Team 9	Team 10	Team 11	Team 12	Team 13	Team 14	Control Team 15	Team 16	Team 17	Team 18	Team 19	Priority
SP1.1	3,0	1	1	M	M	M	M	M	M	M	M	M	M	MH	M	MH	M		M	M	M	M	P1
		2	1											M	L				M	M	M	M	P1
		3	0,5																				P2
		4	0,5																				P2
SP1.1 Average				16,67	16,67	16,67	16,67	16,67	16,67	16,67	16,67	16,67	16,67	25,00	16,67	25,00	16,67	0,00	33,33	25,00	33,33	16,67	
SP1.2	1,5	1	1				M	M	M			M		MH	MH						L		P1
		2	0,5											MH	MH								P2
SP1.2 Average				0,00	0,00	0,00	33,33	33,33	33,33	0,00	0,00	33,33	0,00	75,00	66,67	0,00	0,00	0,00	0,00	0,00	16,67	0,00	
SP1.3	2,0	1	0,5	MH	MH	MH	H	MH	H	MH	MH	H	MH	H	H	MH	H		MH	H	MH	MH	P2
		2	0,5																				P2
		3	0,5											H	H					MH			P2
		4	0,5	M	M	M	M	M	M	M	M	M	M	M	M	M	M		M	M	M	M	P2
SP1.3 Average				31,25	31,25	31,25	37,50	31,25	37,50	31,25	31,25	37,50	31,25	62,50	56,25	31,25	37,50	31,25	31,25	56,25	31,25	31,25	
SP1.4	2,0	1	1			L											L			L			P1
		2	0,5																				P2
		3	0,5																				P2
SP1.4 Average				0,00	0,00	12,50	0,00	0,00	0,00	0,00	0,00	0,00	0,00	0,00	0,00	0,00	12,50	0,00	0,00	12,50	0,00	0,00	
SP1.5	2,0	1	0,5																				P2
		2	0,5																				P2
		3	0,5																				P2
		4	0,5																				P2
SP1.5 Average				0	0	0	0	0	0	0	0	0	0	0	0	0	0	0	0	0	0	0	
REQM Average with P1				12,50	12,50	18,75	25,00	25,00	25,00	12,50	12,50	25,00	12,50	37,50	31,25	18,75	31,25	18,75	12,50	31,25	31,25	12,50	21,53
REQM Average with P1 + P2				10,71	10,71	13,10	16,67	15,48	16,67	10,71	10,71	16,67	10,71	29,78	25,00	13,10	19,05	13,10	10,71	22,82	17,86	10,71	15,61

H	High coverage	MH	High-Medium Coverage	M	Medium coverage	L	Low Coverage
	Not Covered	P1	Priority 1	P2	Priority 2		

were more focused on the planning of the project rather than on the elicitation and description of the requirements for the demanded solution. This is also a quite frequent behavior observed in the industrial practitioners (case study 2 confirms this). The teams have focused their work mainly on the elaboration of the Product Breakdown Structure (PBS) and the Work Breakdown Structure (WBS).

For the REQM process area averages with P1 and P2 subpractices are between 10,71% and 29,76%, and averages with only P1 subpractices are between 12,50% and 37,50%. These results are quite disappointing from the perspective of the quality of the teams work. By using the surveys we concluded that the teams have neglected essential RUP tasks needed to ensure the complete coverage of the required subpractices to the elaboration of project proposals. With the direct observation we could perceive a quite different set of activities performed by each regular team that may justify the obtained results for the REQM process area, by the considerable RUP tailoring effort that each team had to perform. The control team performed two of the four P1 subpractices and two P2 subpractices. The results of the regular teams and the control team are quite similar. Even not using RUP the control team performed the elicitation and description of the requirements similarly to the other teams. These similarities demonstrate the pertinence to explicitly inform practitioners about two different levels of priorities for REQM subpractices to help them better decide what subpractices to perform even in strongly constricted contexts for the elaboration of project proposals.

In the second case study, we have evaluated eight real project proposals elaborated by the consulting team of the EPMQ Laboratory at the CCG/ZGDV Institute. The CCG/ZGDV Institute is the frontend of the University of Minho for elaborating projects for the ICT local industry. In the CCG/ZGDV Institute, the EPMQ Laboratory is responsible for the software engineering and information systems domain. The EPMQ Laboratory is permanently enrolled in around a dozen of ICT projects.

The ICT projects considered for the second case study were divided in three types of funding source: IST European projects; QREN National projects (big projects with the local industry supported by the Portuguese Economics Ministry); and Vale IDT projects (small projects with the local industry supported by the Portuguese Economics Ministry). Table 12 presents the funding source of each project considered in this case study.

The evaluation was performed by a survey with a set of questions directly related with the CMMI REQM and PP subpractices. The survey was applied to the project manager of each project proposal. Table 13 presents the results of the projects assessment.

In what considers the PP process area, we can observe similar results across the projects: averages with P1 and P2 subpractices are between 11,94% and 68,41%, and averages with only P1 subpractices are between 14,29% and 83,04%.

The elaboration of project proposals for IST European calls is more exhaustive and demanding than for other calls. Those projects are usually more complex, have longer duration, higher number of partners and are usually focused in a mix of applied research and technology transfer. Therefore, the average of PP process area for those projects is much higher than the QREN national projects and the Vale IDT projects.

Table 12. Case study 2: Projects Characterization

	Funding Source		
	IST European Project	QREN National Project	Vale IDT Project
Project 1		X	
Project 2			X
Project 3		X	
Project 4	X		
Project 5		X	
Project 6		X	
Project 7	X		
Project 8			X

In what concerns the REQM process area, we can observe a decrease of effort when compared with the PP process area. Across the 8 projects we have obtained averages for P1 and P2 subpractices between 0% and 14,29%, and averages with only P1 subpractices between 0% and 37,50%. As said before, the industrial practitioners are also more focused on the planning of the project rather than on the elicitation and description of the requirements; so, the results for the REQM process area were also quite weak like in the case study 1. Like in the PP subpractices, the results for the REQM process area shows that the IST European projects have a better result, since in these projects a proper definition of the project scope is fundamental to get a successful project.

When comparing the results of case study 1 and case study 2 , we can conclude that the performance of case study 2 is better in both the calculated averages, P1 and P1+P2 subpractices (see Figure 1). Since the project planning tasks are directly related with the budget to be approved, it is completely understandable why in real projects the subpractices of the PP process area are better performed than in academic environment. It is also possible to admit that academic projects performed by students is not a perfect emulating environment to motive a detailed project planning, at least when elaborating project proposals.

When we analyze to the REQM process area, we obtain two different situations: (1) case study 1 performed better in P1+P2 subpractices; (2) case study 2 performed P1 only subpractices. We believe that in constricted contexts of the elaboration of project proposals, industrial practitioners are more effective in selecting and performing higher priority subpractices, since they know that the elicitation and the description of requirements have to be reworked when the project is approved. Therefore, they perform the minimum requirements-related tasks required to elaborate a project proposal. In opposition, students in academic projects are more motivated to perform less priority REQM tasks since they know that every additional effort will be counted positively for their academic assessment. Students do not make choices with exactly the same criteria as industrial practitioners.

Table 13. Case study 2: Project Planning and Requirements Management Assessment

	Specific Practices	SP weight	Subpractice	Subpractice weight	Project 1	Project 2	Project 3	Project 4	Project 5	Project 6	Project 7	Project 8	Priority
PP (Category: Project Management)	SP1.1	4,0	1	1	H	H	H	MH	H	MH	H		P1
			2	1	M	H	H	MH	H	MH	H		P1
			3	1	H	H	H	MH	H	MH	H		P1
			4	1			H	M	H	MH	MH		P1
	SP1.1 Average				62,50	75,00	100,00	68,75	100,00	75,00	93,75	0,00	
	SP1.2	3,0	1	1	H	H	H	MH	H	MH	H	H	P1
			2	1	L						H	L	P1
			3	1	MH	MH	H	MH	MH	MH	H	L	P1
	SP1.2 Average				66,67	58,33	66,67	50,00	58,33	50,00	100,00	50,00	
	SP1.3	1,0	1	1	H	H	H	MH	MH	MH	H		P1
	SP1.3 Average				100	100	100	75	75	75	100	0	
	SP1.4	3,0	1	1		H	H	M	MH	MH	MH	L	P1
			2	1	H	H	H	MH	MH	MH	H	MH	P1
			3	1				MH	MH	MH	MH		P1
	SP1.4 Average				33,33	66,67	66,67	66,67	75,00	75,00	83,33	33,33	
	SP2.1	6,0	1	1	H	H	H	H	H	MH	H		P1
			2	1	MH	H	M	H	H	MH	H		P1
			3	1	M	MH	M	M	H	MH	H		P1
			4	1	H	H	MH	MH	H	MH	H		P1
			5	1	MH	MH	MH	M	H	MH	H	MH	P1
			6	1									P1
	SP2.1 Average				66,67	75,00	58,33	62,50	83,33	62,50	83,33	12,50	
	SP2.2	4,0	1	1		MH			MH	MH	MH	H	P1
			2	1		MH			MH	MH	MH	H	P1
			3	1		MH							P1
			4	1									P1
	SP2.2 Average				0,00	56,25	0,00	37,50	37,50	37,50	50,00	0,00	
	SP2.3	2,0	1	1	M	MH	MH	MH	H	MH	H		P1
			2	0,5									P2
			3	0,5									P2
	SP2.3 Average				25	37,5	37,5	37,5	50	37,5	50	0	
	SP2.4	2,0	1	0,5									P2
			2	0,5									P2
			3	1	MH	MH	MH	H	H	MH	H	MH	P1
	SP2.4 Average				37,5	37,5	37,5	50	50	37,5	50	37,5	
	SP2.5	3,0	1	1	H	MH	MH	H	H	MH	H		P1
			2	0,5									P2
			3	1				H	H	MH	H		P1
			4	0,5									P2
	SP2.5 Average				33,33	25,00	25,00	66,67	66,67	50,00	66,67	0,00	
	SP2.6	1,0	1	1				MH	H	MH	H		P1
	SP2.6 Average				0	0	0	75	100	75	100	0	
	SP2.7	1,0	1	1	MH	MH	MH	MH	H	MH	H		P1
	SP2.7 Average				75	75	75	75	100	75	100,0	0	
	SP3.1	1,0	1	1									P1
	SP3.1 Average				0	0	0	0	0	0	0	0	
	SP3.2	0,5	1	0,5									P2
	SP3.2 Average				0	0	0	0	0	0	0	0	
	SP3.3	2,5	1	0,5									P2
			2	0,5									P2
			3	0,5									P2
			4	0,5									P2
			5	0,5									P2
	SP3.3 Average				0	0	0	0	0	0	0	0	
	PP Average with P1 only				48,21	62,50	55,36	62,50	75,89	61,61	83,04	14,29	57,92
	PP Average with P1 and P2				39,80	51,87	45,90	51,24	62,44	50,75	68,41	11,94	47,79
REQM (Category: Engineering)	SP1.1	3,0	1	1	MH	MH	MH	MH	MH	MH	M		P1
			2	1	M						MH	M	P1
			3	0,5									P2
			4	0,5									P2
	SP1.1 Average				0,00	41,67	25,00	25,00	25,00	25,00	50,00	33,33	
	SP1.2	1,5	1	1				MH					P1
			2	0,5									P2
	SP1.2 Average				0	0	0	50	0	0	0	0	
	SP1.3	2,0	1	0,5									P2
			2	0,5									P2
			3	0,5									P2
			4	0,5									P2
	SP1.3 Average				0	0	0	0	0	0	0	0	
	SP1.4	2,0	1	1									P1
			2	0,5									P2
			3	0,5									P2
	SP1.4 Average				0	0	0	0	0	0	0	0	
	SP1.5	2,0	1	0,5									P2
			2	0,5									P2
			3	0,5									P2
			4	0,5									P2
	SP1.5 Average				0	0	0	0	0	0	0	0	
	REQM Average with P1 only				0,00	31,25	18,75	37,50	18,75	18,75	37,50	25,00	23,44
	REQM Average with P1 and P2				0,00	11,90	7,14	14,29	7,14	7,14	14,29	9,52	8,93

H	High coverage	MH	High-Medium Coverage	M	Medium coverage
	Not Covered	L	Low Coverage	P1	Priority 1	P2	Priority 2

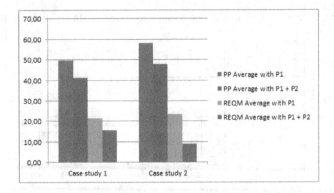

Fig. 1. Case Study 1 and Case Study 2 Performance Analysis

7   Conclusions

CMMI is an approach used to assess the maturity of software development process. RUP provides guidelines for activities, artifacts, roles and responsibilities. However, both intersect in regards to software quality and hence customer satisfaction. A review of the literature shows that RUP does not provide full coverage of CMMI PP and REQM process areas.

When we are elaborating project proposals, we are executing a set of tasks and/or activities that are framed within to the REQM and PP process areas. We have identified the subpractices of REQM and PP process areas that help in the elaboration of project proposals. We have assessed several teams that adopt RUP (both in educational and in industrial settings) when elaborating project proposals. The assessment was based on the adoption of the CMMI-RUP mapping (mainly in what regards the REQM and PP subpractices) that has been thoroughly described and justified in this paper. The comparison of the results obtained for the two case studies allowed us to conclude that practitioners adjust their PP effort taking into account the kind of project and that REQM tasks are generally neglected in the context of elaborating project proposals.

As future work, we will extend this mapping to the remaining process areas of CMMI ML2 and ML3 process areas, since we will focus next our work in the project development phase. We will also change the educational case study: students will be organized in big teams to emulate a real software house.

References

1. Niazi, M., Wilson, D., Zowghi, D.: Critical success factors for software process improvement implementation: An empirical study. SPIP 11, 193–211 (2006)
2. Manzoni, L.V., Price, R.T.: Identifying extensions required by RUP to comply with CMM levels 2 and 3. IEEE TSE 29, 181–192 (2003)

3. Marchewka, J.T.: Information technology project management. John Wiley and Sons (2009)
4. Chen, C.-Y., Chong, P.P.: Software engineering education: A study on conducting collaborative senior project development. Journal of Systems and Software 84, 479–491 (2011)
5. Carvallo, J.P., Franch, X., Quer, C.: Supporting CMMI Level 2 SAM PA with Non-technical Features Catalogues. SPIP 13, 171–182 (2008)
6. Kruchten, P.: The Rational Unified Process: An Introduction. Addison-Wesley (2003)
7. CMMI Product Team: CMMI for Development version 1.2, CMU/SEI-2006-TR-008, ESC-TR-2006-008 (2006)
8. CMMI Product Team: CMMI for Development version 1.3, CMU/SEI-2010-TR-033, ESC-TR-2010-033 (2010)
9. IBM, Rational Unified Process: Best practices for software development teams, http://www.ibm.com/developerworks/rational/library/content/03July/1000/1251/1251_bestpractices_TP026B.pdf (accessed August 30, 2012)
10. Chrissis, M.B., Konrad, M., Shrum, S.: CMMI(R): Guidelines for Process Integration and Product Improvement, 2nd edn. The SEI Series in Software Engineering. Addison-Wesley Professional (2006)
11. Ahern, D.M., Clouse, A., Turner, R.: CMMI Distilled: A Practical introduction to Integrated Process Improvement. Addison-Wesley (2004)
12. IBM, RUP for small projects, version 7.1, http://www.wthreex.com/rup/smallprojects/ (accessed August 30, 2012)
13. What Is a Project Proposal?, http://www.wisegeek.com/what-is-a-project-proposal.html, (accessed August 30, 2012)
14. Nebiu, B.: Project Proposal Writing, http://documents.rec.org/publications/ProposalWriting.pdf (accessed August 30, 2012)
15. Procter, R., Rouncefield, M., Poschen, M., Lin, Y., Voss, A.: Agile Project Management: A Case Study of a Virtual Research Environment Development Project. In: CSCW, vol. 20, pp. 197–225 (2011)
16. Kurbel, K.E.: Developing Information Systems: The Making of Information Systems, pp. 155–234. Springer, Heidelberg (2008)
17. Monteiro, P., Machado, R.J., Kazman, R.: Inception of Software Validation and Verification Practices within CMMI Level 2. In: ICSEA 2009, pp. 536–541. IEEE (2009)
18. SEI, Published Appraisal Results, http://www.sei.cmu.edu/cmmi/casestudies/profiles/pdfs/upload/2010MarCMMI.pdf (accessed August 30, 2012)
19. IBM, RUP for Large Projects, version 7.1
20. Uttangi, R.V., Rizwan, R.S.A.A.: Fast track to CMMI implementation: Integrating the CMMI and RUP process frameworks, http://www.ibm.com/developerworks/rational/library/oct07/uttangi_rizwan/index.html (accessed August 30, 2012)
21. Grundmann, M.: A CMMI Maturity Level 2 assessment of RUP, http://www.ibm.com/developerworks/rational/library/dec05/grundmann/ (accessed August 30, 2012)

22. IBM, IBM Rational Unified Process with CMMI Compliance Support, Version 7.5.0.1, `http://www.ibm.com/developerworks/rational/downloads/07/rup_cmmi_v1/` (accessed August 30, 2012)
23. Gallagher, B., Brownsword, L.: The Rational Unified Process and the Capability Maturity Model – Integrated Systems/Software Engineering, `http://www.sei.cmu.edu/library/assets/rup.pdf` (accessed August 30, 2012)
24. Monteiro, P., Borges, P., Machado, R.J., Ribeiro, P.: A Reduced Set of RUP Roles to Small Software Development Teams. In: ICSSP 2012, pp. 190–199. IEEE Computer Society Press (2012)
25. Borges, P., Monteiro, P., Machado, R.J.: Mapping RUP Roles to Small Software Development Teams. In: Biffl, S., Winkler, D., Bergsmann, J. (eds.) SWQD 2012. LNBIP, vol. 94, pp. 59–70. Springer, Heidelberg (2012)
26. Borges, P., Monteiro, P., Machado, R.J.: Tailoring RUP to Small Software Development Teams. In: SEAA 2012, pp. 306–309 (2012)

Development and Evaluation of Systems Engineering Strategies: An Assessment-Based Approach

Fritz Stallinger[1], Reinhold Plösch[2], Robert Neumann[1],
Stefan Horn[3], and Jan Vollmar[3]

[1] Software Competence Center Hagenberg, Process & Quality Engineering, Hagenberg, Austria
{fritz.stallinger,robert.neumann}@scch.at
[2] Kepler University Linz, Business Informatics - Software Engineering, Linz, Austria
reinhold.ploesch@jku.at
[3] Siemens AG, Corporate Technology, Erlangen, Germany
{stefan.horn,jan.vollmar}@siemens.com

Abstract. Linking process improvement with the business and strategic goals of an organization is a key prerequisite for enabling such process improvement initiatives to generate appropriate value for the organization. However, process improvement methods themselves typically do not deal in detail with the provision of guidance for the derivation of business focused process improvements. Therefore, we provide a best practice-based approach for developing and evaluating systems engineering strategies, based on a conceptual framework for defining and representing such engineering strategies. The resulting engineering strategies are aligned with corporate strategies and business goals. Strategy objects as a core element of our approach can be associated with the process areas and processes of existing process improvement frameworks. The presented approach thus allows that any process improvement action can consequently be systematically aligned with the strategy objects of the developed systems engineering strategies and thus with the business and strategic goals of the enterprise.

Keywords: Systems engineering, industrial engineering, engineering strategy, functional strategy, strategy development, strategy evaluation, process improvement, CMMI.

1   Introduction, Background, and Overview

Linking process improvement initiatives with the business and strategic goals of an enterprise is regarded a key success factor for process improvement and a prerequisite for enabling such improvement initiatives to generate value for the organization. A lot of research and development work has been performed on elaborating and validating best practice models for system lifecycle as well as software lifecycle activities (e.g. [1], [2], [3], [4]) and on methods for guiding process improvement. This ranges from the provision of guidance for single improvement actions (e.g. [5], [6]) to the provision of frameworks for the management of overall improvement programs (e.g. [7], [8]).

D. Winkler, S. Biffl, and J. Bergsmann (Eds.): SWQD 2013, LNBIP 133, pp. 215–229, 2013.

All these frameworks and methods generally assume the existence of business and strategic goals at organizational or enterprise level and stress the importance of aligning any process improvements with these goals. Nevertheless, they generally provide little and typically only generic guidance on how to actually define the implementation details of and evaluate, prioritize, and select process improvements.

Within this context, this paper presents the results of investigations on engineering strategies for the industrial solutions business as a specialization of systems engineering. Engineering strategies describe how *'Engineering'* as a functional area of an organization will support the achievement of the organization's business goals. Other functional areas include for example marketing, human resources, or customer service. The industrial solutions business is concerned with the provision of highly customer-specific and complex systems like power plants, airports, rail systems, chemical plants, or substantial parts of such systems.

The main goals of this work are to understand the role of engineering strategies in the overall strategy development and implementation framework of an enterprise, to identify the conceptual framework and key elements for describing engineering strategies, to identify best practice examples for engineering strategies in systems engineering, to provide a model and method to assess and, if necessary, improve the quality of an engineering strategy in a systematic and efficient way, and to validate and identify the alignment of the developed engineering strategy model against a selected process improvement framework.

The paper builds on work on developing software engineering strategies [9] and extends this work from the software engineering domain to the systems engineering domain using industrial engineering or the industrial solutions business as an example. The major enhancements refer to an extension of the underlying meta-model for strategy representation by grouping dimensions for strategy objects and the widening of the scope of strategy definition from software engineering to industrial and systems engineering, respectively. This results in the revision and extension of the number and type of strategy objects to consider and the provision of an assessment-based method for engineering strategy evaluation and improvement.

The remainder of the paper is structured as follows: section 2 elaborates the role of engineering strategies in the overall strategy development context of an organization and introduces the basic elements and the conceptual framework for strategy definition; section 3 presents typical strategy objects relevant for the industrial solutions business domain; section 4 presents and discusses the development and assessment process for engineering strategies; section 5 maps the identified strategy objects to the process areas of CMMI [4] and discusses support through the presented approach for process improvement; section 6 provides the status on application and validation of the proposed approach; section 7, finally, summarizes and concludes the paper.

2   Conceptual Framework for Defining Engineering Strategies

Understanding strategy development at systems engineering level from an overall strategy development point of view is quite similar to understanding software engineering strategy development. We first relate engineering strategies to the overall strategy development efforts within an enterprise. Fig. 1 illustrates the overall strategy development process of an organization. Engineering strategies are developed within the *'Development of functional strategies'* process step. Detailed explanations on the steps of this process are provided in [10] and [11]. According to [11], a distinction can be made between the corporate strategy, various division strategies, and various functional strategies which can be characterized as follows (cf. [9]):

- *Corporate Strategy*: The central issue on this level is to determine which market segments should be addressed with which resources. This has to be understood against the background of the core tasks of a company – resource allocation, diversification decisions, and the coordination of the more or less independent divisions.
- *Division Strategy*: The division strategy refines the corporate strategy. The major questions to be addressed by the division strategy are how to develop a long-term unique selling proposition compared to the market competitors and how to develop a unique product or service. For generating competitive advantages a division has to take its capabilities and resources as well as customer needs and market structures into consideration.
- *Functional Strategy*: Functional strategies define the principles for the functional areas of a division in accordance with the division strategy and, therefore, refine the division strategy in the distinct functional areas. Examples of such functional areas whose principles can be defined by means of functional strategies are marketing, finance, human resources, software or systems engineering, etc.

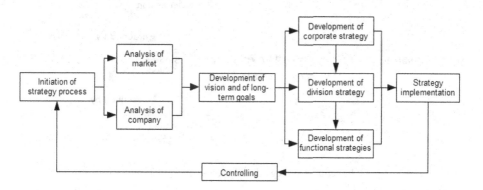

Fig. 1. Overall strategy development process (adapted from [11])

Functional strategies can be developed independently from each other, but must all adhere to the division strategy and, therefore, also to the corporate strategy. On the corporate and on the division level the emphasis is on the effectiveness (doing the right things) of the corporation or division, while the functional strategies have their focus on the efficiency (doing the things right) of the respective functional areas. The distinction between the different levels of strategies ensures the translation of business goals from the corporate level down to the functional level.

The implied structure of different kinds of strategies on the corporation and division level might not be applicable for all companies but depends on the companies' size and organizational structure. Especially in smaller companies there might be no distinction between corporate strategies and division strategies.

The corporate and division strategy is one part of the context relevant for the development of functional strategies. Furthermore, other aspects have to be considered like the market of the organization, human resources, or budgets. It is important to notice that the impact of these aspects changes over time and situation; the resulting relevant driving forces typically also determine the focus of the engineering strategy and thus the emphasis with respect to content.

In a next step one has to understand the structure of functional engineering strategies. In our model a functional strategy consists of strategic goals, strategy objects, and strategic statements. In extension to [9] we allow, that strategy objects can be prioritized and grouped. Fig. 2 depicts the conceptual framework for the description of functional strategies also showing the relations between these elements.

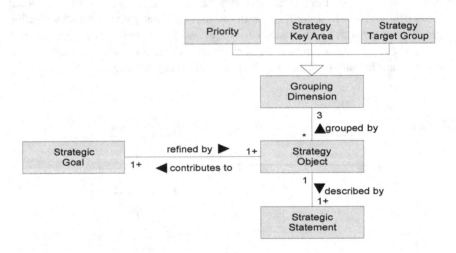

Fig. 2. Functional strategy description - conceptual framework

A *strategic goal* describes a desired state in the future and specifies a framework for actions on a strategic level. The strategic goals formulated in the functional strategy are refinements of strategic goals on the corporate and divisional level mapped on the respective functional area. Table 1 shows the attributes used to describe strategic goals and provides an example description from a real-world project.

Table 1. Example description of a strategic goal (adapted from [9])

ID:	G-SALE
Priority:	A
Strategic Goal:	Selected software products have to be sellable separately, i.e. without selling the underlying hardware product.
Explanation of strategic goal:	The selected software products must meet conditions, so that they can be sold independently of other products (hardware and software) on the automation market.
Description how to reach the strategic goal:	This is achieved by appropriate abstraction of the runtime environment, isolation and independence from other products, extensive tests, appropriate actions for the protection of intellectual property, documentation and consulting and support offers.
Description how to measure the realization of the strategic goal:	Guideline for achieving this goal is that by the end of the first quarter of 2011 product X is sellable alone and independently of other products.

The verbalization of strategic goals should be based on knowledge from a detailed analysis of the organization. A strategic goal of a functional strategy must not violate or determine corporate or division goals or visions. Strategic goals are refined by and linked to strategy objects. These links help to identify affected strategic goals or strategy objects when changing either of them.

A *strategy object* refines one or more strategic goals and groups strategic statements targeting one common topic or theme. As the strategy objects and the strategic statements are targeted towards the functional strategic goals it is also assured that the divisional and corporate goals are not violated. Examples of strategy objects that are typically refined during the strategy development process include architecture management, quality management, requirements management, standards management, etc. Table 2 shows the attributes used for describing strategy objects and provides an example of a description of a strategy object from a real-world project.

Table 2. Example description of a strategy object (adapted from [9])

ID:	O-WORK
Name:	Work Organization
Definition:	Work Organization is the systematic arrangement of effective and efficient software development and project execution.
Set of strategic statements:	1 **A** - In the areas of Firmware (incl. Technology), Human-Machine-Interface and Tools the following developer teams have to be formed: OEM development, product development, and maintenance
	2 **B** - Each software developer is member of one of these teams. For capacity reasons a developer may temporarily join another team, but the number of these developers should be kept low.

A *strategic statement* provides specific instructions for supporting the associated strategy object within the organization and is described by a consecutive number, priority, and the actual statement.

The *grouping of strategy objects* facilitates understanding strategy objects on a more abstract level. Additionally, the assessment or development process for engineering strategies (cf. section 4) benefits from additional abstractions, as assessment or development can be carried out in a focused way. We structure strategy objects simultaneously along three dimensions:

- *Strategy Key Areas*: The key areas used are *People, Process, Products and Services*, and *Methods and Tools*. We identified these key areas to be important from several functional strategy development projects. Each strategy object is assigned to one or more of these key areas, but a leading key area is marked.
- *Strategy Target Group*: A strategy target group denotes the typical business function or role responsible for a strategy object. Strategy target groups have to be denoted organization-specific, but generally comprise e.g. *Product Management, Product Development, Project Execution, Organization/Resources, Sales,* or other.
- *Priority*: This grouping dimension considers priorities. Strategy objects are grouped by priorities along the ordinal scale *Priority A, Priority B, Priority C,* with *Priority A* denoting the highest priority.

These grouping dimensions can be used in different scenarios of a strategy assessment project, e.g. to easily cross-check to what extent the strategy objects that fall into a specific category are considered in actual strategies or to focus the assessment to strategy objects within a specific group.

3   An Industrial Engineering Strategy Objects Reference Model

This section provides the results of the identification and definition of strategy objects that can be considered generally relevant for the industrial engineering. As a starting point, strategy objects identified in the software engineering domain (cf. [9]) were evaluated and adapted for their use in the industrial solutions business. Additional strategy objects were identified by research and investigation in the industrial engineering and industrial solutions business domain and validated by discussions with and review through industrial and academic experts from the industrial engineering domain. These additionally identified strategy objects for the industrial engineering domain are *Claim Management, Product Life Cycle Management, Competence Management, Tool and Data Integration, Reuse Management, Solutions Building, Supplier Management, and Value Chain Management* (cf. Table 3).

A *strategy object* in the context of an engineering strategy, i.e. in the context of a functional strategy, can be understood as a subject area that needs to be dealt with on a strategic level. Our intention here is to identify and describe to the widest generic coverage the typical strategy objects for industrial engineering. Nevertheless, in the course of a strategy development process additional strategy objects might be identified, triggered by characteristics of the organization, domain, market, or concrete specialization of systems engineering.

Table 3 provides an overview on the identified set of typical and possible strategy objects for the industrial engineering. On this general and abstract level it is not possible to distinguish more and less important or related strategy objects. Therefore, the strategy objects are ordered alphabetically – ascending by their unique ID. Moreover, the generic assignment of the strategy object to the strategy key areas *'People' (P)*, *'Engineering Processes' (EP)*, *'Engineering Methodology' (EM)*, *'Solution Structure, Solution Modules' (SS,SM)* and *'Engineering Tools Support' (ETS)* is provided with a black square denoting a major assignment (i.e. the leading key area) and a grey square indicating a subordinate assignment.

Table 3. Strategy objects for industrial engineering

Strategy Object	P	EP	EM	SS,SM	ETS
O-ARCH: Architecture Management	□	□	□	■	□
O-CHAN: Change Management	□	■	□	□	
O-CLAI: Claim Management	■	□		□	
O-COMP: Component Management	□	□	□	■	□
O-CONF: Configuration Management	□		■	□	□
O-COPA: Competence Management	□	■	□		
O-CYCL: Product Life Cycle Management	□	□	■		
O-DOCU: Document Management	□	□	■		
O-DOMA: Domain Engineering	□	□	□	■	
O-INNO: Innovations Management	□	□	□	■	
O-INTE: Tool and Data Integration	□	□	□		■
O-METH: Methods Management	□	□	□	■	
O-PROC: Process Management	□	■			
O-PROD: Product Management	□	□	□	■	□
O-PROM: Project Management	■	□			□
O-QUAL: Quality Management	□	■		□	
O-REQM: Requirements Management	■	□	□	□	□
O-REUS: Reuse Management	□	□	■	□	□
O-RSKM: Risk Management	□	■	□		□
O-SOLB: Solutions Building	□	□	□	■	
O-STND: Standards Management	□			■	
O-SUPL: Supplier Management		□	□	■	
O-TEST: Test Management	□	□	■	□	□
O-TOOL: Tools Management	□	□			■
O-VALU: Value Chain Management	□	■		□	
O-WORK: Work Organization	□	■	□		

Table 4 provides a sample description for the strategy object *Product Management*. For each strategy object we try to give a definition that – of course – has to be adapted to the context of a specific organization. The definition should show what kind of topics and issues should be addressed within the strategy object. Besides the definition we provide a selection of typical topics dealt with in 'real-word' engineering strategies. Last but not least, some examples of strategic statements are given, extracted from annual business and similar reports.

Table 4. Description of strategy object ‚Product Management'

ID:	O-PROD
Name:	Product Management
Definition	*Product Management* in the context of industrial solutions is the development of product ideas, the definition of product requirements, their commercial calculation and the assignment of engineering development efforts over the whole life span. Product Management covers demand-driven as well as supply-side product development.
Typical Topics	• Elicitation and documentation of product requirements • Integration of product development and solutions development – management of synergies, reuse of product or solutions innovations. • Interplay of sales and distribution (product management) and engineering concerning the products • Responsibilities for product management in the context of the solution processes. • Methods and tools for domain engineering (product line engineering).
Examples of Strategic Statements	• „In product development ABB uses standardized Life Cycle Assessment procedures, a handbook for environmentally aware design, a check-list to identify potential sustainability risks, and a list of prohibited and restricted substances to ensure the company's sustainability objectives are embedded into product development." [12] • „Establish a Product Matrix and Implementation Plan for modifications to Siemens THRI and TLRI Generators in the UK." [13]

4   Developing and Assessing Engineering Strategies

The aim of this section is to outline a methodology for the systematic assessment of existing engineering strategies. The general approach is to conduct a strategy development process with an assessment emphasis. As the assessment method simulates parts of a strategy development process, consequently it is inevitable to have the management responsible for strategy development in a division or company at hand. The result of this assessment is a qualitative report that indicates:

• the general maturity of the engineering strategy, taking into account – among others – the form of the engineering strategy, the structuredness of the strategic descriptions, and the appropriateness for the respective business
• those strategy objects that should be considered in the engineering strategy
• the completeness and maturity of strategic statements for each important strategy object
• those strategy objects where strategic statements exist but the coverage of the given strategy object's topics is too low
• gaps in the engineering strategy, i.e. those strategy objects where no strategic statements exist but that are of importance for the company or division.

The strategy assessment method is described in more detail in subsection 4.3 below. As the assessment process is related to the strategy development process, we first present the typical strategy development process and an approach to prioritize strategy objects.

4.1   Developing Engineering Strategies

The strategy development process for engineering strategies is embedded in a more global process. When developing an engineering strategy the organization's business strategy and general conditions must be taken into account. The results of the strategy development process lead to different strategic actions. The impact of these actions on the development process, on the quality, on the work organization, etc. is monitored and analyzed to identify needed changes, which then again must be considered in engineering strategy development and refinement.

The detailed strategy development process is shown in Fig. 3. It is systematically structured into the development of strategic goals and strategy objects. Strategic goals and objects are chosen and defined in cooperation of external consultants with the responsible management of the organization (cf. Fig. 3, *'External Experts'* and *'Customers'*, respectively). It has to be ensured that the strategic goals adhere to and do not violate the more general divisional or corporate goals. For strategic goals and statements a prioritization has to be performed. The strategy itself must state how it is developed further. The management then formally enacts the strategy.

The ideal detailed engineering strategy development process is typically performed in a sequential order. Feedback is gathered and adjustments can be made at certain points of the development process – especially for the intermediate products (*Strategy Structure*, *First Strategy Concept* and *Second Strategy Concept*). The process of finding strategic goals and defining strategy objects is interactive. External experts should make suggestions, which then are refined and finalized in workshops together with the management (cf. Fig. 3, activity *'Strategy Tuning'*). We consider this external view important to achieve a comprehensive view on the engineering strategy.

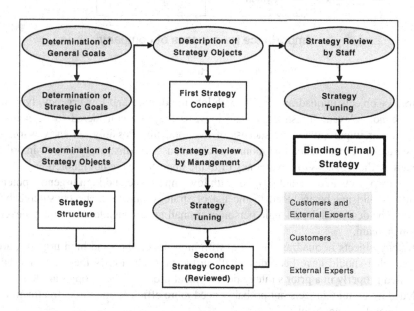

Fig. 3. Detailed process of engineering strategy development

4.2   Prioritizing Strategy Objects

One major step during the strategy development process is to select the appropriate strategy objects (cf. Fig. 3, activity *'Determination of Strategy Objects'*). From a methodic point of view the selection of strategy objects should be driven by the importance and by the urgency of the respective strategy object [11].

According to [11], all strategy objects should be placed in a portfolio with the two axes *importance* (for the success of the company) and *urgency* (see Fig. 4). This allows us to identify a standard procedure for dealing with the different strategy objects depending on their position in the portfolio.

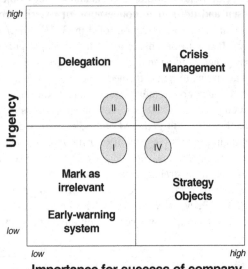

Fig. 4. Portfolio of strategy objects

- Strategy objects in quadrant (I), i.e. with low importance and low urgency, typically are not relevant for strategic decisions, as they are considered to be neither urgent nor important for the success of the company. Possibly, an early warning system can be established that monitors relevant aspects of strategy objects in order to assure that changes to the urgency or to the importance are not ignored.
- Strategy objects in quadrant (II), i.e. with low importance and high urgency, potentially should not be included in the list of strategy objects to be considered but should be dealt with by a single person or a small group outside the strategy development team.
- Strategy objects in quadrant (III), i.e. with high importance and high urgency, are topics that should have been dealt with in the past. Obviously they were not addressed properly in a prior strategy development process. These topics are to be included as strategy objects but probably need more efficient and direct treatment by the general management.

- Strategy objects in quadrant (IV), i.e. with high importance and low urgency, are optimal candidates for strategy objects as they are important and not yet so urgent that they cannot be dealt with properly in the course of the strategy development process.

The assignment of strategy objects to the different quadrants cannot be deducted systematically or automatically according to some meta-criteria, but is a creative task that has to be carried out during a strategy workshop. Besides intensive discussions simple voting mechanisms can be used to determine the importance and urgency of each strategy object.

4.3   Assessing Engineering Strategies

The method for assessing engineering strategies consists of four main activities that are described in detail in a structured way using the elements *purpose, involved roles, output,* and *tasks.* In this section – for reasons of space – we only provide an overview on these assessment steps.

- *Engineering Strategy Assessment – Kickoff:* The purpose of this activity is to find out which strategy objects are relevant for the company or division and which information sources can be used by the assessment team. The management representatives responsible for strategy development have to attend this meeting. – The major output of this activity is the list of strategy objects that are considered to be important in the engineering strategy of the company/division. The second major output is a list of documents where engineering strategy related statements can be found. In cases where no written engineering strategy is available, interview-partners have to be nominated that can provide the information to the evaluators.
- *Evaluation of Strategy Objects:* The purpose of this activity is to assign existing strategic statements to the selected strategy objects, to assess the maturity of each strategy object and to identify gaps in the engineering strategy. This activity is carried out by the external experts based on the data provided and does not involve the management of the company/division under investigation. Optionally, the interview partners selected in the previous activity have to be consulted. – The output of this activity is an assessment document that describes the selected strategy objects and shows the assignment of strategic statements to them. Additionally, each selected strategy object is assessed. For this purpose the number and contents of the strategic statements are set into relation to the definition of the strategy object.
- *Consolidation of the Evaluation of Strategy Objects:* The purpose of this activity is to adjust the assignments of strategic statements as well as the assessment of the strategy objects with the management responsible for the development of engineering strategies. – The output is a revised assignment of strategic statements to strategy objects.
- *Finalization and Presentation of Assessment Results:* The purpose of this activity is to finalize the assessment document and to present the results of the assessment to the management. – The output comprises a presentation that summarizes the assessment results, a document with the assigned strategic statements to strategy objects, including overall recommendations.

5   Relationship of Strategy Objects to Process Improvement

In section 3 we identified a number of candidate strategy objects that can be used for the development of functional engineering strategies. On the one hand, the question arises whether the identified strategy objects satisfactorily cover relevant organizational processes and are in this sense 'valid'. On the other hand, for use of the developed engineering strategies in process improvement a mapping or traceable links of the processes and process areas to the strategy objects is desirable.

To answer or support both issues we performed a mapping of the identified strategy objects to the process areas of CMMI [4] as a major process improvement and maturity model for the development of products and services. Latest versions of the model aim at a wide coverage of engineering disciplines. CMMI is widely and successfully applied. It can be assumed that the process areas described within CMMI cover a wide range of organizational processes.

Table 5 presents the summary of the results of the performed mapping. A strategy object maps to a process area if it addresses issues or topics of that process area. The mapping is quantified by an N-P-L-F-scale as defined in [3], i.e. 0% – 15% (N, not mapped), 16% – 51% (P, partially mapped), 52% – 85% (L, largely mapped), and

Table 5. Coverage of CMMI Process Areas by strategy objects

ID	Description	Coverage	Strategy Objects
CAR	Causal Analysis and Resolution	P	O-QUAL
CM	Configuration Management	F	O-CONF
DAR	Decision Analysis and Resolution	P	O-ARCH, O-COMP, O-INNO
IPM	Integrated Project Management	F	O-PROM, O-WORK
MA	Measurement and Analysis	P	O-QUAL, O-PROC
OID	Organizational Innovation and Deployment	F	O-INNO, O-VALU
OPD	Organizational Process Definition	F	O-PROC, O-WORK
OPF	Organizational Process Focus	F	O-PROC, O-VALU
OPP	Organizational Process Performance	F	O-PROC, O-QUAL
OT	Organizational Training	F	O-COPA, O-PROM, O-WORK
PI	Product Integration	L	O-COMP, O-QUAL, O-TEST
PMC	Project Monitoring and Control	F	O-PROM
PP	Project Planning	F	O-PROM
PPQA	Process and Product Quality Assurance	L	O-QUAL
QPM	Quantitative Project Management	P	O-QUAL, O-PROC
RD	Requirements Development	L	O-COMP, O-PROD, O-DOMA
REQM	Requirements Management	F	O-REQM, O-CHAN
RSKM	Risk Management	F	O-RSKM
SAM	Supplier Agreement Management	F	O-SUPL
TS	Technical Solution	L	O-ARCH, O-COMP, O-DOMA
VAL	Validation	L	O-QUAL
VER	Verification	F	O-QUAL, O-TEST

86% – 100% (F, fully mapped). The detailed underlying mapping study additionally identifies which topics of CMMI are covered by the strategy objects. The topics of CMMI process areas that were not covered were identified and their importance for the completeness analysis was judged in order to suggest additional strategy objects. - All in all, it can be concluded that the CMMI process areas are well addressed by the presented strategy objects.

Additionally, the analysis showed that a series of topics, which are covered by strategy objects, are beyond the scope of or not extensively covered by CMMI and therefore, the following strategy objects are not fully reflected in Table 5: *Claim Management (O-CLAIM), Product Life Cycle Management (O-CYCL), Document Management (O-DOCU), Domain Management (O-DOMA), Tool and Data Integration (O-INTE), Methods Management (O-METH), Product Management (O-PROD), Standards Management (O-STND),* and *Tools Management (O-TOOL).*

6   Validation and Experience

The starting set of strategy objects taken over from the software engineering domain has been applied in a series of more than eight software engineering strategy development projects by the institution of the second author, including at organizations with more than 100 developers.

The strategy objects added or changed in the course of the adaptation and extension of the approach to the industrial engineering domain have been validated through discussion with and reviews by experts from the industrial engineering domain. The respective feedback has been incorporated into the version of the strategy objects reference model as presented in section 3.

Some good practices from our experience in developing software engineering strategies are:

- Suggestions for strategic goals and objects should be made by external experts. They are refined and finalized in a workshop together with the management.
- Consultants also suggest and verbalize strategic statements with consideration of the organization and the organization's domain and goals. They must be prioritized and finalized in a workshop together with the management.
- Workshops should be organized into blocks of four hours each, typically scheduled for four to five appointments.
- Documents should be editorially edited by consultants.
- Strategy development should be accompanied by consultants, especially during workshops.

Overall, the approach represents a structured means that helps focusing on strategic goals. As the strategy objects are linked to the strategic goals, the strategic statements are automatically targeted towards the goals of the organization. The approach further helps in the identification and closure of gaps of existing engineering strategies in a focused manner and supports the identification and removal of contradictions within existing strategies as well as the systematic documentation of strategies.

The discovery of those topics, where the organization has to improve, forms the basis for the identification of improvement potentials and functions as a driver for business focused process improvement.

7   Summary and Conclusions

Based on experience in applying strategy development in software engineering and through additional investigation into the industrial engineering domain and discussion with and review through domain experts, we defined a meta-model for describing functional engineering strategies and identified a set of strategy objects for industrial engineering that are typically of interest for organizations. Using this underlying model we outlined an assessment-based approach for developing such engineering strategies.

For purposes of further validation of the proposed strategy objects and in order to support process improvement by providing traceable links to functional engineering strategies that are derived from business and organizational goals, we mapped the process areas of CMMI to the identified strategy objects. The result shows that most process areas are connected with and their topics thus covered by the strategy objects of our approach. Based on these results, process improvements can be systematically aligned with the strategic specifications. This provides the possibility to systematically cross-check, whether process improvements are aligned with strategic decisions and goals. The presented mapping defines in detail which process areas (i.e. improvements of a process area) have to be aligned with which parts of the engineering strategy.

From experience in applying the strategy development process and the conceptual framework in software development organizations we can draw the conclusion, that the proposed structure helps focusing on the strategic goals. Further, as the strategy objects are linked to the strategic goals, the strategic statements are automatically targeted towards the goals of the organization. Additionally, the mapping of the CMMI process areas to strategy objects allows aligning identified process improvements to the strategy objects and - by means of the link of the strategy objects to the strategic goals - to the business and strategic goals of the organization.

Acknowledgments. The work extending the approach for developing and evaluating engineering strategies from the software engineering to the industrial engineering domain has been performed within the *SISB* project (Systematic Improvement of the Solutions Business) carried out in cooperation between Siemens AG Corporate Technology, Johannes Kepler University Linz, and the Process and Quality Engineering Group of the Software Competence Center Hagenberg. The project aimed at the development of concepts and methods for exploiting the improvement potentials of engineering organizations and for increasing engineering maturity in general.

References

1. ISO/IEC 15288:2008. Systems and software engineering - System life cycle processes. International Standards Organization (2008)
2. ISO/IEC 12207:2008. Systems and software engineering - Software life cycle processes. International Standards Organization (2008)
3. ISO/IEC 15504:2003: Information Technology - Process Assessment. International Standards Organization (2003)
4. CMMI for development, version 1.2. Technical Report CMU/SEI-2006-TR-008, Software Engineering Institute, Carnegie Mellon University, Pittsburgh, PA (2006)
5. Shewhart, W.A.: Economic control of quality of manufactured product. D.Van Nostrand Company, New York (1931)
6. Dion, R.: Process improvement and the corporate balance sheet. IEEE Software 10(4), 28–35 (1993)
7. McFeeley, B.: IDEAL: A user's guide for software process improvement. Handbook CMU/SEI-96-HB-001, Software Engineering Institute, Carnegie Mellon University, Pittsburgh, PA (1996)
8. ISO/IEC 15504-7:1998: Information Technology - Software Process Assessment – Part 7: Guide for use in process improvement. International Standards Organization (1998)
9. Plösch, R., Pomberger, G., Stallinger, F.: Software Engineering Strategies: Aligning Software Process Improvement with Strategic Goals. In: O'Connor, R.V., Rout, T., McCaffery, F., Dorling, A. (eds.) SPICE 2011. CCIS, vol. 155, pp. 221–226. Springer, Heidelberg (2011)
10. Simon, H., von der Gathen, A.: Das große Handbuch der Strategieinstrumente – Alle Werkzeuge für eine erfolgreiche Unternehmensführung. Campus, Frankfurt/Main (2002) (in German)
11. Venzin, M., Rasner, C., Mahnke, V.: Der Strategieprozess – Praxishandbuch zur Umsetzung im Unternehmen. Campus, Frankfurt/Main (2003) (in German)
12. ABB Annual Report 2006 – Sustainability review – Power and productivity for a better world, ABB (2006)
13. Siemens: Fit For The Future update Strategic Goals, Siemens PG (January 2007)

Improving Completeness of Measurement Systems for Monitoring Software Development Workflows

Miroslaw Staron[1], Wilhelm Meding[2], and Micael Caiman[2]

[1] Department of Computer Science and Engineering
University of Gothenburg
miroslaw.staron@ituniv.se
[2] Ericsson SW Research and SW Metrics Team
Ericsson AB
{wilhelm.meding,micael.caiman}@ericsson.com

Abstract. Monitoring and controlling of software projects executed according to Lean or Agile software development requires, in principle, continuous measurement and use of indicators to monitor development areas and/or identify problem areas. Indicators are specific kind of measures with associated analysis models and decision criteria (ISO/IEC 15939). Indicating/highlighting problems in processes, is often used in Lean SW development and despite obvious benefits there are also dangers with improper use of indicators – using inadequate indicators can mislead the stakeholders towards sub-optimizations/erroneous decisions. In this paper we present a method for assessing completeness of information provided by measurement systems (i.e. both measures and indicators). The method is a variation of value stream mapping modeling with an application in a software development organization in the telecom domain. We also show the use of this method at one of the units of Ericsson where it was applied to provide stakeholders with an early warning system about upcoming problems with software quality.

1   Introduction

Software development organizations like Ericsson rely, among others, on measures and indicators for controlling, monitoring and managing products and projects. Indicators and measures are usually used in measurement systems [1, 2] which are dedicated to support stakeholders in achieving their operational goals [3-5]. The fact that measurement systems are built for a specific stakeholder, who usually is a team-, line-project- or product- manager, is well-grounded in practice as it is the stakeholder who has the mandate to act/react upon the specific status of the indicator or measure. Dedicated to one stakeholder, single indicators usually monitor a small number of entities and a limited number of their attributes (e.g. product performance in field, test progress). It is caused by the fact that stakeholders usually manage one entity, i.e. an organization, a product or a project.

Although these two aspects of indicators (being dedicated for one stakeholder and monitoring small number of entities) made them into an effective operative tool for

D. Winkler, S. Biffl, and J. Bergsmann (Eds.): SWQD 2013, LNBIP 133, pp. 230–243, 2013.
© Springer-Verlag Berlin Heidelberg 2013

stakeholders, but they also pose certain risks. One of the risks is the fact that indicators for single stakeholders can lead to sub-optimizations of the whole system since each stakeholder monitors only part/-s of process/es – e.g. optimizing efficiency of the development part of Lean software development program and "forgetting" to monitor test progress, which may lead to decreased efficiency of the complete program or deteriorated quality of the products. To illustrate this, let us consider an example of an indicator for monitoring the quality of software product – an indicator that shows the number of defects discovered during in-house testing of a telecom product (also presented in [6]). If the number of defects discovered is too high then the indicator warns about problems with quality. When the number of defects decreases the indicator shows that the quality of the product is good enough. However, for the whole product development project this indicator might lead to sub-optimizations since the number of defects depends among other factors on the test progress. Developing two indicators – one for controlling quality and one for controlling test progress – provides a more complete picture of the situation. Furthermore we can reason that decreasing of the pace of testing (decreased test progress) is a warning signal of potentially coming problems with quality – as it could also be the case that it is the delays in integration that might cause big-bang integration problems and thus decrease of quality.

As shown in the example, the quality indicator certainly helps the organization to decrease the number of known defects, but it might cause the organization to miss problems with test progress. In this paper we present a method for assessing whether the indicators developed for monitoring projects and the developed product show *a complete view, i.e. provide the stakeholders with the possibility to monitor all (relevant to the stakeholder/-s) activities in the workflow.*

Our method is based on combining models of software development processes together with a number of models of measurement systems according to ISO/IEC 15939 [7]. The method was evaluated as part of an action research project at a software development organization at Ericsson with a few hundred engineers in close cooperation with a number of stakeholders who work with the process, e.g. designers, team leaders, product managers, a measurement program leader. By interviews with these stakeholders we elicited the de-facto development process and visualize it using assembly stations, similar to the Value Stream Mapping modeling [8]. By linking the software development process models with measurement system models (presented in [9]) we could analyze how complete information provided by measurement systems was w.r.t. the measured process and its underlying product. By analyzing time-frame of the modeled process and empirical dependencies between parts of the process (and thus between the indicators linked to these parts) we reasoned about how each indicator warned the stakeholders who managed/monitored subsequent parts of the process, about potential problems.

The action research was conducted in three research projects at one of the units of Ericsson, for creating early warning systems for one of the software development programs. As part of those research projects the method was used in software product development, which is shown in the paper. Based on using our method, several measurement systems were redesigned to increase the completeness of information to the level satisfactory for the stakeholders.

The remaining of the paper is structured as follows: section 2 presents the most relevant related work in the area. Section 3 describes the theoretical background for measuring completeness of the measurement systems. Section 4 presents the research design, which we followed and section 5 presents the method for assessing completeness. Section 6 summarizes the results from the evaluation of the method – its use at one of the large product development units at Ericsson.

2   Related Work

Value Stream Mapping [10] models are commonly used in Lean Development in other domains to model processes and link them to such concepts as customer value or cost. The as-is workflow modeling can be done using Value Stream Mapping/Modeling and complemented with the other parts of our method – information needs and indicators – thus creating a powerful tool for analyzing efficiency, completeness, cost and predictiveness of software development processes.

Modeling of measurement systems has already been proposed by Kitchenham et al. [11, 12] where the authors provide a method for combining metrics of different kinds using a graphical notation. Another example of using models when designing software metrics is provided by a recent work of Monperrus et al. [13] where the authors propose a modeling notation for modeling metrics. Although the approach is interesting and model-driven (in the sense that it provides possibilities to "model metrics and to define metrics for models" [13]), the approach does not cover the most important aspect of our work – linking metrics and process models.

Completeness of information is often a part of the overall information quality and its evaluation. The basis for our research is one of available frameworks for assessing information quality – AIMQ [14]. The framework contains both the attributes of information quality, methods for measuring it and has been successfully applied in industry in the area of data warehousing. In our research we have taken the method one step further and developed a method for automatic and run-time checking of information quality in a narrowed field: measurement systems [15]. In this work we present a method for assessing how complete the information products are; this is a part of requirements for having high-quality metrics. There exist several alternative (to AIMQ) frameworks for assessing information quality, which we also investigated, for example Kahn et al. [16], Mayer and Willshire [17], Goodhue [18], Serrano et al. [19]. The completeness of information is present in all of them in different forms. The AIMQ framework was chosen as it was previously used in our research on information quality – where the information completeness is a part of.

Caballero et al [20] developed a data quality information model based on the ISO/IEC 15939 information model. Caballero et al.'s research aims to standardize the nomenclature in data information quality and provide an XML schema for generating data quality measurement plans. In the contrast with Caballero et al.'s research for measurement plans, our approach is dedicated for measurement systems, is based on a different platform (MS Excel), a narrower domain (measurement systems) and takes the information quality one step further – runtime, automatic assessment of a subset of information quality. Generation of a schema-like textual specification is possible in our method as it is based on the existing framework [2] which allows automatic generation of specifications of metrics (including information quality).

Burkhard et al. [21] found that although the indicators are presented visually, people are surrounded by overwhelming information and miss the big picture. This "bigger picture" in the context of monitoring of software product development means that the stakeholders need to monitor entities that they formally do not manage. For example project managers monitor projects but also need to understand how the "product has it", for example what the quality of the developed product is. For stakeholders responsible for parts of product development that means that they need to understand what the situation "upstream" is – i.e. whether there are any potential problems that might affect their work after a period of time.

3   Combining Measurement Systems with Workflow Modelling

The research presented in this paper addresses the industrial needs for efficient adoption of measurement standards like ISO 15939 [22], which describes how measurement processes should be executed in software and system development organizations. The notion of completeness of information is adopted from the AIMQ framework [14].

3.1   Measurement Systems and ISO 15939

The current measurement processes in software engineering are prescribed by ISO/IEC 15939:2007 standard, which is a normative specification for the processes used to define, collect, and analyze quantitative data in software projects or organizations. The central role in the standard is played by the information product which is a set of one or more indicators with their associated interpretations that address the information need [23]. The information need is an insight necessary for a stakeholder to manage objectives, goals, risks, and problems observed in the measured objects [23]. These measured objects can be entities like projects, organizations, software products, etc. characterized by a set of attributes. We use the following definitions from ISO/IEC 15939:2007 [22]:

- Indicator – measure that provides an estimate or evaluation of specified attributes derived from a model with respect to defined information needs.
- Information need – An insight necessary to manage objectives, goals, risks and problems
- Stakeholder - An individual or organization that sponsors measurements and provides data or is a user of the measurement results. In the case of the studied organization at Ericsson, the stakeholder is a person who has the mandate and ability to act upon the value of the indicator.

The view on measures presented in ISO/IEC 15939 is consistent with other engineering disciplines, the standard states that it is based on ISO/IEC 15288:2007 (Software and Systems engineering - Measurement Processes) [24], ISO/IEC 14598-1:1999 (Information technology - Software product evaluation) [25], ISO/IEC 9126-x [26],

ISO/IEC 25000 series of standards, or International vocabulary of basic and general terms in metrology (VIM) [22].

One of the key factors for every measurement system is that it has to satisfy an information need of a stakeholder – i.e. there is a person/organization who/which is dependent on the information that the measurement system provides. Typical stakeholders are project managers, organization managers, architects, product managers, customer representatives, and similar [27-30]. The indicator is intended to provide information along with interpretation, which implies the existence of an analysis model that eases the interpretation. The analysis model is a set of decision criteria used when assessing the value of an indicator – e.g. describing at which value of the indicator we e.g. set a red flag signaling problems in the measured object. The derived measures (based on the definition of the derived quantity) and base measures (based on the definition of the base quantity) are used to provide the information for calculating the value of the indicator.

3.2 Workflow Modeling

We model workflows based on process models used in software development projects. The method places the stakeholder downstream and all related activities upstream. By doing this:

- we optimize the number of activities/states that have to be described,
- we optimize the number of metrics and indicators used,
- we organize the dependencies of listed activities
- we quantify listed activities time wise

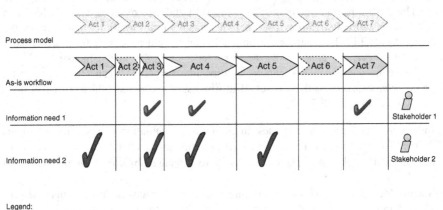

Fig. 1. Process modeling and information needs of stakeholders

Figure 1 outlines how a process model, a workflow model and stakeholders' information needs relate to each other. The *process model* at the top of the figure denotes the prescribed software development process used in the project with activities which should be followed. The *as-is workflow* describes how the process is instantiated in the particular project, which means that it includes activities that are fully automated and includes actual lengths of activities. Each stakeholder in the project (*Stakeholder 1* and *Stakeholder 2*) have distinct roles, distinct information needs and therefore they have distinct needs to monitor different activities.

3.3 Completeness

The AIMQ framework defines completeness of information as information possessing the necessary values [14]. The definition in the AIMQ framework is rather general although its roots are in the ontological definition of information quality presented by Wand and Wang [31] who use the notion of data deficiency to explain different quality attributes. The deficiencies addressed by information completeness are related to incomplete representation of the real-world entities with metrics. This means that in the context of the study presented in this paper the completeness of a measurement system is the possibility to monitor all activities in a process (workflow).

As an example let us consider a toy workflow presented in Figure 2 with three activities in release planning – i.e. Requirements elicitation, Requirements prioritization and Product release planning. The stakeholder for that workflow is the release manager who is responsible for releasing the product with the right features and the right quality. That particular stakeholder is interested in two of the three activities – denoted with a tick under the activities.

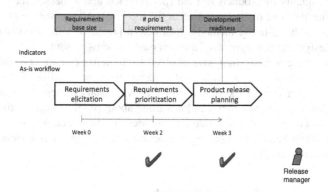

Fig. 2. Mapping workflow elements to indicators

Each of these three activities is linked to one indicator – Requirements base size, # (number of) priority 1 requirements and Development readiness with the status of the indicators - green, yellow and red respectively. If the stakeholder considers the workflow model to be complete, then the measurement system with the three indicators provides the stakeholder with the complete "picture" of the workflow. The "picture" is complete since the indicators are defined according to ISO/IEC 15939 and the standard requires proper construction of metrics. This proper construction means that such properties of metrics/indicators as the empirical mapping criterion (defined by Fenton and Pfleeger [32]) are fulfilled.

4   Research Context and Method

In this section we describe the organization where the need for this new method was identified, implemented and verified. We also briefly present the action research project which we followed in this study.

4.1   Organizational Context

The organization and the project within Ericsson, which we worked closely with, develops large products for the mobile telephony network. The size of the organization is several hundred engineers and the size of the projects can be up to a few hundreds[1]. Projects are more and more often executed according to the principles of Agile software development and Lean production system referred to as Streamline development (SD) within Ericsson [33]. In this environment various disciplines are responsible for larger parts of the process compared to traditional processes: design teams (cross-functional teams responsible for complete analysis, design, implementation, and testing of particular features of the product), network verification and integration testing, etc.

The organization uses a number of measurement systems for controlling the software development project (per project) described above, a number of measurement systems to control the quality of products in field (per product) and a measurement system for monitoring the status of the organization at the top level. All measurement systems are developed using the in-house methods described in [1, 2], with the particular stress on models for design and deployment of measurement systems presented in [4, 9].

The needs of the organization have evolved from metric calculations and presentations (ca. 5 years before the writing of this paper) to assure quality of measures (see [15]) towards measurement systems which provide stakeholders with information about how much in advance they can be warned about problems (predictive information) and how complete the information provided by their measurement systems is. These needs have been addressed by the action research projects conducted in the organization, since the 2006.

4.2   Research Method – Action Research

We followed the principles of action research in our research project [34, 35]. Action research is characterized by the fact that research is embedded in normal activities performed by an organization or an individual. In our case our actions were embedded in the operations of one of the units of Ericsson with several ongoing large projects[2].

---

[1] Due to the confidentiality agreement we are not allowed to provide the exact numbers here.
[2] Due to the confidentiality agreement with Ericsson we are not able to provide the exact numbers of the organization, its products or the geographical location.

Action research is usually conducted in so-called cycles, which are often characterized as:

- Action planning: recognizing the nature of the problem in its natural environment. In our case we needed to investigate the changed reality of using Lean/Streamline in software development, in order to understand, if, and to what extent, the previous approaches and statistical methods (e.g. [36, 37]) apply. We used the knowledge from our previous research projects and the dialog with practitioners to find potential limitations and understand them. The result of the action planning was the choice of Domain Specific Modeling as technology to implement our method on a mid-size software development program where the models were to be used. Close cooperation with the quality manager resulted in précising the requirements for the method – e.g. ease of use, accuracy.
- Execution: acting upon the identified problem and improving the practices. In our case we needed to develop new methods alongside with the practitioners based on the new reality of Lean/Streamline development. The result of action execution was the new modeling method (based on [4, 9]) developed in a close cooperation with stakeholders in a series of interviews and workshops.
- Evaluation: evaluating the action in the real setting. In our case we introduced the method into a mid-size software project at Ericsson and calculated information completeness.

Each of the cycles results in improvements of the current practice and each of them is intended to provide the basis for further improvements. In this short paper we only focus on the final result and its evaluation at Ericsson.

5   Complete Measurement Systems

The method presented in this paper is mostly suitable for assessing the completeness of measurement systems for monitoring workflows, since we use temporal dependencies and process-wise dependencies between activities of a process.

In short, the main principles of our method are: (i) to create a process model of the existing workflow, (ii) link appropriate and necessary measures to activities in this process, (iii) link the time scale to the process and calculate the completeness of information provided by the measurement systems. The method results in

a. time frame for how long in advance the indicators warn about problems, and
b. percent of completeness of measurement systems w.r.t. monitoring of activities

We present the three parts of our method together with an illustrative example.

Step 1: Develop de-facto process descriptions of the workflow. This measurement system should address the following information need – *what do you need to know in order to warn the stakeholder in the subsequent phase about coming problems?* Therefore the model should contain all activities that are relevant for this information need. The description should be in form of a model, for example a model presented in Figure 3(which is UML-like). The model should show the de-facto ways of working in the workflow and should be at the abstraction level of activities, not tasks. The flow depends on the stakeholder, and the process description covers only the aspects that are important from the perspective of the information need of the stakeholder. This means that the workflows are not prescriptive (as process models) but descriptive.

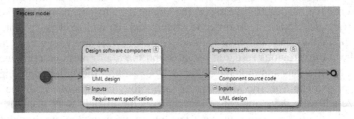

Fig. 3. Process model – an example

The figure shows two activities in an example process description – design software component and implement software component. This is how the stakeholders describe their contribution to the overall company product development, although there might be a number of smaller tasks which are part of these activities.

Step 2: Design measurement systems and link them to activities in the workflow. After describing the process the measurement system for monitoring the workflow is designed. This measurement system should address the following information need – *what do you need to know in order to warn the stakeholder in the subsequent phase about coming problems?* We propose to use a method developed in one of our previous research projects, which uses the ISO/IEC 15939 information model as the basis for the specification of measurement system [1, 7]. An example of this link between process model and metrics specification is presented in Figure 4.

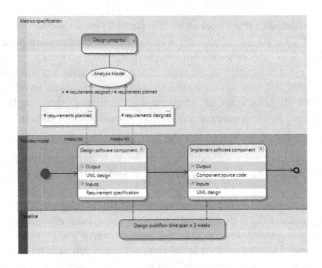

Fig. 4. Measures linked to process elements

The figure shows the design of the measurement system for monitoring the workflow for this process. The measurement system monitors one of the two activities through three measures – number of requirements planned and number of requirements included in the design. It also contains one indicator – design process progress. The reason for having just this indicator is that the indicator warns the stakeholders downstream about the status of this activity and about the potentially coming problems.

Step 3: Add a timeline for the workflow and assess how much time each stakeholder (e.g. a team leader) has to prevent the problem that he/she is warned about. When the measurement system is designed in the model, a timeline is added to show the time frame between activities in the process. The resulting model shows how predictive the measurement system is. It shows that the early warning in the first available measure can warn about potential problems later on in the process. By adding the timeline we can reason about how far away into the future we can have an impact.

5.1   Completeness

In order to perform the assessment of how complete the measurement system is we propose the following formula:

$$compl. = \frac{\# \; activities \; with \; measures \; or \; indicators}{\# \; activities \; in \; total} \cdot 100\%$$

 # activities with measures or indicators in this context means that we count also activities which have only measures (i.e. base or derived measures). This is dictated by the fact that sometimes it is not possible to set static decision criteria (in the analysis model) to develop an indicator, but a derived or base measure still holds an important information about the status of the measured activity. The measurement system which provides measures or indicators for all activities in the monitored process is 100% complete. That number of indicators is given by the number of activities defined by the Info Need of the stakeholder that is downstream. That is why the number of activities and related measures vary given the stakeholder.

In the example presented in in this paper the information is 50% complete as only one of the two activities is monitored – Develop software component.

6   Evaluation: Use of the Method at Ericsson

We have evaluated our method in two projects at Ericsson. Table 1 summarizes the results from the evaluation in three projects. The last column contains the feedback from the stakeholder, whether the completeness of information is enough for their purposes or not (i.e. information needs).

Table 1. Results from using our method the studied organization

Project	# measures	Completeness	Stakeholder's view
A	11	56%	N/A
B	28	60%	The number of measures and indicators satisfies the stakeholder's information needs
C	28	60%	The number of measures and indicators satisfies the stakeholder's information needs

The table shows that in practice the completeness of the information provided by measurement systems was about 60%. The reason for this 60% was the fact that the other activities were fully automated and there was no need of monitoring them separately (furthermore, the stakeholder also claimed to have an everyday update of the status of these activities in other ways). Their outcome was monitored as part of other activities. The 60% completeness means that if a problem appears in ca. 40% of activities in the monitored workflow, the measures cannot show that until the problem reaches an activity which is monitored. However, the stakeholders deemed this as a satisfactory level.

7 Conclusions

In this paper we presented and industrially evaluated a method for monitoring workflows in Lean-like software development based on combining as-is process models, ISO/IEC 15939-based measurement systems and information quality. Since metrics are important in industry to support decisions and to allow for objective monitoring and control, by monitoring workflows we take it one step further – we can monitor the status of product under development and provide stakeholders with the information on the status of projects in objective way. By providing completeness as information to the stakeholders, we add information/knowledge to overall metrics picture equal to the importance of information quality.

One of the shortcomings of measurement systems used in industry previously was the lack of overall picture that combined activities, metrics and indicators in a single view. The lack of such a picture made it difficult to assess how complete a measurement system is from the perspective of an information need of a stakeholder. Thanks to the method presented in this paper we address this shortcoming by identifying the key activities from a vast number of activities ongoing in a software development project. The key activities are linked to those few metrics and indicators needed to fully ascertain the completeness of the information need by the stakeholder.

Another shortcoming of methods used previously was that the measurement systems were static in the sense that they presented reactive information to the stakeholders. By including timeline in the workflow model our method enables the measurements systems to be both reactive and proactive. The proactive means to foretell what might happen in the workflow if no actions are taken by the stakeholder.

The success of this method was mainly due to the fact that it is based on the ISO/IEC 15939 standard and that it lies on the fundaments of UML-like modeling. It can be used to both small and large projects as it was evaluated at Ericsson. As the presented method is based on a small number of steps it has shown itself to be effective for a number of projects in the organization. In particular it has led to improvements of the quality of measurement systems and the elevated awareness of the limitations of the measures provided by the measurement systems. The method can be used for all different stakeholder roles, and at the same time it is limited to the as-is and relevant-only process description.

Acknowledgements. The authors would like to thank Ericsson and Software Architecture Quality Center for the support of this study. The authors would also like to express gratitude to the stakeholders who took part in the evaluation of the presented method.

References

[1] Staron, M., Meding, W., Karlsson, G., Nilsson, C.: Developing measurement systems: an industrial case study. Journal of Software Maintenance and Evolution: Research and Practice (2010)
[2] Staron, M., Meding, W., Nilsson, C.: A Framework for Developing Measurement Systems and Its Industrial Evaluation. Information and Software Technology 51, 721–737 (2008)
[3] McGarry, J.: Practical software measurement: objective information for decision makers. Addison-Wesley, Boston (2002)
[4] Meding, W., Staron, M.: The Role of Design and Implementation Models in Establishing Mature Measurement Programs. Presented at the Nordic Workshop on Model Driven Engineering, Tampere, Finland (2009)
[5] van Solingen, R., Berghout, E.: The Goal/Question/Metric Method. A Practical Guide for Quality Improvement of Software Development. McGraw-Hill, London (1999)
[6] Staron, M., Meding, W.: Defect Inflow Prediction in Large Software Projects. e-Informatica Software Engineering Journal 4, 1–23 (2010)
[7] International Standard Organization and International Electrotechnical Commission, ISO/IEC 15939 Software engineering – Software measurement process, International Standard Organization/International Electrotechnical Commission, Geneva (2007)
[8] Brockers, A., Differding, C., Threin, G.: The role of software process modeling in planning industrial measurement programs. In: The 3rd International Software Metrics Symposium, pp. 31–40 (1996)
[9] Staron, M., Meding, W.: Using Models to Develop Measurement Systems: A Method and Its Industrial Use, Presented at the Software Process and Product Measurement, Amsterdam, NL (2009)
[10] Dolcemascolo, D.: Improving the extended value stream: lean for the entire supply chain. Productivity Press, New York (2006)
[11] Kitchenham, B., Hughes, R.T., Linkman, S.C.: Modeling Software Measurement Data. IEEE Transactions on Software Engineering 27, 788–804 (2001)
[12] Lawler, J., Kitchenham, B.: Measurement modeling technology. IEEE Software 20, 68–75 (2003)

[13] Monperrus, M., Jézéquel, J.-M., Champeau, J., Hoeltzener, B.: A Model-Driven Measurement Approach. In: Czarnecki, K., Ober, I., Bruel, J.-M., Uhl, A., Völter, M. (eds.) MoDELS 2008. LNCS, vol. 5301, pp. 505–519. Springer, Heidelberg (2008)

[14] Lee, Y.W., Strong, D.M., Kahn, B.K., Wang, R.Y.: AIMQ: a methodology for information quality assessment. Information & Management 40, 133–146 (2002)

[15] Staron, M., Meding, W.: Ensuring Reliability of Information Provided by Measurement Systems. In: Abran, A., Braungarten, R., Dumke, R.R., Cuadrado-Gallego, J.J., Brunekreef, J. (eds.) IWSM 2009. LNCS, vol. 5891, pp. 1–16. Springer, Heidelberg (2009)

[16] Kahn, B.K., Strong, D.M., Wang, R.Y.: Information Quality Benchmarks: Product and Service Performance. Communications of the ACM 45, 184–192 (2002)

[17] Mayer, D.M., Willshire, M.J.: A Data Quality Engineering Framework. In: International Conference on Information Quality, pp. 1–8 (1997)

[18] Goodhue, D.L., Thompson, R.L.: Task-technology fit and individual performance. MIS Quarterly 19, 213–237 (1995)

[19] Serrano, M., Calero, C., Trujillo, J., Luján-Mora, S., Piattini, M.: Empirical Validation of Metrics for Conceptual Models of Data Warehouses. In: Persson, A., Stirna, J. (eds.) CAiSE 2004. LNCS, vol. 3084, pp. 506–520. Springer, Heidelberg (2004)

[20] Caballero, I., Verbo, E., Calero, C., Piattini, M.: A Data Quality Measurement Information Model Based on ISO/IEC 15939 (2007),
http://mitiq.mit.edu/iciq/PDF/

[21] Burkhard, R., Spescha, G., Meier, M.: "A-ha!": How to Visualize Strategies with Complementary Visualizations. In: Conference on Visualising and Presenting Indicator Systems (2005)

[22] International Bureau of Weights and Measures, International vocabulary of basic and general terms in metrology = Vocabulaire international des termes fondamentaux et généraux de métrologie, 2nd edn. International Organization for Standardization, Genève (1993)

[23] International Standard Organization and International Electrotechnical Commission, Software engineering – Software measurement process, ISO/IEC, Geneva (2002)

[24] International Standard Organization, Systems engineering – System life cycle processes 15288:2002 (2002)

[25] International Standard Organization, Information technology – Software product evaluation 14598-1:1999 (1999)

[26] International Standard Organization and International Electrotechnical Commission, ISO/IEC 9126 - Software engineering – Product quality Part: 1 Quality model, International Standard Organization/International Electrotechnical Commission, Geneva (2001)

[27] Umarji, M., Emurian, H.: Acceptance Issues in Metrics Program Implementation, p. 20 (2005)

[28] Gopal, A., Mukhopadhyay, T., Krishnan, M.S.: The impact of institutional forces on software metrics programs. IEEE Transactions on Software Engineering 31, 679–694 (2005)

[29] Umarji, M., Emurian, H.: Acceptance issues in metrics program implementation, p. 10 (2005)

[30] Kilpi, T.: Implementing a Software Metrics Program at Nokia. IEEE Software 18, 72–77 (2001)

[31] Wand, Y., Wang, R.Y.: Anchoring data quality dimensions in ontological foundations. Commun. ACM 39, 86–95 (1996)

[32] Fenton, N.E., Pfleeger, S.L.: Software metrics: a rigorous and practical approach, 2nd edn. International Thomson Computer Press, London (1996)

[33] Tomaszewski, P., Berander, P., Damm, L.-O.: From Traditional to Streamline Development - Opportunities and Challenges. Software Process Improvement and Practice 2007, 1–20 (2007)

[34] Baskerville, R.L., Wood-Harper, A.T.: A Critical Perspective on Action Research as a Method for Information Systems Research. Journal of Information Technology 1996, 235–246 (1996)

[35] Susman, G.I., Evered, R.D.: An Assessment of the Scientific Merits of Action Research. Administrative Science Quarterly 1978, 582–603 (1978)

[36] Fenton, N., Krause, P., Neil, M.: Software measurement: uncertainty and causal modeling. IEEE Software 19, 116–122 (2002)

[37] Fenton, N.E., Neil, M.: Software metrics: successes, failures and new directions. Journal of Systems and Software 47, 149–157 (1999)

Exploiting Natural Language Definitions and (Legacy) Data for Facilitating Agreement Processes

Christophe Debruyne and Cristian Vasquez

Semantics Technology and Applications Research Lab (STARLab),
Vrije Universiteit Brussel,
Pleinlaan 2, B-1050 Brussels, Belgium
{chrdebru,cvasquez}@vub.ac.be

Abstract. In IT, ontologies to enable semantic interoperability is only of the branches in which agreement between a heterogeneous group of stakeholders are of vital importance. As agreements are the result of interactions, appropriate methods should take into account the natural language used by the community. In this paper, we extend a method for reaching a consensus on a conceptualization within a community of stakeholders, exploiting the natural language communication between the stakeholders. We describe how agreements on informal and formal descriptions are complementary and interplay. To this end, we introduce, describe and motivate the nature of some of the agreements and the two distinct levels of commitment. We furthermore show how these commitments can be exploited to steer the agreement processes. Concepts introduced in this paper have been implemented in a tool for collaborative ontology engineering, called GOSPL, which can be also adopted for other purposes, e.g., the construction a lexicon for larger software projects.

Keywords: Hybrid Ontologies, Collaborative Ontology Engineering.

1 Introduction

In this paper, we extend a method for reaching a consensus on a description of the world – or an approximation thereof - within a community of stakeholders. This method exploits the natural language communication between the stakeholders. Even though the method adopted is intended for ontology engineering; aimed at producing application-independent descriptions of the world for semantic interoperability between autonomously developed information systems, the ideas presented here are easily extrapolated to other domain in which modeling (and the agreements leading those models) are critical for a successful project. [16] observed communication and comprehension problems within projects with groups whose members had different (IT) backgrounds. It is this problem that we wish to address in this paper. The better the understanding within (and even across) communities, the more likely that the (ontology) project will be successful. Thus methods will need to take into account the social processes and means used by the community to reach those agreements. Since the most advanced means of communication between humans is natural language, it will be beneficial to exploit this natural language communication in the agreement processes.

D. Winkler, S. Biffl, and J. Bergsmann (Eds.): SWQD 2013, LNBIP 133, pp. 244–258, 2013.

Starting from an existing framework for collaborative ontology engineering that takes into account both formal and informal descriptions of concepts, which we will describe later on, we ask ourselves the following questions: 1) what is the nature of the meaning agreements (esp. across communities), 2) are there different levels of committing to these models and can these be exploited for driving agreement processes.

The paper is thus organized as follows: starting from a brief introduction to ontologies, ontology engineering and related work, we move to the method in Section 3. Section 3 starts with a description from the hybrid ontology engineering framework and method we adopted in this paper, which is based on earlier work. In Section 3, we also describe how the nature of agreements across communities and propose to make a distinction between two types of ontological commitment: at community level, and at the level of a specific application. Ensuring proper business – or proper semantic interoperation – will be the motivation of this separation. We furthermore explain how the commitments can be used to drive the social interaction within the community that will lead to agreements. Section 4 presents the tools implementing these ideas and we conclude this paper in Section 5.

2   Related Work

An ontology is commonly defined as a formal, explicit specification of a shared conceptualization and ontology engineering is a set of tasks related to the development of ontologies for a particular domain. The semantics of an ontology stem not from the ontology language in which the ontology is implemented[1], but from the *agreements* of a community of stakeholders with a particular goal. Those agreements are achieved by interactions within the community leading the ontology to better approximate the domain over time.

We stated what ontologies are. The problem, however, is not what ontologies are, but how they become *community-grounded* resources of semantics, and at the same time how they are made operationally relevant and sustainable over longer periods of time. Quite a few surveys on the state of the art on ontology engineering methods exist [7,16,17]. Some collaborative methods provide tool support such as HCOME [9], DILIGENT [20] and Business Semantics Management[2] [2]. There even exists collaborative ontology engineering platforms, such as, Collaborative Protégé [18], that are not tailored to one specific method. Concerning methods, we noticed a between providing means for supporting social processes (in ontology engineering) and a special linguistic resource to aid these processes [4]. This gap was addressed in [3], which provided a framework for hybrid ontology engineering. Then, a method and tool were developed on top of this method, called GOSPL [4], which stands for Grounding Ontologies with Social Processes and Natural Language.

---

[1] Although some constructs can be reserved a special meaning used for inference, e.g., the relation denoting subsumption.

[2] http://www.collibra.com/products-and-solutions/products/
business-semantics-glossary

3   Method

In conceptual modeling, the natural language aspect helps us to keep a close communication link between the distinct stakeholders and the systems and/or business specifications. This has already been shown before in database design methods and techniques such as NIAM [21], which allows users to model their world by means of fact-types[3] expressed in natural language. In this section, we explain how we adopted fact-orientation for ontology engineering and use distinct levels of "precision" for describing concepts, informal and formal, with the formal level also being grounded in natural language This hybrid aspect is useful since we need informal descriptions to support high level reasoning among humans (i.e. discussions) and at the same time, formal descriptions to be used by machines.

3.1   A Framework and Method for Hybrid Ontology Engineering

Whenever two or more autonomously developed information systems need to interoperate, agreements over the concepts implicitly shared by those systems are made explicit, allowing the mapping of the conceptual schemas onto an ontology. Agreement processes thus co-exist at an organizational level and across organizations. The construction of an ontology can be supported by the same natural language fact-oriented modeling techniques. In fact, a framework for fact-oriented ontology engineering was proposed in [12] that adopted NIAM. This method was extended to include a special linguistic resource, called a glossary, to support the social processes in ontology engineering [3]. The social processes result in changes in the ontology and have been parameterized with the community, thus resulting in a well-defined hybrid aspect on ontologies. A Hybrid Ontology Description [3] contains:

- A lexon base Λ, i.e. a finite set of lexons. A lexon is a binary fact-type that can be read in two directions: t_1 playing the role of r_1 on t_2 and t_2 playing the role of r_2 on t_1 in some community referred to by $\gamma \in \Gamma$, where $t_1, t_2 \in T$ are term-labels and $r_1, r_2 \in R$ are role-labels. Communities are used to disambiguate agreements. An example of a lexon is *<Ticket Community, Ticket, has, of, Price>*.
- A glossary G, a finite set of functions mapping lexon or terms in lexons to natural language descriptions. For instance, the *Ticket Community* can agree to *articulate* the term *Price* with the gloss *"The sum or amount of money or its equivalent for which anything is bought, sold, or offered for sale."* The functions g_1 and g_2 map respectively community-term pairs and lexons to glosses.
- $ci: \Gamma \times T \to C$ a partial function mapping pairs of community-identifiers and terms to unique elements of C, a finite set of concepts.
- A finite set of ontological commitments K describing how one individual application commits to a selection of the lexon base, the use of this selection (constraints) and the mapping of application symbols to that selection. The elements of K will be described in the next section.

---

[3] A fact-type is the generalization of facts, a collection of objects linked by a predicate. "[Person] knows [Person]" would be an example of a fact-type, and "[Christophe] knows [Cristian]" would be a fact in this example.

In [4], a collaborative method on top of aforementioned framework was described, called GOSPL. Fig. 1 depicts the processes in GOSPL. Communities define the semantic interoperability requirements, out of which a set of key terms is identified. Those terms need to be informally described before the formal description (in terms of lexons) can be added. In order for a lexon to be entered, at least one of the terms needs to be articulated. The terms and roles in lexons can be constrained. The community can then commit to the hybrid ontology by annotating an individual application symbols with a constrained subset of the lexons. At the same time, communities can interact to agree on the equivalence of glosses and the synonymy of terms. Important here is that the community first needs to "align" their thoughts and ideas by means of the informal descriptions before formally describing the concepts. This aids in avoiding misunderstandings and changes on the formal descriptions are then less likely to occur.

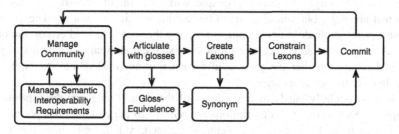

Fig. 1. The GOSPL method

Important in GOSPL is that each "phase" corresponds with a number of social processes within a community. These social processes are there to discuss whether changes will contribute the community in achieving their goal. Rather than immediately change the ontology and discuss the change, the community needs to approve the proposed changes. Only when changes are accepted, they are carried out on the ontology. As the social processes are described and stored, we have added an additional dimension to traceability; the discussion and decisions made by the community.

3.2   The Nature of Agreements

Communities can agree that glosses used to describe terms can refer to the same concept as well as terms in lexons, gloss-equivalence (at gloss-level EQ_G) and synonymy respectively (at lexon-level $\equiv_C$). The elements in C contain the agreements of communities that a particular label refers – for all the members of a community – to the same concept. Every community-term pair refers to at most one concept, otherwise the community would be divided. Communities can agree that their terms could refer to the same concept and those agreements are captured. Given two community-term pairs $(\gamma_1, t_1), (\gamma_2, t_2) \in \Gamma \times T$, $ci(\gamma_1, t_1) \equiv_C ci(\gamma_2, t_2)$ denotes the agreement between communities γ_1 and γ_2 that their terms t_1 and t_2 refer to the same concept. The function g_1 maps every community-term pair to at most one gloss. Given communities $\gamma_1, \gamma_2 \in \Gamma$ and terms $t_1, t_2 \in T$, we say that two term-glosses $g_1(\gamma_1, t_1)$ and

$g_1(\gamma_2, t_2)$ are gloss-equivalent EQ_G if the two communities agree that the described terms refer to the same abstract concept. A hybrid ontology is glossary-consistent if for every two pairs $(\gamma_1, t_1), (\gamma_2, t_2) \in \Gamma \times T$:$EQ_G(g_1(\gamma_1, t_1), g_1(\gamma_2, t_2)) \rightarrow ci(\gamma_1, t_1) \equiv_C ci(\gamma_2, t_2)$. The converse does not necessarily hold.

Note that when the two communities agree that the glosses used to describe their terms are gloss-equivalent, that this does not automatically imply that $ci(\gamma_1, t_1) \equiv_C ci(\gamma_2, t_2)$ is asserted. We motivate the reason to have both agreements established separately as follows: Gloss-equivalences are on the level of the glossary whereas $\equiv_C$ resides on the formal descriptions of the concepts (i.e. the lexons). To assert $\equiv_C$, the term must appear in a lexon. Communities can start gradually building their glossary before formally describing their concepts. However, nothing should prevent the community for having agreements on the "sameness" of descriptions across or within their own community. Another reason is validation of the equivalences. The glossary-consistency principle will pinpoint the descriptions used for terms that are EQ_G, but whose terms in those communities are not $\equiv_C$ The glossary-consistency principle does not become a property that needs to hold or else the ontology project fail, instead it becomes a tool to drive the community in establishing $\equiv_C$, double checking whether the gloss-equivalence was not misleading and both terms really do refer to the same concept.

This is particularly handy as the validity of the natural language descriptions and the equivalence of two such descriptions are relative to the communities partaking in these discussions. If glosses have been ill defined, yet agreed upon, the second agreement while the terms are formally described are more than welcome and the community will be able to rectify the mistakes.

Important to note is that assertions of gloss-equivalences and synonymy are only symmetric, reflexive and transitive *within one agreement process*. This measure is taken to avoid unwanted synonymy and gloss-equivalences to be propagated across communities. If communities A, B and CA all get together and agree that their terms tA, tB and tC are synonymous, the following assertions are added: $ci(A, tA) \equiv_C ci(B, tB)$, $ci(B, tB) \equiv_C ci(C, tC)$ and $ci(A, tA) \equiv_C ci(C, tC)$. However, if community C and D afterwards agree that $ci(C, tC) \equiv_C ci(D, tD)$, then this does not imply that $ci(A, tA) \equiv_C ci(D, tD)$ or $ci(B, tB) \equiv_C ci(D, tD)$. The agreements on synonymy can be followed will be followed by the other communities, allowing them to start interactions to state the terms are indeed synonymous. The same holds for gloss-equivalences.

3.3   Community- and Application Commitments

In GOSPL, a finite set of ontological commitments K contain descriptions on how individual applications commit to a selection of the lexon base (with constraints and mappings). We feel, however, the need to make a distinction between two types of commitments: community-commitments and application-commitments. The first is an engagement of the community members to commit to the lexons and constraints agreed upon by the community. The latter is a selection of lexons that are constrained (according to how the application uses these lexons) and a set of mappings from application symbols to terms and roles in that selection.

The introduction of a community commitment is motivated by the need for proper semantic interoperation between information systems. Depending on the goal of the ontology, instances shared across different autonomous information systems need to some degree to be compared for equivalence. One example is joining information about an instance across heterogeneous sources. In order to achieve this, the members of the community have to agree upon a series of attributes that uniquely, and totally identify the concepts they share. In other words, the conceptual reference structures[4]. By sharing the same reference structures, the information systems are able to interpret information describing instances and find the corresponding instance in their data store (of that of a third system). Application commitments refer to community commitments and can contain additional lexons and constraints. For instance, lexons needed to annotate application specific symbols (e.g., artificial IDs, often found in relational databases) to ensure that instances of concepts are properly aligned (e.g., a proper annotation of the foreign keys in a join-table). Both community- and application commitments also store information about the agreements across communities.

The application-commitment language we have adopted is Ω-RIDL [19], and extended to include references to community commitments. Take for example the ER-diagram for a fictitious database storing information about artists and works of art in Fig. 2. The corresponding application commitment is shown in Fig. 2. Notice the reference to the "Cultural Domain" community, which will include all lexons and constraints currently agreed upon by that community. This particular commitment furthermore includes some application specific knowledge to annotate the artificial IDs. The commitment describes how these IDs uniquely and totally identify instances of artists and works of art. Furthermore the terms "Artist" and "Work Of Art" inside the application's lexons are declared to be synonymous with that of the community. The lexons of the community 'Cultural Domain' g in this example were assumed to include:

```
<g, Art Movement, with, of, Name>        <g, Gender, with, of, Code>
<g, Artist, with, of, Art Movement>       <g, Artist, having, of, Name>
<g, Artist, born in, of birth of, Year>   EACH Name IS LEXICAL.
<g, Work Of Art, with, of, Title>         EACH Code IS LEXICAL.
<g, Work Of Art, made in, of, Year>       EACH Year IS LEXICAL.
<g, Artist, with, of, Gender>             EACH Title IS LEXICAL.
<g, Artist, contributed to, with contributor, Work Of Art>
```

The lexical constraints limit instances of concepts denoted by a term to "things" that can be printed on a screen.

---

[4] Similar to identifications schemes in databases.

250   C. Debruyne and C. Vasquez

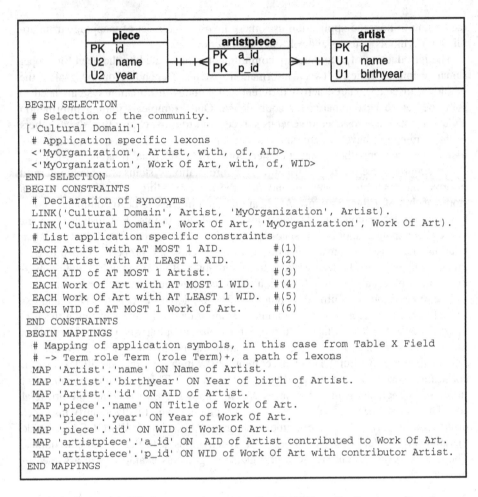

Fig. 2. Example ER diagram and corresponding Ω-RIDL application-commitment

3.4   Exploiting Application Commitments

The application commitments – next to describing how the application symbols are related to the shared lexons – are useful for practical things such as: 1) the publishing of data in other formalisms and 2) the validation of one applications' data with respect to the concepts and constraints agreed upon by the community.

The GOSPL hybrid ontology engineering aims to facilitate the engineering of ontologies and the reduction of a knowledge engineer's involvement in the processes, diminishing the effort spent by experts. The framework aims to be ontology language agnostic. The grounding in natural language and restricting the knowledge building blocks to fact-types instead of making a distinction between classes and properties (or entities and relations) and having those fact-types expressed in natural languages leverages the modeling task. Hybrid ontologies are easily transformed into other formalisms and can be used in conjunction with those other formalisms currently used within semantic technologies. For instance, the ontologies are transformed into the Web Ontology Language (OWL 2 [8]) and used with the R2RML language [1] to offer a virtual SPARQL [13] endpoint over the mapped relational data, or generate RDF [10] dumps, or offer a Linked Data[5] interface.

Not only can hybrid ontologies by transformed to other formalisms, the application commitments also aid the transformation of data locked in closed information systems. [19] even described how mappings can be used to generate SQL queries for relational databases. Another implementation of Ω-RIDL - provided by Collibra NV/SA[6] - allow also the annotation of XML. No matter the formalism, a link with the hybrid ontologies is kept. This link allows exploiting the annotation to see to what extent the individual application comply with the constraints agreed upon by the community as well as those that are application specific. Transforming each constraint into a query does this.

The application mappings are changed according to each closer approximation of the observed world by the communities. As the hybrid ontology grows, so will the data unlocked by means of these commitments. In GOSPL, the constraints that are currently proposed in the community commitment can be tested against the data inside the closed information systems in the same way that the constraints inside a commitment can be tested.

Also the hybrid ontologies and the additional lexons and constraints in application commitments are examined with a reasoner. This is particularly important for application commitments, as the annotations – being the responsibility of the representatives of that particular application – are human and thus inconsistencies could arise.

3.5   Queries as Concept Definitions

Lexons in a community commitment (or even an application commitment) can be used to query information by means of sentences created by concatenating lexons. We created a fact-oriented query language for RDF - called R-RIDL. For this, we adopted the fact-oriented query language RIDL [11]. RIDL, which stands for Reference and IDea Language, was a formal syntactic support for information and process analysis, semantic specification, constraint definition and a query/update language at a conceptual level in the early eighties. The RIDL language manipulated, defined and restricted information structures and flows described using the NIAM method (restricted to binary relations). RIDL was one of the first query languages to access the data via the conceptualization, which resulted from a natural language discourse between the users (of an information system). Because of its groundings in natural language, it was easier for users to retrieve information out of the system. A guide and description of the RIDL grammar are described in [6].

RIDL is a Controlled Natural Languages (CLN), which are less expressive subsets of natural language whose grammars and lexicons have been restricted, making it less

---

[5] http://www.linkeddata.org/
[6] http://www.collibra.com/

complex and ambiguous [15]. CLNs make information retrieval and ontology engineering tasks easier on the user by hiding some of the complexity (e.g., learning standards such as XML, RDF and OWL) [15]. RIDL also inspired Ω-RIDL. Using a concatenation of lexons, sentences can be constructed to describe those application symbols.

Statements entered by the user are parsed following a grammar based on the original RIDL language; the part concerned with information retrieval and refined to cope with Hybrid Ontology Descriptions[7]. Below, we will give two examples of queries in R-RIDL with their equivalent expression in SPARQL. For the queries in SPARQL, the OWL translation of the community commitment is assumed to be available somewhere[8]. We omit the namespaces for the SPARQL queries for simplicity's sake. We assume the prefix of the OWL implementation of the community commitment to be myOnto0. Using the same example as the previous section:

- Return the artists that are not male

R-RIDL:	LIST Artist NOT with Gender with Code = 'M'
SPARQL:	SELECT DISTINCT ?a WHERE { ?a a myOnto0:Artist. OPTIONAL { ?g myOnto0:Gender_of_Artist ?a. ?g myOnto0:Gender_with_Code ?c. } FILTER(?c != "M" || !bound(?c)) }

In this example we wish to list all the artists not having a gender with code `M`. This includes the artists whose gender was not explicitly stated. For the equivalent SPARQL query, we thus need to specify that gender is optional. This is done with the OPTIONAL clause, which will leave the variables unbound if no such information is available. But merely testing the whether variable ?c doesn't equal `M` does not suffice. As apart from bound, all functions and operators that operate on RDF will produce a type error if any arguments are unbound. Thus the result of a Boolean test can be true, false or error. Testing whether ?c != `M` will thus result in an error and the result will thus not taken into account for this query. We therefore need to test whether the variable doesn't equal `M` *or* the variable is unbound.

- Return all the names:

R-RIDL:	LIST Name.
SPARQL:	SELECT DISTINCT ?n WHERE { {?a myOnto0:Artist_having_Name ?n.} UNION {?a myOnto0:Art_Movement_with_Name ?n.}}

---

[7] Details of R-RIDL can be found on
http://starlab.vub.ac.be/website/node/756/edit

[8] For this example, the OWL translation can be found on
http://starlab.vub.ac.be/staff/chrdebru/GOSPL_ATOMIZER/art.owl

> In R-RIDL, if we want to have the set of all names, we merely need to use that term label. This is not possible in SPARQL as lexical attributes result in object properties with their ranges being instances of `rdfs:Literal`. To achieve the same effect, i) one needs to look up all the lexons in which that term plays a role, ii) find the corresponding data properties and iii) construct the SPARQL query using the UNION operator for each of those data properties.

There are two types of statement: LIST and FOR-LIST. The LIST statement returns a set of instances, which can be regarded as a set of unary tuples. The FOR-LIST statement allows the user to create queries returning a set of tuples of arity n>1.

R-RIDL transforms parts of the lexon-paths in these queries into SPARQL queries, and then applies relation algebra to construct the result set. The drawback of this approach is that queries in R-RIDL are indeed slower than in SPARQL, but the added value is an understandable - and at certain points more expressive - query language for RDF fitting an ontology engineering method.. Where SPARQL is suitable for building services, R-RIDL allows for language-grounded exploration of data.

GOSPL allows agreements to be made at two levels: at description level and at the level of the formalism (i.e., lexons). Even though the method supports both high level reasoning by humans with the natural language descriptions and low level reasoning by machines with the formal part, the ontology engineering processes can benefit from the hybrid nature of R-RIDL; the queries looking like natural language sentences become concept definitions. The definition/query can be defined, as the results can be explored, examined and discussed by the community. Those definitions correspond with the *subtype definitions* of ORM, in which subtypes of concepts are defined in terms of the roles of lexons played by its super-types. For instance:

- EACH Female Artist IS IN **LIST Artist with Gender with Code** = 'F', Or
- EACH Female Artist is a **Artist with Gender with Code** = 'F'

4   Tool and Demonstration

The following principles have been included in a tool called GOSPL [5,4]. Fig. 3 depicts a screenshot of the GOSPL prototype, and shows some lexons and constraints currently residing in the "Venue Community", which aimed to describe the venues in which cultural events take place. The tabs in this figure direct the user to:

- **Ontology.** The lexons and constraints currently agreed upon by the community. This is actually the community-commitment
- **Glossary.** The natural language descriptions for terms and lexon currently agreed upon by the community. This page also displays the current gloss-equivalences and to what extent the hybrid ontology is glossary-consistent.

- **Discussions.** The social processes as discussions to evolve the hybrid ontology, as well as the semantic interoperability requirements.
- **Members.** Community management. We choose not to assigned roles denoting a hierarchy; instead we choose to treat all members equal. This simplifies teaching the method.
- **Commitment.** The list of application-commitments. Such commitments can exist without the platform knowing about its existence. However, for the system to be able to query data or test constraints proposed by the community, the systems needs to keep track of applications whose application symbols are annotated. Users are able to manage application commitments expressed in Ω-RIDL and SPARQL-endpoints, with the latter preferably providing triples using predicates from the OWL implementation of the hybrid ontology.
- **OWL/RDFS.** The OWL implementation of the hybrid ontology
- **Activity.** A log of this particular community

Fig. 4 depicts a simple "scenario" with the tool. After logging in, users a presented a list of communities (A), users can take a look in each community – for instance the Venue community in (B) and the discussions of that community (C). The image in (B) corresponds with the screenshot in Fig. 3. Depending whether the user is a member of a community, the user has access to a number of social processes he can start within that community. In (D), we show how a discussion to add a gloss is started. The discussion presented in (E) stems from the experiment we will describe later on. Once a term is articulated, lexons can be built around this term (F) and constraints on the created lexons (G). After a while, the community has obtained a closer approximation of their domain and can start creating/updating their application-commitments (H). These commitments can be (users are not obliged) registered to the platform, which can then be used to test statements made in a discussion, e.g., by looking for counter-examples (H). When users are not part of a community, the interactions they can start only involves general requests (e.g., request an edit, or request to become a member), they have no access to requests on the glossary or lexon base. If that user is part of another community, he can trigger processes to discuss the "sameness" of glosses or terms.

Information on synonymy and gloss-equivalences are shown on a separate page (a community-term page), accessible by - for instance - clicking on one of the terms of the accepted lexons. The GOSPL tool supports a community in *applying* the method for ontology engineering, but its purpose is indeed not to replace other means of interaction that can be more effective when possible (e.g., face-to-face meetings when community members are near, or even teleconferences). The outcome of these interactions outside of the tool, however, needs to be properly written down when concluding a discussion.

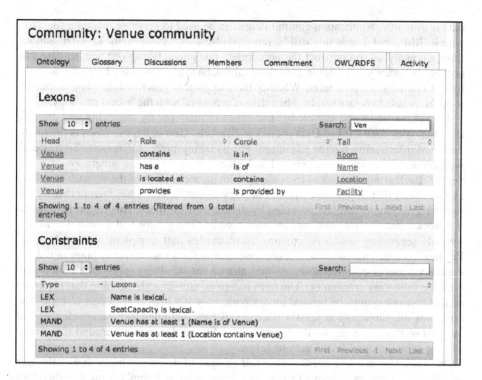

Fig. 3. Screenshot lexons and constraints in a community

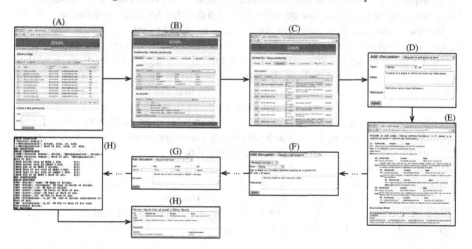

Fig. 4. Different social processes supported by the tool

In the previous section, we described how the lexons in the hybrid ontology-engineering framework could be used to create controlled natural language queries. Given a commitment and the SPARQL end-point, the first tells the client to which community-commitments this application is committing two and the latter where the data is available. Application-commitments can be used to generate mapping files, e.g. with R2RML, but details this will be reported elsewhere. In short, the Ω-RIDL annotations are analyzed to construct the appropriate mappings, taking one special case into account: whether join-tables in the relational database are represented by a lexon in the hybrid ontology, or as a term. Whether the mapping is generated, or done manually, R-RIDL is able to return results when data is annotated with the hybrid ontology.

GOSPL provides the knowledge management platform for managing and creating the ontologies for a Linked Data project in Brussels. One of the use cases is the publication of information related to cultural events taking place in Brussels. To this end, we conducted an experiment with 41 volunteers, each divided in subgroups of 3 to 4 people. Each group was asked to come up with an application in the domain of cultural events and then to create a hybrid ontology to enable semantic interoperability between their systems and one provided by the use case partners. This experiment lasted 7-8 weeks, and several communities were created. The groups had a natural tendency towards separating concerns, creating communities that complemented each other. For instance, the creation of a "Ticket" community for a general description of tickets, conditions and prices. We analyzed the interactions involving terms in a community with the following criteria: (1) The term had to be non-lexical, meaning that instances of this concept cannot be printed on a screen, only it's lexical attributes can. (2) The term was the subject of at least 4 interactions (not including gloss-equivalences and synonyms, thus focusing on the formal and informal descriptions around this term). (3) The term took part in at least one lexon.

We took into account terms with a fair amount of activity. This is due to the fact that the communities employed terms only relevant to their application, and therefore only inspired discussions within that group. These discussions are not interesting as the community tended to agree on what has been decided for their application.

We then analyzed how much of these terms changed in terms of their formal description if a gloss was immediately provided. With these criteria, we identified 49 terms. Of these 49 terms, 38 started with the natural language description as described by the GOSPL method. Of these 38 terms, 11 of them had changes in their formal description (29%). And of the remaining 11 terms that did not start with the informal description, 5 of them changes in their formal description (45%).

The reason we left out lexicals is that they often play in an attributive role. Lexons are supposed to be entered when at least one of the terms is informally described. At the start, the key-terms are often described first. And when the second term concerns a lexical in an attributive role, the community tends to agree on the meaning of this attribute based on the label of that term. If we were to take lexicals into account, we again observe that terms that did not start with an informal description are more likely to change its formal description: 18 terms out of 46 that started with a gloss and 6 terms out of 12 that did not start with a gloss.

5   Conclusions

In any project in which agreements within a heterogeneous community of stakeholders are vital, the natural language aspects in communicating knowledge and aligning ideas are key for success. In this paper, we described – in the context of ontology engineering - how agreements within and across communities are facilitated by natural language descriptions. The ideas presented in this paper are easily extrapolated to other domain, e.g., large software projects, in which the construction of a lexicon for use between developers, users, and other stakeholders will be used throughout the project.

We introduced the notions of community- and application commitments. The first captures the agreements by one community necessary to achieve the community's goals, the latter to ensure proper interoperation by one application. Application commitments even provide additional information if the owners of that application wishes to. This layered approach is also easily applicable in different domain, where the community commitment will contain fact-types and business rules that should always hold and application-commitments contain additional fact-types and rules for specific application (e.g., the rules to which an instance of a concept must comply with in different stages of that entities lifecycle management). We described the nature of agreements; the "sameness" of term-labels or glosses is considered an equivalence relation only within the communities participating in one agreement process.

We furthermore described how these application commitments aid the ontology engineering processes in guiding the interactions within the community. Hypotheses are transformed into queries that returning instances that do not support the hypothesis. The application commitments that co-evolve with the community commitments, allow 1) to publish information in those applications as structured data on the web and 2) users to also explore already annotated data and examine any other annotation on these instances (not necessarily with knowledge from the community). The latter is done by means of R-RIDL, a fact-oriented query language on top of RDF. R-RIDL is a controlled natural language using the natural language fact-types agreed upon by the community. Expressions in R-RIDL allow describing how instances are classified by means of a query, much like subtype-definitions used in ORM.

We implemented these concepts in a tool for hybrid ontology engineering, called GOSPL, and conducted an experiment. One problem we encountered was a tendency by the communities to forget describing the lexical terms with a natural language description. However, it is important – for some concepts – to agree on how some lexical entities should be represented (in terms of format, encoding, etc.). The tool should thus be altered in such a way that communities are still encouraged to describe all of the term in an informal way, even when they're "merely" lexical attributes. The prototype was developed with respect to the method. Some freedom, however, was granted to the users; e.g., terms did not have to be articulated for lexons to be created around it. In a next experiment, we will impose this constraint and examine the users' reactions on this change. At the same time, we will investigate how we should put emphasis on this issue while teaching the method to the participants.

Acknowledgements. This work was partially funded by the Brussels Institute for Research and Innovation through the Open Semantic Cloud for Brussels Project.

References

1. Das, S., Sundara, S., Cyganiak, R.: R2RML: RDB to RDF Mapping Language. W3C Working Draft (May 29, 2012), http://www.w3.org/TR/r2rml/
2. De Leenheer, P., Christiaens, S., Meersman, R.: Business semantics management: A case study for competency-centric HRM. Computers in Industry 61(8), 760–775 (2010)

3. Debruyne, C., Meersman, R.: Semantic Interoperation of Information Systems by Evolving Ontologies through Formalized Social Processes. In: Eder, J., Bielikova, M., Tjoa, A.M. (eds.) ADBIS 2011. LNCS, vol. 6909, pp. 444–459. Springer, Heidelberg (2011)

4. Debruyne, C., Meersman, R.: GOSPL: A Method and Tool for Fact-Oriented Hybrid Ontology Engineering. In: Morzy, T., Härder, T., Wrembel, R. (eds.) ADBIS 2012. LNCS, vol. 7503, pp. 153–166. Springer, Heidelberg (2012)

5. Debruyne, C., Reul, Q., Meersman, R.: GOSPL: Grounding Ontologies with Social Processes and Natural Language. In: Latifi, S. (ed.) ITNG 2010, pp. 1255–1256. IEEE Computer Society (2012)

6. De Troyer, O., Meersman, R., Ponsaert, F.: RIDL user guide. Research report (available from the authors). Int. Centre for Information Analysis Services, Control Data (1983)

7. Gómez-Pérez, A., Fernández-López, M., Corcho, Ó.: Ontological Engineering with examples from the areas of Knowledge Management. In: e-Commerce and the Semantic Web. Springer-Verlag New York, Inc., Secaucus (2003) ISBN: 1852335513

8. Hitzler, P., Krotzsch, M., Parsia, B., Patel-Schneider, P.F., Rudolph, S.: OWL 2 Web Ontology Primer. W3C Recommendation (October 27, 2009), http://www.w3.org/TR/owl2-primer/

9. Kotis, K., Vouros, A.: Human-centered ontology engineering: The hcome methodology. Knowledge Information Systems 10(1), 109–131 (2006)

10. Manola, F., Miller, E.: RDF Primer. W3C Recommendation (February 10, 2004), http://www.w3.org/TR/rdf-primer/

11. Meersman, R.: The RIDL conceptual language. Research report (available from the authors). Int. Centre for Information Analysis Services, Control Data (1982)

12. Meersman, R.: The use of lexicons and other computer-linguistic tools in semantics, design and cooperation of database systems. In: Zhang, Y., Rusinkiewicz, M., Kambayashi, Y. (eds.) The Proceedings of the Second Int. Symposium on Cooperative Database Systems for Advanced Applications (CODAS 1999), pp. 1–14. Springer (1999)

13. Prud'hommeaux, E., Seaborne, A.: SPARQL Query Language for RDF. W3C Recommendation (January 15, 2008), http://www.w3.org/TR/rdf-sparql-query/

14. Sahoo, S.S., Halb, W., Hellmann, S., Idehen, K., Thibodeau, T., Auer, S., Sequeda, J., Ezzat, A.: A survey of current approaches for mapping of relational databases to RDF (2009), http://www.w3.org/2005/Incubator/rdb2rdf/RDB2RDF_SurveyReport.pdf

15. Schwitter, R.: A Controlled Natural Language Layer for the Semantic Web. In: Zhang, S., Jarvis, R.A. (eds.) AI 2005. LNCS (LNAI), vol. 3809, pp. 425–434. Springer, Heidelberg (2005)

16. Simperl, E.P.B., Tempich, C.: Ontology Engineering: A Reality Check. In: Meersman, R., Tari, Z. (eds.) OTM 2006. LNCS, vol. 4275, pp. 836–854. Springer, Heidelberg (2006)

17. Siorpaes, K., Simperl, E.: Human intelligence in the process of semantic content creation. World Wide Web 13(1-2), 33–59 (2010)

18. Tudorache, T., Noy, N., Tu, S., Musen, M.: Supporting Collaborative Ontology Development in Protégé. In: Sheth, A.P., Staab, S., Dean, M., Paolucci, M., Maynard, D., Finin, T., Thirunarayan, K. (eds.) ISWC 2008. LNCS, vol. 5318, pp. 17–32. Springer, Heidelberg (2008)

19. Verheyden, P., De Bo, J., Meersman, R.: Semantically Unlocking Database Content Through Ontology-Based Mediation. In: Bussler, C.J., Tannen, V., Fundulaki, I. (eds.) SWDB 2004. LNCS, vol. 3372, pp. 109–126. Springer, Heidelberg (2005)

20. Vrandecic, D., Pinto, H.S., Sure, Y., Tempich, C.: The DILIGENT knowledge processes. Journal of Knowledge Management 9(5), 85–96 (2005)

21. Wintraecken, J.: The NIAM Information Analysis Method, Theory and Practice. Kluwer Academic Publishers (1990)

Author Index

Beer, Armin   125
Broy, Manfred   1
Burger, Martin   55

Caiman, Micael   230
Curtis, Bill   3

Dallmeier, Valentin   55
Debruyne, Christophe   244
Duarte, Francisco J.   147
Dulz, Winfried   89

Felderer, Michael   10, 125
Fernandes, João M.   147
Ferreira, Nuno   168

Gašević, Dragan   168
Gleirscher, Mario   104

Horn, Stefan   215

Kazman, Rick   191

Lima, Ana   191

Machado, Ricardo J.   147, 168, 191
Meding, Wilhelm   230

Monteiro, Paula   191
Mordinyi, Richard   30
Moser, Thomas   30

Neumann, Robert   215

Orth, Tobias   55

Plösch, Reinhold   215

Ramler, Rudolf   10
Ribeiro, Pedro   191

Santos, Nuno   147, 168
Simões, Cláudia   191
Sneed, Harry M.   70
Soley, Richard Mark   3
Stallinger, Fritz   215
Staron, Miroslaw   230
Sunindyo, Wikan   30

Vasquez, Cristian   244
Vollmar, Jan   215

Winkler, Dietmar   30

Zeller, Andreas   55